A Turbulent Time

BLACKS IN THE DIASPORA

Darlene Clark Hine, John McCluskey, Jr., and David Barry Gaspar

GENERAL EDITORS

A Turbulent Time

THE FRENCH REVOLUTION AND THE GREATER CARIBBEAN

EDITED BY
David Barry Gaspar
AND
David Patrick Geggus

Indiana University Press

BLOOMINGTON AND INDIANAPOLIS

The paper used in this publication meets the minimum requirements of
American National Standard for Information Sciences—Permanence of
Paper for Printed Library Materials, ANSI Z39.48-1984.

MANUFACTURED IN THE UNITED STATES OF AMERICA

Library of Congress Cataloging-in-Publication Data

A turbulent time : the French Revolution and the Greater Caribbean /
    edited by David Barry Gaspar and David Patrick Geggus.
        p.   cm. — (Blacks in the diaspora)
    Includes bibliographical references and index.
        ISBN 0–253–33247–8 (alk. paper). — ISBN 0–253–21086–0 (pbk. :
    alk. paper)
        1. West Indies—History. 2. Caribbean Area—History—To 1810.
    3. France—History—Revolution, 1789–1799—Influence. 4. Slavery—
    West Indies—Insurrections, etc. 5. Slavery—Louisiana—
    Insurrections, etc. 6. Louisiana—History—To 1803. 7. Florida—
    History—To 1821. I. Gaspar, David Barry. II. Geggus, David
    Patrick. III. Series
    F1621.T85 1997
    972.9—dc20   96–33248

1 2 3 4 5 02 01 00 99 98 97

CONTENTS

Maps appear on pages 76 and 77.

For Darryk, Trevor, Garreth
and
For Josiane and Sarah

INTRODUCTION

THE ABOLITION OF NEGRO SLAVERY AND THE CIVILIZATION OF THIS LONG OPPRESSED
RACE OF HUMAN BEINGS WILL PROBABLY IN AFTER-AGES BE CONSIDERED TO DATE FROM
THE ERA OF THE FRENCH REVOLUTION. IN THE MIDST OF ALL THE MISCHIEF AND MISERY
OCCASIONED BY THE ERUPTION OF THAT VOLCANO OF THE MORAL WORLD THE FIRST GERM
OF NEGRO EMANCIPATION WAS UNINTENTIONALLY PLANTED IN THE ISLAND OF ST.
DOMINGO . . . WHENCE IT CAN HARDLY FAIL TO SPREAD ITS ROOTS, IN THE COURSE OF NO
VERY DISTANT PERIOD, THROUGH THE WHOLE OF THE . . . ANTILLES.

Quarterly Review 42 (1819)

People who lived through the age of the French Revolution often felt
the world had entered a chaotic new era, when for better or worse old
constraints and old certainties no longer applied. Welding a dynamic
ideology of liberty and equality, a new concept of state power, and a
nascent sense of nationalism, revolutionary France and its Napoleonic
successor plunged Europe into a quarter-century of warfare and tumultuous change. Outside of Europe, the region most threatened and in
some ways most affected by this upheaval was the colonial plantation
zone surrounding the Caribbean Sea, which was then of extreme importance to the European and North American economies.[1] Devoted to the
export of tropical staples, Europe's Caribbean colonies had always been
vulnerable in times of war. Built precariously on the massive exploitation of slave labor, organized according to the doctrine of racial discrimination, and tied to their metropolises by mercantilist bonds and
imperial fiat, they proved peculiarly vulnerable to the libertarian message of the French Revolution.

That message was all the more potent because it coincided with the
emergence of the antislavery movement in the Atlantic world and
interacted with local traditions of resistance among the region's slaves,
free coloreds, and white colonists.[2] Separate struggles in the French
Caribbean colonies for colonial autonomy, racial equality, and slave
emancipation progressively forced these issues into the program of the
revolution in France and enormously magnified its threat to the Caribbean status quo.[3] The French banning of racial discrimination in 1792
and abolition of slavery in 1794 were milestones in American history.
What perhaps mattered most for people who lived in the Caribbean was
that these legislative victories were won by force of arms in vicious local

conflicts, particularly in the hugely destructive and large-scale slave revolt that took place in Saint Domingue. The epic transformation of Saint Domingue—the region's wealthiest colony—into the independent black state of Haiti (1791–1804) was an inflammatory example of self-liberation and a dramatic symbol of resistance. It was a major revolution in its own right.[4]

This book examines several dimensions of the impact of these two interconnected revolutions on what may be called the Greater Caribbean. We have added the Gulf Coast states to the traditional spatial definition of the Circumcaribbean to reflect the political, economic, and social realities of the period. By the later eighteenth century, the various colonial societies of this wider region constituted basically similar worlds within a larger spatial and cultural sphere that Charles Wagley called Plantation America.[5] These colonial worlds were shaped by developments centered in the Caribbean, principally the establishment and expansion of plantation slavery and crop production which spawned contests for power between competing European states, between masters and slaves, and between whites, blacks, and people of mixed ancestry. There was an interconnectedness about this wider region, in which networks of trade and mobility of the free and the enslaved populations made it possible for news to spread from one corner to another and to produce results that could clearly transcend national, linguistic, and geographic boundaries.[6]

By the start of the revolutionary period with which the chapters in this book are concerned, Florida and Louisiana were not only parts of the Spanish empire administered from Havana and Santo Domingo, but their economies were also oriented southward and increasingly driven by plantation slavery.[7] Until 1794 Louisiana traded more with the French islands than with the mainland, reflecting a Caribbean interdependence that belied the mercantilist claims of the colonial powers in Europe.[8] Contraband and progressive liberalization of trade connected the dispersed segments of the Greater Caribbean and, in this period, permitted the nascent United States to assume an unparalleled role in its commerce. To the south, Venezuela also reflected "Caribbean" characteristics in its social and economic structure.[9] Like the Spanish West Indies, Venezuela had important links with British and French islands through the clandestine livestock trade.[10] The reliance of the Spanish colonies, in return, on foreigners for slaves and manufactured goods made the Spanish silver dollar the common currency throughout the region.

The upheavals of the revolutionary era proved a further source of integration within the Greater Caribbean. Saint Domingue and the rest of the French colonies released waves of refugees; Santo Domingo and Venezuela also experienced substantial emigration. These refugees and their slaves had significant economic, and sometimes cultural, impacts in Louisiana, Cuba, Puerto Rico, Jamaica, and Trinidad. Foreign military occupations and transfers of sovereignty added to the region's cosmopolitanism, notably in the Guianas and south Caribbean. The independence of Venezuela and the absorption of Louisiana and Florida by the United States, however, helped sunder the unity of the Greater Caribbean. The independence and economic decline of Haiti, the abolition of the slave trade, and the declining use of livestock in sugar cultivation all had a similar effect.

The chapters of this volume are not meant to cover every corner of the Greater Caribbean but rather to examine developments within several societies during the revolutionary period to illustrate the pervasive and multilayered impact of the revolutions on the region. In chapter 1, David Patrick Geggus presents a careful and probing overview of the revolutionary and Napoleonic years in the Greater Caribbean that stresses three themes: resistance, migration, and economic growth. He explores the impact of abolitionism, revolution, and war on Caribbean slavery and surveys the incidence of violent resistance across the region, seeking to place the influence of the French and Haitian revolutions in perspective. Against this background of themes and shaping forces which are approached regionally, the particular concerns of the remaining chapters fall into place.

Carolyn E. Fick in chapter 2 focuses on the influence and impact of the revolution in France on colonial revolutionary movements in Saint Domingue. Fick places the great slave revolt that began in 1791 in the context of the colonial revolt to show that to understand the revolutionary accomplishments of the slaves it is necessary to begin with the revolt of the white planters and free people of color who provided the initial explosive context within which the slaves seized their own destiny and shaped the revolution. Through their revolt the slaves placed slavery and emancipation on the agenda of the French Revolution, which had not been concerned with such issues.

In chapter 3, Michael Duffy shifts attention to British attitudes to the Caribbean colonies during the revolutionary period. Duffy shows that once France declared war on Britain in early 1793, Britain capitalized on the internal disruption of the French Caribbean colonies that accompanied the metropolitan revolution to seize these major colonies and acquire a decisive maritime superiority. The impact of the revolution in the Caribbean, however, also caused disruption within the British colonies. The costly crisis that followed brought into sharper focus British attitudes to colonial wealth and to the plight of the black slaves whose labor helped supply it. Duffy considers how these developments of the revolutionary period affected the termination of the British slave trade, Britain's alienation from formal empire during the early 1800s, and the shift of its imperial attention to the East.

Among the many Caribbean colonies whose affairs were disrupted dramatically during this period was Saint Lucia, which was under the French flag when the French Revolution began. For that colony, David Barry Gaspar explores in chapter 4 the consequences of the successful British invasion of 1796 and the reestablishment of slavery after the French declaration of abolition in 1794. Unwilling to return to slavery, many of the Saint Lucia blacks, organized by French patriots or republicans or by other blacks, joined or supported a spirited and protracted resistance to the British, who for many months were unable to truly claim that the colony was fully conquered. Gaspar links this revolutionary situation, and primarily its effect on the slave and black population, to the insistence of older slaves in early 1838—who remembered and called attention to the events of 1794-1796—that they preferred to purchase their freedom rather than wait for Britain to fulfill its promise of emancipation later that year. Connecting the two emancipations throws light on issues related to the collective memory of the slaves and their political reading of important events that affected their lives.

In chapter 5, David Patrick Geggus returns to the issue of slave resistance, exploring developments in the Spanish Caribbean during the mid-1790s. He argues that during this period the Caribbean experienced one of the most remarkable upsurges in slave resistance in the Americas. Based on a detailed examination of evidence from the contrasting cases of burgeoning Cuba and sleepy Santo Domingo, Geggus reassesses prevailing scholarship about the Spanish West Indies and uses these cases to test general models about the development of slave insurrection. He shows that even within the context of the impact of the Haitian Revolution, ethnic forces continued to shape slave resistance in the Spanish Caribbean significantly. Thus the influence of the French and Haitian revolutions, he concludes, is not a reliable enough "principle for typologizing slave revolts."

Jane G. Landers shifts the focus in chapter 6 to Spanish Florida on the northern boundary of the Greater Caribbean. Here too the French and Haitian revolutions left their mark. The Spanish were unable to preserve Florida from the influence of revolutionary ideology. In 1795 Citizen Genet raised an army of American backwoodsmen and invaded the province. Spain was able to reestablish order soon, but that same year a group of Black Auxiliaries of Carlos IV in Santo Domingo, under General Jorge Biassou, arrived in Saint Augustine, Florida, having been sent into exile after Spain ceded Santo Domingo to France by the Treaty of Basle. Landers traces the career of Biassou, a slave who rose to become an army commander, during the early stages of the Haitian Revolution. Biassou, who outranked Toussaint Louverture at the time, allied himself with the Spanish against the French planters and remained loyal. The elite of Spanish Florida regarded Biassou and his men as dangerous persons who might contaminate the slaves with revolutionary ideas; moreover, these newcomers were prone to bypass the authority of Florida's administrators with appeals to the captain general of Cuba. Nevertheless, they proved to be of great value to the governors of Florida because their military skills were badly needed on Florida's unstable frontiers, and they also increased the effectiveness of the black militias.

During this period of war and revolution, ideas and events generated by both also gravely disturbed the Spanish administrators of Louisiana, where a large proportion of the population, who were born there during the French regime or were immigrants, maintained strong loyalties to France. Threats of internal subversion and invasion exacerbated tensions in the colony which was divided by conflicting loyalties. In chapter 7, Kimberly S. Hanger probes into the meaning and significance of such loyalties among the free population of color in New Orleans. As members of the free pardo and moreno militias, many of these people, loyal Spanish subjects, served in defending Louisiana from a feared French invasion and from internal commotions stirred up by sympathizers with the French. Pierre Bailly, a free mulatto officer of the Compañía de Pardos de las Nueva Orleans, was one such sympathizer or agitator who was tried and found guilty of supporting French revolutionary principles. By closely examining the testimony of witnesses in the case, Hanger reveals many of the frustrations free blacks dealt with in racially stratified Louisiana society, and their striving for the equality and brotherhood revolutionary France offered.

Robert L. Paquette draws attention in chapter 8 to the influence of the slave revolution in Saint Domingue on Napoleon's decision to sell Louisiana to the United States in 1803, and on the affairs of territorial Louisiana later. Paquette shows that interpretations of the Louisiana purchase that do not take full account of the role of the slave revolt are seriously flawed. He also shows that the authorities of territorial Louisiana were troubled by the possible contamination of local slaves with revolutionary principles brought by slaves imported from Saint Domingue, or who arrived with émigré masters from that embattled place and also from Cuba in 1809 after Napoleon invaded Spain. Against the background of growing concern in Louisiana about the possibility that social conflicts might reproduce the revolutionary drama of Saint Domingue, Paquette explains the significance of the slave revolt that took place in lower Louisiana in 1811, the largest such occurrence in the history of the United States.

In chapter 9, Roger N. Buckley explores an important but not sufficiently recognized set of consequences of the French revolutionary and Napoleonic wars in the Caribbean. During the seventeenth and eighteenth centuries, Britain relied upon the labor of slaves and free blacks to support its military forces in the region. The role of blacks had expanded dramatically, however, by the 1790s, when they were used in virtually all branches of the imperial army as well as in colonial military establishments, even as professional soldiers, who, however, remained slaves. Black manpower helped Britain achieve success over France, but Buckley points out that it also had "its most tangible effect on the conduct of court-martial proceedings." The attachment of slaves to the army gave rise to concern about whether their testimony was admissible at courts-martial. Colonial custom said it was not. In 1809, however, the British government ruled in favor of accepting the testimony of slaves at its military courts, and in this way began to undermine one of the principal foundations of colonial slavery and the privilege of whites. Thus the expanded roles of slaves in the British military forces in the Caribbean during the French revolutionary and Napoleonic period ultimately contributed to the gradual process of subverting and later abolishing slavery.

We would like to express our thanks and appreciation to the contributors of this volume for their understanding and patience in seeing this project through. Much research and writing on related subjects about this fascinatingly complex historical period remains to be done. If these chapters succeed in generating such results, then one of the primary objectives for bringing them together will have been achieved. Finally, we thank Jenna Golnik and Jane Twigg for word processing and acknowledge the interest that many of our colleagues have shown in this project, whose work, however, is not represented here, especially Anne Pérotin-Dumon and Julius S. Scott.

THE EDITORS

NOTES

1. Jean Tarrade, *Le Commerce colonial de la France à la fin de l'Ancien Régime*, 2 vols. (Paris: Presses Universitaires de France, 1972); Seymour Drescher, *Econocide: British Slavery in the Era of Abolition* (Pittsburgh: University of Pittsburgh Press, 1977); Javier Cuenca Esteban, "Statistics of Spain's Colonial Trade, 1792–1820," *American Historical Review* 61 (1981): 381–428; John Coatsworth, "American Trade with European Colonies in the Caribbean and South America, 1790–1812," *William & Mary Quarterly* 24 (1967): 243–266.

2. David Brion Davis, *The Problem of Slavery in the Age of Revolution, 1770–1823* (Ithaca: Cornell University Press, 1975); Robin Blackburn, *The Overthrow of Colonial Slavery, 1776–1848* (London: Verso, 1988).

3. Yves Bénot, *La Révolution française et la fin des colonies* (Paris: La Découverte, 1987).

4. Carolyn Fick, *The Making of Haiti: The Saint Domingue Revolution from Below* (Knoxville: University of Tennessee Press, 1990).

5. Charles Wagley, "Plantation America: A Culture Sphere," in *Caribbean Studies: A Symposium*, ed. Vera Rubin (Seattle: University of Washington Press, 1971), pp. 3–13.

6. Julius Sherrard Scott III, "The Common Wind: Currents of Afro-American Communication in the Era of the Haitian Revolution," Ph.D. diss., Duke University, 1986 (Ann Arbor: University Microfilms, 1989).

7. Gwendolyn Midlo Hall, *Africans in Colonial Louisiana: The Development of Afro-Creole Culture in the Eighteenth Century* (Baton Rouge: Louisiana State University Press, 1992), chap. 9; Robin Fabel, *The Economy of British West Florida, 1763–1783* (Tuscaloosa: University of Alabama Press, 1988); Helen H. Tanner, *Zéspedes in East Florida, 1784–1790* (Jacksonville: University of North Florida Press, 1989).

8. Jesús Lorente Miguel, "Commercial Relations between New Orleans and the United States, 1783–1803," in Jacques Barbier and Allan J. Kuethe, eds., *The North American Role in the Spanish Imperial Economy, 1760–1819* (Manchester: Manchester University Press, 1984), pp. 177–191.

9. Historians disagree whether the slave trade to Venezuela increased or decreased in the late eighteenth century; see Miguel Izard, "Período de la independencia," in *Política y economía en Venezuela, 1810–1976* (Caracas: Fundación John Boulton, 1976), pp. 3–7.

10. Little has been published on the subject. See Jean Tarrade, "Le Commerce entre les Antilles françaises et les possessions espagnoles d'Amérique à la fin du XVIIIe siècle," in Paul Butel and Bernard Lavallé, eds., *Commerce et plantation dans la Caraïbe, XVIIIe et XIXe siècles* (Bordeaux: Maison des Pays Ibériques, 1992), pp. 27–43; Eduardo Arcila Farias, *Economía colonial de Venezuela* (Pánuco: Fondo de Cultura Económica, 1946), pp. 403–405; Federico Brito Figueroa, *La Estructura económica de Venezuela colonial* (Caracas: Universidad Central, 1963); pp. 231–232, 247–249.

A Turbulent Time

1

Slavery, War, and Revolution in the Greater Caribbean, 1789–1815

DAVID PATRICK GEGGUS

Just when the system of plantation slavery in the Caribbean was reaching its apogee at the end of the eighteenth century, it faced an unprecedented series of challenges. The emergence of the antislavery movement in Europe in the 1780s and the outbreak of the great universalist revolution in France were soon followed by a long period of war and a wave of internal insurrections among the region's racially oppressed groups and occasionally among its white colonists. This combination of forces created enormous disruption in the Caribbean, and in the case of Saint Domingue (modern Haiti) destroyed its wealthiest colony, bringing slave emancipation and independent statehood to the region for the first time. After 300 years of unchecked growth, colonialism and slavery, the defining institutions of the Caribbean, were annihilated precisely where they had most prospered.

However, long after Haitian independence in 1804 and the withdrawal from slave trading during the same decade by most of the region's carriers,[1] slavery and colonialism remained entrenched in the Caribbean. It is true that Haitian aid and French revolutionary inspiration contributed to the secession of the Spanish colonies of the region's southern rimland after 1811 and their eventual abolition of slavery. Yet throughout this period the plantation economy worked by slave labor continued to expand toward new frontiers, in Cuba, Puerto Rico, and the mountains of Jamaica, in Trinidad, the Guianas, and Louisiana. Longer-settled areas also showed unexpected signs of vigor. Most of this development, moreover, took place within the context of colonial empires. If expansion of the United States to the Gulf Coast (between

1803 and 1819) diminished the area under European control, it also further stimulated the growth of plantation slavery in the region. The Haitian Revolution thus remained something of a turning point before its time.

Reform, revolution, war, insurrection, and economic development all interacted but followed different chronologies, thus denying these years of turbulent upheaval any neat unity. If the rise of Napoleon Bonaparte brought both the French and Haitian revolutions to a close in 1804, their influence lived on in the Caribbean, and the insurrectionary movement continued unabated past the end of the European war in 1815. Antislavery did not climax until after 1830. For want of better-defined limits, this chapter will concentrate primarily on the period 1789–1815 and the interlocking struggles to destroy, defend, and extend plantation slavery during a period of widespread military conflict.

From the beginning of European rule in the Caribbean, war and slave rebellion were prominent motifs in the region's history. However, the decades flanking the turn of the nineteenth century, themselves flanked by the mainland revolutions to the north (1776–1783) and south (1811–1824), were quite exceptional. Most colonies suffered either foreign invasion or internal revolt when, from 1793 to 1802, and with lesser intensity to 1815, war between the European powers sent tens of thousands of soldiers into the region, displaced thousands of refugees, and disrupted local shipping on a massive scale. Yet what distinguished this war and made it by far the bloodiest, was that racial inequality and slavery, the twin pillars of white rule in the Caribbean, and eventually European rule itself, were themselves being challenged in an unprecedented manner both within the region and from outside.[2]

After centuries of indifference in the capitals of the imperial powers, slavery came to be seen increasingly as an evil in the eighteenth century, and in the 1780s sectors of European and North American opinion began to mobilize against it.[3] In Pennsylvania and Massachusetts, which had strong maritime links with the Caribbean, slavery was abolished. In England a multiclass abolitionist movement was launched in 1787 that within five years forced a bill abolishing the slave trade through the House of Commons. Encouraged by developments in England, the elite Amis des Noirs society was founded in Paris in February 1788.[4] At the same time colonial governments began to intervene between slaves and their owners to implement limited protective reforms. Over virulent protests from planters, new slave laws were passed for the French islands in the mid-1780s, then for some British colonies, and in 1789 for the entire Spanish empire. The attempts at reform, like the abolitionist movements, were initially failures.[5] They are important, however, for the way they influenced slave resistance in the Americas during the next forty years, creating what Michael Craton has called a "rumour syndrome" centered on imaginary emancipation decrees.[6] Before 1790, as Julius Scott rightly emphasizes, the American Revolution, British abolitionism, and Spanish reformism (and, I would add, French reformism and abolitionism) helped form in slave communities a "culture of expectation [that] anticipated and helped to fuel the outbreak of revolution in the heart of Afro-America."[7]

Antislavery was also important because of its impact on the French Revolution. Though the two movements sprang partially from similar social and intellectual currents, they do need to be distinguished. The one antedated and long outlived the other, and their supporters were far from always the same people. Whatever the implications of the Declaration of the Rights of Man of August 1789, revolutionary egalitarianism in the 1790s by no means necessarily implied racial equality or slave emancipation. Democrats both in France and its colonies were slow to take up these issues, which of course had a relevance to American blacks quite beyond that of any other aspect of the revolution.[8]

In few other societies can the ideals of liberty, equality, and fraternity have seemed so dangerous as in these plantation systems founded on bondage, inequality, and prejudice. The threat from France, however, became much more direct once antislavery became part of the revolutionary mainstream. Legislating for the French colonies in the decrees of April 4, 1792, and February 4, 1794, radicals in Paris first brought racial equality and slave emancipation to the heartland of slaveowning America.[9] Thereafter, in the middle and late 1790s, the French Republic made real its latent threat to slaveowners in general by pursuing a policy, "unjustifiable and barbarous" according to the British war minister, of offering liberation to the nonwhites of enemy colonies.[10] The revolution's impact in the realm of ideas was no doubt real, but it is exceedingly difficult to demonstrate, especially among Caribbean slaves. Its material impact, however, including the disruption of the power structure in the French (and some of the Dutch) colonies and the bringing of war to the whole region, cannot be in question. Affecting all classes of society, the French Revolution did not merely inflame latent aspirations but, more important, undermined the institutions that had held them in check.

The French Revolution's adoption of antislavery and antiracism was primarily a pragmatic response to events in the West Indies. Yves Benot and Robin Blackburn have reemphasized the importance of metropolitan idealist and political influences on the revolution's colonial policy in sophisticated analyses that balance domestic and overseas narratives.[11] But few would disagree that the evolution of that policy was in large measure shaped by developments in Saint Domingue, particularly by the massive slave revolt of 1791. The revolution in Saint Domingue itself evolved out of complex interaction with events in France, but far more than metropolitan pressure groups or Enlightenment ideology, it was responsible for forcing the politicians in Paris belatedly to live up to their ideals when confronting the "colonial question." In so doing, it posed a powerful and different threat to New World slavery, presenting close to home a destructive spectacle of self-liberation, first by the colony's free colored community (1790–1792), then by its slaves (1791–1793). Their defeat of French, British, and Spanish armies and their achievement of national independence in 1804 were inflammatory examples and object lessons to those in bondage and, according to some historians, the source of actual attempts to export the black revolution to other American societies.

In a seminal study of slave resistance in the Americas, Eugene Genovese gives striking centrality to the French Revolution and its impact on Saint Domingue, seeing a transformation from "restorationist" rebellion to "bourgeois-democratic" revolution beginning in Haiti.[12] Many historians of Haiti, on the other hand, seek to downplay the impact of revolutionary France and stress instead continuity of resistance and indigenous factors such as voodoo and marronage in the genesis of the Haitian Revolution.[13] For the British Caribbean, Michael Craton and Michael Mullin also adopt a mainly internal perspective, emphasizing the impact on resistance of creolization, though this view is rejected by Seymour Drescher, who sees phases of rebellion shaped first by the French Revolutionary War and then by abolitionism.[14] Christianity is another factor whose influence on resistance is disputed but whose importance certainly grew in this period, when Protestant planters belatedly accepted evangelization as a means of social control. In addition, the tremendous increase in slave imports during the late eighteenth century and the rapid growth throughout the Caribbean of the free colored population perhaps suggest that the 1790s might have brought increased conflict to the region, whatever happened in Europe.

The relationship between the antislavery movement, the French Revolution, and the forces of black self-liberation is difficult to disentangle, and historians vary in the importance they attach to each of these challenges to the Caribbean status quo. Primarily the product of social and intellectual change in Europe, early antislavery, some argue, also owed a good deal to black resistance in the Caribbean.[15] During the period covered by this chapter (1789–1815), antislavery had a significant impact on black resistance and on the French Revolution but can be seen as subordinate to them, since together they greatly boosted the antislavery movement in France, giving it a forum and compelling arguments, while most scholars agree they set abolitionism back by more than a decade in Britain.[16] However, beginning with the banning of the British slave trade in 1807, abolitionism proved to be the most powerful of the three forces in changing the shape of Caribbean society.

√ In the period 1789–1815 we find two sets of conflicts in the Greater Caribbean. One was the international rivalry between the British, French, and Spanish. The other consisted of mainly domestic struggles waged by the region's three main social groups—slaves seeking freedom, free coloreds fighting racial discrimination, and colonial elites seeking autonomy or independence. They were not discrete developments; one often impinged on another. Slave rebellion encouraged white secessionism and foreign intervention in Saint Domingue but dampened desires for independence among *criollos* in Cuba and western Venezuela. Fear of slave emancipation was probably the biggest obstacle to ending discrimination against free coloreds, although free colored–white conflict, imperial rivalry, and white independence movements all opened up opportunities for slaves. Many of these issues came together in the Grenada and Saint Vincent rebellions of 1795 and the South American revolutions, but only the Haitian Revolution embodied them all. χ

Black resistance to slavery took a variety of forms in this period. Generally, the most massive or protracted conflicts, the ones that most severely challenged colonial rule, were those in which emancipated slaves resisted attempts to reenslave them (Saint Domingue, 1793–1798, 1802–1803; Saint Lucia, 1795–1797; Guadeloupe, 1802; Prospect Bluff, Florida, 1815–1816), or where free coloreds or Black Caribs made common cause with slaves in a joint war of liberation (Grenada and Saint Vincent, 1795–1796). These were usually epic contests, featuring pitched battles, staggering death tolls, and episodes of striking heroism. Also unnerving for colonial regimes were the war against the Boni maroons in Surinam (1789–1793) and the Jamaican Maroon War of 1795–1796, though there slavery was less directly at issue.[17] It is significant that none of these contests strictly speaking was a slave revolt. Each profited greatly from organization, experience, and weaponry available only outside the state of slavery.

The table "Slave Rebellions and Conspiracies, 1789–1815" at the end of this chapter is an attempt to identify what may be most properly termed slave revolts and conspiracies, those which proportionately involved slaves more than other groups, whose principal target was the slave regime, and which were organized within slavery rather than outside it. It is still not a well-defined category and far from homogeneous, with events in Saint Domingue dwarfing all the others put together in magnitude, consequences, and duration. No restrictive criteria regarding size were applied, as information on this was often lacking. A few of the cases perhaps do not meet the standard of ten participants used in Herbert Aptheker's pioneering study of slave rebellions in the United States.[18] On the other hand, small numbers of slaves executed, punished, or even arrested indicate planter parsimony and prudence as often as the true dimensions of a conspiracy or revolt.

Further problems of definition are posed by certain borderline cases. The 1802 Dominica mutiny of soldiers in the Second West India Regiment might have been included, since the legal status of black troops in the British Army was then still unsettled, and fear of being sold motivated the mutineers.[19] Another group of uncertain status, persons who successfully asserted their claim to freedom at this time, were the 1,000 Cobreros of eastern Cuba, though theirs was largely a nonviolent rebellion.[20] The hundreds of fugitive slaves armed by the British in the War of 1812 who raided frontier plantations and later held a fort in the Florida panhandle against a U.S. Army force similarly do not fit usual categories; nor do the thousands of bondsmen who joined both sides in the Spanish American War of Independence.[21] The "Swiss" slaves who joined the free coloreds of west Saint Domingue in their early struggles were omitted from the table because they and their interests remained subordinated to the free coloreds, though they evidently hoped to gain their own liberty.[22] The long resistance of the Dominica maroon bands in 1809–1814 and the "rebellious runaways" of northern Jamaica in 1798, whose activities fell halfway between insurrection and marronage, provide other cases. So, too, do the one or two hundred slaves who apparently joined the Trelawny Maroons in the war of 1795.[23]

What constituted a conspiracy also can be problematic. Some historians question the existence of several of the plots listed in the table and attribute them to the imagination of nervous colonists or to slaves' discussing fantasies of retribution.[24] The Jamaica 1791 conspiracy and the Puerto Rico conspiracy of 1812 may fall in this category, as might the 1795 Trinidad plots mentioned by V. S. Naipaul.[25] Evidence for some of the revolts is also scanty.[26] I have omitted several cases mentioned in recent historiography that I judged to be spurious.[27] On the other hand, it is possible I have overlooked conspiracies or small rebellions that contemporaries sought to cover up.

With these limitations in mind, we may suggest that slave revolts and conspiracies in the Greater Caribbean averaged at least two per year during the period 1789–1815 and nearly four per year in the 1790s, with revolts more numerous than conspiracies that did not reach fruition. About a dozen of the rebellions involved one hundred or more slaves. Outside of Saint Domingue, the only insurrections to mobilize 1,000 slaves occurred in Guadeloupe (August 1793) and in tiny Curaçao (1795 and 1800), though thousands of slaves joined in the multiclass risings in the British Windward Islands in 1795. Initially slave resistance was most prominent in France's colonies. Then, in the mid-1790s, the Spanish Caribbean saw an upsurge of activity. Another spate occurred in 1811–1812, though in general overt resistance diminished considerably after 1800. This pattern clearly had much to do with the impact of the French Revolution, though some historians have exaggerated its importance. Certainly, two other causal factors need to be taken into account: the variations in military strength experienced by different colonies and the influence of European antislavery and reformism.

In the British Caribbean the years 1789–1815 paradoxically constitute something of a low point in the history of autonomous black resistance. Although the mid-1790s revolts of the Black Caribs, Windward Islands free coloreds, and Jamaican Maroons held center stage, and although a number of plots were discovered in Jamaica after 1800, independent slave rebellions and conspiracies were more prominent in the preceding and succeeding decades.[28] Slave participation in the multiclass conflicts provides only a partial explanation of this apparent downturn. Contemporaries pointed to the high degree of creolization, and therefore stability, of the older colonies as an inhibiting factor, but the great "creole" rebellions of 1816–1831 undermine the theory's plausibility.[29] Michael Craton has suggested instead that tensions between demographically balanced African and creole communities in this period made cooperation in revolt difficult.[30] However, the best general explanation might be found in the exceptionally high concentrations of troops maintained in the British colonies through the years 1789–1815. A quite impressive and fairly detailed correlation can be found between diminishing garrison strength and slave rebellion in this period and others, and not just in the British West Indies.[31] The striking upsurge of resistance that occurred in 1795, and the resistance of 1811–1812 as well, seem partly linked to falling troop levels in the Spanish colonies and the region in general. Unsurprising but neglected, this very concrete aspect of social control helps explain both the spatial and chronological distribution of organized slave resistance.

Antislavery and reformism appear as significant influences on black resistance at this time because of a remarkable series of revolts and conspiracies that featured false rumors of an emancipation law. More than twenty occurred in the years 1789–1832, most of them in the Greater Caribbean.[32] Coeval with the heyday of the abolitionist movement in Europe and chiefly associated with creole slaves, the phenomenon emerged well before the French abolition of slavery or the Saint Domingue uprising, even before the Declaration of the Rights of Man. A few comparable examples occurred earlier in the century,[33] but the series in question began with an attempted rebellion on Martinique in August 1789. Slaves claimed that the government in Europe had abolished slavery but that local slaveowners were preventing the island governor from implementing the new law. The pattern would be repeated again and again across the region for the next forty years and would culminate in the three large-scale insurrections in Barbados, 1816, Demerara, 1823, and Jamaica, 1831.[34] Together with the Saint Domingue insurrection of 1791, these were the biggest slave rebellions in the history of the Americas.

Rumors of an official liberation that was being covertly sabotaged, present in at least one-third of the slave insurrections and conspiracies between 1789 and 1815, were clearly a strong mobilizing force. Corrosive of whatever hegemonic values a slaveowning class managed to impose, they both suggested new political strategies to slave dissidents and exacerbated the sense of injustice that Barrington Moore isolated as a crucial component of rebellion.[35] Sometimes the rumors circulated without stimulating revolt, as in Saint Domingue at the end of 1789 or in France's Indian Ocean colony of Bourbon, where the rumors arrived a year later.[36] Early in 1790, however, minor rebellions broke out in Tortola, Venezuela, and Cuba, apparently caused by the anger and confidence generated by talk of an obstructed decree. That April the governor of Guadeloupe similarly interpreted an aborted local revolt.[37] There followed at the start of 1791 two rebellions in Dominica, conspiracies in southern Saint Domingue and Guadeloupe, then the great uprising in northern Saint Domingue in August, followed by a shadowy conspiracy in Jamaica, all of which featured false rumors of emancipation. Similar rumors resurfaced two years later in the major insurrection around Saint Anne, Guadeloupe, and then in mid-1795 in the spate of slave resistance affecting the Spanish empire at Pointe Coupée (Louisiana), Coro (Venezuela), Puerto Príncipe (Cuba), and distant La Plata.[38] The extensive revolt on Curaçao that summer provides another case, according to some accounts. In 1811–1812 the Spanish colonies again were affected, this time Cuba, Puerto Rico, and Santo Domingo, as was once more Martinique. Thereafter, the "rumor syndrome" was limited mainly to the Anglophone world, as was abolitionism.

By 1789 angry colonists and alarmed officials were complaining that antislavery literature and artifacts were circulating in both the French and the British West Indies and were attracting the excited attention of slaves.[39] Incautious table talk by colonists, dockside conversations with newly arrived seamen, and overly optimistic letters from slaves in Europe were further sources of information and misinformation regarding antislavery. Caribbean blacks henceforward were aware that cracks were appearing in what formerly had seemed the monolithic structure of white rule, divisions that perhaps might be exploited. In some cases, shrewd leaders apparently manufactured rumors of emancipation to mobilize resistance. However they started, the rumors seem to have been widely believed. This is partly why a number of rebellions in this period began peacefully as strikes or demonstrations; slaves hoped they might negotiate their way to freedom.[40] Sometimes the supposedly beneficent intentions of the distant metropolitan power were projected onto its local representative, the colonial governor. In Puerto Príncipe, Cuba, in 1811, slaves feared local planters had poisoned the local governor in order to block the emancipation decree. In 1791 Guadeloupe slaves, contrarily, supposed the governor was keeping quiet about the new law until he could sell his own slaves.[41]

Enslaved men and women were willing to believe talk of an abolition law not only because it fulfilled their deepest aspirations but also because numerous contemporary developments combined to give it an air of plausibility. Both before and after 1789, governmental efforts to reform slavery or the slave trade, along with slaveowners' hostile reactions to such measures, signaled to slaves that they had potential allies. Discussions of improving the status of free coloreds were also liable to misinterpretation. The British, French, and Spanish governments had in the past all granted de facto freedom to certain indomitable maroon communities, and the long-standing Spanish sanctuary law (freeing foreign runaways) became an object of critical international attention in 1789–1790 prior to its withdrawal in May 1790.[42] The American Revolution had already begun the process of outlawing slavery, and Lord Dunmore's recruiting of fugitive slaves as soldiers (some of whom were resettled in the Caribbean) set an important example: fighting for a king against rebellious colonists was a path to freedom.[43] This was the role the Saint Domingue rebels claimed for themselves in 1791.

These twenty or so rumor-inspired conspiracies and rebellions display a good deal of variation. In some cases, the sources present belief in an obstructed decree as a prime motive force; for others, it appears as a peripheral aspect competing with several other ostensibly causal factors. Taken together, however, they constitute a type of slave revolt closely associated with the period 1789–1832 and, I would argue, with European antislavery more than with French libertarianism. If the two factors are difficult to separate in some of the early cases, this is not true later. Moreover, there is a fundamental difference between asserting a universal right to individual liberty and claiming a freedom bestowed by royal writ. The supposed agent of liberation was usually a king, and where the rebels' discourse is represented in the sources it is more often of a traditionalist than a "bourgeois-democratic" nature—not least among the slave insurgents of Saint Domingue.[44] When distant echoes of the Cortes of Cádiz reached Cuban plantations in 1811–1812, word went round that "the king had granted freedom," even though the king of Spain had been deposed three years earlier.[45]

In the Port Salut plot and first Dominica rebellion, both of January 1791, the rumor was not of full emancipation but of the granting of three free days per week. Such a rumor was echoed later that year in northern and western Saint Domingue and around Basse Terre, Guadeloupe, in April 1793.[46] This variant rumor first appeared in Martinique in the fall of 1789; it may derive from a French abolitionist tract of that year, and was usually communicated to slaves by free colored activists.[47] Like other "news" of interest to slaves, it was no doubt carried from island to island, as Julius Scott suggests, through networks of seamen and migrant free coloreds.[48] In the three Spanish West Indian cases of 1811–1812 the rumors of emancipation derived from a real proposal made by a Mexican deputy to the Cortes of Cádiz.[49] In early 1790, on the other hand, the reforming Código Negro Español of May 1789 was mistaken for an abolitionist measure. This was partly because colonial administrations sought to keep the decree secret while trying to get Madrid to withdraw or modify it.[50] Urban slaves were often well informed of the Código's real nature, and in Caracas some protested against the cover-up; but in the countryside wishful thinking appears to have distorted the news.

In Martinique, news of antislavery activity and ministerial efforts at reform both played a part in producing the Saint Pierre rising of August 1789. Reports of the initial phase of the French Revolution must also have encouraged slaves' expectations of radical change; but contrary to what some historians have written, the popular revolution of July was then unknown in the colony, where the Old Regime was yet to be challenged.[51] The talk of emancipation surrounding the Guadeloupe conspiracy of May 1791 doubtless owed more to the activity of the National Assembly in Paris—ironically, since the legislators voted that month never to tamper with slavery—but contemporaries still blamed the abolitionists and royalists for the rumors.[52] Scholars often link the disturbances in the Spanish colonies between April and August 1795 to the French abolition of slavery in February 1794. Indeed, the insurgents at Coro, Venezuela, called for "the law of the French." Even in this case, however, where French revolutionary influence was strong, historians disagree about the importance of rumors regarding a cover-up of a Spanish abolition decree.[53] Dating back to the 1770s, such speculations were given new life by the official abandonment of the Código Negro in late 1794 and the hostile reception accorded reforms favoring free coloreds passed in February 1795.[54] This sudden upsurge in nonwhite resistance from Buenos Aires to Louisiana, a full year after the decree of 16 pluviôse and nearly two years after slavery was abolished in Saint Domingue, strongly points to the importance of causes internal to the Spanish empire.[55]

It was against this background of attempted reform and nascent abolitionism that the French Revolution broke upon the Caribbean, and slaves interpreted it in this context. The prior existence of these trends helped foster the impression that the revolution was antislavery long before it actually was, just as the revolution in France and its colonies would encourage slaves to misinterpret reform proposals as being more than they really were. The revolution's threat to Caribbean slavery was both ideological and political. In the realm of ideas, it proclaimed an inspirational doctrine of liberty and equality, which belatedly came to include antiracism (1792) and then antislavery (1794). At the same time, the revolution weakened the material structure of white power in the colonies by causing widespread conflict among the free population, then war, and finally direct attempts to spread the revolution beyond French possessions. The clustering of slave revolts and conspiracies in the French islands in the period 1789–1793 constitutes the revolution's chief impact on the world of Caribbean slaves, and in all some 40 to 50 percent of the revolts and conspiracies listed in the table might be linked with the French Revolution.

That linkage seems to have been more political than ideological; the revolution promoted resistance probably less through the propagation of libertarian ideas than by affecting, or appearing to affect, the distribution of power. In the French colonies as of September 1789 the revolution in Europe split the white population into hostile factions, causing conflict between colonists and metropolis, military mutinies, and struggle between whites and free coloreds. All factions armed slaves to fight for them. A comparable though less dramatic scenario developed in some of the Dutch colonies from mid-1795, when the Batavian Republic was forcibly allied to France. Furthermore, between 1795 and 1800 French officials in the islands and their free colored and white radical supporters sought to spread slave rebellion to British, Spanish, and Dutch possessions.[56] Exactly how slaves perceived libertarian ideology is a difficult issue. Like antislavery rumors, though less directly, it doubtless reinforced existing aspirations for freedom, "boosting their legitimacy," as Michel Martin and Alain Yacou put it,[57] and exacerbating a sense of relative deprivation. But this alone was not enough. The risk of almost certain death that came with violent resistance required a material improvement in the chances of success. Moreover, when slaves did revolt, they did not often employ the language of the French revolutionaries. Rather unusual were the insurgents on Curaçao, who in August 1795 sang French revolutionary songs, and those at Coro and Maracaibo, who demanded "la ley de los franceses," a republic, and the abolition of slavery, the sales tax, and the aristocracy.[58]

When "the first decrees of the Nation" (the Declaration of the Rights of Man, the abolition of serfdom, etc.) reached Martinique in the fall of 1789, the emancipation rumors that already had provoked the Saint Pierre rising were intensified, but no revolt resulted from the ensuing agitation.[59] In Guadeloupe, slaves apparently did rise the following spring, taking advantage of the governor's departure for Martinique with a large military expedition. The rebel leaders supposedly claimed they were authorized to overthrow slavery since the whites had overthrown the king. As late as August 1793, however, after several more plots, a bloody revolt, and a year of civil war and with Jacobins in power locally and in France, Guadeloupean rebels still hesitated, during the major insurrection in Sainte Anne parish, to claim freedom as a right.[60] In Saint Domingue, slaves saw the tricolor cockade as the sign of "the emancipation of the whites." "The white slaves in France," they were reported as saying, "had killed their masters and, now free, were governing themselves and taking over the land."[61] Nevertheless, when they rebelled in 1791, seeking their own emancipation, they adopted a counterrevolutionary stance difficult to reconcile with the ideals of 1789. These did not impinge on the slave revolution in a significant manner until the French Republic abolished slavery and the free black leader Toussaint Louverture rallied the slave insurgents to its cause.[62] This was the turning point of the Haitian Revolution, and it transformed the war in the Caribbean. Henceforth the forces of black self-liberation were combined with the resources of a modern state under the banner of antislavery. The transformation came about not through the French exaltation of individual liberty but because of France's adoption of an abolitionist policy and offer of political support.

It is significant that Toussaint Louverture was not a slave but a member of the lower ranks of the free colored sector.[63] So, too, were the chief conspirators at Coro and Maracaibo, and apparently also the domestic servants who organized the April 1790 conspiracy in Guadeloupe.[64] Free colored leadership is found in about a dozen of the slave revolts and conspiracies of this period, notably those where the impact of libertarian ideology was most in evidence.[65] Across the Americas, it seems that free coloreds were more likely than slaves to respond to the message of the French Revolution.[66] Indeed, a sort of continuum existed, with creole slaves predominating in plots and rebellions exhibiting some degree of outside influence, while those of largely local inspiration were more likely to be dominated by Africans.[67]

French revolutionary influence usually coincided with the expectation of intervention by French colonial forces. Saint Domingue privateers played a prominent role in the Maracaibo conspiracy of May 1799, and according to Federico Brito Figueroa, they were implicated in the Coro rising four years earlier.[68] Another likely case is the great insurrection that spread across western Curaçao in 1795; its field slave leader claimed to be in touch with the mulatto general André Rigaud in Les Cayes, Saint Domingue, and he also took his name.[69] It is additionally probable that, in Spanish Louisiana, the Pointe Coupée conspirators of 1795 were encouraged by France's attempts, organized by ambassador Genêt, to invade and force retrocession of its former colony.[70] French military intervention, however, materialized only in the multiclass risings in the British Windward Islands (1795) and Curaçao (1800).[71]

Notwithstanding the important roles French and Dutch Jacobins played, the Curaçao invasion and the Maracaibo conspiracy were by-products as much of the Haitian as of the French Revolution. The French government and local French naval officers in fact opposed both actions because the Dutch and Spanish were then France's allies. Saint Domingue mulattoes were in large measure behind both events, and most of the troops that invaded Curaçao were black (albeit from Guadeloupe). In Maracaibo, the French Jacobin seamen spoke of decapitating the king, while their nonwhite comrades recommended guillotining "the large landowners and poor whites."[72]

Though independent Haiti was not yet in existence, one might identify a "Haitian" influence on the Caribbean from 1791 onward, the year of the devastating slave insurrection in northern Saint Domingue and of the more immediately successful revolt of the free colored communities of its west and south provinces. Nothing remotely comparable in magnitude or outcome had happened before in an American slave society. The French Revolution proclaimed the ideals of liberty and equality, but the Haitian Revolution showed African Americans that these ideals could be won by force of arms. Successive victories over armies of the chief colonial powers dramatized the message. In 1796 an ex-slave became deputy governor of the region's wealthiest colony. By 1804 a black state existed in the heart of the Caribbean. As John Bauer concluded, the psychological impact on American slaves of this war of liberation will never be fully fathomed, but it was apparently widespread.[73] From Charleston to Bahia slaveowners complained of a new "insolence" shown by slaves, which they often attributed to awareness of a successful black revolution.[74] Some doubts remain about how much news penetrated rural regions.[75] Yet the basic facts of the Haitian Revolution seem to have been rapidly disseminated along regional trade routes. Sailors, refugees, and proselytizing privateers spread tales of apocalyptic destruction and a new world in the making, and planters everywhere voiced fears of "another Saint Domingue." From Jamaica to Trinidad, slaves celebrated in song the triumph of the Haitian insurgents.[76] In 1800, the year Toussaint Louverture became governor of Saint Domingue, slaves sang in the streets of Kingston, "Black, white, brown. All de same."[77]

That this represented a profound change of consciousness is far from certain, and one needs to beware of overrating the Haitian example as a factor stimulating other revolts. Even so, several cases are known where conspirators made reference to the Saint Domingue rising or sought to learn from it, and there were presumably more.[78] Saint Domingue's influence on Curaçao's rebels has already been mentioned, and it is doubtless significant that José Chirino, leader of the Coro insurrection, had visited the French colony. Individuals with French names frequently showed up among conspirators and rebels in Spanish or British colonies. Not all played prominent roles or were necessarily from Saint Domingue.[79] However, three definitely were: Charles Deslondes, the driving force behind the Louisiana (1811) slave uprising, the largest in North America; Auguste Bonhomme, who organized the Marie Galante conspiracy (1791); and a "brown priest" involved in the Igbo conspiracy on Jamaica (1815). The free mulatto Edmond Thétis, a leader of the Martinique rebellion of 1811, had served several years in the army of Henry Christophe, who that year was crowned king of Haiti. The elaborate coronation of the former slave and his founding of a Haitian aristocracy must have caught the imagination of many black people across the Caribbean. In Puerto Rico, where one planter called it "a consummate evil for the West Indies," the news became confused with the emancipation rumor then circulating, so that in one district Christophe was perceived as the liberating monarch.[80]

The Haitian Revolution's most obvious impact was on the extensive Aponte conspiracy that was based in Havana but apparently was linked to plots in many other parts of Cuba. José Antonio Aponte, a free black carpenter and Shango priest, owned portraits of Christophe, Toussaint Louverture, and the Haitian emperor Dessalines (as well as George Washington). Besides spreading rumors of an emancipation decree, he and his group of free black organizers looked back to the Saint Domingue uprising for inspiration and led their followers to believe that help would come from Haiti. One organizer seems to have pretended to be Jean François, the main leader of the 1791 insurrection, who had long been an object of black pride in Havana. The conspirators certainly sought information from Gil Narciso, an ex-subaltern of Jean François who was then visiting Havana, and they may have drawn him into the plot.[81]

Haitian citizens traveling in the Caribbean no doubt tended to be outspoken critics of slavery and racism. So were their governments. The politics of survival, however, probably prevented Haitian statesmen from seeking to spread slave rebellion elsewhere. Endless rumors circulated regarding the activity of Haitian "agents," and these are given credence by some scholars.[82] In his postindependence proclamations, Dessalines declared his solidarity with the still-enslaved blacks of the remaining French colonies, and his attempt in 1805 to annex Santo Domingo strengthened fears of Haitian aggrandizement and subversion. Yet his supposed involvement in the 1805 Trinidad conspiracy seems quite spurious. Early Haitian rulers could not afford to provoke a maritime blockade by the slaveholding powers that would cut off their source of arms. To maintain good relations with Britain, Toussaint Louverture in 1799 betrayed an attempt by French agents to raise Jamaican slaves—an ironic clash between the French and Haitian revolutions—and Christophe similarly denounced a supposed plot by his enemy Alexandre Pétion, the president of the south Haitian Republic.[83]

As noted, south coast mulattoes were implicated in several conspiracies or revolts during the 1790s, and Pétion himself, with 200 of André Rigaud's officers, had participated in the invasion of Curaçao in 1800.[84] Haitians living on Curaçao were implicated in the Martinique rebellion of 1811, though it is not clear they had any state support. The rebellion in Santo Domingo the following year was, according to some scholars, aimed at facilitating intervention by Pétion, and again involved the shadowy figure of Gil Narciso.[85] All in all, those who did most to export liberty from Haiti were not the ex-slave rulers who dominated the north (and who continued to purchase African workers through the slave trade) but the free-born and light-skinned *anciens libres* of the south, who had no inhibiting links with the British. Paul Verna shows that Dessalines had nothing to do with the Miranda expedition that sailed from Haiti in 1806 to end Spanish rule in Venezuela. Pétion, however, in return for vital munitions, ships, and men, persuaded Simón Bolívar a decade later to initiate slave emancipation in northern South America.[86] This contribution to decolonization and liberation on the mainland may have been the Haitian Revolution's most enduring influence on the Greater Caribbean.[87]

Free coloreds thus played a prominent role in slave resistance in this period and proved particularly receptive to the messages of the French and Haitian revolutions. Especially striking was the alliance of free coloreds, slaves, and Black Caribs in the Windward Islands; it almost drove the British from Grenada and Saint Vincent in 1795. With assistance from Guadeloupe and Saint Lucia, the persecuted Francophone population of these former French islands combined across class and ethnic lines under the banner of the Republic and were defeated only after a year.[88] Though their numbers increased rapidly in these years and they proved excellent soldiers, free coloreds were outnumbered by whites in most colonies. Alliance with slaves thus made tactical sense for those determined to change the status quo. This was particularly true for those free coloreds who, regarding themselves as the only indigenous inhabitants of the islands, were developing aspirations toward independence.[89] Espousal of abolitionism, however, threatened free colored slaveowners and greatly complicated the free coloreds' basic demand for racial equality. Emancipation might diminish the stigma attached to their origins, but more surely it weakened their status as free persons in a world of slaves and exposed them to new rivals. As a group, therefore, free coloreds were not abolitionists, and even the most radical proved ambivalent in their attitudes to slavery and ex-slaves.

The conspiracy organized around Bayamo, Cuba, in August 1795 by the mulatto smallholder Nicolás Morales has sometimes been regarded as antislavery, since its aims included distributing land to the poor. Yet Morales made no mention of slavery and had no contact with slaves or maroons, only with free coloreds and disgruntled whites. Moreover, though the local presence of French refugees encouraged speculation among Cubans that the island had been sold to France, Morales seems to have been motivated less by the example of Saint Domingue's free coloreds, who had achieved equality more than three years earlier, than by the *gracias al sacar* law of the preceding February. Wrongly believing it granted full equality and was being concealed by the local governor, Morales planned an armed demonstration to force its implementation—once again, the reform and rumor syndrome. The sales tax was also an issue, as in other Spanish colonial rebellions that year.[90] The minor revolt on Martinique in 1800 led by Colonel Jean Kina, an ex-slave from Saint Domingue, has sometimes been called a slave revolt, and its leader did voice concern about the mistreatment of slaves. The revolt almost solely involved freemen, however, and was an attempt to reverse recent legislation against them.[91] In Saint Domingue Kina had been a staunch defender of the slave regime, fighting for the white planters against slave and free colored insurgents. His rebellion was thus a product of the Haitian Revolution, but an indirect one.

The Declaration of the Rights of Man had an immediate impact on French free coloreds, encouraging them to organize politically in Paris, where they evoked an embarrassed evasiveness, and in the colonies, where they faced lynch mobs. Only in Saint Domingue, where they were most numerous, did they rise in revolt. Initially they aligned themselves with royalist forces, traditionally a limiting influence on popular racism, but after the fall of the monarchy and the winning of political equality in 1792 they changed sides to become a mainstay of republican rule in the colonies.[92] A similar development occurred during the revolution in Venezuela between 1811 and 1815.[93] In each case, the need for free colored military assistance (against rebel slaves or Spanish royalists) forced the dismantling of racial discrimination in the face of ingrained fear and prejudice. In the French colonies the reforms did not survive the revolution.

Elsewhere free coloreds had to pursue less dramatic strategies aimed at achieving modest improvements in their civil status. In 1792 a petition of Jamaican freemen for small changes in discriminatory laws created alarm among white colonists, and four years later produced some limited results. A more widespread free colored activism appeared in the British islands in the period 1810–1815, foreshadowing the mobilization that would bring racial equality after 1830.[94] Two factors that generally favored the free coloreds were a rapidly growing population (whereas white communities were usually shrinking) and the importance in this time of war and slave rebellion of nonwhite militias. In the Spanish colonies especially, militia service provided an avenue of social advancement, and reliance on free colored defenders inhibited governmental desires to discriminate. Since it provided military training, influential whites in Cuba sought to abolish the black militia in the 1790s, but the government retained it, fearing white separatism as well as slave revolts and foreign invasion. In 1812 the black battalion of the Havana militia felt able to petition for equal treatment with white soldiers, though it met only with a worried silence from the administration.[95]

In all colonies, free colored militias helped in the suppression of slave rebellions, and in the Spanish colonies several conspiracies were betrayed by members of the mulatto militia. Although the importance of internal divisions within the free colored sector is not well understood, it appears that the freemen most closely allied with slave rebels tended to be those closest to them in wealth, culture, and appearance— black freedmen with little or no stake in slaveholding, such as Aponte, Chirino, and Toussaint Louverture (or Denmark Vesey in the United States).[96] In Saint Domingue, some communities of free coloreds became caught up in the 1791 revolt, and opportunistic alliances were made and unmade. However, until slavery was abolished in the French colonies, the main free colored leaders did not support general emancipation, even if some displayed sympathy for the slaves' plight. Following emancipation, the two groups jockeyed sometimes violently for power. In Saint Domingue and Guadeloupe many collaborated in the Napoleonic reconquest of their islands in 1802, until it became apparent that only independence could guarantee the preservation of both equality and liberty. In Guadeloupe the freemen Delgrès and Ignace fought a heroically hopeless campaign to the death, while in Saint Domingue Pétion and Dessalines combined in a fragile alliance to finally oust the French.

It was probably a free colored who suggested "Haiti" as the name of their new state.[97] The choice of an Amerindian word to celebrate the rupture with Europe and the massacre of surviving white colonists underscored the point that Haitian independence carried a more radical message than did that of the United States two decades earlier. Haiti was a symbol of black achievement in a world dominated by Europeans, where slavery and racism were gaining strength. For pro- and antislavery forces it became a crucial test case regarding ideas about race, slavery, and the future of the Caribbean, a debate to which Haitian publicists and statesmen contributed.[98]

Envisaging a very different type of independence, some French writers had predicted the secession of Saint Domingue even before the revolution, pointing to its economic strength and the autonomist tendencies of its white planters. The French Revolution promptly gave white colonists extensive political (though not economic) concessions, but its growing radicalism and perceived threat to slavery increased the planters' separatist aspirations and channeled them toward Great Britain. After several attempts at secession, autonomist and counterrevolutionary groups colluded in inviting British forces into the main French colonies once war broke out in Europe (1792–1794).[99] British rule, however, did not bring self-government, and no more planter legislatures were created in the West Indies. The British planter classes, weakened by absenteeism and already possessing considerable political autonomy, proved relatively quiescent through this period. Though embittered by the progress of the antislavery movement, their dependence on imperial protection, both commercial and naval, severely limited their room for maneuver. Moreover, the class conflict that racked the French colonies' white communities produced only a few weak echoes in those of the British, who generally affected a bluff disdain for the doings of the "French maniacs."[100] As France had a much larger population than either England or Spain but far fewer colonial outlets, young and indigent white males were exceptionally numerous in its West Indian possessions.[101] These *petits blancs* challenged planters and administrators and fueled fierce racial conflict, until later, as Jacobins, they rallied to the egalitarian republic. This radical trend was both expressed and facilitated by military mutinies of varying importance in most of the French islands.[102]

Spain's Caribbean colonies proved socially more stable, but its absolutist rule was particularly vulnerable to the doctrines of revolutionary France, at least in its mainland colonies, where whites were less inhibited than in the islands by fear of slave revolts and naval blockade.[103] Hostile even to moderate liberalism, the Spanish government sought from the beginning of the French Revolution to ban French publications and restrict immigration from foreign colonies. Rumors of white rebellion circulated in Cuba as early as 1794, but members of its prospering elite gave only a passing thought to autonomy when the monarchy fell in 1808 and to annexation by the United States when slave emancipation was feared in 1811. A minor proindependence plot among Havana creoles was easily suppressed in 1810.[104] Far more fragile was Spain's hold on New Orleans and the Floridas, which were largely settled by foreigners.[105] Yet it was Venezuela that generated most secessionist activity. This consisted of a republican (and antislavery) plot in 1797, the exile Miranda's incessant canvassing for foreign assistance, his invasion of 1806, and the war for independence launched in 1811. The strength of the colonial military and administration made it a long struggle, and only revolution in Spain in 1820 clinched the outcome.[106] Venezuela thus produced the only Caribbean planter class to emulate Virginia's in winning self-determination.

For some other social groups the encroaching plantation frontier brought about a complete loss of autonomy. In the Gulf Coast hinterland the Creek nation was destroyed by the U.S. Army following the War of 1812 and the curious attempt to establish the multiethnic state of Muskogee.[107] In the West Indies, the Cuban Cobreros won official title to land and liberty, but the Dominica maroons were finally subdued, as were the Boni in Surinam. The Black Caribs were deported from Saint Vincent to Central America, and the Trelawny Maroons from Jamaica to Canada.

Most scholars regard the Jamaican Maroon War as the product of local causes, though a few have argued that French revolutionary influence was behind it.[108] Some Maroons did claim belatedly to be seeking slave emancipation, but the conflict essentially expressed their particularist interests. They attracted relatively few supporters and were opposed by the rival Accompong Maroons. Similarly, the Djuka Maroons in Surinam helped the Dutch repress the rebellious Boni, and the Maniel/Dokos of Saint Domingue followed a strictly opportunist policy through the Haitian Revolution. Co-opted by timely concessions, the Dominica maroons did not join in the local revolts of 1791 and 1795 or the French invasion in 1805, though they fought against planter encroachment before and afterwards.[109] Established maroon bands had separate interests and identities from those of the surrounding slave populations. They thus tended to fight their own battles, not those of the slave population in general.[110] Nevertheless, they remained a potent symbol. On both Jamaica and Dominica, maroons were regarded by slave conspirators as potential allies in revolt.[111] During the Haitian Revolution, black, white, and mulatto revolutionaries referred in their proclamations to the example of earlier maroon struggle (in Jamaica rather than Saint Domingue), though the popular belief that bands of fugitive slaves played a major role in launching the revolution is largely mythological.[112]

Even in this age of revolution, the strength of the colonial regimes resided not just in their ability to wield overwhelming force and their willingness to use terror but also in their ability to divide their opponents and persuade them the costs of accommodation were less than those of resistance. Everywhere the deadliest enemy of conspiracy was the common government tactic of rewarding betrayal with grants of freedom, land, or cash pensions. Most of the conspiracies listed in the table were betrayed, as were those of whites and free coloreds. Moreover, colonial governments were able to recruit thousands of enslaved blacks as armed defenders of the status quo. Though this usually provided a path to freedom for the slave soldiers, it divided the black population while adding to the regimes' strength. Independence was achieved in Haiti and Venezuela only after the negotiation of multiclass alliances. In the British Windward Islands, a shared Francophone identity also helped cement a multiclass alliance of oppressed groups that yielded only to massive military pressure. Among Anglophone blacks, however, French invaders often encountered a hostility to outsiders built upon the creoles' growing sense of identification with their particular islands. This constituted another obstacle confronting Caribbean rebels.[113] Black refugees from Saint Domingue met with resentment from slaves in Jamaica; Barbadian slaves celebrated British victories over the French Republic.[114] Then as now, migration provided an antidote to small island parochialism, and it is striking that numerous rebels had previously traveled in the region.[115] Yet there is no reason to believe whites had a monopoly on xenophobia.

The ruling classes were at war with one another for much of this period, and in the French and mainland Spanish colonies they were rent by revolutionary divisions. The intersection of international rivalries and race war complicated calculations of self-interest, but as a rule, colonial policies switched from displays of transnational race/class solidarity in peacetime to the sponsoring of revolutionary upheaval in time of war. In 1791 the governors of Jamaica and Santiago de Cuba sent assistance to Saint Domingue planters, their commercial rivals, albeit with mixed emotions.[116] The governors of Havana and Santo Domingo were certainly less helpful, but there seems no truth to the charge leveled by contemporaries and some historians that the British and Spanish governments encouraged the destruction of the French colony.[117] Spanish individuals undoubtedly traded with the rebel slaves, but there is no evidence of official intervention until war broke out in 1793. Then both powers sought to annex the colony, not to destroy it. Nonetheless, Spain's recruitment of the 1791 rebels as auxiliary troops and, in a different way, the British intervention of 1793–1798 did much to advance the black revolution.[118] Defeat then led the British to assist Toussaint Louverture against the French, until peace with France caused a cynical reversal of this policy, permitting the Napoleonic invasion of 1802.

The Spanish, for their part, sent soldiers to Grenada to help the British against Julien Fédon, and they provided the Jamaican government with hunting dogs to suppress the Trelawny Maroons.[119] During the Anglo-Spanish wars between 1796 and 1808, the British assisted Spanish American revolutionaries seeking to throw off rule from Madrid, but the return of peace prevented the insurgents from obtaining help when the revolution got under way. Both British and Spanish colonies gave French refugees a nervous welcome; conservative white property owners were favored, and many were naturalized, but others were intermittently excluded or expelled. Napoleon's invasion of Spain in 1808 led to the large-scale expulsion of French residents from Cuba, though it caused less drastic results in Puerto Rico. Spain's century-old sanctuary policy of welcoming runaway slaves from foreign colonies was withdrawn in 1790, and the following year a treaty with the Dutch sought to close the Orinoco to fugitives.[120] This closing off of traditional havens to runaway slaves possibly helped increase the likelihood of slave rebellions in the non-Hispanic Caribbean.

The French Revolutionary War differed from previous wars in the Caribbean, partly because it combined traditional imperial rivalries with a bitter civil war and unprecedented racial struggle. A contest between opposing world views, in which opponents were dehumanized, it generated exceptional brutality, as did the later struggle in Venezuela. Both white and black troops tortured their prisoners and collected severed heads as trophies.[121] Blacks were fighting for their freedom, colonial whites for their way of life. French republicans regarded colonists who collaborated with foreign invaders as traitors, and their opponents viewed them as low-born saboteurs of social order. In Guadeloupe, Saint Domingue, and Venezuela, royalists and republicans executed hundreds of their compatriots. The French government, moreover, ordered no quarter be given to British soldiers, just as Bolívar later ordered war to the death against belligerent Spaniards. Yet it was the black population that suffered the worst atrocities. These reached a peak in the Haitian war of independence, in which the Napoleonic army waged what amounted to a war of genocide. Europeans who believed in the progressive civilization of mankind found cause for reflection.[122]

The war was also unusual as regards the Europeans' degree of reliance on black soldiers, which was a response to the high death rates of European soldiers in the tropics and the need to combat nonwhite insurgents in difficult terrain. Free colored militias and the occasional arming of slaves in wartime had a long history in the region. The second half of the eighteenth century also saw the formation of special nonwhite units to combat maroons, as well as growing concern about military mortality due to disease. The 1790s then brought dramatic change in this area. Royalists, radicals, and free coloreds in the French islands all armed slaves to fight for them in 1791–1792, and after the outbreak of war in 1793 more formal corps appeared that mixed former rebels with other recruits. The French organized *légions* and *demi-brigades* of emancipated slaves; the British raised Chasseur regiments on the plantations of occupied colonies, and in a desperate gamble that soon went awry, the Spanish recruited *tropas auxiliares* among the Saint Domingue insurgents of 1791.[123] In the War of 1812, the British armed slave fugitives, as they had in the American War of Independence; and ephemeral corps of rangers were used in the West Indies down to 1815. The major development, however, was the foundation in 1795 of the

West India Regiments as regular units of the British army. Recruited mainly from slave ships, they numbered twelve regiments in the middle years of the war and came to constitute one-third of British forces in the Caribbean.[124] Comparable developments occurred after 1811 in Venezuela, where the Haitian example at first made both sides reluctant to arm slaves, but circumstances soon changed their minds.[125]

Though frequently opposed by planters, the military demanded the arming of blacks because of their degree of immunity to tropical diseases and their superior performance in mountainous and forested terrain. As a result, much of the fighting between the British, French, and Spanish actually involved blacks in combat with blacks. The nature of the conflict consequently was rather different from that of most previous Caribbean wars. Often fought in the interior of the islands, it was more mobile, more adapted to the landscape, using surprise attack and rapid dispersal—guerrilla warfare a decade before the term was coined. Orthodox assumptions sometimes had to be reversed. Cavalry, not previously a key element in Caribbean warfare, became critical for controlling the plains, where most slaves lived. Port cities usually considered indefensible from the landward side were able to hold out for years against attackers lacking in artillery skills; whereas, deprived of their naval support, the ports now proved vulnerable to assault from the sea.[126] Until guns were widely distributed, Africans, accompanied by drumming and chanting, fought with bows and arrows and lances; they yelled and whistled to frighten their enemies. Provided with uniforms, they underwent a degree of Europeanization, but according to Moreau de Jonnès, even regimented black troops always fired in a prone position.[127] Many perhaps saw their tricolor cockades or royalist cap badges as amulets rather than political symbols. If John Thornton is right that many had been soldiers in Africa, they were doubtless more experienced than some of the hastily raised European corps sent against them.[128]

The war at sea, too, was mainly of an informal type, centered on privateering rather than fleet actions. Reviving an old regional tradition, swift coasting vessels were converted into corsairs and wrought havoc among regional shipping. Far more than in earlier wars, nonwhite seamen now played prominent roles, especially in the French islands, in Tortola, and later in Spanish America. Off the coast of Saint Domingue, armed barges crammed with fighting men of all colors became the terror of becalmed shipping. British Caribbean commerce lost some 500 vessels per year in the period 1793–1805. However, of the more than 700 captured by Guadeloupe privateers in the mid-1790s, half belonged to neutrals, as did most of those taken before British Vice-

Admiralty Courts. The Danish merchant Johan Nissen was plundered seventeen times during the war.[129] North American losses led to the Quasi War between France and the United States in 1798–1800. Neutral trade nevertheless flourished.[130] Privateers, we have seen, also spread the message of revolution, and seaborne propaganda was a novel feature of this war. Victor Hugues arrived in Guadeloupe with a printing press, and Pétion sent one back with Bolívar to Venezuela. The British in Trinidad also funneled seditious writings into Spanish America. Driven from the French Windward Islands in 1809–1810, French corsairs moved northward to New Orleans and at the end of the period were operating out of Cartagena and Les Cayes with Yankee, Haitian, and Spanish creole brethren. The privateering milieu spanned the hemisphere and provided continuity between the revolutionary movements of the age.[131]

The amount of blood and treasure expended by the European governments in defending their Caribbean empires has never been calculated. According to Michael Duffy, the campaigns of 1793–1801, excluding the expenses of the Royal Navy, cost the British government perhaps thirty million pounds.[132] This was equivalent to a year's prewar tax revenue, or somewhat less than the market value of one year's British Caribbean exports during the period in question. Military mortality has been a very controversial topic, but it is now clear that, of the European troops sent to the Caribbean by Britain alone, some 70,000 died there between 1793 and 1815. The turbulent years of the great military expeditions, 1793–1798, claimed just over half this number. Nearly 33,000 died in the relatively uneventful years that followed. The defense of Jamaica, which was never attacked, cost more than 8,000 British lives. In the period 1793–1801, 50 percent of European troops in British pay died and another 14,000 were discharged or deserted, while the British navy lost more than 30,000 total casualties.[133] The vast majority of military deaths—certainly more than 95 percent—were due to disease, chiefly yellow fever, which fed on the massive influx of nonimmunes and subsequent movements of population throughout the region.[134] Battle casualties, Duffy shows, were "relatively trivial" even in the 1790s.[135] European troops generally died without seeing combat at all. Not even the Crimean War provides a comparable example, though death rates were probably not very different from those in earlier Caribbean conflicts.[136]

Much less is known about French and Spanish losses. Of the approximately 60,000 soldiers and national guardsmen sent from France to Saint Domingue in the period 1791–1803, most never returned. The majority perished of fever, though in the first half of the Haitian War of

Independence battle casualties approached 20 percent of total French military dead.[137] At the beginning and end of the French wars Spain had the largest garrison in the Caribbean, but its military losses were probably the smallest. Cut off from its colonies and near bankruptcy for much of the period, Spain sent relatively few forces to the region between 1793 and 1811. Spanish troops, moreover, had the reputation of suffering the lowest mortality and morbidity rates. Only a minority were native to the Caribbean, but soldiers from southern Europe had a significant degree of immunity to malaria, as the French also found.[138] Even so, Spanish losses to disease in Santo Domingo were very heavy, and garrisons dwindled everywhere. All in all, the regular armed forces of the main colonial powers must have lost at least 180,000 dead in defending or seeking to expand their Caribbean empires in the period 1791–1815. The losses of the local populations in resisting or assisting their ambitions will probably never be known.

This enormous inflow of European troops and seamen formed part of a multifarious movement of population within the Greater Caribbean that is one of the notable characteristics of this period. Germans, Poles, Catalans, and Irish, as well as British, French, and Spanish, they added to the ethnic diversity of the region. Although the army was the ultimate deterrent against slave uprisings, slaves and soldiers had a certain amount in common. Similarly regimented and punished, they both were employed for heavy manual labor and they had a tendency to become fugitives. In garrison towns they lived in close proximity. They also had the reputation of stealing from plantation provision grounds and retailing stolen property.[139] More than ever the military was a salient presence in Caribbean societies, patrolling and mounting guard, parading on town squares, and thronging the markets, bars, and brothels of the seaports. Much of the military's later influence on Caribbean popular culture perhaps dates from these years, when slave secret societies organized as "regiments" and "convoys," and the carnival Jonkonnu figure changed from a horned beast to a European soldier.[140]

Colonial refugees and their slaves were another source of population movement. From 1791 to 1804 successive cataclysms in Saint Domingue sent thousands of whites and free coloreds back and forth between the French colony and Jamaica, Cuba, and the south Caribbean, as well as permanently to North America and Europe. There were reputedly 10,000 to 18,000 French in Santiago de Cuba in 1803. By mid-1804 scarcely a member of the former ruling class remained behind in independent Haiti.[141] Santo Domingo similarly lost most of its white inhabitants when it was transferred to French rule in 1795; they went chiefly to Cuba, Puerto Rico, and Venezuela, though some returned in

1809.[142] Beginning in 1790, alternating waves of royalists and republicans also fled the French Windward Islands, overwhelming small neighbors such as Saint Eustatius and Saint Kitt's. In the summer of 1793, Dominica received 5,000 to 6,000 refugees from Martinique. Arriving sometimes in rowing boats, often destitute, refugees had to be housed on porches and in sheds, and everywhere became the object of government relief and public subscriptions. Together with thousands of prisoners of war crammed into jails and prison ships, they stretched local food supplies and helped spread the pandemic of yellow fever that ravaged the entire region for much of this period. Large numbers died.[143]

In the Spanish colonies, even conservative French refugees sometimes met with widespread hostility. This was caused first by their worldly behavior and by popular perceptions of them as radical heretics, and later by anger at the Napoleonic invasion of Spain. Their harshness toward their slaves occasionally also attracted comment.[144] In the British islands, too, foreigners were frequently feared as a political threat, particularly the free coloreds and the slaves. In early 1795, 900 of the 1,500 "French" in Antigua were slaves. Colonial governments periodically passed laws to exclude or expel nonwhites. However, if some sang revolutionary songs, others were considered "inoffensive" and a valuable economic resource. This was especially so in underdeveloped regions such as Puerto Rico, eastern Cuba, Trinidad, and Louisiana. Only 30 percent of the Saint Domingue refugees who moved to New Orleans when expelled from Cuba in 1809 were whites.[145] Just as the social accomplishments of the French colonists tended to impress their hosts, the skills of their pastry cooks and laundry women also were appreciated. Some French refugees were able to set up in colonial trade and made quick fortunes, as in Saint Thomas, where more than 1,500 foreigners were naturalized in the period 1792–1801. In Santo Domingo French colonists opened bars and gaming houses. Other refugees turned to privateering, as in Puerto Rico and Santiago de Cuba. Whites, free coloreds, and slaves made important contributions to the sugar industry in Cuba and Louisiana and to the expansion of coffee cultivation (till then largely a French monopoly) in Cuba, Puerto Rico, and Jamaica. Their most lasting impact, perhaps, was in the reinforcing of Francophone culture in Louisiana and Trinidad.[146]

A peculiarly embarrassing refugee problem for colonial administrations was the resettling of demobilized black regiments. How could former slaves with military experience be integrated into a slave society? The problem was especially acute in the case of the Santo Domingo auxiliary troops, who as rebel slaves had devastated northern Saint

Domingue in 1791 and as mutineers had massacred 700 colonists three years later. When the Spanish surrendered Santo Domingo in 1795, a hard core of 800 black soldiers refused to be left behind. After the governors of Cuba and Trinidad refused to accept them, they were distributed between coastal Honduras, Campeche, Portobelo, and Florida—marginal regions with few slaves and a need for additional defense. The policy proved a success. The blacks in Honduras played a key role in defending Trujillo against a British attack in 1797, and on the Florida frontier the former rebel leader Biassou defended Spanish plantations against the incursions of Creek Indians led by a white American eccentric.[147] The British faced problems similar to those faced by the Spanish when they too withdrew from Saint Domingue. The Chasseur regiments they raised were turned away from Jamaica and many were sent back to plantation labor under Toussaint Louverture. Some were captured at sea and incorporated into the army of Guadeloupe; the rest went to Trinidad and helped ensure that colony remained Francophone in culture under British rule. Trinidad and British Honduras later became preferred locations for settling black levies from the War of 1812 and retirees from the West India regiments.[148]

Spanish, British, and French all used Central America's sparsely settled Caribbean coast for disposing of groups they feared. In 1791 Saint Domingue colonists deported some 200 slaves, known as "the Swiss," who had been armed by free colored insurgents. Intended for the Mosquito Shore of Nicaragua, they were dumped instead on the tiny islet of English Key, which led to their repatriation by the alarmed colonists of British Honduras. Others followed in succeeding years, including survivors of Fédon's rebellion on Grenada, and perhaps other black prisoners of war.[149] (Already by 1794 black prisoners from Saint Domingue filled the jails of Kingston, Havana, and La Guaira, and though the military sometimes tried to sell those it did not kill, recruit, or use for forced labor, purchasers could not always be found.)[150] The largest group of forced migrants to Central America comprised the Black Caribs deported from Saint Vincent in 1797. The British moved more than 2,000 to Roatan, along with black rebels from Martinique. With the help of the *tropas auxiliares* recently arrived from Saint Domingue, the local Spanish transferred them to the mainland, whence they spread westward to their present homes.[151]

The war thus occasioned substantial population movements in the Greater Caribbean, some of lasting consequence. By far the most significant, however, was the continuing importation of enslaved Africans. About 800,000 arrived in the period 1789–1815, not counting the approximately 240,000 sold in the southern states of North America.

Despite the removal of the huge Saint Domingue market, slave imports to the Caribbean fell by less than 20 percent in the 1790s from their peak level in the 1780s. In the following decade abolition reduced them to one-third of their peak level (or, including the United States, one-half). Among new arrivals, adolescents from the Congo basin were more prominent than ever; captives from the Bight of Benin were markedly fewer.[152] This continuing inflow of new laborers fueled an economic growth that financed the huge costs of colonial defense and helped make them acceptable to European governments.

Economic growth came from three other main sources apart from this infusion of new labor. New lands were brought into production, notably in the Spanish islands, the Guianas, and Louisiana. Improved agricultural and manufacturing techniques, sometimes diffused by refugees, raised productivity even in the oldest colonies. And sugar production everywhere received a fortuitous boost from the adoption of the high-yielding Tahiti cane. The opening of the slave trade to the Spanish colonies in 1789 and the generalized relaxation of trade restrictions in wartime further aided expansion.[153] War drove up production costs considerably, but it also did the same for commodity prices. The decimation of Saint Domingue's output, together with population growth and urbanization in Europe and the United States, reinforced the trend. Though not the only factor at work, and though its losses were not quite as dramatic as sometimes suggested, the revolution in Saint Domingue powerfully affected markets for coffee, sugar, and cotton, stimulating production across the Americas.[154] The other colonies where fighting was fiercest (Grenada, Saint Lucia, Venezuela), or where for other reasons export production collapsed (French Guiana, Dominica, Santo Domingo) were in general not major producers. Regional output of tropical products was thus higher at the end than at the beginning of this period, notwithstanding the ruin of the Caribbean's most important colony.

Not only did Spanish West Indian sugar production triple, but expansion in the British and Danish colonies more than compensated (in weight traded) for the fall in French and Dutch production, which itself experienced substantial recovery by the late 1820s.[155] Saint Domingue's coffee output was less easily replaced, but by 1815 expansion in Jamaica and Cuba had gone far in making up losses.[156] Similarly, though Venezuelan cacao suffered irreparable damage after 1811, this stimulated production in Grenada, Trinidad, and Saint Vincent. Caribbean cotton, moreover, flourished for most of the war years. If one further takes into account increases in market prices, increases in customs duties, freight and insurance rates, and the subsequent processing of raw cotton and sugar, the growing value of Caribbean commerce during the French wars is all the more impressive.[157]

War and revolution encouraged expansion outside the region as well, of course. Although Caribbean sugar output increased, its share of the world market diminished somewhat between 1791 and 1815. This was due largely to the economic revival of Brazil; the Indian Ocean colonies and European beet sugar were then still negligible competitors.[158] The take-off of coffee cultivation in Brazil would eventually prove a severe blow to Caribbean planters, but as with sugar, its impact was not fully felt till the 1820s. The most formidable competition came from the spread of short staple cotton across the interior of the U.S. South, but cotton had never been a major crop in the Caribbean. Although production was shifting to new areas within and outside the region, when peace came the world's leading exporter of tropical staples was still Jamaica. As late as 1807 it exported three times as much sugar and seven times as much coffee as Brazil.[159]

In all types of agriculture, numerous small-scale or marginal producers went out of business. Yet this was by no means new. With war's end European farmers faced similar problems. Consolidation was a continuing process. Lowell Ragatz's thesis that the British West Indies faced inevitable decline in 1790 and was reprieved only by the Haitian Revolution is thus difficult to accept. The critical economic change in this period, Seymour Drescher demonstrates, was the ending of the British slave trade in 1808. The Greater Caribbean had substantial reserves of new land, and Barbados, oldest of the sugar islands, showed that profitability and expanding production did not depend on virgin soil. Abolition, however, limited expansion and increased labor costs, thus giving external competitors extra advantage over British and British-occupied territories. J. R. Ward argues that profit margins, though trimmed, remained competitive in the British colonies through the 1820s. Nonetheless, by 1815 the British Caribbean was set on a downward path, and the region as a whole faced increasing competition, and counted for less, in a much-expanded world market.[160]

The war period thus had paradoxical results. It brought Great Britain a considerable accession of political power, the eclipse of its European rivals, and increased control of international commerce. Yet, just when its colonies attained their maximum importance to the home country, the abolition of the slave trade undercut their precarious prosperity and ensured their economic decline.[161] Spain, on the other hand, suffered great political losses but saw its remaining possessions assume unprecedented economic importance, though at the price of sharing control of their trade. Only the United States managed to combine economic and political gains (on the Gulf Coast) while consolidating its position in regional commerce.

Colonialism and slavery remained the defining institutions of the Caribbean, but they had received heavy blows and were henceforth on the defensive. The Haitian Revolution freed a half-million slaves and shattered France's status as a major colonial power. The fusion of black resistance, abolitionism, and secular libertarianism achieved in the French colonies in the 1790s proved of short duration, but a weaker amalgam was forged in the Spanish American Wars of Independence. Spain's hold on its mainland possessions was far from broken by 1815, but thereafter the South American insurgents were committed to the policy of racial equality, military manumission, and eventual slave emancipation that was to bring them success within a decade. Florida, invaded several times from the north, would be sold to the United States in 1819. Meanwhile only Haiti achieved independence and only Louisiana joined it in escaping European rule. Although the Danish, Dutch, British, and North American slave trades were ended, the number of slaves in the Caribbean declined only slightly and thousands of transported Africans would be sold there annually for almost another half-century.

Colonial rule after 1815 brought an uneven movement toward economic liberalization, combined with tighter political control. Mercantilist restrictions, abandoned during the war, were reimposed, and planters continued to sell in a protected home market at the price of heavy taxation. Spain, however, soon granted a large measure of free trade to its islands in recognition of their burgeoning position in the world market and its own political and economic weakness. The British introduced similar though less radical reforms in 1822. Colonial representation in metropolitan legislatures, briefly allowed in France (1789–1799) and Spain (1811–1814), was not continued. The French government rejected not only the innovations of the revolution but even the advisory colonial assemblies granted in the 1780s. British opinion also favored greater control of colonial affairs. Representative government was not introduced into the new colonial conquests, and the Colonial Office, founded in 1803, took an increasingly interventionist stance, which helped pave the way toward the abolition of British slavery in 1833.[162]

Slavery changed for the better and for the worse. Demographic rates benefited in the long term from the increasing creolization of the slave population, but this was interrupted by the massive imports of the 1790s and counteracted by the increasing concentration on sugar cultivation and the shift in settlement toward the unhealthy environments of the south Caribbean. More efficient work regimes in the British West Indies gave plantation slaves shorter working hours and more food, according to J. R. Ward, and on Guadeloupe the abolition of night work proved a durable legacy of the revolutionary period.[163] Changing European manners, abolitionist scrutiny, and the threat of rebellion probably helped reduce flagrant atrocities against slaves. Wartime also brought those with access to urban markets better prices for their forage, firewood, and foodstuffs, and the influx of troops and seamen no doubt increased prostitution.[164] The consequent flow of earnings may have increased acts of self-purchase, which along with manumission for military service contributed to the rapid growth of the free colored population in these years. The free nonwhite proportion of the population grew everywhere except in Cuba, where it was outstripped by white and African immigration. An expanding free colored sector perhaps increased some slaves' hopes for freedom, but more generally it must have enhanced the sense of relative deprivation among those in bondage.

If an end to slavery was hardly in sight in 1815, its elimination by either violent or peaceful means was much easier to imagine than it had been a quarter-century earlier. Though the antislavery movement had yet to adopt emancipation as a political goal, it enjoyed a burst of success in 1814–1817 in obtaining slave registration in the British colonies and agreements to end the slave trade from all remaining carriers. Slaves in the nineteenth century knew slavery was under attack; they were exposed to the growing European preoccupation with individual liberty; and the searing drama of Saint Domingue had demonstrated, to them and their owners, the possibility of successful revolt. Since 1791 colonial whites had been complaining that Caribbean blacks exhibited a "new temper and ideas" or were "no longer the same people."[165] Slave conspirators and rebels now usually articulated demands for general emancipation, which they felt they could extract from a white society in which they knew they had allies. Henceforward, however, central government politics, not slave consciousness or planter morale, would be the critical element in ending Caribbean slavery. Although black resistance or war often formed part of the process, peaceful means were usually to predominate. The Haitian case, the product of a unique combination of war and revolution, was not easily forgotten but would never be emulated.

Caribbean slaves might secretly revere the black state in their midst,[166] but its contribution to the broader emancipation process remains controversial. Robin Blackburn makes strong general claims for its impact, but outside of Venezuela and Santo Domingo, these seem difficult to substantiate precisely. Seymour Drescher's rigorous analysis of the British antislavery campaign suggests the Haitian Revolution had no decisive or long-lasting influence on it.[167] Michael Duffy argues persuasively that the Haitian Revolution removed a fundamental obstacle to abolition by lessening British concern that Britain's losses would benefit its traditional enemy, but he seems to suggest the Anglo-French war had an even greater effect.[168] To an uncertain degree the Haitian struggle enhanced European opinions of blacks; but proslavery writers rationalized Haitian achievements, and both the revolution and subsequent national development fueled contradictory propaganda. The contrast between the export-oriented, forced-labor regime of King Christophe's northern kingdom and the peasant agriculture of Alexandre Pétion's southern republic further complicated assessments. The striking enthusiasm for Haiti evinced by the conservative *Quarterly Review*, cited in the introduction, proved short-lived, and after 1820 Haiti's centrality to the European debate over emancipation gradually diminished.[169]

NOTES

1. The Danish, Dutch, and (temporarily) the French slave trades ended in 1803, those of Britain and the United States in 1808. The slave trade to Venezuela was banned in 1811. According to David Eltis, *Economic Growth and the Ending of the Transatlantic Slave Trade* (New York: Oxford University Press, 1987), p. 56, British and United States involvement in the Cuban slave trade had largely ceased by 1820.

2. The two classic studies of the wider political and intellectual context are David Brion Davis, *The Problem of Slavery in the Age of Revolution, 1776–1823* (Ithaca: Cornell University Press, 1975), and Robin Blackburn, *The Overthrow of Colonial Slavery, 1776–1848* (London: Verso, 1988).

3. Seymour Drescher, *Capitalism and Antislavery: British Mobilization in Comparative Perspective* (New York: Oxford University Press, 1986), emphasizes mobilization rather than the temporal shift in attitudes stressed in David Brion Davis, *The Problem of Slavery in Western Culture* (Ithaca: Cornell University Press, 1966).

4. On the links between British and French antislavery, see Jacques-Pierre Brissot, *Discours sur la nécessité d'établir à Paris une Société . . .* (Paris, 1788); Benjamin Frossard, *La cause des esclaves nègres*, 2 vols. (Lyon, 1789).

5. Gabriel Debien, *Les esclaves aux Antilles françaises aux XVIIe et XVIIIe siècles* (Basse-Terre: Société d'Histoire de la Guadeloupe, 1974), pp. 485–487, 493–494; Robert Southey, *Chronological History of the West Indies* (London, 1827), vol. 3, pp. 18, 21–22; R. C. Dallas, *History of the Maroons* (London, 1803), vol. 2, p. 444; José Torre Revello, "Origen y aplicación del Código Negrero en la América Española (1788–1794)," *Boletín del Instituto de Investigaciones Históricas* (Buenos Aires) 15, no. 53 (July 1932): 42–50.

6. Michael Craton, "Slave Culture, Resistance and the Achievement of

Emancipation in the British West Indies, 1783–1838," in *Slavery and British Society, 1776–1838*, ed. James Walvin (London: Macmillan, 1982), pp. 105–106.

7. Julius S. Scott III, "The Common Wind: Currents of Afro-American Communication in the Era of the Haitian Revolution," Ph.D. diss., Duke University, 1986, pp. 122, 158.

8. David Geggus, "The French and Haitian Revolutions, and Resistance to Slavery in the Americas: An Overview," *Revue Française d'Histoire d'Outre-Mer* 56 (1989): 107–124. Of those revolutionaries in the Caribbean who did most to advance the cause of nonwhites, Victor Hugues and Admiral Lacrosse subsequently betrayed them, moving with the political tide after 1800. On France, see Yves Bénot, *La Révolution française et la fin des colonies* (Paris: La Découverte, 1989). On the ideological limitations of the Patriots in the Tropics, see Anne Pérotin Dumon, "Les Jacobins des Antilles ou l'esprit de liberté dans les Iles-du-Vent," *Revue d'Histoire Moderne et Contemporaine* 35 (1988): 275, 284–290, 302–304.

9. Though racial equality had been mandated in the French Code Noir of 1685, it had largely been ignored.

10. Cited in David Geggus, "The Enigma of Jamaica in the 1790s: New Light on the Causes of Slave Rebellions," *William & Mary Quarterly* 44 (April 1987): 279.

11. Bénot, *Révolution française;* Blackburn, *Overthrow of Colonial Slavery*, chaps. 5 and 6.

12. Eugene Genovese, *From Rebellion to Revolution: Afro-American Slave Revolts in the Making of the Modern World* (Baton Rouge: Louisiana State University Press, 1979); also see David Patrick Geggus, chap. 5 in this volume.

13. For recent discussion, see Carolyn E. Fick, *The Making of Haiti: The Saint Domingue Revolution from Below* (Knoxville: University of Tennessee Press, 1990), chap. 2; David Geggus, "Voodoo, Marronage, and the Saint Domingue Slave Revolt of 1791," in *Proceedings of the 15th Meeting of the French Colonial Historical Society, Martinique and Guadeloupe, 1989*, ed. Patricia Galloway and Philip Boucher (Lanham: University Press of America, 1992).

14. Michael Craton, "The Passion to Exist: Slave Rebellions in the British West Indies," *Journal of Caribbean History* 13 (1980): 1–20; Michael Craton, *Testing the Chains: Resistance to Slavery in the British West Indies* (Ithaca: Cornell University Press, 1982); Michael Mullin, *Africa in America: Slave Acculturation and Resistance in the American South and the British Caribbean, 1736–1831* (Urbana: University of Illinois Press, 1992); Drescher, *Capitalism and Antislavery*, pp. 104–109.

15. Michèle Duchet, *Anthropologie et histoire au siècle des lumières* (Paris: Flammarion, 1977), chap. 3. This view is rejected in Drescher, *Capitalism and Antislavery*, p. 99.

16. However, one can argue that by weakening French commercial competition, the Haitian Revolution was a vital precondition for abolitionism's success in Britain; see n. 168.

17. I capitalize those maroon communities recognized by colonial treaties, which granted free status in exchange for the recapture of fugitive slaves. The Boni fought for such treaty recognition; see Wim Hoogbergen, *The Boni Maroon Wars in Suriname* (Leiden: Brill, 1990). Already free for a half-century, the Trelawny Maroons fought principally for their own particularist ends; see Geggus, "Enigma of Jamaica," pp. 279–285.

18. Herbert Aptheker, *American Negro Slave Revolts*, 5th ed. (New York: International Publishers, 1987), p. 162.

19. Roger N. Buckley, *Slaves in Red Coats: The British West India Regiments* (New Haven: Yale University Press, 1979), pp. 76–77.

20. Formerly slaves of the Crown but left largely to their own devices since the seventeenth century, the Cobreros periodically took to the hills when attempts were made to reenslave them. In 1788 they sent a representative to Spain to plead their case. When tensions mounted in 1795, a group of them ambushed a patrol, killing an official, but they were pardoned two years later. In 1800 the government gave way and recognized them as free. See José Luciano Franco, *Las Minas de Santiago del Prado y la rebelión de los Cobreros* (Havana: Editorial Ciencias Sociales, 1975); José Luciano Franco, *Los Palenques de los negros cimarrones* (Havana: Colección Historia, 1973), pp. 57–87.

21. John Milligan, "Slave Rebelliousness and the Florida Maroon," *Prologue: The Journal of the National Archives* 6 (1974): 8–18; Blackburn, *Overthrow of Colonial Slavery*, chap. 9.

22. Most were probably recruited by the free coloreds, and the majority were forced back onto their plantations once the freemen had gained their ends. They apparently revolted when this was first attempted, but this (bloodless) rebellion may also have been a free colored maneuver to extract arms from their opponents. See letter by Bauvais, 22 September 1791, Caradeuc Papers, Georgia Historical Society, Savannah.

23. Geggus, "Enigma of Jamaica," pp. 279–287. On the Dominica maroons, see Craton, *Testing the Chains*, pp. 226–231. For another case, omitted for lack of evidence, see n. 36.

24. For example, see Léo Elisabeth, "Gens de couleur et révolution dans les Iles du Vent (1789–janvier 1793)," *Revue Française d'Histoire d'Outre-Mer*, 282–283 (1989): 90; W. J. Gardner, *A History of Jamaica* (London: Elliot Stock, 1873), pp. 243–244; V. S. Naipaul, *The Loss of Eldorado* (London: André Deutsch, 1969), pp. 250–257; E. L. Joseph, *History of Trinidad* (Port of Spain, 1838), p. 226. Keith Laurence notes that in Tobago and Trinidad conspirators exploited social organizations, not all of whose members were aware of the rebellions being planned; see Laurence, "The Tobago Slave Conspiracy of 1801," *Caribbean Quarterly* 28 (1982): 7.

25. See table for references to individual revolts and conspiracies. The most detailed work on this period of Trinidad history mentions a wave of marronage following the outbreak of the Grenada uprising, slaves discussing liberty and equality, and unconfirmed rumors of mutiny, but nothing more; see Jesse Noel, "Spanish Colonial Administration and the Social and Economic Foundations of Trinidad," D.Phil. diss., Cambridge University, 1966, pp. 283–284. Cf. Gustave Borde, *Histoire de l'île de la Trinidad sous le gouvernement espagnol* (Paris, 1882), p. 246.

26. The case of Demerara 1795 is usually described as a rebellion, but it looks more like slave cooperation with maroon attacks than an actual revolt; see Alvin Thompson, *Some Problems of Slave Desertion in Guyana, c. 1750–1814* (Barbados, 1976), pp. 27–28. For the Guadeloupe 1790 case, see n. 37.

27. Reference to Cuban revolts in 1792–1793 in Jorge Dominguez, *The Breakdown of the Spanish Colonial Empire* (Cambridge: Harvard University Press, 1980), p. 160, derives from a confusion with later events. Revolts in Bayamo and in Holguín in 1811–1812 referred to in Allan Kuethe, *Cuba, 1753–1815: Crown, Military, and Society* (Knoxville: University of Tennessee Press, 1986), p. 171, apparently were plots that did not reach fruition, to judge from José Luciano Franco, *Ensayos históricos* (Havana: Editorial de Ciencias Sociales, 1974), pp. 167–173, though this work (pp. 133–134) exaggerates Cuban resistance in the

1790s. Alain Yacou, "Le Péril haïtien," *Chemins Critiques* 2 (1992): 85–92, misleadingly presents the 1805 Trinidad plot and 1798 Trinidad (Cuba) plot as major revolts. The incident of August 1798 on the Peñalver estate near Havana (see Geggus, chap. 5 in this vol., n. 38) was in my view a work strike rather than a revolt. I can also find no evidence of the Jamaican risings of 1793 or the French invasion that stimulated them, mentioned in Genovese, *Rebellion to Revolution*, p. 21. The revolt mentioned in Henri Bangou, *La Révolution et l'esclavage à la Guadeloupe* (Paris: Messidor, 1989), p. 42, occurred in Guadeloupe not Martinique.

28. Geggus, "Enigma of Jamaica," pp. 274–276.

29. Add. Ms. 58906, 115–116, British Library, London. This report of 1791 quite successfully predicted which islands were to be most at risk. It contrasted the unfavorable terrain, strong defense forces, and creolized slave populations of Barbados, Saint Kitts, and Antigua with the almost entirely African slave population of Grenada and the "impassable woods" found there and on Dominica and Saint Vincent. Grenada had one of the highest black-to-white ratios in the region.

30. For discussion, see David Geggus, *Slave Resistance Studies and the Saint Domingue Slave Revolt: Some Preliminary Considerations* (Miami: Florida International University, Occasional Papers Series, 1983), pp. 17–20.

31. Geggus, "Enigma of Jamaica," pp. 288–299. To the cases reviewed in this article, some of the Guadeloupe revolts could be added, notably that of April 1790, which followed immediately the departure of a military expedition of 1,000 men from the island. Robert Paquette, *Sugar Is Made with Blood: The Conspiracy of La Escalera and the Conflict between Empires over Slavery in Cuba* (Middletown: Wesleyan University Press, 1988), p. 293, denies that an increase in garrison strength coincided with a lull in slave resistance in Cuba in 1799–1804, "because slave uprisings occurred in 1798 and 1799." However, whether or not the incident of February 1799 on the Ponce de León estate was a strike or a revolt (see chap. 5 in this vol., n. 38), the following five years were apparently peaceful, in marked contrast to the previous five-year period. After declining substantially for six years, the island garrison was reinforced in 1799 (from Mexico and Santo Domingo) and again (from Spain) in 1802.

32. Those occurring outside the region include a three-day strike in Buenos Aires, 1795; a conspiracy of Brazilian slaves in Upper Peru, 1809; the 1822 Vesey conspiracy in Charleston; and a conspiracy on Bourbon (Reunion) in 1832; see Lesley Rout, *The African Experience in Latin America* (Cambridge: Cambridge University Press, 1976), p. 120; "El alzamiento de Santa Cruz, 1809," in *Obras completas de Humberto Vásquez-Machicado y José Vásquez-Machicado*, ed. Guillermo Ovando Sanz and Alberto Vásquez (La Paz: Don Bosco, 1988), vol. 7, pp. 617–620; William Freehling, *Prelude to Civil War: The Nullification Controversy in South Carolina, 1816–1836* (New York: Harper Torchbooks, 1965), pp. 53–61; Hubert Gerbeau, "De Saint-Domingue à Bourbon," *Revue de la Société Haïtienne d'Histoire et de Géographie* 163 (1989): 55–62.

33. In Virginia, 1730, Venezuela, 1749, and Peru, 1779. Emancipation rumors without evidence of plotting were reported in Martinique in 1768, Venezuela in the 1770s, and the French Caribbean in 1775. See Aptheker, *Slave Revolts*, p. 79; Federico Brito Figueroa, *Las Insurrecciones de los esclavos negros en la sociedad colonial venezolana* (Caracas: Editorial Cantaclaro, 1961), pp. 49–53, 59; Wilifredo Kápsoli Escudero, *Sublevaciones de esclavos en el Perú* (Lima: Universidad Ricardo Palma, 1975), p. 67; Lucien Peytraud, *L'Esclavage aux Antilles françaises* (Paris: Hachette, 1897), p. 372; Debien, *Les Esclaves*, pp. 387–

388. The Cobreros community of eastern Cuba, which had long asserted its freedom, began in 1788 claiming knowledge of a royal decree in its favor; see n. 20.

34. Geggus, "French and Haitian Revolutions," 119–121. On the three late British Caribbean insurrections, see Craton, *Testing the Chains*, pp. 254–321.

35. Barrington Moore, *Injustice: The Social Bases of Obedience and Revolt* (New York: Sharpe, 1978).

36. Letter, 1 December 1789, Colonies, C9A/162, Archives Nationales, Paris (hereafter, AN); Claude Wanquet, *Histoire d'une révolution: La Réunion, 1789–1803* (Marseille: Jeanne Laffitte, 1980), pp. 398–399. Unspecified "disturbances" did occur on some Saint Domingue plantations, however. On Bourbon, the rumors were particularly associated with *esclaves du roi*, belonging to the government.

37. AN, C7A/44, 25–32, 36. Though he used the word "insurrection," it is not apparent any violence occurred. An ambitious conspiracy was discovered that had been preceded by widespread marronage and (apparently verbal) confrontations between slaves and whites.

38. Unfortunately no details are available concerning the Aguadilla rebellion in Puerto Rico, which occurred probably in July, or about the Trinidad conspiracies of 1795. On dating the Aguadilla affair, see chap. 5, n. 23.

39. Wedgwood ceramics featuring a kneeling slave with the caption "Am I not a man and a brother?" or "Ne suis-je pas ton frère?" appeared in Saint Domingue and Jamaica. In both colonies literate free coloreds were said to have read pamphlets to slaves. On Martinique, town slaves were described as gathering in groups to hear pamphlets read. See letter of 10 October 1789, C9A/162, AN; David Geggus, "Jamaica and the Saint Domingue Slave Revolt, 1791–1793," *The Americas* 38 (October 1981): 222; Scott, "Common Wind," pp. 134–135; Pierre-François Dessalles, *Historique des troubles survenus à la Martinique*, ed. Henri de Frémont (Fort-de-France: Société d'Histoire de la Martinique, 1982), pp. 17–26.

40. This was true of the revolts in Martinique (1789), Dominica (1791), Guadeloupe (1793), Curaçao (1795), Demerara (1823), and Jamaica (1831). The Puerto Príncipe rebels of 1795 claimed to have had the same intention. Barbados (1816) presents a similar case. Craton, *Testing the Chains*, p. 291, gives other comparable examples.

41. Franco, *Ensayos*, p. 156; Anne Pérotin-Dumon, *Etre patriote sous les tropiques* (Basse-Terre; Société d'Histoire de la Guadeloupe, 1985), p. 277. In 1789 Martinique slaves generally favored the governor, though some expressed doubts: F3/30, 74, AN.

42. Its renewal in 1789 gave rise to complaints from British colonists and diplomats, as well as confusion in Saint Domingue: Colonial Office (hereafter, CO) 137/88–89, Public Record Office, London (hereafter, PRO); letter of 23 October 1789, C9A/162, AN. For U.S. complaints, see Jane G. Landers, chap. 6 in this volume.

43. Significantly, in view of what later happened in Saint Domingue, the initiative for this policy came as much from the slaves as from Dunmore; see Sylvia Frey, *Water from the Rock: Black Resistance in a Revolutionary Age* (Princeton: Princeton University Press, 1991), chap. 2. As governor of the Bahamas, Dunmore visited northern Saint Domingue in 1789 and dined on the Galliffet estate, where the 1791 uprising would begin; letter of 12 April 1789, 107 AP 128, AN.

44. David Geggus, *The Saint Domingue Slave Revolt and the Rise of Toussaint Louverture*, forthcoming. The insurgents did not speak with one voice, and what

they did was no doubt more important than what they said. Nevertheless, the church and king rhetoric of their leaders, even if opportunist or bogus, suggests that French revolutionary ideology was not an important influence on the 1791 revolt. Cf. n. 51.

45. Franco, *Ensayos*, p. 156; also see chap. 5 in this volume.

46. Fick, *Making of Haiti*, pp. 91, 137–138; Scott, "Common Wind," pp. 193–199; "Jugement en dernier ressort," 19 August 1793, D XXV 129/1008, AN. In 1797 the demand for free days reappeared in Marie Galante, voiced by the ex-slaves subjected to forced labor; see Jacques Adélaïde-Merlande, *La Caraïbe et la Guyane au temps de la Révolution et de l'Empire* (Paris: Karthala, 1992), p. 120.

47. See n. 51. The tract is Abbé Sibire, *L'Aristocratie négrière* (Paris, 1789). In the "Swiss" affair in western Saint Domingue, the rumored three days sometimes appeared as a royal reform, but sometimes were explicitly part of a deal between slave and free colored rebels; report of 4 October 1791, D XXV 61/610, and doc. 59, D XXV 1/12, AN.

48. Scott, "Common Wind," esp. pp. 193–199. The Port Salut conspiracy followed the Dominica rebellion by two weeks. Southern Saint Domingue had close commercial links with the south Caribbean, particularly Dominica, Curaçao, and Saint Thomas. Only twenty miles separate Dominica and Martinique. The rumor reappeared in Bourbon in 1832.

49. Franco, *Ensayos*, pp. 151–153; Guillermo Baralt, *Esclavos rebeldes: Conspiraciones y sublevaciones de esclavos en Puerto Rico* (Rio Piedras: Ediciones Huracán, 1985), pp. 21–23; Carlos Esteban Deive, *La Esclavitud en Santo Domingo* (Santo Domingo: Museo del Hombre Dominicano, 1980), vol. 2, p. 479; Eleázar Córdova-Bello, *La Independencia de Haití y su influencia en Hispanoamérica* (Caracas: Instituto Panamericano, 1967), pp. 146, 150.

50. In Venezuela, Cuba, Santo Domingo, Louisiana, and New Granada, colonial governments protested against the decree: Torre Revello, "Origen y aplicación," pp. 44–47; Scott, "Common Wind," pp. 150–157. In Florida, too, the Spanish administration seems to have quietly avoided publishing it; communication from Sherry Johnson.

51. David Geggus, "The Slaves and Free Coloreds of Martinique during the Age of the French and Haitian Revolutions: Three Moments of Resistance," in *Parts beyond the Seas: The Lesser Antilles in the Age of European Expansion*, ed. Robert L. Paquette and Stanley L. Engerman (Gainesville: University Press of Florida, 1996).

52. Pérotin-Dumon, *Etre patriote*, p. 277; Bangou, *La Révolution*, p. 46.

53. Cf. Pedro Arcaya, *Insurrección de los negros en la serranía de Coro* (Caracas: Instituto Panamericano de Geografía y Historia, 1949); Miguel Acosta Saignes, *Vida de los negros esclavos en Venezuela* (Caracas: Hespérides, 1978), p. 279; Federico Brito Figueroa, *El Problema tierra y esclavos en la historia de Venezuela*, 2d ed. (Caracas: Ediciones de la Biblioteca, 1985), pp. 225–232; Scott, "Common Wind," p. 158. On the Puerto Príncipe rebellion, see chap. 5 in this volume.

54. The French law of May 15, 1791, enfranchising some free coloreds probably helped create the emancipation rumors surrounding the Saint Domingue uprising of the following August, especially as the colonists forced the governor to reject it.

55. A recent increase in the sales tax was certainly a major grievance of the Coro rebels, who demanded its abolition, as did free colored rebels in Cuba in August. The Louisiana conspiracy doubtless owed something to French attempts to seize the colony, but the often-asserted involvement of French agents has never been proved. On Puerto Rico, see n. 38.

56. Victor Hugues on Guadeloupe and Goyrand on Saint Lucia assisted

rebellions on Grenada, Saint Vincent, and Dominica in 1795 with soldiers and guns. Hugues's successor Bresseau invaded Curaçao in 1800 (though without approval from Paris). Agent Roume in Saint Domingue attempted to organize a rising on Jamaica in 1799, and he perhaps was behind the Santo Domingo plot of 1795. French involvement in the Coro and Maracaibo movements was apparently unofficial. Commissaire Sonthonax in Saint Domingue pretended he had established links with Jamaica, but French involvement in the Second Maroon War has not been proved; see Geggus, "Enigma of Jamaica," pp. 279–287.

57. *De la Révolution française aux révolutions créoles et nègres,* ed. Michel Martin and Alain Yacou (Paris: Editions Caribéennes, 1989), pp. 10, 15.

58. See nn. 68, 69. In the 1800 rising on Curaçao, town slaves also sang "Down with those who trample on the people's rights," and in 1797 three mulatto slaves from Curaçao were deported from La Guaira for singing revolutionary songs; see Roberto Palacios, "Ansia de Libertad," *Lanternu* 1 (1983): 20–27; Carlos Edsel, "Trois mulâtres de Curaçao, chantres de la liberté," in *Révolution française,* ed. Martin and Yacou, pp. 61–68.

59. F3/30, 116–119, AN.

60. Pérotin-Dumon, *Etre patriote,* pp. 137–138, 274–282; Lucien-René Abenon et al., *Antilles 1789: La Révolution aux Caraïbes* (Paris: Nathan, 1989), pp. 163–166; *Independent Chronicle* (Boston), October 17, 1793. However, the governor thought the April 1790 conspirators genuinely believed they had been freed; see n. 37.

61. Letter of 10 October 1789, C9A/162, AN.

62. This was the opinion of the first Haitian historian, Thomas Madiou, *Histoire d'Haïti* (1847–1848; 2d ed., Port au Prince: Département de l'Instruction Public, 1922), vol. 1, p. 490. It also seems to be the argument of Genovese, *Rebellion to Revolution,* p. 90. Both Toussaint's and France's commitment to general emancipation came about in two stages, marked by the local abolition in Saint Domingue by Commissioner Sonthonax in August 1793 and the Convention's decree of the following February. See David Geggus, "From His Most Catholic Majesty to the Godless Republic: The 'Volte-Face' of Toussaint Louverture and the Ending of Slavery in Saint Domingue," *Revue Française d'Histoire d'Outre-Mer* 65 (1978): 481–499; Geggus, "French and Haitian Revolutions," 116–119.

63. David Geggus, "Toussaint Louverture and the Slaves of the Bréda Plantations," *Journal of Caribbean History* 20 (1985–1986): 30–48. The original slave leaders of the 1791 insurrection continued their counterrevolutionary campaign in opportunistic alliance with the proslavery Spanish.

64. Anne Pérotin-Dumon, "The Emergence of Politics among Free Coloureds and Slaves in Revolutionary Guadeloupe," *Journal of Caribbean History* 25 (1993): 109. The governor of Guadeloupe, however, thought they were slaves; C7A/44, 36, AN.

65. Others include the Dominica rising led by the mulatto Apollinaire and the Marie-Galante plot (1791); the Curaçao (1800) and Martinique (1811) rebellions; the Havana and Bayamo conspiracies and Guanabo rising in Cuba; and the Santo Domingo rebellion (1811–1812). The "French negroes from captured ships" who conspired in Nassau in 1797 and spoke of Saint Domingue must have been (re)enslaved freemen. Free coloreds also played a role in the Port Salut conspiracy and northern plain rebellion in Saint Domingue (1791), the risings in Guadeloupe (August 1793) and Curaçao (1795), the conspiracies in Louisiana (1795), Cartagena (1799), Tobago (1801), Trinidad (1805), Puerto Rico, Puerto Príncipe, and New Orleans (1812), and Jamaica (1815). Here I am not

counting the free colored revolts that also included slaves, as in Grenada and Dominica (1795).

66. Geggus, "French and Haitian Revolutions," pp. 109–113. The statement in José Luciano Franco, *Revolución y conflictos* (Havana: Academia de Ciencias, 1965), p. 11, that the Jamaican Maroon War resulted from Victor Hugues's propaganda seems without foundation.

67. In the latter category were the Louisiana (1791) plot; the revolts at Boca Nigua (1796) and Puerto Príncipe (1798); and the Carúpano (1798), Demerara (1807), and Jamaica (1806–1807) conspiracies. The claim in Bridges, *Annals of Jamaica*, p. 284, unsupported by other sources, that the latter plot and that of 1809 were linked with French refugees may be doubted given the work's highly xenophobic stance. The Bayamo conspiracy (1812) primarily involved Africans of the local cabildos, free and slave. Though motivated by Aponte's propaganda concerning an emancipation decree, it apparently was set off by a local incident of brutality by a military patrol and was weakened by ethnic rivalries. The Igbo plot on Jamaica (1815) did have some links with British abolitionism and a mulatto priest from Saint Domingue, but otherwise had a traditional appearance, as defined by Michael Craton or Eugene Genovese.

68. Brito Figueroa, *Problema*, pp. 225–235; Brito Figueroa, *Insurrecciones*, pp. 60–79. Not infrequently privateers were former contraband traders, and southern Saint Domingue had close commercial links with Curaçao and the Venezuelan coast.

69. Two of the leaders, Louis Mercier and Toussaint, who declared "Nous sommes ici pour vaincre ou mourir," were probably from Saint Domingue. See Johann Hartog, *Curaçao: From Colonial Dependence to Autonomy* (Aruba: De Wit, 1968), pp. 125–128; Cornelis Goslinga, *The Dutch in the Caribbean and Surinam, 1791/95–1942* (Assen: Van Gorcum, 1991), pp. 1–20.

70. Gwendolyn Hall, "The 1795 Conspiracy in Pointe Coupée," *Proceedings*, ed. Galloway and Boucher, pp. 130–141; Jack Holmes, "The Abortive Slave Revolt at Pointe Coupée, Louisiana," *Louisiana History* 11 (1970): 341–362. The Tobago conspiracy of 1801 is a comparable case. With peace negotiations in progress, the conspirators may have hoped to force the colony's return to French rule.

71. Though the latter was a multiclass insurrection, I have classed it among the slave revolts, since it seems to have included the autonomous involvement of the entire rural slave population but only a minority of local free coloreds and whites, who nonetheless played key roles; see Palacios, "Ansia de libertad," pp. 20–27.

72. Brito Figueroa, *Problema*, pp. 234–235. Moreover, among the leaders of the Curaçao revolt were (as in 1795) a local black named Rigaud and residents from Saint Domingue.

73. John E. Bauer, "International Repercussions of the Haitian Revolution," *The Americas* 26 (April 1970): 417; Scott, "Common Wind," chap. 4; Kieran Kleczewski, "Martinique and the British Occupation, 1794–1802," Ph.D. diss., Georgetown University, 1988, pp. 331–332.

74. Geggus, "French and Haitian Revolutions," pp. 110–112; Gardner, *Jamaica*, p. 239; *Révolution française*, ed. Martin and Yacou, pp. 38–39; Alain Yacou, "Le Projet des révoltes serviles de l'Ile de Cuba dans la première moitié du XIXe siècle," *Revue du CERC* 1 (1984): 51. I do not think this means slaves were "well-informed" as argued in Hall, "Pointe Coupée." Even literate whites lived in a world of rumor and uncertainty. Cf. the Pierre Bailly case described by Kimberley Hanger, chap. 7 in this volume.

75. J. R. Ward, *British West India Slavery, 1750–1834* (Oxford: Clarendon

Press, 1988), p. 229; Jacques Adélaïde-Merlande, *Documents d'histoire antillaise et guyanaise* (n.p., 1979), p. 52.

76. Geggus, "Enigma of Jamaica," 276–277; Lionel Fraser, *History of Trinidad* (Port of Spain, 1891–1896), vol. 1, p. 268.

77. *Slavery, Abolition and Emancipation: Black Slaves and the British Empire*, ed. Michael Craton, James Walvin, and David Wright (London: Longmans, 1976), p. 138. The same year, the Spanish government suddenly found it prudent to recognize the freedom of the fractious Cobrero community, no doubt because of eastern Cuba's close links with Saint Domingue; see n. 20.

78. Such cases include the conspiracies in Jamaica (1791), Santo Domingo (1793), Tobago (1801), Trinidad (1805), Havana, Bayamo, and Puerto Rico (1811–1812), and the rebellions in Santo Domingo (1796) and Barbados (1816). In Trinidad (1795) and Tobago black resistance in Grenada and Guadeloupe was also held up as an example.

79. Apart from the Curaçao cases and those discussed in chap. 5, examples include the conspiracies in the Bahamas (1795, 1797), Cartagena (1799), Havana, Bayamo, and Puerto Rico (1811–1812), and, less surprisingly, Louisiana (1795) and Tobago (1801). The leader of the fugitives who fought U.S. troops at Prospect Bluff, Florida, in 1816 was a Pensacola slave named Garson; see Milligan, "Slave Rebelliousness," p. 14; Jane Landers, "Slave Resistance on the Southern Frontier: Fugitives, Maroons, and Banditti," unpublished paper.

80. Baralt, *Esclavos rebeldes*, p. 27. In northeast Brazil, free colored militiamen were discovered wearing cameo portraits of Dessalines a year after he was crowned emperor, and in a later rebellion they sang of emulating Christophe; see Luiz Mott, "A revolução dos negros do Haiti e o Brasil," *Mensario do Arquivo Nacional* 13 (1982): 5; Franco, *Ensayos*, p. 184.

81. Franco, *Ensayos*, pp. 154–180. Prominent among the conspirators was Hilario Herrera from Azua on the Santo Domingo frontier, who had lived through the Haitian Revolution. Another owned a copy of one of Christophe's proclamations.

82. Jean Fouchard, "Quand Haïti exportait la liberté," *Revue de la Société Haïtienne d'Histoire et de Géographie* 143 (1984); Palacios, "Ansia de libertad," pp. 20–27; Yacou, "Le Péril haïtien," pp. 85–92; Baralt, *Esclavos rebeldes*, pp. 17–20.

83. Geggus, "Enigma of Jamaica," 287–288.

84. Defeated by Toussaint Louverture, they were fleeing to France.

85. See n. 51; Franco, *Ensayos*, p. 183; Deive, *Esclavitud*, vol. 2, p. 479.

86. Paul Verna, *Pétion y Bolívar: Cuarenta años de relaciones haitiano-venezolanas* (Caracas: Oficina Central de Información, 1969), pp. 87–298. Once again, Curaçao radicals such as Luis Brión were key intermediaries. A gradual emancipation law had already been passed by insurgents in New Granada but it remained without effect; Blackburn, *Overthrow of Colonial Slavery*, p. 348.

87. In a contrary sense, the destruction of Saint Domingue inhibited moves toward independence in Cuba and encouraged the expansion of slavery elsewhere.

88. Edward Cox, *The Free Coloreds in the Slave Societies of St. Kitts and Grenada, 1763–1833* (Knoxville: University of Tennessee Press), pp. 76–91; Craton, *Testing the Chains*, pp. 180–210.

89. The French free coloreds' club founded in Paris in September 1789 was called the Société des Colons Américains. For much of the 1790s free colored commanders in Saint Domingue enjoyed de facto independence in their localities.

90. Franco, *Ensayos*, pp. 95–100. Misdating the plot to 1796, Paquette,

Sugar, pp. 75, 124–125, underestimates its immediate causes, I think, and limitations.

91. David Geggus, "La Révolte de Jean Kina à Fort-Royal, décembre 1800," *Revue de la Société Haïtienne d'Histoire et de Géographie* 140 (September 1983): 12–25; see n. 51.

92. David Geggus, "Racial Equality, Slavery, and Colonial Secession during the Constituent Assembly," *American Historical Review* 94, no. 5 (December 1989): 1297–1303; Elisabeth, "Gens de couleur," pp. 79–93.

93. Blackburn, *Overthrow of Colonial Slavery,* pp. 341–347.

94. Geggus, "Enigma of Jamaica," 278–279; Cox, *Free Coloreds,* pp. 96–100.

95. See chaps. 6 and 7 in this volume; Kuethe, *Cuba,* pp. 166–168, 172.

96. Most of Aponte's and Chirino's co-conspirators were blacks. Other examples include José Ortiz of the Cartagena conspiracy, Joseph Suárez at Maracaibo, many minor figures such as Jean-Baptiste Cap and Romaine Rivière in Saint Domingue, and the free blacks who administered a ritual "conspirators' drink" to the Curaçao rebels of 1795. Mulattoes were more prominent in the Maracaibo plot (which is perhaps best classified as a free colored rather than slave conspiracy), the Martinique (1811) rebellion, one of the Dominica revolts, and the Marie Galante plot. Charles Deslondes of Louisiana was thought to be a free mulatto, but Robert Paquette (chap. 8 in this volume) shows that he was a slave.

97. Before the revolution, a white southerner had already suggested the name in a proposal for political reform; see anon., *Essai sur l'administration des colonies françoises* (Antonina [Les Cayes], 1788), p. 12.

98. David Nicholls, *From Dessalines to Duvalier: Race, Colour and National Independence in Haiti* (Cambridge: Cambridge University Press, 1979), chap. 2; Alfred Hunt, *Haiti's Influence on Antebellum America* (Baton Rouge: Louisiana State University Press, 1988), chaps. 3–5; Karin Schüller, *Die deutsche Rezeption haitianischer Geschichte in der ersten Hälfte des 19. Jahrhunderts* (Cologne: Böhlau, 1992); David Brion Davis, "American Equality and Foreign Revolutions," *Journal of American History* 76 (1989): 747–749; David Geggus, "Haiti and the Abolitionists: Opinion, Propaganda and International Politics, 1804–1838," in *Abolition and Its Aftermath: The Historical Context 1790–1916,* ed. David Richardson (London, 1985), pp. 113–140.

99. Henri Lémery, *La Révolution française à la Martinique* (Paris: Larose, 1936); David Geggus, *Slavery, War and Revolution: The British Occupation of Saint Domingue, 1793–1798* (Oxford: Clarendon Press, 1982), chap. 3; Pérotin-Dumon, *Etre patriote,* chaps. 5–9.

100. Geggus, "Jamaica and the Saint Domingue Revolution," pp. 225–229. Note, however, that English and French "republicans" upset the authorities in Havana with their celebrating together the success of the revolution; *Royal Gazette* (Kingston), 1792, no. 42, p. 22.

101. French colonial productivity, along with overmanning in the merchant marine, contributed to the effect.

102. Rioting troops burned the capital of Tobago in 1790. Those of the Port au Prince regiment killed their colonel in 1791.

103. The Coro-Maracaibo region was an exception. The revolt of 1795 helped ensure the failure of Miranda's invasion in 1806.

104. See chap. 5, n. 13; Kuethe, *Cuba,* pp. 156–162, 171; Blackburn, *Overthrow of Colonial Slavery,* p. 388.

105. Ernest Liljegren, "Jacobinism in Spanish Louisiana, 1792–1797," *Louisiana Historical Quarterly* 22 (1939): 49–97; Thomas Abernethy, *The South in the*

New Nation (Baton Rouge: Louisiana State University Press, 1961), pp. 330–366. A rebellion of North American settlers in 1810 extended along the Gulf Coast U.S. gains from the Louisiana purchase. Another revolt in 1812, in East Florida, misfired.

106. Naipaul, *Loss of Eldorado*, pp. 135–154; Blackburn, *Overthrow of Colonial Slavery*, pp. 340–350; Verna, *Pétion y Bolívar*, pp. 76–298.

107. The creation of Augustus Bowles, an ex-Loyalist secretly backed by Bahamian merchants, Muskogee lasted from 1799 to 1803. With Governor Dunmore's support, Bowles had invaded Florida in 1788 and 1791; see Lyle McAlister, "William Augustus Bowles and the State of Muskogee," *Florida Historical Quarterly* 40 (1962): 317–328.

108. Cf. Franco, *Revolución y conflictos*, p. 11, and Geggus, "Enigma of Jamaica," pp. 279–287.

109. Craton, *Testing the Chains*, pp. 226–231.

110. A possible exception might be found in Demerara in 1795; see n. 26.

111. Craton, *Testing the Chains*, pp. 224–225; Geggus, "Enigma of Jamaica," p. 277.

112. Geggus, "Voodoo, Marronage," pp. 23–28.

113. Craton, *Testing the Chains*, pp. 165–168.

114. Geggus, "Enigma of Jamaica," p. 292; Hilary Beckles, *Black Rebellion in Barbados* (Bridgetown: Antilles Publications, 1984), pp. 60–61.

115. On the diaspora of Francophone blacks, see n. 79. Aponte had done militia service in Florida, and possibly with Miranda in the American War of Independence. His lieutenant Hilario Herrera, "el Inglés," was from Santo Domingo and later participated in the 1812 rebellion there. The Venezuelan freemen Chirino and González had respectively visited Saint Domingue and Curaçao; the latter had been to Spain; and their companion José Ortiz featured in both the Coro and Cartagena conspiracies. The 1798 plot in Trinidad, Cuba, involved slaves from Curaçao and Jamaica.

116. Geggus, *Slavery, War and Revolution*, p. 93; José Luciano Franco, *Documentos para la historia de Haití en el Archivo Nacional* (Havana, 1954), p. 81.

117. E.g., Jules Saintoyant, *La Colonisation française pendant la Révolution* (Paris: La Renaissance du Livre, 1930), vol. 2, pp. 77–84; Tadeusz Lepkowski, *Haití* (Havana: Casa de las Américas, 1968–1969), vol. 1, pp. 62, 69; Franco, *Revolución*, pp. 29, 31.

118. Geggus, "The Great Powers and the Haitian Revolution," in *Tordesillas y sus consecuencias*, ed. Berndt Schröter and Karin Schüller (Madrid: Iberoamericana, 1995), pp. 114–122; Geggus, *Slavery, War and Revolution*, chaps. 3, 4, 15; also see chap. 5, n. 43, in this volume.

119. The Cuban administration would not, however, provide dogs or cattle to help the British in Saint Domingue: Franco, *Revolución*, p. 45; Geggus, *Slavery, War and Revolution*, p. 164.

120. Scott, "Common Wind," pp. 188–189; Thompson, *Some Problems*, p. 27.

121. Bernard Foubert, "Les volontaires, de l'Aube et de la Seine-Inférieure à Saint-Domingue," *Bulletin de la Société d'Histoire de la Guadeloupe* 51 (1982): 30; Pierre Pluchon, *Toussaint Louverture: Un Révolutionnaire noir d'Ancien Régime* (Paris: Fayard, 1989), pp. 491–492; Geggus, *Slavery, War and Revolution*, pp. 282–284; Verna, *Pétion y Bolívar*, pp. 125–129.

122. Marcus Rainsford, *An Historical Account of the Black Empire of Hayti* (London, 1805), introduction.

123. Fick, *Making of Haiti*, pp. 161–166; Geggus, *Slavery, War and Revolution*, pp. 103, 315–325; chap. 5, n. 43. Spanish policy reflected long traditions of

arming blacks and welcoming foreign slave fugitives, as well as local dislike of the French, hatred of the French Revolution, and the desire to reconquer what had been Spain's first American colony.

124. Buckley, *Slaves in Red Coats*, p. 55, estimates about 13,400 Africans were purchased for the regiments down to 1808. At least another 6,000 slaves were purchased for the Chasseurs in Saint Domingue. The combined cost exceeded 1.25 million pounds.

125. Davis, *Age of Revolution*, p. 80; Verna, *Pétion y Bolívar*, p. 97.

126. In the Haitian Revolution the development of a black artillery took time, notwithstanding Alexandre Pétion's personal virtuosity in the matter. The departing British would have retained two coastal towns in 1798 (for strategic reasons) but for this development. No battery was dressed against Cap Français until November 1803; the city surrendered the next day, so ending colonial rule. This is one reason I think the comments in Roger N. Buckley, *The Haitian Journal of Lieutenant Howard* (Knoxville: University of Tennessee Press, 1985), pp. 137–138, are misplaced.

127. Alexandre Moreau de Jonnès, *Essai sur l'hygiène militaire des Antilles* (Paris: Migneret, 1816), p. 19; Geggus, *Slavery, War and Revolution*, pp. 318–319; Foubert, "Volontaires," p. 30.

128. John Thornton, "African Soldiers in the Haitian Revolution," *Journal of Caribbean History* 25 (1993): 58–80.

129. M. W. B. Sanderson, "English Naval Strategy and Maritime Trade in the Caribbean, 1793–1802," Ph.D. diss., London University, 1969, chaps. 3–4; Anne Pérotin-Dumon, "Commerce et travail dans les villes coloniales des Lumières: Basse-Terre et Pointe-à-Pitre, Guadeloupe," *Revue Française d'Histoire d'Outre-Mer* 75 (1988): 65; Johan Nissen, *Reminiscences of a 46 Years' Residence in the Island of St. Thomas* (Nazareth, Pa., 1838), pp. 38, 58; Vice-Admiralty Court papers, 1793–1794, Jamaica Archives, Spanish Town.

130. John Coatsworth, "American Trade with European Colonies in the Caribbean and South America, 1790–1812," *William & Mary Quarterly* 24 (1967): 243–266; Nissen, *Reminiscences*, pp. 16, 50, 61.

131. Anne Pérotin-Dumon, "Course et piraterie dans le Golfe de Mexique et la Mer des Antilles: L'Ultime épisode, ou la contribution des 'corsarios insurgentes' à l'indépendance de l'Amérique," *Bulletin de la Société d'Histoire de la Guadeloupe* 53–54 (1982): 49–69.

132. Michael Duffy, *Soldiers, Sugar, and Seapower: The British Expeditions to the West Indies and the War against Revolutionary France* (Oxford: Clarendon Press, 1987), p. 372. Also see David Geggus, "The Cost of Pitt's Caribbean Campaigns, 1793–1798," *Historical Journal* 26 (1983): 704–705.

133. See Duffy, *Soldiers, Sugar, and Seapower*, pp. 329–334, for the period 1793–1801; garrison returns for 1799–1815, War Office (WO) 17/1733, 1875–1879, 2490–2504, PRO; and for Jamaica, WO 17/1985–2005, PRO. The total of military dead is 71,640, but Duffy included deaths en route to the Caribbean. Buckley, *Slaves in Red Coats*, p. 99, arrived at a similar figure using different sources. His estimate that 97,000 European troops in British pay served in the Caribbean in this period probably needs increasing by about one-third.

134. Buckley, *Slaves in Red Coats*, p. 100, contends that lead poisoning was more important than fevers, but this seems improbable for many reasons; see David Geggus, "The Destruction of the British Army in the West Indies: Some Further Comments," *Journal of the Society for Army Historical Research* 61, no. 4 (1978): 238–240.

135. Duffy, *Soldiers, Sugar, and Seapower*, pp. 337–338; Geggus, *Slavery, War*

and Revolution, pp. 364–365. In 1809, the year Martinique was captured, British losses in the south Caribbean were 24 killed in action and 2 dead from wounds out of 1,910 total dead: WO 17/2499, PRO.

136. Geggus, *Slavery, War and Revolution*, pp. 363–364. Frank and Andrea Cook, *Casualty Roll for the Crimea* (London: Haywood & Son, 1976), pp. 243, 245, show 19.3 percent of British forces in the Crimea died "in the east" (20,707), and that of these 13 percent were killed in action. The French army lost a larger proportion, but of its 95,000 dead, 10.5 percent were killed in action and 15.7 percent died of wounds; René Guillemin, *La Guerre de Crimée* (Paris: France-Empire, 1981), p. 316.

137. Pluchon, *Toussaint Louverture*, p. 572.

138. Moreau de Jonnès, *Essai*, pp. 22–23, 26; Geggus, *Slavery, War and Revolution*, p. 364.

139. Yvan Debbasch, "Le Marronage: Essai sur la désertion de l'esclave antillais," *L'Année Sociologique* (1961): 39; Charles Frostin, "Papiers des Antilles III," *Cahiers des Amériques Latines* (1966): 183; Scott, "Common Wind," pp. 50–53.

140. Judith Bettelheim, "Jamaican Jonkonnu and Related Caribbean Festivals," in *Africa and the Caribbean: The Legacies of a Link*, ed. Franklin Knight and Margaret Crahan (Baltimore: Johns Hopkins University Press, 1979), pp. 81, 86, 95; Naipaul, *Loss of Eldorado*, pp. 250–257.

141. Philip Wright and Gabriel Debien, "Les Colons de Saint-Domingue passés á la Jamaïque," *Notes d'Histoire Coloniale* 168; Alain Yacou, "La Présence française dans la partie occidentale de l'île Cuba au lendemain de la Révolution de Saint-Domingue," *Revue Française d'Histoire d'Outre-Mer* 84 (1987): 149–188; Alain Yacou, "Esclaves et libres français à Cuba au lendemain de la Révolution française," *Jahrbuch für Geschichte von Staat, Wissenschaft und Gesellschaft Lateinamerikas* 28 (1991): 163–197.

142. See chap. 5, n. 46.

143. *Boston Independent Chronicle*, January 31, 1793; Lowell J. Ragatz, *The Fall of the Planter Class in the British Caribbean, 1763–1833* (New York: Century, 1928), pp. 236–238; Anne Pérotin-Dumon, "Révolutionnaires français et royalistes espagnols dans les Antilles," *Revue Française d'Histoire d'Outre-Mer* 56 (1989): 125–158; Geggus, *Slavery, War and Revolution*, pp. 95–97.

144. Santo Domingo 1110, Portillo to Acuña, 25 September 1793, AGI, Sevilla; Angel Sanz Tapia, *Los Militares emigrados y los prisioneros franceses en Venezuela durante la guerra contra la revolución* (Caracas: Instituto Panamericano, 1977), pp. 74, 106, 132–133; María Luque de Sánchez, "Colons français réfugiés à Porto Rico," in *Révolution française*, ed. Martin and Yacou, pp. 41–48; Blackburn, *Overthrow of Colonial Slavery*, p. 388; Gabriel Debien, "Les Colons de Saint-Domingue réfugiés à Cuba, 1793–1815," *Revista de Indias* 13 (January 1954): 559–605; (June 1954): 11–36.

145. Robert Dallas, *The Maroons of Jamaica* (London, 1803), vol. 2, p. 456; Borde, *Trinidad*, p. 246; Gardner, *Jamaica*, p. 239; Ragatz, *Fall of the Planter Class*, p. 237; Paul Lachance, "The Politics of Fear: French Louisianians and the Slave Trade, 1786–1809," *Plantation Societies in the Americas* 1 (1979): 162–197.

146. Nissen, *Reminiscences*, pp. 16, 50, 90; Chapman Milling, "The Acadian and San Domingan French," *Transactions of the Huguenot Society of South Carolina* 62 (1957): 33–34; Gabriel Debien, "De Saint-Domingue à Cuba avec une famille de réfugiés," *Revue de la Faculté d'Éthnologie* 8 (1964): 18; Manuel Moreno Fraginals, *El Ingenio: Complejo económico social cubano del azúcar* (Havana: Editorial de Ciencias Sociales, 1978), vol. 1, pp. 71–72. Also see n. 141 above.

147. Estado 5/23, 24, 28, etc., AGI, Sevilla; n. 154 below; chap. 6 in this volume.

148. CO 319/6, 118, 126, PRO; Geggus, *Slavery, War and Revolution*, pp. 379–381; Buckley, *Slaves in Red Coats*, pp. 136–317.

149. CO 123/13, PRO; Nancie L. Gonzalez, *Sojourners of the Caribbean: Ethnogenesis and Ethnohistory of the Garifuna* (Urbana: University of Illinois Press, 1988), p. 53; Cox, *Free Coloreds*, p. 80.

150. Sanz Tapia, *Militares emigrados*, pp. 78–103, 147, 173, 263–264; Geggus, *Slavery, War and Revolution*, pp. 265, 282–284, 324. After the Napoleonic reconquest of Guadeloupe in 1802, 2,000 black soldiers were deported and perhaps sold; Adélaïde-Merlande, *La Caraïbe*, p. 162.

151. Guatemala 805, AGI, Sevilla; *Gazeta de Guatemala* no. 15, 21 (1797); Gonzalez, *Sojourners*, pp. 39–41. Some Black Caribs remained hiding on Saint Vincent down to 1800; WO 1/89, 493, 567, PRO.

152. Data from Eltis, *Economic Growth*, p. 249. The more recent figures in David Richardson, "Slave Exports from West and West-Central Africa, 1700–1809: New Estimates of Volume and Distribution," *Journal of African History* 30 (1989): 1–22, suggest a less abrupt shift between the 1780s and 1790s and that Caribbean imports may have peaked in the 1760s.

153. Ward, *British West Indian Slavery*, chap. 4; Moreno Fraginals, *El Ingenio*, vol. 1, pp. 71–72, 78–95.

154. Seymour Drescher, *Econocide: British Slavery in the Era of Abolition* (Pittsburgh: University of Pittsburgh Press, 1977), pp. 76–91, 116. The production figures presented for Saint Domingue in the 1790s usually omit the output of either the Republican or British-occupied zone; those of 1800–1801 were probably deliberately understated. On the importance of rising demand, see Eltis, *Economic Growth*, pp. 37–38.

155. Data in Noel Deerr, *History of Sugar* (London: Chapman & Hall, 1949), vol. 1, pp. 112, 131, 193–203, 212, 245; Francisco Scarano, *Sugar and Slavery in Puerto Rico: The Plantation Economy of Ponce, 1800–1850* (Madison: University of Wisconsin Press, 1984), p. 7; Dale W. Tomich, *Slavery in the Circuit of Sugar: Martinique and the World Economy, 1830–1848* (Baltimore: Johns Hopkins University Press, 1990), pp. 15, 24, 30, 42. Note, however, these figures mask the replacement of semirefined sugar exports with those of low-value muscovado.

156. Data in Francisco Pérez de la Riva, *El Café: Historia de su cultivo y explotación en Cuba* (Havana: Jesús Montero, 1944), p. 51; Drescher, *Econocide*, p. 79; James Leyburn, *The Haitian People* (New Haven: Yale University Press, 1966), p. 320.

157. Barry Higman, *Slave Populations of the British Caribbean, 1807–1834* (Baltimore: Johns Hopkins University Press), pp. 55–63; Drescher, *Econocide*, chaps. 5–9; Duffy, *Soldiers, Sugar, and Seapower*, p. 380.

158. Data in Stuart Schwartz, *Sugar Plantations in the Formation of Brazilian Society* (Cambridge: Cambridge University Press, 1985), pp. 422–434; Moreno Fraginals, *Ingenio*, vol. 1, pp. 40–42, vol. 2, p. 173.

159. Data in *Colonial Brazil*, ed. Leslie Bethell (Cambridge: Cambridge University Press, 1987), pp. 314, 327–328.

160. Ragatz, *Fall of the Planter Class*, p. 206; Drescher, *Econocide*, passim; Ward, *British West Indian Slavery*, chap. 3.

161. Britain gained Saint Lucia and Tobago from France, Trinidad from Spain, and much of the Dutch Guiana colonies. Direct trade between British Caribbean colonies and Britain rose from one-fifth to one-quarter of total

British trade, then fell back to one-fifth by 1815: Duffy, *Soldiers, Sugar, and Seapower,* pp. 378–393; Drescher, *Econocide,* chap. 8.

162. David J. Murray, *The West Indies and the Development of Colonial Government, 1801–1834* (Oxford: Clarendon Press, 1965), chaps. 4–7; Henri Blet, *Histoire de la colonisation française* (Grenoble: Arthaud, 1946), vol. 2, pp. 47–52, 60–64; Louis Pérez, *Cuba: Between Reform and Revolution* (New York: Oxford University Press, 1988), p. 72; Scarano, *Sugar and Slavery,* p. 18; Ragatz, *Fall of the Planter Class,* pp. 338–339.

163. Higman, *Slave Populations,* passim; Ward, *British West Indian Slavery,* chap. 6; Blackburn, *Overthrow of Colonial Slavery,* p. 478.

164. Nissen, *Reminiscences,* p. 39; Geggus, *Slavery, War and Revolution,* p. 279.

165. See n. 74; Geggus, "Enigma of Jamaica," p. 277; Craton, *Testing the Chains,* p. 225. Cf. Pierre Dessalles, *La Vie d'un colon à la Martinique au XIXe siècle,* 2d ed., ed. Henri de Frémont (Courbevoie: De Frémont, 1988), pp. 86, 187; Blackburn, *Overthrow of Colonial Slavery,* p. 384.

166. In 1836 the Cuban government discovered that the banner of Bayamo's Carabalí *cabildo* bore a plumed cocked hat (as worn by Haitian officials) in place of the royal crown; Franco, *Ensayos,* p. 185.

167. Blackburn, *Overthrow of Colonial Slavery,* pp. 30, 300–315, 527; Drescher, *Capitalism and Antislavery,* pp. 98–99, and *Econocide,* pp. 168–169, 214–223.

168. Duffy, chap. 3 in this volume; Duffy, *Soldiers, Sugar, and Seapower,* pp. 391–393. Cf. Franklin Knight, *The Caribbean: Genesis of a Fragmented Nationalism,* 2d ed. (New York: Oxford University Press, 1990), p. 212; Blackburn, *Overthrow of Colonial Slavery,* p. 145. Even Drescher observes that in 1792 "never before in the eighteenth century did the French colonies seem less likely to be serious rivals"; *Econocide,* p. 119.

169. David Geggus, "British Opinion and the Emergence of Haiti, 1791–1805" in *Slavery and British Society,* ed. Walvin, pp. 123–149; Geggus, *Slavery, War and Revolution,* pp. 285–289; Geggus, "Haiti and the Abolitionists," pp. 113–140; Drescher, *Capitalism and Antislavery,* pp. 98–99.

Slave Rebellions and Conspiracies, 1789–1815

Time and Place	Revolt (R) or Conspiracy (C)	Details
1789		
1. August, Martinique	R	Saint Pierre district. 300–400 slaves.
2. Demerara	R	1 plantation. Widespread conspiracy.
1790		
3. January, Cuba	R	1 plantation.
4. April, Guadeloupe	R?	Petit Bourg, etc. 100+ punished.
5. Spring? Venezuela	R	1 plantation. 1 overseer killed.
6. May, Tortola	R	1 plantation. 2 slaves executed.
7. October–December, Martinique	R	West coast. Pillage and killing.

1791

8. January 1, Saint Lucia	C	Soufrière. 1 plantation.
9. Early January, Dominica	R	Work stoppage/desertion/con-frontation.
10. Mid-January, Dominica	R	Free colored leader. 1 white killed.
11. January, Saint Domingue	C	Port Salut. 200 slaves.
12. May, Guadeloupe	C?	Saint Anne. Led by mulatto slave.
13. June–July, Saint Domingue	R	Separate revolts on 3 estates.
14. July, Louisiana	C	Pointe Coupée. 17 slaves arrested.
15. August, Marie-Galante	C	Saint Domingue free colored hanged.
16. August–November, Saint Domingue	R	North Province. 100,000+.
17. November–December, Jamaica	C?	North Coast.

1792+

18. Saint Domingue	R	Revolt spreads beyond North. 1,000s.

1793

19. March, Santo Domingo	C	Hinche. 19 arrested. No executions.
20. April, Guadeloupe	R	Trois Rivières. 200. 20 whites killed.
21. April, Guadeloupe	C	Baillif. 5 death sentences.
22. April, Guadeloupe	C	Basse-Terre region. 14 punished.
23. August, Guadeloupe	R	Saint Anne. 1,000? slaves and freemen.
24. Saint Lucia	R	

1794

25. February, Martinique	R	Saint Luce. During British invasion.

1795

26. Early, Santo Domingo	C	Samaná. 7 blacks, 3 French whites.
27. Trinidad	C?	2 conspiracies in south and north.
28. April, Louisiana	C	Pointe Coupée. 23 slaves executed.
29. May, Bahamas	C	Nassau. Francophone slaves.
30. May, Venezuela	R	Coro. 300 slaves and free blacks.
31. July, Cuba	R	Puerto Príncipe. 15 slaves.
32. July? Puerto Rico	R?	Aguadilla. A few slaves.
33. August, Curaçao	R	2,000 slaves? 29 slaves executed.
34. Demerara	R	Cooperation with maroon attacks.

1796
35. February–April, Louisiana C   Pointe Coupée, German Coast. 3 plots?
36. May, Cuba   C   Puerto Príncipe. 5 "French" slaves.
37. October, Santo Domingo   R   Boca Nigua. 100 slaves. 7 executed.

1797
38. August, Bahamas   C   Nassau. "French" slaves. 5 executed.

1798
39. January, Venezuela   C   Carúpano/Cumaná. African slaves.
40. June, Cuba   R   Puerto Príncipe. 20 slaves punished.
41. July, Cuba   C   Trinidad. 5 slaves tried, 2 hanged.
42. October, Cuba   R   Güines. 23 slaves on 1 estate.

1799
43. April, New Granada   C   Cartagena. French slaves, freemen.
44. May, Venezuela   C   Maracaibo. French and local freemen.

1800
45. September, Curaçao   R   Large multiclass rising.

1801
46. December, Tobago   C   7 or 16 estates. 7 slaves executed.

1803
47. June, Jamaica   C   Kingston. 2 executed.

1805
48. December, Trinidad   C   4 slaves executed.

1806
49. Jamaica   C   Saint George's. 1 slave executed.
50. Puerto Rico   R   Humacao. Slaves attack guardhouse.

1807
51. December, Demerara   C   20 slaves arrested. 9 executed.

1809
52. March, Jamaica   C   Kingston. 2 executed.

1811
53. January, Louisiana   R   German coast. 400–500 slaves.
54. September, Martinique   R   Saint Pierre. 15 executed.
55. Cuba   C   Widespread, centered on Havana.

1812

56. January, Puerto Rico	C?	Widespread. 16 punished.
57. January, Cuba	R	Puerto Príncipe. 8 hanged; 73 whipped.
58. February, Cuba	C	Bayamo. Probably part of Aponte plot.
59. March, Cuba	R	Guanabo. 1 estate.
60. August, Louisiana	C	New Orleans. 1 white executed.
61. August, Santo Domingo	R	Eastern region. 3 executed.

1815

62. December, Jamaica	C	Saint Elizabeth. 250 Africans. 1 hanged.

SOURCES: 1. David Geggus, "The Slaves and Free Coloreds of Martinique during the Age of the French and Haitian Revolutions: Three Moments of Resistance," in *Parts Beyond the Seas: The Lesser Antilles in the Age of European Expansion*, ed. Robert L. Paquette, and Stanley L. Engerman (Gainesville: University Press of Florida, 1996, 300–321). 2. Thomas Southey, *Chronological History of the West Indies* (London, 1827), vol. 3, pp. 22–23. 3. Julius Scott, "The Common Wind," Ph.D. diss., Duke University, 1986, p. 151. 4. Anne Pérotin-Dumon, *Etre patriote sous les tropiques* (Basse-Terre: Société d'Histoire de la Guadeloupe, 1985), pp. 137–138. 5. Scott, "Common Wind," p. 157. 6. Elsa Goveia, *Slave Society in the British Leeward Islands* (New Haven: Yale University Press, 1965), pp. 95–96. 7. Pierre-François-Régis Dessalles, *Historique des troubles survenus à la Martinique pendant la Révolution*, ed. Henri de Frémont (Fort-de France: Société d'Histoire de la Martinique, 1982), pp. 315–316, 364–366. 8. David Barry Gaspar, chap. 4 in this volume. 9 and 10. Scott, "Common Wind," pp. 193–199. 11. Carolyn Fick, *The Making of Haiti* (Knoxville: University of Tennessee Press, 1990), pp. 137–138. 12. Pérotin-Dumon, *Etre patriote*, p. 277. 13. Jean-Philippe Garran Coulon, *Rapport sur les troubles de Saint-Domingue* (Paris: 1797–1799), vol. 2, p. 215. 14. Ulysses S. Ricard, Jr., "The Pointe Coupée Slave Conspiracy of 1791," in *Proceedings of the 15th Meeting of the French Colonial Historical Society*, ed. Patricia Galloway and Philip Boucher (Lanham: University Press of America, 1992), pp. 116–129. 15. Anne Pérotin-Dumon, "The Emergence of Politics among Free Coloureds and Slaves in Revolutionary Guadeloupe," *Journal of Caribbean History* 25 (1993): 115. 16. Fick, *Making of Haiti*, chap. 4. 17. David Geggus, "Jamaica and the Saint Domingue Slave Revolt, 1791–1793," *The Americas* 38 (1981): 223–225. 18. Fick, *Making of Haiti*, chaps. 5–7. 19. David Patrick Geggus, chap. 5 in this volume. 20. *General Advertiser* (Philadelphia), June 10, 1793. 21 and 22. Archives Nationales, Paris, DXXV/129/1008. 23. Pérotin-Dumon, *Etre patriote*, pp. 278–282. 24. Lucien Abenon et al., *Antilles 1789: La Révolution aux Caraïbes* (Paris: Nathan, 1989), p. 174. 25. Kieran Kleczewski, "Martinique and the British Occupation, 1794–1802," Ph.D. diss., Georgetown University, 1988, p. 143. 26. Carlos E. Deive, *La Esclavitud en Santo Domingo* (Santo Domingo: Museo del Hombre Dominicano, 1980), vol. 2, p. 471. 27. V. S. Naipaul, *The Loss of Eldorado* (London: Penguin, 1973), p. 138. 28. Gwendolyn Hall, "The 1795 Slave Conspiracy in Pointe Coupée," in *Proceedings*, ed. Galloway and Boucher, pp. 130–141. 29. Michael Craton and Gail Saunders, *Islanders in the Stream: A History of the Bahamian People* (Athens: University of Georgia Press, 1989), vol. 1, p. 208. 30. Pedro Arcaya, *Insurrección de los negros en la serranía de Coro* (Caracas: Instituto

Panamericano de Geografía y Historia, 1949). 31. Geggus, chap. 5 in this volume. 32. Archivo General de Indias, Sevilla, Estado 10/1. 33. Cornelis Goslinga, *The Dutch in the Caribbean and Surinam, 1791/95–1942* (Assen: Van Gorcum, 1991), pp. 1–20. 34. Michael Craton, *Testing the Chains: Resistance to Slavery in the British West Indies* (Ithaca: Cornell University Press, 1982), p. 272. 35. Paul Lachance, "The Politics of Fear: French Louisianians and the Slave Trade," *Plantation Society in the Americas* 1 (1979): 168. 36 and 37. Geggus, chap. 5 in this volume. 38. Craton and Saunders, *Islanders*, pp. 211–212. 39. Federico Brito Figueroa, *El Problema tierra y esclavos en la historia de Venezuela* (Caracas: Ediciones de la Biblioteca, 1985), pp. 233–234. 40 and 41. Geggus, chap. 5 in this volume. 42. Archivo General de Simancas, GM 6855 (courtesy of Allan J. Kuethe). 43. Allan Kuethe, *Military Reform and Society in New Granada* (Gainesville: University of Florida Press, 1978), pp. 178–179. 44. Brito Figueroa, *Problema*, pp. 234–235. 45. Roberto Palacios, "Ansia de libertad," *Lanternu* 1 (1983): 20–27. 46. Keith Laurence, "The Tobago Slave Conspiracy of 1801," *Caribbean Quarterly* 28, no. 3 (1982). 47. Southey, *History*, vol. 3, p. 248. 48. Lionel Fraser, *History of Trinidad* (Port of Spain, 1891–1896), vol. 1, pp. 268–271. 49. W. Gardner, *A History of Jamaica* (London, 1873), pp. 243–244; George Bridges, *Annals of Jamaica* (London, 1828), p. 284, gives 1807 as the date. 50. Guillermo Baralt, *Esclavos rebeldes* (Rio Piedras: Huracán, 1985), p. 18. 51. Thomas Saint Clair, *A Soldier's Sojourn in British Guiana* (Georgetown, 1947), pp. 237–240. 52. Southey, *History*, vol. 3, p. 469. 53. Robert L. Paquette, chap. 8 in this volume. 54. Geggus, "Slaves and Free Coloreds of Martinique," 300–321. 55. José Luciano Franco, *Ensayos históricos* (Havana: Editorial de Ciencias Sociales, 1974), pp. 125–190. 56. Baralt, *Esclavos*, pp. 21–29. 57–60. Franco, *Ensayos*, pp. 160–183. 61. Deive, *Esclavitud*, vol. 2, p. 479. 62. Richard Hart, *Slaves Who Abolished Slavery* (Kingston: Institute of Social and Economic Research, 1985), pp. 225–227.

2

The French Revolution in Saint Domingue
A Triumph or a Failure?

CAROLYN E. FICK

In only one case throughout the millennial history of slavery in the world did slave rebellion actually escalate into a genuine revolutionary movement that not only succeeded in abolishing slavery but, in the process, also proved that slave emancipation, once achieved, would be permanent. This occurred during the course of the French Revolution in France's prized sugar colony, Saint Domingue. But it was also in the ultimate consolidation of France's new bourgeois republic under the governance of Napoleon Bonaparte that members of the French bourgeoisie sought the restoration of slavery, and with it the regeneration of their colonial fortunes. That attempt pushed the struggle of the ex-slaves in Saint Domingue toward one of national independence from which the former French colony emerged in 1804 as the New World's second independent nation, Haiti.

When the events in Saint Domingue are examined from the vantage point of the colonial revolution, it becomes immediately evident that they are intertwined with and even partially dependent upon those of the metropolitan revolution in France. Yet the sheer paucity, if not the near-total absence, in French revolutionary historiography of any substantive treatment of the colonial question, of the slave trade, or of slavery itself—indeed, of those interlocking spheres of activity forming the economic underpinnings of the rising French bourgeoisie—would lead one to assume that, from the vantage point of the French Revolution, these issues were, at best, of only peripheral importance to the vital political and social problems facing revolutionary France.[1] That the abolition of slavery, the "most radical step of the Haitian Revolution and perhaps even of the French Revolution," as one historian has

recently affirmed,[2] should occupy so trivial a place in the overall histo-
ries of the revolution is no doubt a stubborn and persistent reflection of
the inability of the French revolutionaries themselves to confront the
issue of slavery head on in the legislative assemblies, and to do so
forthrightly in the name of those principles guiding the revolution—
that is, the universalist principles of liberty and equality. But what did
these ideals really mean, and what did they mean to whom?

In France, as in Saint Domingue, such an ideology obviously signi-
fied different and often opposing goals for different social groups or
parties, depending upon the class interests at stake. For the port merchants, the slave traders, and the absentee planters—that is, the enslav-
ing bourgeoisie—liberty and equality were not only political matters,
but ones that would also ensure the unhampered continuation of the
slave trade and of commerce in slave-produced commodities. Though
they were members of the revolutionary bourgeoisie, their interests
were tied nonetheless to the maintenance of slavery, to the colonies, and
to the economic derivatives of the colonial system, all of which constituted a major cornerstone of France's prerevolutionary political
economy. This may largely explain why the issue of abolition of both the
slave trade and of slavery, when it was debated, was never seriously
approached on economic grounds, as it would be in Britain some forty
years later.

In this vein, it has been suggested that if revolutionary France (at
least up to the war with Britain in 1793) experienced such impregnable
difficulties in dealing with the economic problems of abolition, it was
not so much because the revolution was a bourgeois one as because it
was not yet bourgeois to the limit.[3] Indeed, during the latter decades of
the eighteenth century, slavery and the colonies were still primary
factors in the development of France's economy, and only eventually, by
mid-nineteenth century, would the ending of slavery mark, as it did in
Britain, the beginning of its real expansion. Abolitionism in revolutionary France thus found its expression, for the most part, in relatively
benign philosophical terms. Even the Société des Amis des Noirs, the
one group that did advocate the immediate abolition of the slave trade
and, by extension, though far less forcefully, the eventual ending of
slavery, found it more politically judicious to pose its arguments on
humanitarian and moral grounds. For to directly attack the economic
foundations of these issues would be to attack the legitimacy of key
sectors of the national economy and a formidable source of the nation's
wealth. Port merchants, traders, shipbuilders, outfitters, financiers,
insurance brokers, not to mention sugar refiners, all depended, directly
or indirectly, upon the maintenance of slavery and the slave trade.

Nowhere in France was the slave trade more central to the economy than in the city of Nantes, the country's chief slaving port. As early as 1750, Nantes alone accounted for over 50 percent of the entire French slave trade, and throughout the remainder of the Old Regime its economic activity centered increasingly on the trade, to which eventually all other economic activity, including that of colonial commerce, became subordinate. By the final decade of the Old Regime, between 1783 and 1792, during which time some 350 slave ships had been equipped by Nantes outfitters, slave trading was largely responsible for sustaining the city's commercial trade, as one-third to one-half of all colonial products entering Nantes represented payments for slaving debts to Nantes merchants.[4] Additionally, the slave trade either stimulated or directly financed other sectors of the Nantes economy, notably shipbuilding but also textiles, iron manufacturing, and sugar refining. Even in Bordeaux, where the trade was not a prime factor in a thriving economy which was based essentially upon colonial imports and exports, profits from slave trading as an auxiliary activity were hardly negligible during the 1783–1792 decade.[5]

So if France's economy placed the country in a favorable position among the nations of Europe by the eve of the Revolution and strenghtened the bid of its own bourgeoisie to bring down the feudal regime, why then should its foundations be questioned or, even worse, swept away in the name of revolutionary principle? Not one of the Jacobin clubs, not Robespierre, Camille Desmoulins, nor any of the radical left-wing revolutionaries in France, Marat notwithstanding, wanted to touch the burning question of the slave trade openly.[6] In fact, prior to the February 4, 1794, abolition of slavery by the National Convention, the most that would be conceded on the issue was the suspension in July 1793 and removal in September of the slave trade subsidy.[7] Not a word was spoken about the abolition of the slave trade itself. Why, then, did France abolish slavery in its decree of February 4, at the height of the revolution's most radical phase? What factors led France's legislators to take such a step that otherwise would have been seen as both inconsistent with and contrary to the economic forces impelling the nascent bourgeois republic? The answers do not lie in the French Revolution but emerge out of the complex web of events that beset revolutionary Saint Domingue at the opposite end of the mercantile system. There, revolutionary notions of liberty and equality were interpreted by the diverse classes and racial castes composing its slave society in ways that overtly exposed the contradictions and inequalities upon which that society was built—and in the name of which it would also be utterly destroyed.

For the resident planters of Saint Domingue, as for the French maritime bourgeoisie, liberty was seen in economic terms. For the planters liberty meant the removal of metropolitan controls over the affairs of the colony, externally as well as internally. They refused to see their interests as being subordinate to those of the metropolis and, in short, wanted free trade and local political autonomy. Liberty carried meaning that was far more elementary and nonetheless imperative for the racially oppressed sectors of the colonial population. The free coloreds, who were denied civil and political rights under the colonial order because of their color and because of their genealogical links to slavery, demanded their equality with whites. As for the slaves, liberty was a question of outright freedom from slavery and ultimately of the right to define in their own ways the material conditions that should accompany it.

Why was Saint Domingue uniquely ripe for revolution in 1788–1789? Why should the unfolding of the metropolitan revolution in France have so decisive and so far-reaching an impact upon this Caribbean colony and not another? Ideas about liberty and equality, which were circulating so profusely once revolution broke out in France, no doubt served as a catalytic force in impelling the revolts that occurred in each of the indigenous sectors of Saint Domingue's colonial society. But revolutionary ideas alone could not have produced the unfolding of events in the colony. A brief overview of Saint Domingue's exceptional development as a Caribbean slave colony may help to provide a partial explanation for that extraordinary explosion of events.

Saint Domingue was among the last of the Caribbean sugar colonies to be established and exploited by a major European power. It did not become French until the close of the seventeenth century, when the western third of Hispaniola, only sparsely inhabited by buccaneers, pirates, and other sundry elements, in the majority French, was ceded by Spain under the Treaty of Ryswick in 1697. And yet, although a latecomer to the West Indian mosaic of European exploitation colonies, Saint Domingue's rate of development in its incipient stage phenomenally exceeded that of any other colony. Capital derived chiefly from small-scale indigo production was rapidly converted into investment capital for sugar. Where not a single sugar plantation existed in 1689, within a decade and a half and within only seven years of its acquisition by the French crown, there were already 120 in place; over 100 of these had been established in the four-year period from 1700 to 1704.[8] Without having undergone several decades of turbulence and the chronic setbacks that had beset the early British colonies (notably Jamaica and the Leewards) and retarded their growth, Saint Domingue was, by the turn of the century, already entering a period of economic takeoff.

There could be no sugar without slaves. Saint Domingue's rapid conversion from indigo to sugar production also created dramatic changes, both quantitatively and qualitatively, in its slave population. During the formative period of growth, roughly from 1690 to 1720, the number of slaves rose from just over 3,000 to well over 47,000, representing a fourteenfold increase in just thirty years. From 80,000 in 1730, the slave population more than doubled in the next twenty-four years to reach about 172,000; from the end of the Seven Years' War to the eve of the revolution (1763 to 1789), the increase was over 100 percent, rising from 206,000 to the officially cited figure of 465,429, or roughly half a million.[9] If the excessively high mortality rates among slaves in the sugar colonies and the notoriously low birth rates among slave women are taken into account, these increases were, for the greater part, directly attributable to the importation of slaves through the slave trade. In fact, slave imports to Saint Domingue in the final decade of the colonial regime accounted for approximately 80 percent of the imports to the French West Indies for this period, which averaged between 37,000 and 40,000 annually.[10]

The colony's economy, however, did not rest entirely upon sugar. Coffee cultivation, an important secondary sector, in which a significant portion of the colony's free coloreds participated as slaveowning planters by the 1780s, had emerged during the last two decades of the colonial regime. The rise of the free coloreds economically and demographically throughout the eighteenth century (and more dramatically so during these two critical decades preceding the revolution) certainly constitutes a unique situation in the slave colonies of the colonial Caribbean. It also constitutes an important contributing factor in the outbreak of revolution in Saint Domingue and, as such, deserves particular attention.

Prior to the French slave code of 1685 known as the Code Noir, no comprehensive legislation existed that formally regulated the status of free persons of color, and no deliberately discriminatory legislation existed to constrict their social condition for the simple reason that their numbers, still significantly low, posed little threat to colonial slave society.[11] In turn-of-the-century Saint Domingue, they barely numbered six hundred.[12] Initially they competed with lower-class whites for jobs in the skilled or specialized trades on the plantations, but by midcentury their economic advances already began to be perceived by some whites as a dangerous trend which would undermine the hegemony of the white plantocracy and the institutionalized rule of white supremacy. In the decades following the close of the Seven Years' War, many free persons of color had participated in the rise and expansion of coffee production by purchasing land and slaves and bringing under cultivation the relatively undeveloped mountainous areas of the West and South provinces. By this time their numbers had swelled to nearly 7,000 officially; between 1775 and the eve of the revolution in 1789, in merely a decade and a half, the free colored population increased fourfold to reach roughly 28,000. The free coloreds had effectively attained a near-equal balance with the colony's whites, who now numbered just above 30,000.[13] In fact, the number of free people of color in Saint Domingue far exceeded the number of such persons for the British and the rest of the French West Indies combined.[14] Moreover, the free people of color of Saint Domingue now owned one-third of the colony's plantations, one-quarter (over 100,000) of the slaves, and one-quarter of the real estate property. Many had been educated in France by their former masters and occupied fair positions in commerce, the trades, and the military.[15] Nowhere in the eighteenth-century Caribbean was there such a combination of demographic and economic strength among the free colored population as in Saint Domingue.

For this very reason, it became increasingly imperative for colonial and metropolitan authorities to reinforce the code of white supremacy by legislating against the free coloreds' equality with whites, by repressing their political aspirations, and by placing them generally in a socially degraded position. Throughout the eighteenth century, therefore, modifications were made in the Code Noir and date as far back as the 1720s, but the bulk of repressive legislation came during the final decades of the colonial regime in direct response to their demographic explosion and marked economic advances. The manifest aim of the metropolitan, as well as colonial, authorities was to cut off rising expectations of a class which increasingly saw itself as the social equal of its white counterpart. In spite of their status as free persons, and in spite of their education, training, skills, and in some cases financial success, the free coloreds were to understand that their racial and slave origins made it impossible for them to enjoy equality with whites; the slaves, for their part, were also to understand that a state of freedom did not mean equality but rather a continuation of their subjugation by the white ruling class.

In 1788–1789, when the white colonists of Saint Domingue began to agitate in response to news of the calling of the Estates General in France and of the revolutionary stand taken by the Third Estate, claiming their own right to be represented in the metropolis, they also unwittingly opened the door for the tensions and contradictions embedded in the colony's caste and racial structure to be exposed fully. By 1789, with the political conjuncture of the metropolitan revolution, these tensions reached a point of exasperation. It was thus in the emergent ideology of liberty and equality that each of the contending parties saw its own particular interests embodied, and in the name of which each sought to define and to put forth its own demands. In this light, it is important to remember that the Saint Domingue revolution, which saw both the ending of slavery and the emergence of the former French colony as a free black state, began not by slave rebellion but by a revolt of its own ruling class of resident white planters.

A group of wealthy planters in the North province began by organizing themselves around the issue of representation in the metropolitan assembly. Their aim, once represented in France, was to gain significant changes in the economically restrictive areas of the Crown's mercantile policy; in addition, they hoped to achieve greater control over the internal politics of the colony. Opposing them in Saint Domingue were the royalists, who, as members of the bureaucracy or as commanding officers in the army, represented the Crown and therefore supported the status quo. In France, however, the absentee planters organized their own lobby, the Massiac Club, whose interests were supported and capably represented in the National Assembly by Antoine Barnave. With greater affinities to the metropolis and to the port merchants than to their creole counterparts, they were, in general, unfavorably inclined toward the idea of colonial representation, for, as proved to be the case, once that right was granted to the colonies, discussion of the planters' interests on the floor of the national revolutionary assembly would also lead to questions concerning civil rights and social equality for the free coloreds.[16] When the free coloreds, with the aid of Abbé Grégoire, the leading spokesman of the abolitionist Société des Amis des Noirs, mounted a parallel movement for their own representation in France, it became all the more imperative for the planters to prevent open debate of colonial questions in the National Assembly. A colonial deputy from Guadeloupe, de Curt, proposed that a separate committee should prepare legislation for the colonies without preliminary discussion by the assembly of the whole.

It was from the Colonial Committee that the decree of March 8 and the instructions of March 28, 1790, originated concerning the constitutional status of the colonies. Prepared in advance by Barnave, they provided a constitutional framework allowing the colonies considerable internal autonomy and sanctioned the already-existing colonial and provincial assemblies in Saint Domingue. These, of course, had been constituted without a single free colored vote. To complicate matters further, divisions among the whites in Saint Domingue reached their peak. Another organized faction calling itself the "patriot party" emerged. This faction moved beyond the comparatively moderate aims of the colonial representatives and sought virtual independence from France—in part as a solution to the problems posed by colonial representation and the inevitable treatment of the mulatto question in the National Assembly.

The instructions of March 28, 1790, as finally adopted, stated that the right to vote and hold office be granted to all property-owning persons at least twenty-five years of age who fulfilled the tax and residence requirements. However, the prerogative of deciding who was, and who was not, a "person" was left entirely up to the white colonists. On this issue the colonists instinctively set aside their political antagonisms to form a united front of opposition. When the free coloreds in Saint Domingue petitioned Governor Peynier, de Vincent, the military commander of the North province, and also the president of the Provincial Assembly of the North,[17] claiming the rights they believed were implicitly extended to them as persons, they predictably encountered implacable and even violent opposition from nearly every sector of white colonial society. Their movement quickly escalated into armed rebellion. Outnumbered, the rebels were defeated by colonial forces; their leaders, Vincent Ogé and Jean-Baptiste Chavannes, were given a summary trial in February 1791, after which they were publicly executed and decapitated. Their heads were displayed on pikes as a public reminder of the inviolable laws of white supremacy. To grant civil rights to a single free person of color, as the white colonists saw it, was to undermine the racially bound foundations of slavery itself; if these were undermined, so too were their own fortunes and well-being.

Once news reached France about the revolt of the free coloreds in Saint Domingue and the martyrdom of their leaders, it became clear that the March 1790 decrees had, in fact, done far more harm than good, and the Constituent Assembly was once again forced to debate the issue left unresolved by the ambiguities of the March decrees. In May 1791, the Colonial Committee prepared a report which essentially reasserted colonial jurisdiction over the mulatto question. Grégoire, in the name of the Amis des Noirs, bitterly opposed the report. Robespierre addressed the issue vigorously in terms of the very principles upon which the revolution was founded:

> The supreme interest of the nation and of the colonies is that you remain free, and that you do not overthrow, by your own initiative, the basis of that freedom. Perish the colonies if they are to be maintained at the cost of your freedom and glory. I repeat it: perish the colonies if the colonists, by their threats, want to force us to decree that which best suits their own interests! I declare in the name of the Assembly, of those members of the Assembly who do not wish to see the constitu-

tion overturned, and in the name of the entire nation which desires freedom, that we will sacrifice to the colonial deputies neither the nation, nor the colonies, nor the whole of humanity. . . . I ask the Assembly to declare that the free men of color shall enjoy all the rights of active citizens.[18]

Here was Robespierre in all of his revolutionary rhetorical splendor. However, although an egalitarian and an advocate of mulatto rights, he was not an abolitionist. Nor, for that matter, did he wish to see France lose her prize colonies over a principle: neither revolutionary principle, nor the nation, nor the colonies should perish. To save the colonies, civil equality must be extended to all free persons of color. He could afford to address the issue unequivocally in the name of revolutionary virtue because the rights of free coloreds in the colonies was not an economic question, but much closer to the principles of equality embodied in the Declaration of the Rights of Man and Citizen.

The principle of extending the rights of French citizenship to the mulattoes was undeniably an audacious and a noble one, but it also lent itself admirably to the furthering of a sense of national regeneration and of revolutionary self-gratification, in its attack on unjustifiable and abusive privileges, in this case the privileges of the aristocracy of the skin. In this sense, it might be argued that radicals such as Robespierre and Grégoire saw the issue of mulatto rights more in relation to the virtues of the revolution than on undauntedly antiracist grounds, or for the sake of the free coloreds themselves.

In the end, a proposal was put to the Colonial Assembly that would grant political rights to the free coloreds, but only to those born of legally free parents. As such, the law affected only a tiny minority of the free coloreds, perhaps a few hundred, and therefore explicitly excluded the rest, who, although free, were born of a slave parent or parents. It was, in reality, an extremely moderate step that the assembly took, one which sought a compromise between the white supremacist interests of the colonists and the legitimate claims of the free coloreds. As it concerned only a minute number of free mulattoes and free blacks, it was a measure whose consequences, it was hoped, would not necessarily threaten the social stability of the colonies. Although Grégoire and Robespierre both voted against the final proposal because of its restrictive nature,[19] and although virulent opposition came from Barnave (himself a Jacobin) and from others in the Massiac Club because the right to equality of even a small number of free coloreds was allowed, the measure did not ultimately jeopardize the basis of the nation's prosperity. The port merchants, for their part, had far more to fear from the growing strength of the secessionist patriot faction in Saint

Domingue than from the enfranchisement of a few mulattoes. Some merchants actually tended to favor granting political rights to free men of color, but in the interest of preserving the colonies and of safeguarding their own fortunes.[20] At least some of the free coloreds, after all, were themselves plantation owners and slaveholders. By keeping their distance from Barnave and his group, the metropolitan merchants indirectly helped to facilitate the passage of the May 15, 1791, decree granting full rights of French citizenship to a small segment of the colonies' free coloreds. The law was, incidentally, passed only three months prior to the wholly unanticipated outbreak of massive slave rebellion in Saint Domingue's North province on August 22–23, 1791.

The law brought into the open the contradictions it entailed. It would still take much bloodshed and armed conflict in Saint Domingue before all free coloreds would obtain civil liberties and political equality with whites. On April 4, 1792, eight months after the outbreak of the slave revolt in the North, and in the midst of continued warfare between the patriot faction and the free coloreds (now in an alliance of convenience with royalists and, to a lesser extent, with slaves who were beginning to desert their plantations in the West and South provinces), France's legislature finally granted full equality to all free coloreds. It was hoped that once the free coloreds gained their rights and abandoned their royalist allies, thus affirming their allegiance to France, they would then be able to help suppress the slave rebellion and induce the slaves to return to the plantations. At this stage of the French Revolution, the preservation of the colonies for France depended upon the twin components of egalitarianism and slavery. As for the slaves themselves, liberty and equality were simply not a part of the logic of France's bourgeois revolution.

How, then, did the slaves of Saint Domingue interpret these ideals on the eve of the revolution? Why, indeed, did revolutionary France abolish slavery on February 4, 1794? And, once slavery was abolished, what did freedom mean to the ex-slaves, who opposed the postslavery labor regime for its harsh resemblance to slavery and attempted, if only minimally, to forge a new existence based on self-defined goals and aspirations?

For virtually every social group or class in the colonies, the decade surrounding the French Revolution was one of rising expectations which reflected the natural economic interests or political aspirations of each group. The slaves of Saint Domingue thus shared a common vision of change. But for them change also entailed an end to slavery and the death of France's prize colonial possession.

In 1784 and 1785 the French government adopted a number of

reforms to the Code Noir that either reinforced previous measures concerning the obligations of masters toward their slaves or, minimally, conferred new rights upon the slaves. It became necessary to restate an earlier provision concerning the allocation of small plots of land to the slaves for their personal use and profit and to expressly forbid masters to abandon or neglect their responsibility of providing sufficient food rations for the slaves.[21] Pregnant women were to receive a reduction in workload and schedule and, even during the grinding season, they were to be exempted from night work on sugar estates. For the first time, masters were required to limit punishment of their slaves to fifty lashes of the whip; they could no longer mutilate, strike with a rod, or cause the death of their slaves as a result of any of a variety of insidious forms of flagrant brutality. In fact, in the latter event, a master could, by virtue of the 1784 reform legislation, run the risk of the death penalty. Finally, slaves were also allowed to denounce a master before the courts in cases of unrestrained cruelty.[22] However, a slave's testimony in court still could not be taken officially as legal evidence against the master, though it could be used to establish circumstances in any given case.[23]

Particularly revealing in this regard is the often-cited case of Nicolas Le Jeune, a coffee planter in the North Plain parish of Plaisance, who put to death four of his slaves, whom he suspected of poisoning, and tortured two others so brutally under his interrogations that they subsequently died. A group of Le Jeune's slaves brought the case to the magistrate, an investigation ensued, and Le Jeune was forced to stand trial.[24] If we may reasonably assume that news of the slave reform measures—bitterly opposed by the planters—had reached the colony's slaves, then the organized and assertive action of Le Jeune's slaves in bringing their master to trial (despite his threats to kill them if they did) may indeed reflect a new consciousness and rising expectations among the slaves in general.[25] The evidence against Le Jeune was incontrovertible, and the slaves no doubt expected he would be found guilty. If so, he would, theoretically, face the death penalty. A common front of white solidarity and white supremacy ensured Le Jeune's acquittal, but in these final years of the colonial regime, slaves were testing their chains and challenging the system in ways that may, in some measure, have anticipated their full-scale revolt on August 22–23, 1791.

At the same time Spain started to scrutinize its system of colonial slavery more closely. In 1789 fairly sweeping reforms of slavery were introduced. Spanish colonists were also instructed to welcome and protect runaway slaves from the French and British islands if they could produce "a 'legitimate' claim to freedom."[26] In Britain by this time the abolitionist movement was gaining momentum. Under increasing popular pressure, Parliament opened public debates, from 1789 to 1791, on the British slave trade. News of these reform tendencies in Europe, combined with news of the French Revolution and its resounding principles of liberty and equality, not only reached the Caribbean and the slave population, but, as vividly demonstrated in a study by Julius Scott, it spread rapidly throughout the islands by way of ships, sailors, and a vast network of interisland coastal commerce.[27] While British sailors arrived with news of the antislavery movement in England, French sailors, wearing the revolutionary cockade, spoke with even greater excitement of events in France as they worked together with slaves and free blacks loading and unloading ships' cargoes on the waterfront wharves. On market day, plantation slaves might even engage in commerce with the sailors, exchanging what produce they had for goods—and news—from Europe.[28] Persons of color, slave and free, actually participated in a diverse range of seafaring activities. Through several channels of life at sea, information could be transmitted not only from island to island, but sometimes, even more importantly, from one coastal town to another in the same colony. If such networks provided a vital means for the reporting of news and events from one area to another or for the transmission of revolutionary and reform currents in Europe, it also facilitated the spread of rumor. In this context the slaves of Saint Domingue played their own revolutionary part.

Rumors that the French king had granted the slaves three free days per week had been circulating throughout the colony for some time. Following the outbreak of events in 1789, the slaves also had witnessed the revolt of their own masters against the authority of the royal bureaucracy. In 1790, they had witnessed, and a few had even participated in, the armed revolt of Vincent Ogé and his supporters against a colonial order that denied free coloreds civil rights because of their color. Some slaves were no doubt aware of the reforms of slavery decreed by the king only a few years earlier. Slaves who had access to information in the port towns certainly knew that a revolution had broken out in France in the name of liberty and equality. If news also spread that the king had freed the slaves for three days a week, there is little reason to assume that slaves would not believe it to be true and, in the context of ongoing revolutionary upheaval, organize themselves to act upon that belief.

One of the first manifestations of the slaves' organized efforts to claim their three free days from their masters occurred in the South province, the most recently settled and least developed of the colony's three provinces. The movement originated at Port-Salut in the region surrounding the port city of les Cayes, the province's commercial and trading center and seat of its legislative assembly. It was here, too, in this region known as the Plaine-des-Cayes, that roughly half of the province's two hundred sugar plantations were concentrated,[29] and from which much of the revolutionary slave activity of the South was generated. Their movement was formed in January 1791 in response to the armed revolt of Ogé and his supporters in the North, and of intensified activity among the mulattoes of the West and South.[30] From these sources in the South the slaves at Port-Salut learned of the rumor that they had been freed for three days a week but that masters refused to comply. When they offered to join the mulattoes, however, they were told they must act on their own behalf. Some two hundred slaves then armed themselves in a conspiracy to demand that their masters recognize the rights they believed the king had granted them. If the masters refused, they planned to begin the revolt and kill them off. Almost inevitably, the conspiracy was discovered, and the ringleaders were arrested.[31] However, the conspiracy signaled the beginning of the revolutionary struggle of the slaves in the South for general emancipation. It originated in a rumor the slaves believed to be true, expected to be implemented, and for which they were determined to risk their lives.

The same rumor stimulated the organized activities of the slaves in the North as they prepared their massive revolt of August 22–23, six months later. The free coloreds had recently won a partial victory with the May 15 decree. In the face of a united front of white supremacy, outright hostility to and subversion of the law, the mulattoes and free blacks attempted to claim their own limited rights to political equality. By the end of the summer, the new Colonial Assembly, which would convene in le Cap (the capital city of the North) on August 23,[32] had been constituted without the participation of a single free colored elector. In June and July sporadic gatherings of slaves similar to those organized by the Port-Salut slaves in the South began to appear in the West. Plantation managers informed absentee owners that their slaves were becoming unmanageable and were letting things go to their heads at the sight of the cockade; one wrote that "many [slaves] imagine that the king has granted their freedom," and that it was the masters who refused to consent to it.[33] The spread of this rumor gave rise to the Morne Rouge and Bois-Caïman slave assemblies at the Normand de Mézy plantation in the North Plain, when the slaves there made plans for their revolt. The assemblies were held on the night of August 14, one week prior to the definitive outbreak of revolt and the beginning of the black revolution.[34]

At the assemblies false papers were read, reportedly by an unknown mulatto or quadroon, which declared that the king had granted the slaves three free days per week, that the masters refused to consent, and that royalist troops were on their way to execute the decree by force. It was not outright freedom, but in an era of rising expectations, political turmoil, and violent conflict within the colony, it was near enough to freedom to incite the slaves to rebel on their own account. The leader of the Bois-Caïman gathering (at which the plans agreed upon earlier that evening at the Morne Rouge assembly were sanctified by a voodoo ceremony) was Boukman, a former plantation headman and now coachman on the Clément plantation, one of the first to go up in flames when the revolt began in the North Plain district of Acul. Boukman issued the call to arms, combining indigenous elements of slave religion with a secular exhortation to war and liberty. Now it was the freedom of the blacks from slavery that was at stake: "Couté la liberté li palé nan coeur nous tous (Listen to the voice of liberty which speaks in the hearts of all of us)."[35]

For the slaves, the three-free-days-a-week rumor, the exact origins of which (as with rumor generally) may be impossible to determine, was nonetheless associated with the king who supposedly decreed it. It also served the purposes of some elements within the counterrevolutionary royalist faction[36] who would tacitly support slave rebellion and the slave leaders in order to destabilize the colony, defeat the patriot secessionists, return the slaves to their plantations, and restore the power and prestige they derived from the Old Regime. For the slaves these royalists appeared to be useful allies, whose credibility was certainly enhanced by the fact that they represented the king, who was ostensibly on the side of the slaves. Thus the slaves, who were now aware that a libertarian revolution and a counterrevolution had broken out in France, waged their own struggle for freedom under the colors of monarchy and royalism.[37] In this, they later found protectors in the Spanish colonial government of Santo Domingo to the east. It is thus somewhat ironic that, for the slaves of French Saint Domingue, the most pragmatic repercussions of the French Revolution lay not so much in its ideology—for even if news and propaganda about liberty and equality fell upon receptive ears, many slaves hardly needed to be convinced of the validity of their freedom—as in the reactionary forces produced by the revolution. Within an environment of war and counterrevolution, the slaves found the logistical means, the arms, and the allies of convenience with which to wage their struggle to overthrow slavery. Without those conditions, and without the concomitant breakup of the ruling planter elite within the colony, it is difficult to imagine how their revolt could have gained the magnitude and momentum that it did, no matter how carefully organized or how genuinely inspired it may have been.

By early 1793 both Britain and Spain were officially at war with France and were therefore confirmed enemies of the revolution. The rebel slave leaders of the North, Jean-François, Biassou, and Toussaint Louverture, now formalized their alliance with Spain as officers of the Spanish army fighting to promote the interests of the Bourbon monarchy, under which they enjoyed their own freedom. Large portions of the North province, particularly in the northeast, were already occupied by rebel slave forces and nominally, at least, under Spanish control. Britain, in collusion with seditious-minded colonists, was also preparing to invade. Essentially, these colonists hoped to escape the supreme authority of France's two republican civil commissioners, Léger Sonthonax and Etienne Polverel, who had been sent to the colony in September 1792 along with 6,000 troops to restore order and impose a proper respect for metropolitan law, in particular the April 4, 1792, law guaranteeing the full rights of the free coloreds. Refusing to accept these changes to the colonial order, these colonists looked to Britain for protection. By the end of the summer, British forces were in control of the Grande-Anse districts at the western extremity of the South province, as well as Môle St. Nicolas on the western tip of the North; before the end of the year, parts of the coastal region of the West province would also fall into British hands.

The survival of the colony depended not only upon conquering the forces of foreign occupation; internally, the colony was being torn to pieces by the factional power struggles of counterrevolutionary royalists, on the one hand, and secessionist patriots (some of whom had already deserted to the British), on the other. Many from both sides had already been arrested and deported by the commissioners earlier that year, and by June, with the arrival of a new governor-general, Thomas Galbaud, tensions reached their peak. Galbaud's aristocratic leanings and cavalier refusal to accept the authority of the commissioners envenomed the situation to the point where open rebellion, supported by the political enemies of the commissioners and other disparate elements, broke out in le Cap. The commissioners effectively had only the mulattoes and the city's black slave population, some ten thousand strong, to count upon for the defense of the capital. During the fighting, fire broke out and spread rapidly, in the end destroying two-thirds of the city.

Under these circumstances, with the mass of slave rebels in the North fighting against the republic and occupying French territory in the name of Spain, with the threat of an imminent British invasion in the

South, and with over ten thousand black slaves participating in the defense of le Cap, which was in near-total ruin, the commissioners took their first step toward the realization of general emancipation. They declared free those slaves (and subsequently their families) who would choose to join the republican army to fight the enemies of France and the revolution.

However, the extent to which these circumstances helped to determine the commissioners' decision to manumit thousands of slaves in this manner, before Sonthonax finally abolished slavery altogether (on August 29, 1793) in the North, is debatable. It has often been argued that the foreign occupation of large areas of Saint Domingue, coupled with counterrevolutionary and secessionist tendencies operating in combination with the enemy, not to mention the mortality and excessive morbidity of French troops suffering the baneful effects of an adverse tropical climate, left Sonthonax with no other choice than to free the slaves to save the colony. However, it has also been argued that, in fact, the actual position of France in Saint Domingue following the declarations of war against Britain and Spain was far from hopeless and that the real danger to France of the foreign invasion in 1793 has been largely exaggerated by historians who have simply taken the Anglo-Spanish military threat for granted.[38] If this is so, then one must pose the question: Why the need to free the slaves to fight for France if the colony was not in any real danger of falling into enemy hands? Why, indeed, the need for general emancipation at all? Here, other factors must also be considered, which is not to say that Sonthonax's apprehensions of foreign occupation and of counterrevolution were not real, or that they did not contribute to the commissioners' decisions regarding slave emancipation. But Sonthonax was both a philosophical and a practical revolutionary. He can be said to have taken a deliberate step to turn into reality the promise of a long line of European abolitionist thought, and not merely to have reacted to a difficult situation.[39]

Thus it was perhaps not so much that the war situation left Sonthonax with no other alternative than to abolish slavery, but rather that it provided the context within which he could justify an act of genuinely revolutionary proportions—an act that no politician in France wished to consider openly in the National Convention. Under the circumstances that prevailed in Saint Domingue in 1793, the advantages to France of general emancipation could certainly be defended. The most capable fighters in the colony were the slaves, and they were fighting and gaining territory in the name of Spain, the monarchy, and, as far as Toussaint Louverture was concerned, in the name of general emancipation. By abolishing slavery Sonthonax also hoped to win the rebel leaders over to the republican cause, secure the allegiance of the blacks to France, and preempt any practical possibility of losing the colony by virtue of an alliance of rebel slaves with a foreign power. The real danger was, after all, not the Spanish army itself,[40] but the blacks who were fighting in its ranks against France. The argument therefore that France could have held on to Saint Domingue indefinitely without the support of a well-trained black army under the military leadership of a Toussaint Louverture is not absolutely irrefutable. But even more crucial than the slaves' alliance with an enemy power was that they had themselves taken up arms and staged a massive rebellion in the first place. Without their independently organized revolt in the North with their own goals and aspirations, and also their alliance with Spaniards and counterrevolutionaries whom they believed to be (nominally, at least) supportive of those goals, it is hardly conceivable that Sonthonax could have carried off such a sweeping proclamation for general emancipation. Two months after the proclamation in the North province, Polverel followed suit, and slavery in its entirety was abolished throughout the colony.[41]

It can be argued therefore that the abolition of slavery in Saint Domingue resulted from a combination of mutually reinforcing factors that fell into place at a particular historical juncture. No single factor or even combination of factors—including the beginning of the French Revolution with its catalytic ideology of equality and liberty, the colonial revolt of the planters and of the free coloreds, the context of imperial warfare, and the obtrusive role of a revolutionary abolitionist as civil commissioner—warranted the termination of slavery in Saint Domingue in the absence of independent, militarily organized slave rebellion. Without slave rebellion, Sonthonax's philosophy of nongradualism in regard to abolition could not have gone very far in practice. And yet, without all of these external factors, the slave rebellion itself could hardly have succeeded as it did. Toussaint, for his part, remained with Spain for another eight months before finally deserting his former comrades, Jean-François and Biassou, and adopting the republican flag.

From the vantage point of revolutionary France the abolition of slavery seems almost to have been a by-product of the revolution and hardly an issue central to the pressing concerns of the nation. It was Sonthonax who initiated the abolition of slavery in Saint Domingue, not the National Convention. In fact, France only learned that slavery had been abolished in Saint Domingue when the colony's three deputies, Dufay, Mills, and Jean-Baptiste Mars Bellay (respectively a white, a mulatto, and a former free black), arrived in France in January 1794 to take their seats and asked on February 3 that the Convention officially abolish slavery throughout the colonies.

At this point, however, abolitionism in France had become directly associated with the Girondins, the party of Brissot, himself a genuine abolitionist and member of the now defunct Société des Amis des Noirs. Brissot's equivocal stance on the arrest and execution of Louis XVI and consequently on the legitimacy of the new republic—combined with the blatant leanings of the Girondins in favor of the wealthy, propertied bourgeoisie and with their opposition to the domestic controls necessitated by a foreign war they had themselves proclaimed imperative in 1792—led Robespierre and the Jacobins to see the Girondins as covert supporters of France's enemies in order to bring the revolution to a moderate end. Thus the Girondins were accused of having secretly fomented the colonial upheavals to the advantage of England and of supporting abolition in order to ruin France's empire.[42] Under the impetus of the revolutionary Terror, abolitionism was equated with treasonable Girondin politics, and political expediency now prevented even the most radical Jacobins from publicly endorsing the issue or even proposing an open debate on its merits. However, with the arrival of the three colonial deputies (two of them men of color) who announced that slavery was abolished in Saint Domingue, the Convention faced a fait accompli. It could no longer avoid the issue, and on February 4 it proclaimed slavery abolished in all of the colonies. The decree was passed with much fervor and inflated rhetoric about universal liberty, but Robespierre himself was conspicuously absent during the February 4 session and did not sign the decree.[43] No doubt the very recent execution of Brissot and a number of other Girondins known incidentally to have been members of the Amis des Noirs, induced the radicals to keep their silence on an issue that, prior to February 4, had come to be seen as part of a counterrevolutionary Girondin conspiracy. Thus, inside France, the legislative abolition of slavery, even at the height of the revolution's most radical phase, was hardly the resounding victory of revolutionary principle that it ought to have been, but was instead thoroughly enmeshed in the political mechanics of the foreign war and the domestic Terror.

Nevertheless, slavery was an embarrassment to the French Revolution. For if, as it was argued earlier, the organized slave insurrection in Saint Domingue was the essential factor, among other important contributing factors, in determining Sonthonax's general emancipation proclamation of August 29, 1793, it was also the military success of the slave revolt, which was not merely a jacquerie or a colonial version of the Vendée, but a genuine struggle for emancipation, that provided the Convention with the means it lacked for a legislative abolition of slavery. If the slaves themselves had not taken revolutionary initiatives in Saint Domingue, there is no reason to assume that the Convention would have seen the necessity, or even the political expediency, of seriously confronting the issue of slavery in the colonies and of abolishing slavery. By keeping their distance on the question of slavery and abolition, the revolutionary democrats were protecting themselves during the Terror from the political consequences of their past association with the Girondins. Also, it was almost as if, by not addressing the issue of slavery, they were waiting to see whether slavery would survive in Saint Domingue against factors external to those operating in France.[44] Once the three colonial deputies appeared before the Convention to announce general emancipation in Saint Domingue, the Convention approved and sanctioned it, and thus congratulated itself for an act worthy of revolutionary virtue and of national regeneration. For the members of the Convention to have acted otherwise at this stage of the revolution would have been to dishonor the nation and to dishonor themselves, and in this, at least, revolutionary France does deserve recognition.

The crucial link, then, between the metropolitan revolution and the black revolution in Saint Domingue seems to reside in the conjunctural and complementary elements of a self-determined, massive slave rebellion, on the one hand, and the presence in the colony of a practical abolitionist in the person of Sonthonax, on the other.[45] Each side may have discreetly relied upon the other for the fulfillment of its goals, yet without the essential reality of autonomous slave rebellion, it is almost certain that Sonthonax could not have carried off such a sweeping measure as general emancipation, the foreign war notwithstanding. It would be wrong, however, to assume that France's legislative abolition of slavery on February 4, 1794, did not have an impact on the course of the black revolution. The decree did not prove to be the pivotal factor that has often been assumed to have influenced Toussaint Louverture's decision to abandon the Spanish and fight under the colors of France,[46] but one can safely maintain that it was instrumental in confirming and consolidating the military dedication with which Toussaint fought for France, thus effectively keeping the colony both French and free.

What can be said about freedom for the greater mass of average men and women who did not enjoy the prestige and relative ease of life in the military ranks but who, as ex-slaves, were still laboring on the plantations under slavelike conditions, despite the legal change in their status? For these, there was little or no hope at all of achieving, within the framework of the French or the Saint Domingue revolution, their own self-defined vision of emancipation, in which liberty entailed at once a claim to personal "proprietorship" of the land they tilled and, as independent subsistence farmers, an irrevocable shedding of their former slave identity. This world view, in any event, had far more to do with the African origins of the vast majority of the Saint Domingue blacks than with revolutionary notions of bourgeois democratic egalitarianism.[47]

Finally, it may be suggested here that the failure of the French Revolution to deal with the essential problem of slavery and abolition on the grounds of the ideals and political principles that inspired the revolution is embedded in the economic foundations for its very success. For, in the eventual triumph of the propertied bourgeoisie, which looked to Napoleon Bonaparte for the consolidation of its interests, came the reestablishment of slavery by the consular regime in 1802. So, was France's abolition of slavery in 1794 only a circumstantial aberration of the revolution? For the slaves of Saint Domingue, who had embarked upon a course of emancipation in 1791 grounded in the realities of their own lives under slavery, abolition was as permanent as it was inviolable, and their tortuous war for national independence, engaged in response to Bonaparte's attempt to restore slavery, was irrefutable proof.

In this light, one cannot properly speak of any real triumph of the French Revolution in Saint Domingue, but rather of the revolution's role in the unfolding of this thirteen-year liberation struggle. The French Revolution did provide the political conditions within which autonomous slave rebellion could fairly rapidly assume revolutionary proportions; and without the French Revolution there would have been no talk of liberty and equality, no counterrevolution, no ready access to allies and arms for the slaves, no real political leverage for Sonthonax to have taken the audacious step that he did. Without these revolutionary conditions, the terrifying revolt of the slaves on August 22–23, 1791, in the North may have remained just that, a courageous but restricted attempt by Caribbean plantation slaves to liberate themselves, an attempt like so many others throughout the New World that were ultimately defeated. If the dynamics of the black revolution in Saint Domingue have, until very recently, eluded historians of the French Revolution, it is not merely because slavery had become a monumental embarrassment to the revolution in 1794. It is also, more importantly, because Bonaparte's attempt to restore the odious institution in 1802, resulting in Haitian independence, became—probably unconsciously and perhaps even insidiously—an embarrassment to the distinguished field of French revolutionary historiography: in short, *ça gêne*.

NOTES

1. A highly critical survey of this lacuna in the historiography of the French Revolution is presented by Yves Bénot, *La Révolution française et la fin des colonies* (Paris: La Découverte, 1988), pp. 10, 205–217.

2. Robert L. Stein, *Léger Félicité Sonthonax: The Lost Sentinel of the Republic* (Rutherford: Farleigh Dickinson University Press, 1985), p. 79.

3. Bénot, *La Révolution française,* p. 106.

4. Robert L. Stein, *The French Slave Trade in the Eighteenth Century* (Madison: University of Wisconsin Press, 1979), pp. 27, 130–137; Alan Forrest, *Society and Politics in Revolutionary Bordeaux* (New York: Oxford University Press, 1975), p. 52.

5. Forrest, *Society and Politics,* p. 52; Stein, *French Slave Trade,* p. 135.

6. Bénot, *La Révolution française,* p. 102; Michael L. Kennedy, *The Jacobin Clubs in the French Revolution: The First Years* (Princeton: Princeton University Press, 1982), p. 204; Ruth F. Necheles, *The Abbé Grégoire, 1787–1831: The Odyssey of an Egalitarian* (Westport: Greenwood, 1971), p. 121; Stein, *Sonthonax,* p. 109. See also Aimé Césaire, *Toussaint Louverture: La Révolution française et le problème colonial* (1961; revised ed., Paris: Présence africaine, 1962), pp. 175–176. Political opportunism led Desmoulins, in his defense of Robespierre on the war question, to attack and denigrate Brissot (an Ami des Noirs) by indirectly attacking abolition of the slave trade and extolling the virtues of the great port merchants. Bénot, *La Révolution française,* pp. 100–102.

7. Stein, *Sonthonax,* pp. 82, 109.

8. Charles Frostin, *Les révoltes blanches à Saint-Domingue au XVIIe et XVIIIe siècles* (Paris: Ecole, 1975), pp. 138–145.

9. Ibid., p. 28.

10. Pierre Pluchon, *La route des esclaves: Négriers et bois d'ébène au XVIIIe siècle* (Paris: Hachette, 1980), pp. 19–20; Stein, *French Slave Trade,* p. 38. Figures for decadal imports to Saint Domingue are provided in David Eltis, *Economic Growth and the Ending of the Transatlantic Slave Trade* (New York: Oxford University Press, 1987), p. 249.

11. Prior to the Code Noir, it was the practice in Martinique to free automatically mulatto girls at age fifteen and mulatto males at twenty. Lucien Peytraud, *L'esclavage aux Antilles avant 1789* (Paris: Hachette, 1879), p. 402. Under the Code Noir, any mulatto child of a white planter living with a slave woman would similarly become free, as would the slave mother, but only if the master formally married his concubine. M. L. E. Moreau de Saint-Méry, *Loix et constitutions des colonies françaises de l'Amérique sous le vent* (Paris: By the Author, 1784), vol. 1, p. 416.

12. Frostin, *Les révoltes blanches,* pp. 28, 304.

13. Official population figures for the free coloreds are no doubt below the reality and would not have accounted for those individuals whose de facto freedom was not legally established but who were recognized and accepted (as would their children) as free persons. It is possible their numbers may even have exceeded that of whites. On this and other demographic considerations directly related to their population increase over the period after the Seven Years' War, see *Histoire des Antilles et de la Guyane,* ed. Pierre Pluchon (Toulouse: Privat, 1982), pp. 158–159, 175–181, and passim.

14. Population figures for 1788–1789 covering the islands of the French West Indies are presented in Antoine Gisler, *L'esclavage aux Antilles françaises: XVIIe–XVIIIe siècle,* 2d ed. (Paris: Karthala, 1981), p. 35. Tables indicating

overall population growth for the hundred-year period from the 1680s to the 1780s in the economically significant French and British West Indies are presented in Frostin, *Les révoltes blanches*, pp. 28–30. In 1788 there were only 908 free coloreds in Saint Kitts and, in 1783, only 1,125 in Grenada. Edward L. Cox, *Free Coloreds in the Slave Societies of St. Kitts and Grenada, 1763–1833* (Knoxville: University of Tennessee Press, 1984), pp. 13–14. Only in Jamaica in the British West Indies were their numbers comparatively significant: approximately 10,000 in 1787, having risen from 4,100 in 1774. Frank W. Pitman, *The Development of the British West Indies, 1700–1763* (1917; reprint, Hamden: Archon, 1967), pp. 377–378; Richard B. Sheridan, *The Development of the Plantations to 1750: An Era of West Indian Prosperity, 1750–1775* (Barbados: Caribbean Universities Press, 1970), p. 41. Nowhere in 1789 in the French Caribbean did their numbers significantly exceed 5,000. For Martinique, where the population may have risen slightly above this peak in 1789, see Pluchon, *Histoire des Antilles*, p. 175.

15. Léon Deschamps, *Les colonies pendant la Révolution* (Paris: Perrin, 1898), p. 18; Henri Castonnet des Fosses, *La perte d'une colonie: La révolution de Saint-Domingue* (Paris: A. Faivre, 1893), p. 11. See also Micheline Labelle, *Idéologie de couleur et classes sociales en Haïti*, 2d ed. (Montreal: CIDIHCA, 1987), pp. 46–47. Much research still needs to be done to determine what proportion of the roughly 28,000 free coloreds of Saint Domingue owned 30 percent of the plantations and one-quarter of the slaves; that is, the size of the free colored plantocracy remains to be determined. Did they constitute only a small but politically significant elite of the free colored population? See, in any case, Pluchon, *Histoire des Antilles*, p. 183.

16. See Blanche Maurel, *Saint Domingue et la Révolution française: La représentation des colons en France de 1789 à 1795* (Paris: Presses universitaires de France, 1943), p. 2, and Gabriel Debien, *Les colons de Saint-Domingue et la révolution: Essai sur le Club Massiac* (Paris: Armand Colin, 1953), pp. 150–151. Although absentee and resident planters shared common economic goals, namely the preservation of slavery and the sustained growth of profits, the two groups did not see eye to eye on the appropriate strategy to adopt in defense of these goals.

17. Pauléus Sannon, *Histoire de Toussaint Louverture* (Port-au-Prince: Imp. A. Héroux, 1920–1933), vol. 1, pp. 66–67; Étienne Charlier, *Aperçu sur la formation historique de la nation haïtienne* (Port-au-Prince: Les Presses Libres, 1954), p. 46; J. Ph. Garran-Coulon, *Rapport sur les troubles de Saint-Domingue*, Commission des Colonies (Paris: Imp. nationale, 1797–1799), vol. 2, pp. 40–41, 46–48.

18. Maximilien Robespierre, *Oeuvres de Maximilien Robespierre*, ed. M. Bouloiseau, G. Lefebvre, and A. Soboul (Paris: Presses universitaires de France, 1930–1967), vol. 7, pp. 362–363.

19. Necheles, *Abbé Grégoire*, pp. 85–86. See also George Rudé, *Robespierre: Portrait of a Revolutionary Democrat* (New York: Viking, 1975), pp. 140, 210–213.

20. Françoise Thésée, *Négociants bordelais et colons de Saint-Domingue: La maison Henry Romberg, Bapst et Cie, 1783–1793* (Paris: Société française d'histoire d'Outre-Mer et Paul Geuthner, 1972), p. 148.

21. The allocation of small plots of land to the slaves often depended upon the dispositions of the individual planter and the type of plantation. Sometimes, as in the seventeenth century, these plots were situated between the slave huts and were known as *jardins-case*, perhaps "kitchen gardens." By the eighteenth century, as slave dwellings increasingly took on the form of barracks, row upon row, with very little space between them, their garden plots became

geometrically aligned and were situated elsewhere, often on a fairly infertile portion of the plantation property. These gardens, or *jardins-nègre*, were more of an extension or pragmatic modification of the original *jardins-case* (as space was rationalized to maximize cultivation for export) than the comparatively larger provision grounds allocated to slaves in some colonies of the British West Indies. Moreover, the extent to which the allocation of such plots of land to slaves for purely personal use constituted a uniform practice throughout the colony is not at all clear. In the best of cases, as on the Laborde sugar estates in the South province of Saint Domingue in the 1770s, these "squares" measured only one-twentieth of a *carreau* (a *carreau* is approximately three acres), that is, one-sixth of an acre or, roughly, 600 to 640 square meters in squares of 20 paces by 25. See Bernard Foubert, "Les Habitations Laborde à Saint-Domingue dans la seconde moitié du XVIIIe siècle: Contribution à l'histoire d'Haïti (plaine des Cayes)," Thèse de doctorat d'État ès Lettres, Université de Paris IV–Sorbonne (Lille: Atelier national de reproduction des thèses, 1990), vol. 1, pp. 292 n. 3, and 290–302. In Foubert's judgment the contemporary meaning of the word "garden" should be retained in referring to these lots. In my view, the term *provision grounds,* if understood in the sense in which such plots existed in the British West Indies, and especially in Jamaica, where slaves often had an extra free day (usually Saturdays) to work them, would be misleading in the case of prerevolutionary Saint Domingue. Here, the term *provision grounds* would perhaps more appropriately apply to the collective provision grounds (*places à vivres*) which were worked by the slaves under the command of a slave driver to produce the plantation food rations than to the slaves' individual gardens. I use the term *garden,* or *slave gardens,* to refer to these lots, even if they were no longer attached to the slaves' dwellings (as were their minuscule "kitchen gardens," now used, for those that still had them, only to grow occasional vegetables, spices, and sundry food relishes). It was obviously the intention of the 1784 reform legislation to keep the produce of the plantation provision grounds, which was the planters' responsibility, separate from that of the slaves' gardens, which was supposed to belong exclusively to the slaves. In practice, however, slaves were more often than not reduced to feeding themselves partially, if not entirely in times of drought, from their personal gardens, especially during the 1780s. For a more than adequate treatment of this aspect of slave conditions, see Gabriel Debien, *Les esclaves aux Antilles françaises: XVIIe–XVIIIe siècles* (Basse-Terre: Société d'histoire de la Guadeloupe, 1974), pp. 171–218; see also Pluchon, *Histoire des Antilles,* pp. 148–149; Alex Dupuy, *Haiti in the World Economy: Class, Race, and Underdevelopment Since 1700* (Boulder and London: Westview Press, 1989), p. 37. On the provision ground system of Jamaica and the general distinction between "kitchen gardens" and "provision grounds," see Sidney Mintz, *Caribbean Transformations* (Chicago: Aldine, 1974), pp. 180–213, 236–238; also Orlando Patterson, *The Sociology of Slavery* (London: Macgibbon & Kee, 1967), pp. 183–184, 216–221.

22. Moreau de Saint-Méry, *Loix et constitutions,* vol. 6, pp. 657–659, 665, 918–928.

23. Carolyn Fick, *The Making of Haiti: The Saint Domingue Revolution from Below* (Knoxville: University of Tennessee Press, 1990), p. 283 n. 108.

24. For a detailed account and critical assessment of the case, see Gisler, *L'esclavage,* pp. 117–121.

25. In this light, see David Geggus, "Slave Resistance Studies and the Saint Domingue Revolution: Some Preliminary Considerations," Occasional Papers

Series, no. 4. (Miami: Florida International University, Latin American and Caribbean Center, 1983), pp. 13–14.

26. Julius Sherrard Scott III, "The Common Wind: Currents of Afro-American Communication in the Era of the Haitian Revolution," Ph.D. diss., Duke University, 1986 (Ann Arbor: University Microfilms, 1989), p. 185.

27. Ibid.

28. Ibid., pp. 64–65.

29. Bernard Foubert, "Colons et esclaves du Sud de Saint-Domingue au début de la Révolution," Revue française d'histoire d'Outre-Mer 61 (1974): 200.

30. Sannon, Histoire de Toussaint, vol. 1, pp. 69–70, 87.

31. Fick, Making of Haiti, pp. 137–138 and appendix C.

32. See Sannon, Histoire de Toussaint, vol. 1, p. 91; Garran-Coulon, Rapport, vol. 2, pp. 192–193, 232, 235. On August 24, the Colonial Assembly sent dispatches to several neighboring powers for aid, in the form of troops and munitions, to suppress the revolt that broke out on August 22–23. Governor Blanchelande, in a letter to the minister of the marine, M. Bertrand, noted that the "General Assembly of Saint Domingue, which holds its sessions in le Cap," asked him (at the latest on the 24th) to take all necessary measures to restore public security in the face of the slave insurrection that had just broken out. Archives Nationales (AN), DXXV 46, 432, Copies de différentes lettres sur les événements de Saint-Domingue extraites de la gazette anglaise et transmises à Paris, Kingston. M. de Blanchelande à M. Bertrand, Ministre de la Marine, le Cap, September 2, 1791. See also G. Laurent, Le commissaire Sonthonax à Saint Domingue (Port-au-Prince: Imp. de Phalange, 1965–1974), vol. 1, p. 29, citing Charles Tarbé, Rapport sur les troubles de Saint-Domingue; the latter writes that "prior to the convening of the General Assembly on the 22nd, the Provincial Assembly of the North asked M. Blanchelande to be present. . . ."

33. M. Begouën-Demeaux, Mémorial d'une famille du Havre (1743–1831) (Le Havre: Imp. Etaix, 1957), vol. 2, pp. 135, 137.

34. On the composition, organization, leadership, and orientation of the August 22–23 revolt, see Fick, Making of Haiti, pp. 91–117 and appendix B.

35. For the translated text, the implications and possible interpretations of Boukman's controversial Bois-Caïman oration, see Fick, Making of Haiti, pp. 93–94, 104–105, 264–266; but see also the discussion of the controversy in Geggus, "Slave Resistance Studies," pp. 16, 18.

36. See, at any rate, Sannon, Histoire de Toussaint, vol. 1, p. 88.

37. On the role and nature of kings in the political ideology of African-born slaves, especially those from the Congo, and of the relationship of this ideology to the Haitian revolution, see John K. Thornton, "'I am the Subject of the King of Congo': African Political Ideology and the Haitian Revolution," Journal of World History 4 (Fall 1993): 181–214.

38. See David Geggus, "From His Most Catholic Majesty to the godless Republique: The 'volte-face' of Toussaint Louverture and the ending of slavery in Saint Domingue," Revue française d'histoire d'Outre-Mer 65 (1978): 491–494.

39. Stein, Sonthonax, p. 79. Actually, in the view of Aimé Césaire, it was the threat or the perceived threat of the foreign invasion that was put forward as an excuse for Sonthonax's proclamation of general emancipation during his trial before the National Convention. In other words, he was to be exonerated because he had no other choice and, in any event, because his decision was inspired by the higher interests of the nation at war with Spain and Britain. The forthright abolition of slavery as a revolutionary principle in and of itself could not be admitted, and Sonthonax had to be defended on grounds other than the

validity of his philosophical and practical abolitionism. Césaire, *Toussaint Louverture*, p. 197.

40. See Geggus, "From His Most Catholic Majesty," pp. 492–494.

41. For the progression toward general emancipation in the West and South provinces, see Fick, *Making of Haiti*, pp. 163–168; Stein, *Sonthonax*, pp. 86–94.

42. See Necheles, *Abbé Grégoire*, pp. 119–125; Bénot, *Révolution française*, pp. 163–164; Robin Blackburn, *The Overthrow of Colonial Slavery, 1776–1848* (London: Verso, 1988), pp. 171–172; Césaire, *Toussaint Louverture*, p. 172.

43. C. L. R. James, *The Black Jacobins: Toussaint Louverture and the San Domingo Revolution* (1938; 3d ed., London: Allison & Busby, 1980), p. 141; Stein, *Sonthonax*, p. 112. Following its adoption, neither Robespierre nor even Grégoire publicly commented upon the February 4 decree in the press. Necheles, *Abbé Grégoire*, pp. 124–125. What laudatory comment there was in the revolutionary press came chiefly from Hébert in *Père Duchesne* (no. 347), who rejoiced at the abolition of slavery but only published his remarks two weeks after the fact. Césaire, *Toussaint Louverture*, pp. 201–204. As for Danton, he reacted with ambivalence to the decree, which he welcomed in the revolutionary republican spirit but considered disruptive of the colonies if introduced precipitously. At any rate, he found the decree useful in France's war against the British. He is said to have declared: "The English are dead! They will find the French colonies invincible." Stein, *Sonthonax*, pp. 111–112.

44. See Bénot, *La Révolution française*, pp. 149–150.

45. On this point, see the discussion in Fick, *Making of Haiti*, pp. 161–163.

46. The circumstances influencing Toussaint's turnabout have been meticulously researched and documented in Geggus, "From His Most Catholic Majesty," esp. pp. 489–497.

47. These considerations are beyond the scope of this chapter. They are treated in Fick, *Making of Haiti*, chap. 7, and pp. 207–210, 249–250.

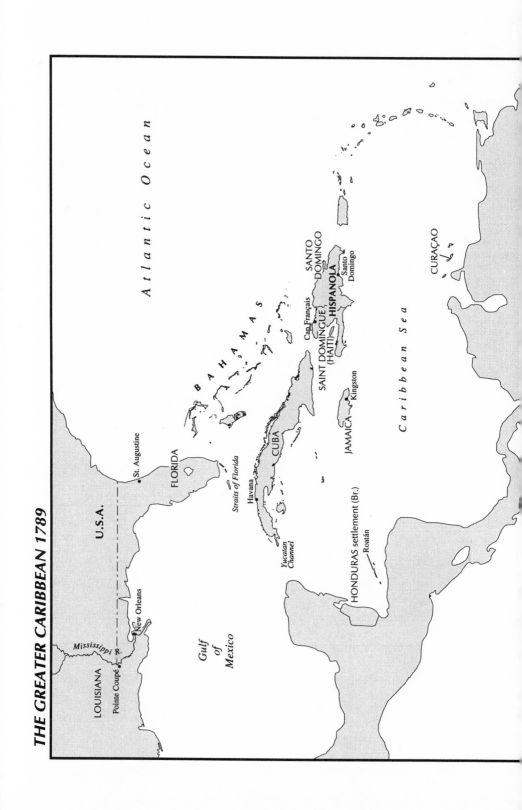

THE GREATER CARIBBEAN 1789

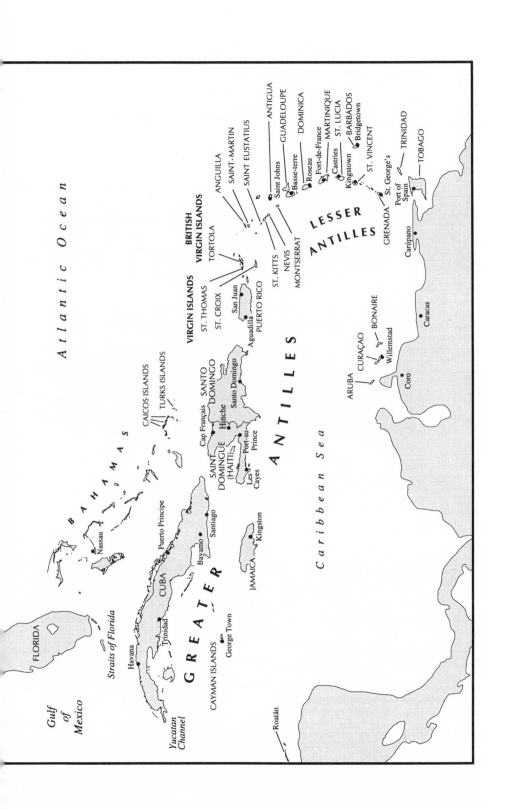

Atlantic Ocean

FLORIDA

Gulf of Mexico

Yucatan Channel

Straits of Florida

Havana

Trinidad

George Town

CAYMAN ISLANDS

CUBA

Bayamo

Santiago

Puerto Principe

Nassau

B A H A M A S

CAICOS ISLANDS

TURKS ISLANDS

G R E A T E R

Kingston

JAMAICA

A N T I L L E S

Caribbean Sea

Cap Français

SANTO DOMINGO

Hinche

Santo Domingo

SAINT DOMINGUE (HAITI)

Port-au-Prince

Les Cayes

Aguadilla

San Juan

PUERTO RICO

VIRGIN ISLANDS

ST. THOMAS

ST. CROIX

BRITISH VIRGIN ISLANDS

TORTOLA

ST. KITTS

NEVIS

MONTSERRAT

ANGUILLA

SAINT-MARTIN

SAINT EUSTATIUS

ANTIGUA

GUADELOUPE

DOMINICA

MARTINIQUE

ST. LUCIA

BARBADOS

ST. VINCENT

Saint Johns

Basse-terre

Roseau

Fort-de-France

Castries

Kingstown

Bridgetown

St. George's

GRENADA

LESSER

ANTILLES

Port of Spain

TRINIDAD

TOBAGO

Carúpano

Caracas

Coro

Willemstad

CURAÇAO

BONAIRE

ARUBA

Roatán

3

The French Revolution and British Attitudes to the West Indian Colonies

MICHAEL DUFFY

In September–October 1789 British colonial governors began reporting back to London news of the tumultuous reaction of French colonists to the revolution in France. These reports drew an instant response from the secretary of state for the Home and Colonial Department, Lord Grenville, who instructed the commander-in-chief in the Leeward and Windward Islands that

> as the late transactions in France may be productive of effects in the West Indies highly important to the interests of this country, I must desire that you will be particularly attentive to transmit to me the earliest intelligence which you may receive of what passes in the different islands with relation to this subject.[1]

It is easy to see why ministerial attention was aroused. The French West Indies were regarded as the most valuable European possessions overseas with the fastest expanding economy. As early as 1756 Malachy Postlethwayt had identified them as the main source of the increase in French shipping and seamen which was threatening British maritime supremacy, and that was before the astonishing expansion of production in Saint Domingue, the richest of all European colonies in the 1770s–1780s, and before the formidable showing of the French navy in the War of American Independence. In 1790 admirals queued up to declare to the House of Commons' Committee of Enquiry into the Slave Trade that "had it not been for the French West India commerce, that nation could not have been in a condition to dispute with Great Britain the empire of the ocean in the last war."[2] Direct French trade with the

West Indies and the marketing of produce through the *cabotage* around the coasts of Europe accounted for two-fifths of France's foreign trade, two-thirds of its ocean-going shipping, and over a third of all trained French seamen.[3]

Participants in the British West Indian trade were not slow to claim its equally important contribution to British seapower. A 1781 pamphleteer described the trade as the "great source of the English navigation," and the planter Bryan Edwards hailed it as "the principal source of national opulence and maritime power."[4] British trade patterns, however, were more widely spread than the French, and the West Indies probably accounted directly and indirectly for about one-fifth of all British foreign trade. These colonies had, however, contributed a large part of the increase in British maritime power in the eighteenth century. From 110 ships of 12,848 tons manned by 1,171 seamen in 1690 that trade had grown to involve 627 ships totaling 139,382 tons and 13,347 seamen in 1787–1788, accounting at that point for one-eighth of Britain's merchant tonnage and of its trained seamen.[5] After the loss of the North American colonies, the West Indies stood as easily Britain's biggest overseas capital investment, no longer simply the jewel in the crown of the British empire, but now virtually the crown itself, as was recognized by the way in which their defenses were built up in the 1780s. During the war scare with France in 1787–1788 the West Indian garrisons were doubled to 6,000 men, and a fortification program was begun which cost £480,000 by 1791, at which time the Caribbean was Britain's biggest overseas military commitment, absorbing considerably more than half the total expenditure for all colonial defense.[6] The value of the West Indies was used as the keystone of the concurrent defense of the slave trade against abolitionist attack. Alderman Newnham bluntly demanded of the Commons in 1790:

> were the House aware that the question of the slave trade involved the very existence of the country? For the preservation of the West India islands depended on it, and our connection with those islands, in his mind, materially concerned the welfare of the country. Were gentlemen prepared to say we could do without the West India islands? He was of opinion that we could not.[7]

Many people in Britain believed equally that France could not do without its West India islands, particularly if it was to remain a maritime power, hence the interest in reports of the colonial reaction to the revolution in France.

There was much indeed to report. The repercussions of the revolution on France's rich Caribbean colonies were both chaotic and violent. Demands from the colonies for *liberté* from central authority—for semiautonomy, for their own assemblies, and for relaxation of the home monopoly of the colony trade—became complicated by demands for *égalité* within the colonies from the poorer whites, followed by the mulattoes and free blacks. The result was the collapse of *fraternité*. While successive French Assemblies vacillated over their colonial policy, various factions within the colonies attempted to take matters into their own hands by armed force. It was not long before these divisions among the free population also encouraged slave insurrection.[8]

To interested onlookers within the British government, these events came as rather a mixed blessing, bringing both opportunity and cause for concern. Opportunity beckoned in that, at the very least, Britain might gain an entry into the rich French colonial trade and expand its own commerce and shipping at the expense of mainland France. In late 1791 the president of the Board of Trade began pressing for an amendment to the Navigation Acts which would allow foreign sugar brought into the British islands in British ships to be refined in Britain and reexported to Europe, so as to break the French hold on the sugar reexport trade. Despite some hostility from the Committee of West India Planters and Merchants, this amendment was enacted in June 1792.[9] The opportunity was there for far more. Governor Orde of Dominica reported in December 1790 that "had there been a war we might have had possession of all the French islands with very little trouble," while, from the Paris embassy, Earl Gower hinted in August 1791 that Britain might support the separatist movement in Saint Domingue, to gain revenge for the loss of the American colonies.[10]

British ministers were not yet ready to go that far, however. A crisis with Spain in 1790 made them eager to isolate that nation by placating its French ally, while a further unsuccessful confrontation with Russia in early 1791 made them lose their appetite for foreign adventures. Instead the British ministers resorted to nurturing the loyalty of the nation against revolutionary subversion by a policy of encouraging domestic prosperity through peace. Hence colonial governors and military commanders were repeatedly instructed to avoid any interference or appearance of partiality in what was happening in the French colonies, and Earl Gower was told that "we are fully persuaded that the islands in the West Indies are not worth to us one year of that invaluable tranquility which we are now enjoying." When, toward the end of 1791, some Saint Domingue planters made approaches seeking British protection for the colony, they were politely but firmly rebuffed.[11]

The danger of this hands-off policy was that the escalating crisis in the French islands might overflow into the British colonies. While Lord Hawkesbury seems to have been happy to entertain the prospect of a Saint Domingue independence movement, others were less sure. Such an example, following that of the thirteen North American colonies, might inspire similar thoughts in the British West Indian colonies, whose jealous concern for the rights of their own assemblies provoked one colonial governor to comment in 1804 that "America is the natural mother of these colonies." British colonists in the early 1790s were feeling particularly aggrieved at the mounting British movement to abolish the slave trade. By 1794 the threat of their disaffection alarmed the home secretary, Henry Dundas, into using "all the influence I possess to prevent any question on the subject being agitated at least during the war," and it may also have been behind Grenville's comment to a further Saint Domingue overture in late 1792 that many circumstances both of British policy and the situation of the islands "made the idea of their [Saint Domingue] independence chimerical and dangerous."[12]

Other aspects of events in the French colonies were even more pressing. The successful campaign of French mulattoes and free coloreds for civic equality led to a petition by their counterparts on Jamaica for the removal of certain legal disabilities in 1792. Especially alarming was the sight of mulattoes, free coloreds, and slaves in arms on the French islands. British colonial officials attributed a plot on Tortola in 1790 and a minor insurrection on Dominica in early 1791 to the influence of events on the adjacent French islands.[13] The West Indian planters and merchants preferred to see the latter, as well as the vast slave rebellion in the North province of Saint Domingue in August 1791, as a response to abolitionist activity in Britain and France. Home Secretary Dundas retorted that there were obvious reasons for slave revolt in Saint Domingue independent of abolitionism in Britain, but the British government demanded reports from its officials on the possibility of such revolts on their islands.[14] The Saint Domingue revolt, with over 100,000 slaves at large and over a thousand sugar, coffee, cotton, and indigo plantations destroyed, far surpassed anything that had gone before, and the possibility of imitation had to be taken seriously.[15]

Reports were for now reassuring. From Jamaica in 1791 acting governor Williamson conceded that the island was alarmed at the slave rising in neighboring Saint Domingue and that thousands of slaves would willingly enter into rebellion if they thought they could succeed, not from oppression or ill usage but merely to become free. Nevertheless, a display of strength in the mobilization of the militia over the sensitive Christmas period set him at ease. In mid-January 1792 he reported that the slaves were perfectly well disposed and obedient and were wondering why the white people were so very busy.[16]

From the Leeward and Windward islands, a thousand miles to the east, came a comprehensive survey by Grenville's relation, Captain Berkeley of the Royal Navy, prophetic in its identification of potential trouble spots. Berkeley considered Barbados, Antigua, and Saint Kitts as safe because they had been long cleared and lacked refuges for rebels to hide or assemble without being instantly prevented. A large white population and a mainly creole slave population accustomed to white ways further secured Barbados, while Saint Kitts was commanded by a military strongpoint and had the best-clothed and best-treated slaves. Antigua had a similar strongpoint, a naval base, along with the powerful influence over the slaves of Moravian ministers who preached passive obedience. Grenada, Saint Vincent, and Dominica, however, were potentially vulnerable. Their uncultivated and impassable wooded interiors made revolt sustainable. Grenada's slaves were nearly all new imports, and half the planters were disaffected Frenchmen, though Berkeley thought that the latter had a common interest with the British in preventing slave revolt, that their present mild treatment by the British was likely to retain their loyalty, and that two regiments in forts at the island's capital made revolt doubtful. Some observers thought revolt was most likely on Saint Vincent, where there was a large disaffected native Carib population, but Berkeley felt that antipathy between the Caribs and the Negroes made revolt less likely. He thought Dominica was most exposed to revolt from its proximity to the French islands, its difficult terrain and scattered plantations, and the presence on the island of sympathizers with the blacks.[17] Each of these last three islands had received French settlement before being acquired by Britain in 1763 and were hence susceptible to French revolutionary influence. Indeed, the increasing number of refugees fleeing to Dominica from the faction fighting on Martinique and Guadeloupe led British ministers to send military reinforcements and orders to evict all undesirable foreigners. While reassured about the unlikelihood of a spontaneous slave insurrection in the British colonies, the British remained concerned about the possibility of disaffection incited by refugees, particularly as relations with France deteriorated in the course of 1792 and as French planter connections sought to attract British intervention by warning of plots by France's revolutionary government to place subversive agents in the British islands.[18]

While sending warnings to colonial governors and orders to restrain the admission of French mulattoes or free blacks, Britain's ministers still held off from direct intervention until after the actual outbreak of war in February 1793. By December 1792 there were representatives of Saint Domingue planters in London, as well as royalists from Martinique and Guadeloupe, which in September had renounced the Paris revolution. To them all, ministers promised help and cooperation once war broke out, but they declined to act until then.[19]

The opportunities and alarms of the Caribbean situation were not the prime factors which led Britain into war with France that February. The prime cause of war from the British viewpoint was the French threat to Britain's interests in Belgium and Holland. However, once war became a serious probability, the attractions of using it to seize the French West Indies encouraged ministers to hold to their firm line toward the French government. In mid-January 1793 the prime minister, Pitt, privately pointed to British possession of the French islands as an advantage of a war which he considered inevitable.[20]

The outbreak of war with revolutionary France fired all the pent-up British ambitions with regard to the French West Indies. Their acquisition would restore the British empire up to and beyond the commercial heights lost when the American colonies won their independence, and would do so, moreover, at the expense of the country whose powerful naval interference was widely regarded as a major cause of that catastrophe. Indeed, the main advantage of seizing the French West Indies was the blow it would give to French naval power, which would be permanently reduced below the strength needed to challenge British seapower in the future. Here was the essence of Pitt's declared war aims of "indemnity for the past, security for the future."[21]

Thus while a British contingent was sent to the Continent to capture from France a new fortress barrier to ensure the security of Belgium and Holland, the war minister, Dundas, admitted that "the principal object proposed by the war in favor of Great Britain as compensation for our charge in it" was to be the destruction of French naval power. He planned to send 17,000 men to capture the French West Indies at the end of 1793, to be followed by an attack to destroy the French naval arsenals at Brest and Toulon in the following year. In this way French naval power would be destroyed and the loss of the West Indies would prevent the French from restoring it.[22] As an enthusiastic Cabinet member, Lord Amherst, confided in his diary about news of the first British landings in Saint Domingue,

by account the nett produce from St. Domingo to France amount to five millions sterling, the other French islands are supposed to give three million, so that the whole amounts to eight million sterl. and whether France or England has the Islands it must give a superiority of the Fleet to the Possessor.

The *Times* (London) also made a similar point in the following July after news arrived about the successes of Sir Charles Grey's expedition:

> in proportion as our territory increases in the West Indies, so must our shipping multiply. The prospect which this holds out, is the happy one of our always having in case of emergency sufficient number of able hands to man our fleets.[23]

The early capture of Tobago in April 1793 was followed by that of Martinique, Saint Lucia, and Guadeloupe (March–April 1794) and most of the South and West provinces of Saint Domingue (September 1793–June 1794). In April 1794 Pitt informed the Committee of West Indian Planters and Merchants of his intention to retain all the French islands after the war "at any price." Lord Hawkesbury, drawing up the plan of a provisional government for the conquered islands, instructed the British commanders "to omit no measure that is calculated to make the inhabitants of these Islands truly British, and to reconcile them to our Government."[24]

Just as Britain stood on the verge of carving out for itself a vast new West Indian empire which would have left it preponderant in the Caribbean and assured of secure maritime supremacy, the fortunes of war with the French Revolution swung dramatically the other way. The needs and opportunities of the European war had led to Grey's expedition to the Caribbean being cut by half just before its departure, so that it fell just short of the strength to give it a clean sweep of all the French colonies in one campaign. Thereafter, the worsening situation of the war in Europe diverted troops to the Continent who might have clinched success in the colonies in the following season. France was therefore given the opportunity to strike back from the small toeholds left to it. The Republic did so by revolutionary means. Lacking the capacity to send a major expedition from Europe to recover its colonies, the Republic sought to mobilize all the resources available within the Caribbean by emancipating the slaves. Initiated as an emergency measure by the Republican commissioners in Saint Domingue in August 1793 and officially established by decree of the National Convention in February 1794, emancipation changed the whole nature of war and politics in the Caribbean.

This revolutionary measure had immediate military consequences in the eastern Caribbean under the inspired leadership of the energetic new Republican commissioner, Victor Hugues. Slipping through the British blockade to Guadeloupe in June 1794, Hugues was able to rally to the Republican cause French colonists who were disillusioned by the rapacious greed for prize money of Grey's expedition, which had signally failed to reconcile them to British rule.[25] Emancipation then gave Hugues manpower vastly superior to the British forces, which were devastated by yellow fever. It enabled him to recover Guadeloupe and Saint Lucia and to carry the attack to the British islands. Hugues applied himself in particular to those colonies whose vulnerability Berkeley had already noted. Although a landing on Dominica in support of a prearranged rising by some French-speaking smallholders and their slaves in May 1795 was foiled when the majority of the colony's slaves stayed loyal to British masters, spectacular results were achieved on Saint Vincent and Grenada. On Saint Vincent, contrary to predictions, French planters and their slaves did join the Caribs and, reinforced by Hugues's black regiments from Saint Lucia, several times overran the colony up to the capital, Kingstown. On Grenada the mild treatment of the French Catholic inhabitants ended in 1792 when the British colonists finally pressed the Privy Council to enforce the original British-based constitution of 1763 and to disallow concessions made to the French in 1768. Many French-speaking coffee planters and smallholders, white and colored, were therefore willing to make contact with Victor Hugues and, taking advantage of the absence of the regular garrison away on the French islands, to rise in revolt in conjunction with half of the 28,000 slaves on Grenada in March 1795 in a particularly bloody and brutal struggle which devastated that productive island.[26]

In the western Caribbean, too, emancipation coupled with devastating casualties from disease reduced the British presence on Saint Domingue to coastal ports in the summer of 1795. At Jamaica overreaction by the new governor, Earl Balcarres, who was fearful of slave insurrection, precipitated a rebellion among the Trelawney-town Maroons in August 1795.[27] Within barely a year (1794–1795) Britain passed from being on the verge of replacing its lost North American colonies with a massive new Caribbean empire to being on the verge of losing to another revolution its old West Indian colonies, the mainspring of its Atlantic commerce and the major component of its remaining overseas empire.

Pitt's government responded to the danger by sending to the Caribbean in the 1795–1796 season the biggest expedition yet to sail from British shores, about 32,000 soldiers. The effort saved the British colonies. It also won the Dutch Guiana settlements on the South American coast, recaptured French Saint Lucia, and temporarily recovered ground in Saint Domingue. But the cost was appalling. Approximately 14,000 troops died and 7,000 more were incapacitated by disease in the Caribbean in the course of 1796. Again, there were neither troops nor time enough to make a clean sweep of the French islands before the end of the campaign.[28]

The expedition of Sir Ralph Abercromby in 1795–1796 was the last major British effort in the Caribbean. By mid-1796 the war minister, Dundas, had largely given up hope of retaining Saint Domingue. In June he talked of offering it to Russia in order to persuade Catherine the Great to intervene in the continental war,[29] and by autumn he considered the capture of Puerto Rico from a new enemy, Spain, to resettle the French Saint Dominguan colonists who had sided with Britain.[30] In 1798 Britain evacuated Saint Domingue by means of a nonaggression pact with Toussaint Louverture, the ex-slave commander-in-chief of a predominantly ex-slave republican army.[31]

The evacuation of Saint Domingue marked the end of Britain's attempt to carve out a new empire of major settled colonies in the Caribbean. By this time Dundas had changed his policy of expanding British commerce (and hence maritime power) through the significant extension of formal empire to the acquisition of entrepôt bases from which to tap the trade of other empires. This was the motive behind the capture of Trinidad and the projected expeditions to La Plata and Chile in 1797, as well as proposals to seize Buenos Aires and New Orleans in 1800.[32] Because of the formidable obstacle presented by the French Revolution's emancipation of the slaves in the West Indies, Dundas considered trying to open up Spanish South American and North American markets instead. However, owing to lack of manpower and to the demands of the war in Europe, little was in practice attempted or achieved with this alternative strategy.

If the French Revolution opened up opportunities for British imperial expansion by the chaos it created in France's Caribbean colonies, it also closed those opportunities again. The revolution caused a diversion of British attention and resources to cope with its unexpectedly dramatic success in Europe. The revolution also armed the Negroes in the West Indies; and in Saint Domingue and Spanish America in the 1800s, it fueled powerful independence movements out of revolutionary upheaval which proved resistant to British takeover. In the 1790s the ex-slaves not only impeded British conquest by their resistance, but they also forced the British to leave large garrisons to continue the struggle and maintain precarious conquests through successive sickly summer seasons. The Caribbean thus sucked in British forces and destroyed them. Of about 89,000 British soldiers in the Caribbean between 1793 and 1801, over 45,000 died (overwhelmingly from disease) and perhaps 14,000 more were discharged as unfit for further service. Deaths of naval and transport seamen may have totaled between 19,000 and 24,000.[33] The overwhelming impression left on British minds by the war against the French Revolution in the Caribbean was of slave rebellion and immense British mortality. In 1797, two books, Hector McLean's *Enquiry into the Nature and Causes of the Great Mortality among the Troops at St. Domingo,* and Bryan Edwards's *Historical Survey of the Island of St. Domingo,* entrenched the view that Saint Domingue was a death trap. A stream of accounts by army and naval doctors between 1799 and 1806 about their attempts to combat tropical disease[34] confirmed Castlereagh's view (in a debate in June 1807) that "certainly there was a strong feeling in the public mind of the great mortality in the army in the West Indies."[35]

Casualties from disease in the Caribbean were expected, but the magnitude of those of the 1790s campaigns staggered everyone. These may have been facilitated by an unfortunate coincidence of the arrival from Africa of a new and virulent strain of yellow fever and successive highly favorable breeding seasons for the mosquito vectors of the killer diseases. However, it was the manpower demands of the new Caribbean warfare which drew tens of thousands of susceptible, nonimmune Europeans into an area of endemic tropical disease that was primarily responsible, and this persuaded the British not to waste lives by further large expeditions from Europe. When, in 1800, Dundas made a last attempt to resurrect his grand Caribbean design by proposing an expedition to Cuba of 20,000 troops, he met with unanimous hostility from king and Cabinet. No subsequent government repeated the proposal.[36] Thereafter, large British forces would only be sent, if necessary, to defend the British islands against threatened French attack (5,000 troops were prepared but not sent in 1805). For offensive operations commanders were allowed only the use of existing garrisons, a policy which effectively confined them to acting against weakly defended enemy colonies. It was not until 1809–1810 that large reinforcements were temporarily brought in from Nova Scotia and Bermuda to seize Martinique and Guadeloupe, with instructions that the object was not permanent conquest but the mopping up of the remaining enemy bases which were tying down British resources and that if the attack was likely to be difficult, then it was not worth the likely losses. At all events, the reinforcements were to be withdrawn before the start of the sickly season.[37] No attempt was made again to gain possession of the very largest Caribbean colonies. Britain's own experience on Saint Domingue and the horrendously deadly failure of Napoleon's attempt to assert his authority and reimpose slavery there with 40,000 troops between 1802 and 1806 put a decisive stop to such ambitions.

In other ways, too, the war against the French Revolution brought changes of attitude in Britain toward the West Indies. One of these was connected with the emergence of the black population as a far more positive factor in the West Indian picture. How far this was a consequence of the successful resistance of the ex-slaves of Saint Domingue has been much debated. In 1804 James Stephen claimed that they broke the myth of European supremacy and African inferiority. Other observers, however, were inclined to attribute white defeat to disease or incompetence and to counterbalance the impact of the success of the blacks' victory with the horror of their atrocities and their manifest failure to restore the economy of what had been Europe's richest colony. The atrocities committed by the slaves liberated by the French Revolution shook their sympathizers. On Saint Lucia General John Moore confided to his diary that "the cause in which they fight is praiseworthy did they not disgrace it by acts which are a shame to human nature," and the abolitionist William Wilberforce was still worried in 1804 "lest some insurrection, or other event with two handles, should turn men against us."[38]

Perhaps more important in changing British attitudes was the way in which Britain responded to the French mobilization of the blacks by raising twelve black West India regiments for the regular army. The planters, who had exploited the slave insurrections to show the essential barbarity and inferiority of blacks, opposed the raising of these regiments tooth and nail. They believed that the regiments would undermine the superior position of whites and destroy the social and moral basis for slavery.[39] However, the casualty rates of the European regulars and the need for light troops to combat the French blacks led the British government to force the measure through, notwithstanding the unanimous opposition of the colonial assemblies. These West Indian regiments were built up to a third of the garrisons of the colonies and soon proved their worth, so much so that Lord Henry Petty stated during the debates which led to the abolition of the British slave trade to foreign islands in 1806 that

> an argument in favor of this Trade . . . is founded upon an idea, that the part of the human race who are its subjects labour under such a total degradation of mental and moral faculties as nothing can cure; and hence a conclusion is drawn, that nature doomed them to slavery. But I would ask, Have not the premises from which this conclusion is

drawn been proved to be false . . . ? Have we not ourselves, put them in a situation, for which it was confidently asserted that their talents were not fit, and have we not experienced the falsehood of that assertion? Have we not, ourselves, made them soldiers? Have we not made them noncommissioned officers? Have we not employed them in every service requiring fidelity and courage, and all the intelligence and virtue which go to constitute a good military character? Certainly we have done all these things, and they have answered the expectation of those who thought the most favourably of them. But now . . . shall it be said that they possess no such capacity; that they are unfit for trust and confidence; that slavery is their doom by nature, and that they are unfit for any other condition?[40]

The logic of such argument, along with legal complications of colonial jurisdiction (through slave laws) over slave units of the British army, ultimately led to the emancipation of the entire 10,000 men of the West India Regiments in 1807.[41] The myths of white supremacy and invincibility and of permanent inferiority of blacks had now been challenged, and though blacks were still far from reaching in public estimation a position of equality, their status as British regular soldiers had at least elevated them above the East India Company sepoys and posed new questions about the inevitability of slavery and the slave trade.

The determined opposition and obstructionism of the colonial assemblies to the recruitment of the regular black regiments also posed questions about the desirability of extending the traditional colonial system of government (governor, council, and independent elected assembly) to any further additions to the empire. The plan of provisional government for the conquered French islands drawn up by Lord Hawkesbury in 1794 avoided the imposition of the rigid traditional system, made the governor all-powerful, omitted any elected assembly, and sought to work with existing political frameworks, particularly in avoiding the religious discriminations of the British Test Acts. The plan was the basis of the system which became known as "Crown colony government." In framing it Hawkesbury recorded that he had particularly in mind to avoid the mistakes made in the acquisition of Grenada in 1763.[42] Within a year rebellion by the French-speaking population of Grenada, the most serious and destructive of the outbreaks in the British colonies, emphasized that point absolutely. Thereafter, constitutional and legal battles over the West India regiments and a running dispute with the Jamaican assembly over the extent to which its contribution to its defense costs entitled it to control military arrangements on the island increased government dissatisfaction with the existing traditional system, so that the alternative Hawkesbury framework was imposed wherever possible thereafter.[43]

In all this, too, there was the basis of a reassessment of the military importance of the West Indies and of its economic value to the British empire, commerce, and overall wealth. From 1793 the British government had launched its expeditions into the West Indies to increase its commerce and shipping by expanding its empire. Yet each grew greatly without the acquisition of a major productive colony such as Saint Domingue or Cuba. Undoubtedly, the increase was facilitated by the smaller conquests (the Dutch Guiana–coast colonies in particular proving unexpectedly lucrative), which accounted for just under a third of shipping and imports from the Caribbean in 1800–1802.[44] However, a very considerable part of the increase came from within the existing British colonies, particularly Jamaica, when production was raised to exploit the higher prices that followed the collapse of the Saint Domingue economy.[45] Was it therefore necessary to seek for more, particularly in view of the likely casualties that would be suffered? The only consideration that might have overcome this formidable drawback would have been the other original motive for the expeditions, namely, the destruction of French seapower. Already in 1799, however, there was support for the argument that French naval performance in the Revolutionary War was poor and therefore not a pressing concern.[46] Dundas's original policy was to destroy existing French seapower and to capture Saint Domingue to prevent France from restoring it. By 1807 both of those aims might have seemed to have been achieved. The French navy was greatly reduced by the British victories of the 1793–1802 war, followed in 1805 by Trafalgar and in 1806 by the annihilation of the last French squadron sent to Saint Domingue. In 1793 the paper strength of the opposing line-of-battle fleets was 76 French against 116 British. By 1807 only 34 battleships remained in French and Dutch hands facing a British battle fleet of 123.[47] Prospects of French maritime recovery seemed removed by the successful resistance of the former slaves of Saint Domingue to French attempts to reassert their authority, which made it unnecessary for Britain to acquire that colony. It is significant that William Playfair, who urged the conquest of Saint Domingue and the other French islands in 1793 to diminish French access to wealth and power, wrote in 1805 that "the British superiority in the West India Trade is so far of a permanent nature, that France never will again be a formidable rival there. Saint Domingo is not only lost, but probably lost forever, while it is expected that Britain may retain her islands."[48]

In the same year another writer reached the same conclusion. Jepson

Oddy described how France had lost both its East and West Indian trade, even though prior to the wars it had greatly more of the latter than Britain. He added that "the island of St. Domingo . . . is now estranged from France, probably forever." France's merchant marine collapsed from over 5,000 long-haul ships in 1785 to 1,500 in 1800 and to only a few hundred in 1814, while Britain's merchant tonnage doubled.[49]

Britain's newly won superiority in the West India trade helped it through the crisis of the Revolutionary War. That superiority also played a part in enabling the country to survive the long struggle of the Napoleonic Wars through its increased contribution to government revenue, credit, and general mercantile wealth.[50] Its proportionate contribution, directly and indirectly, to British foreign trade increased from a fifth to between one-third and two-fifths by 1802. The importance of this contribution and the way in which it had been jeopardized by the French Revolution in the Caribbean, however, raised questions about the desirability of overdependence on such a potentially vulnerable source. In 1803 Henry Brougham urged the advantages of taking over Egypt as an alternative source of production of West Indian commodities; in 1805 another pamphleteer pressed for a general development of Mediterranean trade to balance that of the West Indies; and in 1807, during the slave trade debates, William Roscoe urged removal of the East India Company's trade monopoly with India as an alternative for the body of British merchants.[51] Other critics, including Playfair, pointed to the development of domestic British production as a safer and surer alternative to the colonial trades, and their arguments were backed by a growing mass of statistical evidence which emerged as part of the investigation of Britain's capacity to sustain the fight against the French Revolution and Napoleon.[52] The new data produced in the first decade of the nineteenth century showed an expanding domestic market, a greatly expanded value of domestic exports, and a considerably diminished proportionate contribution of overseas trade to the total national wealth.[53] In this scheme of business the most valuable West Indian contribution to the domestic economy was perhaps its prime position as supplier of raw cotton for British industry, and in this the United States overtook the island colonies by 1804–1806 and passed the combined islands and Guiana coast imports between 1814–1816 and 1824–1826.[54]

The immense European successes of the French Revolution and Napoleon must also be taken into account in this reassessment of the value of the West Indies. As early as 1796 a pamphleteer asserted that the French acquisition of a single Flemish province was of more consequence than the British conquests in the West Indies.[55] At the Peace of Amiens in 1802 all Britain's conquests except Trinidad and Ceylon were restored in a bid to bring Napoleon to moderation in Europe. As French power continued to get increasingly out of control in Europe, it became apparent that it could not be counterbalanced by British success in the Caribbean or anywhere else overseas and that the main object of the war would have to be the creation of a sufficiently powerful European barrier to restrain France within its former borders. To enlist the help of the European powers in this policy, Britain recognized that something would have to be done to overcome their jealousy of the monopoly of overseas trade that it was acquiring through its transoceanic conquests. By 1805 Pitt was willing to offer the surrender of all Britain's overseas conquests for so desirable an object.[56] The success of the final coalition in 1813–1814 was so absolute that Liverpool's government never had to go that far, though it still recognized European sensitivities. After securing the French evacuation of Holland, Liverpool and his colleagues became concerned about France's continued hold on its new naval bases at Antwerp and Flushing. The lord president of the council, Lord Harrowby (Pitt's former foreign secretary), urged that "Antwerp and Flushing out of the hands of France are worth 20 Martiniques in our own hands." Harrowby was worried that the allies might not remove Antwerp from the French "if they expect that we shall remain not only with that thorn taken out of our side, but with a superiority over France in colonial and maritime strength greater (particularly after the annihilation of Saint Domingo) than at any former period, and still further increased by our connection with Holland." He pressed that Britain should still offer to restore its overseas conquests[57] in the event Martinique and Guadeloupe were returned to the French to avoid discrediting the restored Bourbon regime in France. Britain also returned its other Caribbean conquests from France and its former allies except Trinidad (ceded to it at Amiens in 1802), the Dutch Guiana colonies and French Tobago (in each of which there was a considerable British capital stake),[58] and French Saint Lucia, which remained useful as a naval base strategically placed to watch the restored French islands.

The events of the 1790s and their impact on affairs regarding the West Indies both influenced the course of the debate on the British abolition of the slave trade to foreign colonies in 1806, and to Britain's own colonies in 1807. Several scholars have considered that the war with revolutionary France obstructed the course of British abolitionism. It discredited many of the more prominent abolitionists, some of whose radical leanings led to accusations of their sympathy with the national enemy. Other abolitionists, including Wilberforce, seemed unpatriotically opposed to the continuation of the war.[59] The war turned some influential moderates such as Dundas and Windham against abolition for fear of alienating the colonies during this period of national crisis.[60] At all events, after the House of Commons voted in 1792 for gradual abolition by 1796, support for abolition in the House fell away substantially, while the House of Lords remained determinedly hostile.[61] However, it has yet to be proved conclusively that the Commons' votes in 1792 were anything more than a fluke due to an unexpectedly favorable conjunction of circumstances,[62] or that abolition was in any way inevitable in the 1790s.

On the other hand, how the impact of the war in the West Indies facilitated the eventual success of abolitionism has often been ignored. At the very least, the war provided new arguments for the debate and new information hostile to the slave trade from many British officers sent to the Caribbean, information which enabled abolitionists to counter their opponents' charges of ignorance of West Indian conditions.[63] At the most, the war may have provided the clinching arguments which finally undermined the antiabolitionist defense. The antiabolitionist case was fairly consistent from start to finish.[64] One approach was to deny the right of the British Parliament to legislate on matters of such vital social and economic importance to the colonists. Abolitionists were able to retort powerfully that British blood and money poured into saving the colonies from the revolutionary threat of the mid-1790s gave it that right.[65] As early as 1796, Wilberforce had grasped the opportunity created by the terrible casualties of the Caribbean expeditions to observe that "I am strongly of opinion that the expense both of blood and treasure which government has incurred from its West India establishments is so monstrous, that when stated and properly pressed on the public attention, it will produce a rooted disgust of those possessions." This was a theme drummed repeatedly by the abolitionists in the closing years of the campaign, culminating in a passionate declamation by Sheridan in the 1807 debates.[66] The theme made more attractive the abolitionist argument that abolition would ease the defensive requirements of the islands. Whereas the planter lobby asserted that abolition of the slave trade would encourage a Saint Domingue–style revolt among the slaves, the abolitionists argued from the beginning that the Saint Dominque revolt was a result of massive importation of new slaves. By the 1800s the abolitionists were able to point to the West India regiments and to the loyalty of creole slaves in the British colonies throughout the chaos of the 1790s to justify their denial of the danger of revolution.[67]

The fundamental planter defense, however, turned on the importance of the slave trade to the economic prosperity of the West Indies and the importance of the West Indies to British commercial and naval supremacy over France. Each of these might be jeopardized if the slave trade were abolished. But the premises of the planter defense had come into question as a result of the effect of the revolution on the French colonies and the subsequent events of the wars against the French Revolution and Napoleon. Despite temporary trade depressions when military operations periodically disrupted the European market and despite planter complaints at increased expenses and higher sugar duties, the British colonies benefited greatly from the collapse of their Saint Domingue rival. Their economic future seemed assured even without the slave trade.[68] The members of Parliament who abolished the slave trade had no wish to destroy the economy of the British West Indian colonies. In 1806 they combined humanity with self-interest in abolishing the slave trade to foreign colonies, and since at that time Britain virtually monopolized that traffic, this abolition effectively prevented rivals from immediately gaining any advantage over the British colonies. In 1807, the same year that they abolished the slave trade to the British islands, they responded to Napoleon's Berlin Decree (which forbade trade and communication with Britain) by backing the Orders in Council, which allowed freedom of the seas only to ships that put into British ports and paid a 25 percent transit tax. This benefited British West Indian commerce by effectively destroying the price differentials of the remaining non-British West Indian trade carried by neutral (chiefly United States) interlopers, and it was enforced despite the protests of domestic manufacturers whose exports to the United States suffered from U.S. retaliation.[69] In 1808 members of Parliament sought to sustain falling sugar prices by allowing sugar to be used in British distilleries, and they maintained the discriminatory duties against non–West Indian sugar until 1825, when they allowed Mauritius parity, refusing until 1835 parity for East Indian sugar, which had been demanded since the early 1790s. In 1807 they allowed their humanity to prevail in abolishing the slave trade because they believed the British West Indian economy was basically strong enough (with a little alternative help when necessary) to survive abolition.[70]

Equally, in the light of the reassessment that was taking place about the West Indian contribution to British power and of the decline of French seapower, Parliament was no longer ready to admit that either the slave trade or even the West Indies were so crucial to British commercial or naval supremacy. Estimates for the value, shipping tonnage, and seamen employed in the West Indian trade were paraded before Parliament; Castlereagh in the Commons and Admirals Saint Vincent and Hood in the Lords urged the naval necessity; but it was all ignored.[71] Politicians and public alike were less likely to be alarmed by such jeremiads than formerly. British naval superiority now seemed too obvious and unshakable. William Playfair wrote in 1805 that "if we want to make a comparison between the naval power of England and that of France and Spain we must not compare it with the strength of their navies in the year 1780 [1779], when they bid us defiance at Plymouth, but take things actually as they are at this present time."[72] In the succeeding two years the disparity between the naval powers grew still further. In these circumstances arguments of the importance of the slave trade to British naval power lost all their former force. Was it simply coincidence that the slave trade was finally abolished by Britain in the very year that the size of the French navy fell to its lowest point? If the economic expectations of the impact of abolition on the West Indian colonies proved wrong—and Seymour Drescher has claimed the result as "econocide"[73]—the expected lack of impact on British naval power proved substantially correct, and in the last resort that was what above all else mattered to British governments and parliaments of the eighteenth and early nineteenth centuries.

The impact of the French Revolution on British attitudes to the West Indies was thus to raise them to an importance beyond all that had gone before, and then to deflate that importance and divert British attention. Vincent Harlow's concept of a swing to the east of British imperial policy immediately following and consequent upon the loss of the North American colonies has now been largely discounted,[74] but it is significant that he took his account of the founding of the second British empire only up to 1793, thereby missing the start of the attempt to found that empire on a massively expanded position in the West Indies. British military efforts in the 1790s were paralleled by a vastly increased capital investment in new plantations, new crops, and new slaves as the colonists responded to initial British conquests and to the opportunities created by high prices following the revolutionary collapse of French Saint Domingue. In Demerara, for example, 28,000 of the 52,000 slaves held in 1801 had been imported since the British occupation of 1796. The British slave trade reached its peak in the 1790s, and ironically for its abolitionist prime minister, the biggest single purchaser was the British government, which, between 1795 and 1808, paid out about £925,000 for some 13,400 slaves for its black West India Regiments.[75]

The military offensive, however, met an abrupt check in the face of vigorous resistance from emancipated French slaves, French-inspired revolt in Britain's own colonies, massive financial costs and manpower losses through disease, and the mushrooming of a threat closer to home as French revolutionary power broke loose in Europe. Economic expansion was also checked as governments, under abolitionist influence, first restrained sales of confiscated or conquered lands in Saint Vincent and Trinidad and then increasingly limited and ultimately abolished the slave trade.[76] In this context, the abandonment of the attempt to acquire the biggest foreign colonies with large established slave populations was as much part of the "econocide" in the British West Indies, suggested by Drescher, as was abolition.

The efforts of the 1790s thus constitute an attempt at a turning point around which the British empire failed to turn, and indeed ended by turning in a diametrically opposite direction. British governments ceased to try for large acquisitions to their formal empire in the west. The reduced alternative of going for entrepôt-based conquests to catch the trade of others, which got off to a stuttering start in 1797, came to an equally abrupt end with defeat at Buenos Aires in 1807 and at New Orleans in 1815.[77] Thereafter, British merchants looked to informal penetration of American markets. It was not therefore the American Revolution but the War against the French Revolution in the Caribbean which brought the expansion of Britain's western empire to a halt and produced a swing of formal empire to the east, where opportunities were not counterbalanced by such vigorous revolutionary resistance and such devastating mortality.

NOTES

1. Lord Grenville to Lieutenant-General Mathew, December 2, 1789, Public Record Office, Kew, Surrey, *Colonial Office* (hereafter, *CO*) *102/16*.

2. M. Postlethwayt, *A Short State of the Progress of the French Trade and Navigation* (London, 1756), pp. 82–86; S. Lambert, ed., *House of Commons Sessional Papers of the 18th Century* (Wilmington: Scholarly Resources, 1975), vol. 72, p. 183 (Lord Rodney); see also pp. 112, 114, 123, 129, 177, 183, 187.

3. M. Duffy, *Soldiers, Sugar, and Seapower: The British Expeditions to the West Indies and the War against Revolutionary France* (Oxford: Clarendon Press 1987), pp. 22–23.

4. *Observations from a gentleman in town to his friend in the country relative to the sugar colonies proving their importance to England* (London, 1781), p. 8; B. Edwards, *The History, Civil and Commercial of the British Colonies in the West Indies* (4th ed., London, 1807), vol. 1, p. iii.

5. British Library, Additional Manuscripts (hereafter BL, Add. MS) 38351 (Hawkesbury Papers) f. 198v; Duffy, *Soldiers, Sugar, and Seapower*, pp. 15–16, 21.

6. H. T. Manning, *British Colonial Government after the American Revolution 1782–1820* (New Haven: Yale University Press, 1933), pp. 219–234.

7. W. Cobbett, *The Parliamentary History of England from the Earliest Period to the Year 1803* (London, 1817–1819) (hereafter *Parl. Hist.*), vol. 28, col. 314 (debate on the Slave Trade, January 27, 1790).

8. See L. Deschamps, *Les Colons pendant la Révolution* (Paris, 1898); J. Saintoyant, *La Colonisation française pendant la Révolution* (Paris, 1930); H. Lemery, *La Révolution française à la Martinique* (Paris, 1936); D. Geggus, *Slavery,*

War, and Revolution: The British Occupation of Saint Domingue 1793–1798 (Oxford: Clarendon Press, 1982).

9. D. Geggus, "The British Government and the Saint Domingue Slave Revolt, 1791–1793," *English Historical Review* (hereafter *EHR*) 96 (1981): 291.

10. Orde to Grenville, December 13, 1790, *CO 72/4*; Historical Manuscripts Commission, *Manuscripts of J. B. Fortescue, Esq., Preserved at Dropmore* (hereafter *HMC, Dropmore*), vol. 2 (London, 1894), p. 176.

11. Grenville to Orde, October 6, December 16, 1790, April 6, 1791, *CO 72/4*; Grenville to Mathew, December 16, 1790, *CO 102/16*; *HMC, Dropmore*, vol. 2, p. 181; Geggus, "British Government," p. 290.

12. Geggus, "British Government," p. 291; Seaforth to Camden, December 12, 1804, quoted in D. J. Murray, *The West Indies and the Development of Colonial Government 1801–1839* (Oxford: Clarendon Press, 1965), p. 39; R. I. and S. Wilberforce, *The Life of William Wilberforce* (London, 1830), vol. 2, p. 49; PRO, War Office (hereafter *WO*) *1/58*, Minutes of Lord Grenville's meeting with Malouet, January 1, 1793.

13. M. Craton, *Testing the Chains: Resistance to Slavery in the British West Indies* (Ithaca: Cornell University Press, 1982), pp. 224–225; Williamson to Grenville, July 4, 1791, *CO 137/89*; Orde to Grenville, February 12, 1791, *CO 72/ 4*. On the basis of an examination of the rebels' free mulatto leader, Polinaire, Governor Orde explained the revolt on Dominica as a reaction to an intrigue by a white faction against the governor which the slaves misinterpreted as a planter attempt to stop them from being granted three free days a week.

14. London University, Institute of Commonwealth Studies, microfilm M.915, reel 3, Minutes of the Committee of West India Planters and Merchants, April 5, November 3, 1791, March 29, 1792; Dundas to Effingham, January 17, 1792, *CO 137/90*. The demand for information followed the Dominica revolt. Grenville to Williamson and Effingham, April 21, 1791, *CO 137/89*.

15. Circular to colonial governors, November 11, 1791, *CO 5/267*.

16. Williamson to Dundas, September 18, November 6, 1791, *CO 137/89*; January 15, 1792, *CO 137/90*. See also D. Geggus, "Jamaica and the Saint Domingue Slave Revolt, 1791–1793," *The Americas* 38 (1981): 219–233; Geggus, "The Enigma of Jamaica in the 1790s: New Light on the Causes of Slave Rebellions," *William & Mary Quarterly* 44 (1987): 274–299.

17. BL, Add. MS, Grenville Papers: "From Captain Berkeley," November 18, 1791. This interesting letter, of which the author has a full copy, was formerly in Add. MS 59,239 but has since been redisposed and the efforts of both the author and the British Library staff have hitherto failed to relocate it.

18. Dundas to Orde, August 1, 1792, *CO 71/23*; Dundas to Orde, January 5, 1792, *CO 71/24*. For threats to stimulate revolt in the British colonies voiced in the French National Convention, see Duffy, *Soldiers, Sugar, and Seapower*, p. 18.

19. Circular letters to colonial governors, December 8, 1792, January 12, 1793, *CO 5/267*; Dundas to Orde, August 1, 1792, *CO 71/23*, Dundas to Bruce, January 5, 1793, *CO 71/24*; BL, Add. MS 59,239, "Digest of . . . Proceedings . . . December 1792 to December 1793"; Add. MS 38,352, "Minutes by Lord Hawkesbury of a meeting with De Curt . . . ," January 11, 1793; Dundas to Williamson, January 12, 1793, *CO 137/92*.

20. Third Earl of Malmesbury, ed., *Diaries and Correspondence of James Harris, First Earl of Malmesbury* (London, 1844), vol. 2, pp. 501–502.

21. *Parl. Hist.* vol. 30, col. 715. There was strong press support for this policy. See *Times* (London), February 8, 1793; W. Playfair, *Thoughts on the Present State of French Politics and the Necessity and Policy of Diminishing France . . .* (London,

1793); [Willis], *A Short Exposition of the Important Advantages to Be Derived by Great Britain from the War* (London, 1794).

22. National Library of Scotland, MS 11,159 (Minto Papers), Journal of Sir Gilbert Elliot, September 8, 1793; Duffy, *Soldiers, Sugar, and Seapower*, pp. 24–25.

23. Kent Record Office, Lord Amherst's Diary 099/2, entry for December 10, 1793; *Times*, July 19, 1794; see also April 28, 1794.

24. Geggus, "British Government," p. 304; BL, Add. MS 38,310, Hawkesbury to Grey, May 23; Hawkesbury to Williamson, September 9, 1794.

25. Duffy, *Soldiers, Sugar, and Seapower*, pp. 113–134.

26. Duffy, *Soldiers, Sugar, and Seapower*, pp. 136–156; Duffy, "War, Revolution, and the Crisis of the British Empire," in M. Philp, ed., *The French Revolution and British Popular Politics* (Cambridge: Cambridge University Press, 1991), pp. 125–136; Craton, *Testing the Chains*, pp. 180–194, 227; E. L. Cox, *Free Coloreds in the Slave Societies of St. Kitts and Grenada, 1763–1833* (Knoxville: University of Tennessee Press, 1984), pp. 76–91.

27. Duffy, *Soldiers, Sugar, and Seapower*, pp. 149–151; Craton, *Testing the Chains*, pp. 211–219. Alone among the rebellions of 1795, that of the Maroons does not seem to have been deliberately provoked by the French. See Geggus, "Enigma of Jamaica," pp. 280–282.

28. Duffy, *Soldiers, Sugar, and Seapower*, pp. 159–257.

29. BL, Add. MS 38,734 (Huskisson Papers) f.178, Dundas to Huskisson, June 14, 1796. A similar idea was suggested two years later in [Beeke], *Letter to a Country Member on the Means of Securing a Safe and Honourable Peace* (London, 1798).

30. BL, Add. MS 38,734, Huskisson to Dundas, October 30, Dundas to Huskisson, November 3; Dundas to Abercromby, November 13, 1796, *WO 1/85*.

31. Duffy, *Soldiers, Sugar, and Seapower*, pp. 298–311; Geggus, *Slavery, War and Revolution*, pp. 373–381.

32. See n. 30 above; J. S. Corbett and H. W. Richmond, eds., *The Private Papers of George, 2nd Earl Spencer 1794–1801* (Navy Records Society, no. 46, London, 1913), vol. 1, pp. 321–323, 331; Scottish Record Office, Melville Papers GD 51/1/548/3, Dundas to Grenville, November 24, 1799, GD 51/1/725/1, Secret Memorandum, August 14, 1800; National Library Scotland, MS 1075 (Melville Papers), ff. 130–134, Memorandum. See also J. Lynch, "British Policy and Spanish America 1783–1808," *Journal of Latin American Studies* 1 (1969): 11–12.

33. Duffy, *Soldiers, Sugar, and Seapower*, pp. 326–334; J. Stephen,*The Crisis of the Sugar Colonies* (London, 1802), pp. 62–63. Even after the peace of 1802 it was felt necessary to maintain a Caribbean garrison of 14,000 men—more than double the prewar strength (pp. 279–280, *CO 318/26*).

34. See works by J. Anderson (1798), R. Jackson (1798), W. Lempriere (1799), L. Gillespie (1800), C. Chisholm (2 eds. by 1801), T. Clark (1801), B. Moseley (4 eds. by 1803). For the reactions of those sent to the Caribbean, see Duffy, *Soldiers, Sugar, and Seapower*, pp. 343–349.

35. W. Cobbett, ed., *The Parliamentary Debates from the Year 1803* (hereafter *Parl. Debates*), vol. 9, col. 690. Castlereagh pointed out that the reputation survived despite a drop in mortality to only a third of what it had been ten years before.

36. BL, Add. MS 40,102, Secret Memorandum, July 22; Add. MS 40,101, Dundas to George III, July 25; George III to Dundas, July 28, October 5, 1800. Seymour Drescher, in *Econocide: British Slavery in the Era of Abolition* (Pittsburgh: University of Pittsburgh Press, 1977), p. 132, asserts there was a government

attempt to acquire Cuba in 1806, but this is a misreading of a proposal by its peace negotiator, Lord Yarmouth, that Cuba be given to Britain's ally the king of the Two Sicilies in compensation for the loss of his Italian possessions—a proposition which even the prime minister, Lord Grenville, described as "absurd to ask" (*HMC, Dropmore*, vol. 8, p. 245).

37. Camden to Myers, November 1804, *CO 318/25;* Castlereagh to Beckwith, December 14, 1808, *CO 318/34;* November 2, 1809, *CO 318/36;* August 12, 1809, *CO 318/37; HMC, Dropmore*, vol. 8, p. 97.

38. J. Stephen, *The Opportunity; or Reasons for an Immediate Alliance with St. Domingo* (London, 1804), pp. 12–13; Sir J. F. Maurice, ed., *The Diary of Sir John Moore* (London: Edward Arnold, 1904), vol. 1, p. 234; R. I. and S. Wilberforce, *Life of Wilberforce*, vol. 3, p. 181. See also D. Geggus, "British Opinion and the Emergence of Haiti, 1791–1805," in J. Walvin, ed., *Slavery and British Society 1776–1846* (Baton Rouge: Louisiana State University Press, 1982), pp. 123–149; and Geggus, "Haiti and the Abolitionists: Opinion, Propaganda and International Politics in Britain and France, 1804–1838," in D. Richardson, ed., *Abolition and Its Aftermath: The Historical Context, 1790–1816* (London: F. Cass, 1985), pp. 113–140.

39. Roger N. Buckley, *Slaves in Red Coats: The British West India Regiments, 1795–1815* (New Haven: Yale University Press, 1979), pp. 20–52; Inst. Commonwealth Studies., M 915/3, Minutes of the Committee of West India Planters and Merchants, June 27, 1795; Ricketts to Abercromby, January 18, 1797, *WO 1/86;* Resolution of the Antigua Assembly, December 12, 1798, *WO 1/88.*

40. *Substance of the Debates on a Resolution for Abolishing the Slave Trade . . . 1806* (London, 1806; reprint, 1968), p. 47. See also Stephen, *Crisis of the Sugar Colonies*, pp. 69–70.

41. *Parl. Debates*, vol. 8, col. 678; Buckley, *Slaves in Red Coats*, pp. 63–81.

42. BL, Add. MS 38,351, f. 202.

43. Manning, *British Colonial Government after the American Revolution*, pp. 242–247, 342–344; Murray, *The West Indies and the Development of Colonial Government*, p. 33 ff.; J. Millette, *The Genesis of Crown Colony Government: Trinidad 1783–1810* (Curepe, Trinidad: Moko, 1970), pp. 72–101.

44. Sir W. Young, *The West India Commonplace Book* (London, 1807), p. 88 n.; D. Macpherson, *Annals of Commerce* (London, 1805), vol. 4, p. 535.

45. Drescher, *Econocide*, pp. 76–91.

46. See *Thoughts on the Interference of Great Britain with the Political Concerns of the Continent* (London, 1799).

47. W. James, *The Naval History of Great Britain 1793–1820* (London, 1837), vol. 1, appendix 1, vol. 4, appendix 15; N. Hampson, *La Marine de l'an II* (Paris, 1959), pp. 21–22; O. Connelly, *Historical Dictionary of Napoleonic France 1799–1815* (Westport: Greenwood, 1985), pp. 359, 361.

48. See n. 21 above and W. Playfair, *An Inquiry into the Permanent Causes of the Decline and Fall of Powerful and Wealthy Nations* (London, 1805), p. 195.

49. J. J. Oddy, *European Commerce, Shewing New and Secure Channels of Trade with the Continent of Europe* (London, 1805), pp. 462, 475; F. Crouzet, *De la supériorité de l'Angleterre sur la France* (Paris: Perrin, 1985), pp. 300–301.

50. Duffy, *Soldiers, Sugar, and Seapower*, pp. 378–388; J. H. Rose, "British West Indies Commerce as a Factor in the Napoleonic War," *Cambridge Historical Journal* 3 (1929–1931): 34–46.

51. H. Brougham, *An Enquiry into the Colonial Policy of the European Powers* (Edinburgh, 1803), vol. 2, passim; *Remarks on the Probable Conduct of Russia and France towards This Country* (London, 1805), pp. 79–82; *Parl. Debates*, vol. 8, col.

962. See also G. F. Leckie, *An Historical Survey of the Foreign Affairs of Great Britain* (London, 1808), pp. 144–145.

52. Oddy, *European Commerce*, p. 489 ff.; Playfair, *Inquiry*, pp. 199–200, 205; J. E. Cookson, "Political Arithmetic and War in Britain, 1793–1815," *War and Society* 1 (1983): 49–53.

53. The recalculation increased the value of domestic exports by 61 percent and changed the ratio of home exports to reexports in 1805–1807 from 2.7 to 1 (official values) to 4.2 to 1 (real values); Cookson, "Political Arithmetic," p. 56.

54. R. Davis, *The Industrial Revolution and British Overseas Trade* (Leicester: Leicester University Press, 1977), pp. 112–117.

55. D. O'Bryen, *Utrum Horum? The Government or the Country* (London, 1796).

56. See n. 45 above; C. K. Webster, ed., *British Diplomacy 1813–1815* (London, 1921), pp. 389–394; J. H. Rose, "Pitt's Plans for the Resettlement of Europe," in *Napoleonic Studies* (London, 1904), pp. 64–76; M. Duffy, "British Diplomacy and the French Wars 1789–1815," in H. T. Dickinson, ed., *Britain and the French Revolution 1789–1815* (London: Macmillan, 1989), pp. 133, 137–144.

57. BL, Loan 57/7 (Bathurst Papers), Harrowby to Bathurst (secretary for war and acting foreign secretary), January 16, 1814.

58. Tobago had been a British possession between 1763 and 1783 and was recaptured from France in 1793 and 1803. It was asserted that £18 million of British capital was invested in the Guiana colonies of Demerara, Berbice, and Essequibo while they were in British hands between 1796 and 1802. Stephen, *Crisis of the Sugar Colonies*, p. 157 n. See also C. K. Webster, *The Foreign Policy of Castlereagh 1812–1815* (London, 1931; reprint, Bell, 1950), p. 517: Liverpool to Castlereagh, January 20, 1814.

59. R. I. and S. Wilberforce, *Life of Wilberforce*, vol. 2, pp. 18, 54, 72 ff., 135; *Parl. Hist.*, speeches by Burton (vol. 30, col. 515), Cawthorne (col. 1440), Lord Abingdon (vol. 31, col. 467); J. Walvin, "British Popular Sentiment for Abolition," in C. Bolt and S. Drescher, eds., *Anti-Slavery, Religion, and Reform* (Folkestone: Dawson, 1980), pp. 152–153.

60. *Parl. Hist.*, vol. 32, cols. 874, 893.

61. R. Anstey, *The Atlantic Slave Trade and British Abolition 1760–1810* (London: Macmillan, 1975), pp. 255–342; Drescher, *Econocide*, pp. 113–121; D. Porter, *The Abolition of the Slave Trade in England, 1784–1807* (Hamden: Archon, 1970), pp. 70–107.

62. Namely, initial resentment at the high sugar prices after the Saint Domingue slave revolt, complacency and lax preparation by the West India lobby after their overwhelming victory in the previous year, sensational allegations of atrocities by a slave-ship captain, Kimber (subsequently dismissed in the law courts), and Dundas's compromise proposals for deferred abolition (later abandoned).

63. See *Parl. Hist.*, vol. 24, col. 1241 (Phipps), vol. 30, col. 513, vol. 31, col. 1344 (Young) for early charges of inadequate evidence. For military views, see W. Jeffrey, ed., *Dyott's Diary* (London, 1907), vol. 1, pp. 93–94; *Diary of Sir John Moore*, vol. 1, pp. 256–257; C. Willyams, *An Account of the Campaign in the West Indies in the Year 1794* (London, 1796), pp. 12–14; G. Pinckard, *Notes on the West Indies* (London, 1806), vol. 1, pp. 227–238. Pinckard, in particular, was used extensively by abolitionists in the latter stages of the debate; see *Substance of the Debates on a Resolution for Abolishing the Slave Trade . . . 1806*, pp. 172–175, 184–190, 195–196 and W. Wilberforce, *A Letter on the Abolition of the Slave Trade* (London, 1807), p. 331. An extract was sold separately as G. Pinckard, *Interesting Narrative of a Negro Sale at Demarara* (London, 1806).

64. Porter, *Abolition of the Slave Trade in England,* p. 53. I disagree with his similar statement regarding abolitionist arguments.

65. Stephen, *Crisis of the Sugar Colonies,* p. 139.

66. R. I. and S. Wilberforce, *Life of Wilberforce,* vol. 2, p. 175; Stephen, *Crisis of the Sugar Colonies,* p. 58 ff.; Stephen, *Opportunity,* pp. 143–145; Stephen, *Dangers of the Country* (London, 1807), p. 7; Stephen, *New Reasons for Abolishing the Slave Trade* (London, 1807), p. 8; Wilberforce, *Letter on the Abolition of the Slave Trade,* pp. 330–331; *Substance of the Debate on the Bill for Abolishing the Slave Trade . . . 1807* (London, 1808), pp. 258–259.

67. *Parl. Debates,* vol. 8, cols. 951–952 (Howick, February 23, 1807).

68. In contrast to Williams, Drescher has pointed to obstructions at the sales end rather than overproduction at the supply end as the cause of depression in 1806–1807. See Eric Williams, *Capitalism and Slavery* (New York: Russell & Russell, 1961), pp. 149–150, 152; Drescher, *Econocide,* pp. 125–137.

69. See F. Crouzet, "Groupes de pression et politique de blocus: Remarques sur les origines des Ordres en Conseil de Novembre 1807," *Revue Historique* 228 (1962): 45–72; Crouzet, *De la superiorité de l'Angleterre,* pp. 302–308. It is significant of the decline of West Indian influence and the rise of that of the domestic manufacturers later in these wars, however, that the latter finally secured the withdrawal of the Orders in Council in 1812.

70. *Parl. Debates,* vol. 7, col. 32 (Grenville); Drescher, *Econocide,* p. 140; C. Duncan Rice, "'Humanity Sold for Sugar!' The British Abolitionist Response to Free Trade in Slave-Grown Sugar," *Historical Journal* 13 (1970): pp. 402–418. In the same way the West Indian economy had been thought buoyant enough in 1783 to bear the ban on U.S. supplies in order to benefit Canada. Lord Sheffield, *Observations on the Commerce of the American States,* 2d ed. (London, 1783), pp. 88–90.

71. *Substance of the Debates . . . 1806,* p. 17; *Parl. Debates,* vol. 8, cols. 693, 981, 988–989; *Substance of the Debates . . . 1807,* pp. 31–32.

72. Playfair, *Inquiry into the Permanent Causes,* p. 9.

73. Besides Drescher's *Econocide,* see also Drescher's defense against his critics in "Econocide, Capitalism and Slavery: A Commentary," *Boletín de Estudios Latino Americanos y del Caribe* 36 (1984): 49–65, and "The Decline Thesis of British Slavery since *Econocide,*" *Slavery and Abolition* 8 (1986): 3–24.

74. V. T. Harlow, *The Founding of the Second British Empire, 1763–1793* (London: Longmans, 1952–1964), vol. 1, p. 62. See also R. Hyam, "British Imperial Expansion in the Late Eighteenth Century," *Historical Journal* 10 (1967): 113–131; D. L. Mackay, "Direction and Purpose in British Imperial Policy, 1783–1801," *Historical Journal* 17 (1974): 487–501.

75. J. R. Ward, *British West Indian Slavery 1750–1834: The Process of Amelioration* (Oxford: Clarendon Press, 1988), pp. 45, 90–91; Drescher, *Econocide,* pp. 65–98; R. B. Sheridan, "Slave Demography in the British West Indies and the Abolition of the Slave Trade," in D. Eltis and J. Walvin, *The Abolition of the Atlantic Slave Trade* (Madison: University of Wisconsin Press, 1981), pp. 269–274. See also Buckley, *Slaves in Red Coats,* p. 55.

76. Rose to Cuyler, July 8, 1797, *WO 1/86;* Drescher, *Econocide,* pp. 103–104, 106–111.

77. Lynch, "British Policy and Spanish America," pp. 1–30; B. Perkins, *Castlereagh and Adams: England and the United States 1812–1823* (Berkeley: University of California Press, 1964), p. 141.

4

La Guerre des Bois

Revolution, War, and Slavery in Saint Lucia, 1793–1838

DAVID BARRY GASPAR

During the period of the French Revolution and the Napoleonic Wars the inhabitants of several Caribbean colonies, including Saint Lucia, experienced much turmoil and anxiety through invasion, troop movements, battles, slave unrest, and general political destabilization.[1]

The devastation wrought upon Saint Lucia, situated between the island colonies of Martinique and Saint Vincent, from 1789 (when it was in French possession) to 1814 (when it finally came to rest in British hands) took decades to repair. For most of this period the forces of war shaped life on the island; and when Britain and France were in possession of it, both regarded it "more as a Military and Naval Station than as a Colony from which government calculated to raise the expence of its establishment." Writing in 1803, British governor Robert Brereton explained that during the preceding years of turbulence the planters of Saint Lucia had lost most of their male slaves and stock and had ceased cultivation as a result. According to a report of 1824, there had been a church in each of the island's eleven parishes in 1789, but following the revolution five parishes were "almost wholly uninhabited" and their churches had "fallen into total decay."[2]

The decline of the slave population of Saint Lucia, which one report placed, perhaps exaggeratedly, at nearly 70 percent, can be explained largely by the effects of the internal war that developed there between 1794 and 1797. That war is the focus of this study. It was the so-called Brigands' War, in which slaves, who withdrew from the plantations and more or less joined the cause of the revolution, associated themselves with French Republicans in the island's interior to win the colony for revolutionary France against the schemes of royalists and British invaders.[3]

On the eve of the French Revolution Saint Lucia enjoyed some prosperity as a French colony which, with slave labor, produced sugar, coffee, cotton, and cocoa for export.[4] It did not take long for tremors of the revolution to reach the island. When they did, the free inhabitants were split into royalists and self-styled "Patriots." So zealously did the Patriots support the revolution that in 1792 Saint Lucia received the revolutionary title of La Fidèle (The Faithful). In October 1791, the governor of the nearby British colony of Dominica reported receiving information that the "Patriotic Party" of Saint Lucia and the "inferior Military" of the garrison at the main fort of Morne Fortuné had seized the fort. However, the royalist governor succeeded in reestablishing order. Earlier, some of the slaves themselves showed that they had an interest in the possible meanings or outcome of the revolution, particularly in the shape that it might take closer to home.

On January 1, 1791, several slaves on the plantation of M. Viet in the southern quarter of Soufrière planned to lead a revolt involving other plantations of the area if their master did not free them. These rebels believed that the Republicans had succeeded in freeing the slaves over in Martinique. The writer who reported the incident at Soufrière denounced the bad influence the revolutionaries were having on the slaves of Saint Lucia, who he feared could be easily incited to revolt. The Soufrière authorities moved quickly. Before the rebellion could spread, several ringleaders were seized and executed. Their heads were cut off and displayed prominently in different parts of the area.[5]

Finally, later in 1791, the tensions building up within Saint Lucia came to a head when two agents or commissaires sent by the revolutionary government in Paris, Montdenoix and Linger, succeeded in kindling a brighter revolutionary flame when they seized power from the royalist governor Jean-Joseph Soubader de Gimat, who fled, leaving the island to the Patriots. In 1792, after the overthrow of the monarchy in France, the republican commissaire Lacrosse arrived. He circulated "incendiary pamphlets and proclamations" spreading the revolutionary message. One result of this was that many slaves deserted the plantations.[6]

When France declared war on Britain in February 1793, the radical faction was dominant in Saint Lucia. Nearly a year later, in January 1794, a British amphibious force under Lieutenant General Sir Charles Grey and Vice Admiral Sir John Jervis arrived at Barbados and prepared to attack the French islands. By the third week of March they captured Martinique. By early April they took Saint Lucia also, and Sir Charles Gordon was appointed governor. In taking Martinique the British reportedly lost fewer than 200 men, while Saint Lucia fell within twenty-four hours without loss. When Grey reported the capture of the island to authorities in Britain, he referred to its "entire Conquest . . . altho there has been a good deal of Cannonading from the Enemys Batteries and Works." By "entire Conquest" Grey meant that he had managed to seize Morne Fortuné, the island's main defensive post situated near the northwest coast overlooking the principal town and harbor of Carenage or Castries. French troops remained in possession of some of the twenty-four other smaller batteries or fortified posts on the island.[7]

By the time the British forces arrived, support for the revolution had gained more ground among the island's inhabitants. In this situation royalists became losers. Francis Henry Charles de Bexon, a lieutenant colonel and commander of the Royal Corps of Engineers under the French Crown, lost his appointment and his plantation. He sought refuge, like many other royalists, with the British at Dominica. When Grey reached the islands in 1794, he drew upon the vast local experience of de Bexon and others to seize both Martinique and Saint Lucia, and de Bexon regained his plantation.[8] If de Bexon decided to remain a royalist and a friend of the British, he would be able to retain his property only so long as Gordon could complete the conquest of Saint Lucia.

According to the nineteenth-century historian of Saint Lucia H. H. Breen, Saint Lucia "though reduced was far from tranquil. The insurgent slaves had retired to the woods, where they were joined by a number of French soldiers, who had succeeded in making their escape: and these motley masses, organized and instigated by a few democratic whites, carried on a harassing war against the British. . . ."[9] By the end of April 1794, republican resistance was so troublesome in Saint Lucia and the other two captured colonies of Martinique and Guadeloupe that Grey believed it had become "a matter of expediency and necessity" to raise a corps of men in each. These corps were to be called Island Rangers. They were to consist of 250 private men, part cavalry and part infantry, "with Non Commissioned Officers in proportion." Only trusted individuals who were well acquainted with the "most secret recesses" of these mountainous and densely forested islands were to be recruited. "The Brigands being numerous in the Woods, must be rooted out," Grey explained, "which will take up some time to do effectually so as to restore Peace and happiness throughout the Captured Islands; which is already encreasing Hourly, by our pursuit of the wicked and dangerous and adding to the Number of our Prisoners." Grey favored the deportation of free mulattoes and other potentially subversive inhabitants to England.[10]

Though British forces managed to invade Guadeloupe in April 1794, they could not hold the entire colony, which consisted of two contiguous land masses, Grande Terre and Basse Terre. In July the French recovered Grande Terre. With this event began the emergence of Victor Hugues as a major force in the struggle against the British in the Lesser Antilles. Still in his midtwenties, this republican commissaire civil arrived from France with the forces that took Grande Terre. In 1795 and 1796, from his base at Guadeloupe, Hugues, who was determined to reverse British success, sent help to republican fighters in Saint Lucia; he also sent aid to insurgents in Saint Vincent and Grenada, both of which were in British hands when the war started.[11] According to Grey, the success of the French at Guadeloupe boosted the morale of republican sympathizers in the captured islands, where many "Evil minded, dangerous" persons were discovered who deserved to be deported.

In September 1794, fearing that Henry Dundas, secretary of state for war, might be under the erroneous impression that most of the inhabitants of the captured islands were partial to the British, Grey informed him that those places "still abound with numerous Brigands, our inveterate enemy, ready to seize on the first opportunity favorable to their wishes and eagerly looking for a Reinforcement at Grand-Terre from France, which they persuade themselves is at no great distance." Grey also felt that he could hardly count on British sympathizers among the French inhabitants. They are "so extremely timid," he wrote, "as to prove hurtful rather than serviceable to us, under continual apprehension of the Guillotine, and ever apprehensive of an Insurrection amongst the Negroes, in consequence of the Note of Emancipation of the French Government." Nevertheless, short of troops to defend his gains and to carry on the war, Grey fell back on organizing local collaborators. Some British merchants and their white employees in the captured islands agreed to form a corps and to serve at their own expense. Grey issued orders for the reorganization of the island militia "for their own Defence." He also deported many suspected troublemakers, and in Saint Lucia he prepared a new oath of allegiance for recruiting men into the militia. Recruits taking the oath swore to be loyal to the king of Britain by revealing all subversive developments and by defending the island against attacks organized by "a ferocious and destructive enemy," the National Convention of France. The oath was to be "printed, published and inserted in every Paper" with the names of all recruits, so that these persons "finding themselves between death and victory, and convinced that they should have no quarter to expect, if the colony was retaken, they may place their hopes in nothing but the most unshaken resistance."[12]

As Grey saw it, the greatest threat to the British war effort at this juncture came from the decree of the National Convention on 16 pluviôse (February 4, 1794) to abolish slavery in the French colonies. By

September 1794, republican agents were busy circulating the decree (which reached the major French colony of Saint Domingue in June) in the conquered islands. The republican abolition of slavery was above all meant to turn the slave population against the British wherever they might land, thus adding to republican strength.[13] The strategy worked in Saint Lucia. The Brigands' War took concrete shape starting in 1794 as a resistance movement against the British.

It is difficult to trace the particular shape of the ideology that may have motivated hundreds of blacks in Saint Lucia to participate in one form or another in a spirited opposition to the British, but it is not hard to see that in doing so they pursued what they ultimately perceived to be their own advantage, which may have come down simply to the difference between slavery and freedom. They saw the British, according to Roger Buckley, "as the red-coated enforcers of the old slave order." These anti-British, prorepublican freedom fighters who styled themselves "l'armeé français au bois," but whom the British derogatorily called Brigands, were organized at this time under the leadership of two French soldiers, Kermené and Sabathier Saint-André.[14]

The republicans were also able to win support from whites who lived on the island because these people nursed a strong grievance against the British for abusing the prize-money system which Grey and Jervis had allowed. Governor Gordon was accused of taking "protection money from colonists to safeguard them from the general extradition of undesirables and suspect persons" which followed the British occupation.

The British troops under Gordon's command and other local corps were obviously kept busy dealing with resistance. In August 1794, Major Baillie reported an engagement with the insurgents in the Dauphin district to the north, in which a British force of regular soldiers and militia routed them; one soldier was killed, another wounded, and three militiamen were also wounded. After a long night march north from Morne Fortuné, the force had encountered the insurgents at daybreak and attacked. The militia apparently did not perform well under fire. However, the insurgents' losses included eleven men killed or wounded. Two men were also captured and hanged, but most of the rest escaped into the woods. Baillie, analyzing the larger situation of unrest in Saint Lucia, remarked that "the Rascals are in such Numbers and the Woods impenetrable that I am much afraid they will not be easily quelled particularly as I cannot well spare more men from this Garrison." To make his job easier in the northern part of the island, Baillie proposed arming the proprietors there; and, following Grey's instructions, he also agreed to organize the islands's "British Gentlemen" into the Saint Lucia Royal British Volunteers.[15]

By the end of 1794 Lieutenant General Sir John Vaughan replaced Grey as British army commander in the Caribbean. Vaughan, although anxious to receive reinforcements from home, tried to push the campaign against the Saint Lucia insurgents with vigor. After careful evaluation of the difficulties he inherited among the islands, Vaughan concluded that a sensible solution would be "to arm and train a regiment of negroes, obtaining the men either from the various islands, if the local governments would grant them, or, if that were not practicable, to import them direct from Africa."[16] In January 1795, Vaughan sent over the Black Carolina Corps from Martinique to Saint Lucia to try to dislodge the "revolted Negroes" from a mountain post "which being judged to be a Service of more Fatigue than Danger, was a proper Enterprize on which to employ the Blacks, and to save our own Soldiers." These Black soldiers were organized in 1779 from among loyalist slaves and free Negroes in South Carolina during the War of American Independence. A detachment of about seventy men attacked the insurgents' post but were unable to drive them out, losing two officers and twelve men. The insurgents, who reportedly had only one white man among them, lost several men. While Brigadier General Stewart, now in command at Saint Lucia, made plans to resume the attack, the insurgents abandoned their post, which the British troops then destroyed, "burning the Palissades and levelling every thing."

For some reason Stewart believed the rebels might be induced to surrender if they were pardoned. Vaughan went along with this approach, realizing, though, that if it failed, stronger and more effective measures must be used against "this Mischievous set of People" or "Banditti." Stewart issued a proclamation to pardon rebels who surrendered and who were not involved in murder and other serious crimes. It is, therefore, not at all surprising that after several days only eight persons came in. As if this were not a sure indication that the insurgents intended to go on fighting, they soon attacked a detachment of the Black Carolina Corps which was making its way across rugged country from Dennery on the east coast to Choiseul in the southwest, killing or wounding several men. Vaughan quickly sent 120 blacks recruited in Martinique under the command of Captain Malcolm to assist Stewart, his conviction growing that the struggle in Saint Lucia required the organization of "a strong Body of Blacks."[17]

In February 1795, there were also signs that the French were preparing a major Caribbean offensive. Vaughan explained that they might successfully invade the islands because they could depend on disgruntled white inhabitants, as well as most of the blacks, joining them.[18] Reinforced from France after he succeeded in taking the whole of Guadeloupe at the end of 1794, Victor Hugues next made bold efforts to intensify the fight against the British in the Lesser Antilles. Hugues sent troops south to Saint Lucia, Saint Vincent, and Grenada. By March 1795, Saint Vincent and Grenada were, like Saint Lucia, scenes of internal war. J. W. Fortescue, in his military account of the period, called these events "simultaneous insurrections." French soldiers were involved in each island to some degree, and the insurgents maintained contact across the narrow waterways that separated their shores.[19]

Although the black corps under Major Malcolm vigorously pursued the Saint Lucia insurgents, their number and influence only increased. "The inhabitants are alarm'd to the greatest Degree," Vaughan reported, "the greater part are extremely disaffected, and the others overawed by the Threats, made by the Enemy in various Proclamations and there is in short no Dependence to be placed on them." Without reinforcements from home, Vaughan feared the worst. By mid-April 1795, the situation was desperate. Under Commissaire Gaspard Goyrand from Guadeloupe, who brought soldiers and arms, the insurgents had grown stronger and more organized and quickly took control of most of the island, leaving the British in possession of Morne Fortuné and the town of Castries below it. When reinforcements arrived from Barbados, Stewart took the offensive again. He concentrated his attention on the area around Vieux Fort, at the island's southern extremity, where the insurgents had established an important rendezvous and received supplies. Vaughan believed that had it not been for the exertions of the black corps the island would already have been lost.[20]

The general also concluded that the war in the islands had taken on a new character. It was now a "war of posts." In Saint Lucia the enemy could only be engaged at different shifting locations. The insurgents would not commit themselves to an all-out effort to seize the island or to drive out the British in a major concerted effort or "general action." The war had become a protracted, dispersed affair that wore down the British.[21] Hoping for success nonetheless, Vaughan followed closely Stewart's renewed efforts. Stewart soon managed to drive the insurgents from Vieux Fort. He then turned to attack Soufrière, the rebels' principal post a few miles from Vieux Fort along the southwest coast. The attack, which took place on April 20–22, 1795, failed. On the British side, 108 men were killed or wounded; five men were reported missing. "After this," Vaughan mused philosophically three days later, "I have no Expectation of anything being effected in that Island. We must remain upon the defensive, which as in this Climate the European troops are constantly diminishing in Effectives, will probably lead to more disagreeable Consequences." Vaughan pressed Dundas to send out more seasoned troops that had served in Europe. Without such reinforcements he felt he could not be held responsible for the loss of the captured islands within six months. He warned, indeed, that "the time is not far distant, when it will be necessary and unavoidable to evacuate at least Saint Lucia to strengthen other places, and because the Garrison [at Morne Fortuné] will be exposed to a continued Siege or Blockade."[22] Saint Lucia was proving too costly and difficult to hold.

A few weeks later, Vaughan made a quick trip to Saint Lucia from his headquarters at Martinique to reassess the situation and he came away mortified by what he found. He estimated the "very considerable force" of the insurgents at "not less than six thousand" and expected to withdraw his troops before long.[23] The evacuation finally came on the evening of June 18, 1795, when Stewart realized that his situation at Morne Fortuné would be hopeless; the insurgents had taken the British post on Pigeon Island off Gros Islet on the northwest coast, and, more important, they had also overrun another post at Vigie on the northern shore of the harbor of Castries. Without Vigie, communication by sea with the town would be difficult, if not impossible. By the middle of 1795, Saint Lucia was in the hands of the insurgents and their republican allies under Goyrand.[24] One Antigua correspondent, writing about the British evacuation, said that it was "spoke of as one of the most disgraceful Events that ever happened, for we had more Regular Troops in Garrison there, than the whole Brigand Army, and which mostly consisted of Color'd People, and yet such was their precipitate Retreat, that not a Gun or Mortar was spiked, nor did the Enemy know that the Fort was Abandoned till the following Day."[25]

When Vaughan died in June 1795, the command of the British forces passed to Major General P. Irving, who considered the loss of Saint Lucia to be especially damaging because of its strategic location along the chain of islands and its two excellent harbors of "Gros Islet and Grand Carenage" along the northwest coast. Meanwhile, the French quickly capitalized on this success at Saint Lucia. They planned the invasion of Martinique and sent over from the island of Saint Vincent, a few miles to the south, more than two thousand regular troops to assist the anti-British insurgency there. For the time being, at least, the insurgents at Martinique and Grenada could also count on help from Saint Lucia. The situation was so troubling to Irving that, in writing to Dundas, he commented on "a despondency in general in this part of the World," no doubt for the British and their supporters.

Irving also drew attention to "a Circumstance of a very serious Nature, and one that I much fear will be in the last degree injurious to us." This was related to "the change that has taken place in the Conduct of the Enemy, and which has become more humane and soothing, and in spite of every Watch that can possibly be thought of, they contrive to have thrown into the different Islands Proclamations, and other Papers, amounting almost in their tenor to a Promise of Pardon" for all who supported the British. Irving's comment draws attention to Guadeloupe where, when Victor Hugues established control of the whole colony a few months before, he had ordered mass executions of royalists and other supporters of the British who had been forced out. In Saint Lucia, Irving said, Goyrand pardoned "a Mr. Plant, one of the greatest Enemies of the Republic," and restored his property.[26] Plant was more fortunate than de Bexon, whose property, restored by General Grey in 1794, was destroyed and his land confiscated.[27]

The British occupation of Saint Lucia for a little over a year (April 1794–June 1795) had been tenuous at best. The colony had not been pacified. Instead the British stirred up a hornets' nest of republican resistance, which involved large sections of the black population to whom the republic had offered freedom in early 1794 and which Victor Hugues did his best to encourage from Guadeloupe, "the nerve-center for revolution."[28] When the British withdrew, the insurgent former slaves could assert that they had fought to preserve their freedom; at the same time they had won an important victory for revolutionary France. If Britain were to capture Saint Lucia again, the liberated blacks knew they faced reenslavement.

Early in 1796 a new British amphibious force under Major General Ralph Abercromby and Rear Admiral Sir Hugh Cloberry Christian arrived in the Caribbean. Their main objective was to recapture both Guadeloupe and Saint Lucia. Under Goyrand the republican insurgents at Saint Lucia had fortified several strategic hills (*mornes*) overlooking the length of the northwest coast, from Gros Islet to the north to Grand Cul de Sac a few miles south of Castries and Morne Fortuné. These coastal or seaward batteries were meant to command landing points which the invading British had used in 1794 to march upon Morne Fortuné, and which they might use again. Like Grey in 1794, Abercromby landed troops at two places in the north: Longueville Bay near Le Cap and Choc Bay just north of Castries. A third landing took place at Anse la Raye a few miles south of Morne Fortuné. According to Breen, Goyrand's defensive force consisted of "2,000 well-disciplined black soldiers, a number of less effective blacks, and some hundred whites."[29] The British force, which stood at over 9,000 officers and men, would also have to contend with potential enemies among the rest of the island's black population, now free from bondage.

Abercromby's forces reached Saint Lucia on April 26, 1796. By May 25, after overcoming stiff resistance, they captured Morne Fortuné, and the French under General Cottin and Goyrand capitulated. The French had armed all males, of whatever complexion or social origin capable of bearing arms, to turn back the British and distributed the men among different posts across the island. The garrison of Morne Fortuné which marched out at the surrender consisted of about two thousand men, mostly blacks or coloreds (of mixed descent). They were placed on transports to be carried off the island.[30] They fought well. Brigadier General Perryn confessed that he was "ever afraid of those blacks who climb like Monkeys, cutting off our retreat. The Enemy behaved altho black, so well that they stood firing at half Pistol shot with the head of our attack, & only yielded, I verily believe, one Inch of ground, in hopes of getting round us."[31] During a thirty-six-hour interval between when the fighting at Morne Fortuné stopped and when the British formally took possession of it, many of the black and colored defenders eluded the British soldiers and escaped into the woods, some with arms, making for the interior of the island. There, according to a report, "they were soon joined by the garrisons of Soufrière and Vieux Forts" in the south, "who went off with their arms, ammunition, and provisions." Among these were about three hundred French soldiers from Soufrière who left behind eighty British prisoners and three officers.[32] Part of the garrison at Pigeon Island in the north acted similarly, ignoring the terms of capitulation. These men joined the insurgents' army in the woods, determined to make it difficult for the British to consolidate their victory. Thus began what can be called the second phase of the Brigands' War against the British, who were both enemies of republican France and enforcers of black slavery.

Abercromby acknowledged that Saint Lucia was a "barren conquest." Even before the French surrendered, he informed Dundas that "such is the State of this Island that if conquered it can only be considered as a Military Post" which could be preserved best by remaining in possession of the fort at Morne Fortuné. Life on the island was too unsettled by recent events to generate optimism about its future. "The Negroes are completely Masters of the Island," the general elaborated, "and those who are not in M. Fortuné are collected in the different Quarters in Arms, exercising every Act of Cruelty and Oppression; and possessing a Country naturally so strong that several thousand European Troops would find it difficult if not impossible to reduce them."[33] How then, one may ask, could Morne Fortuné be held? In danger of being confined by the enemy to the fort in 1795, Stewart had quit the island with his troops. If Abercromby expected to avoid the possible repetition of such an evacuation, he would have to pursue the insurgents into the wild and rugged backcountry, however disagreeable such a course of action might turn out to be. Guillaume-Albert Lasalle de

Louisenthal of the foreign corps among the British troops shared Abercromby's reluctance to carry out a campaign against the insurgents in a daunting environment of "Pointes, sommets, pitons, hautes montagnes, rocs, failles." However, these conditions suited the insurgents. They used a guerrilla-style warfare which wore down the British troops. Abercromby did not mention climate, but this, too, was a factor working against his troops. The rainy season which was beginning was sure to cause widespread sickness among them.[34] "I regret very much having come to this Country," Perryn fretted miserably.[35]

At the end of May 1796, Abercromby left Brigadier General John Moore in command at Saint Lucia to deal with the insurgents and restore tranquillity. Moore had distinguished himself in the attack on Morne Fortuné. "From the good sense & spirit of Gen. Moore much may be expected," Abercromby noted; "everything that is practicable will be done." Moore's troops numbered over three thousand. Already "several hundred Blacks" were said to be "in a hostile state" on the island's windward or eastern side. On the first day of June, Moore, reflecting on his predicament, in much the same way perhaps as his predecessor Charles Gordon in 1794, wrote in his journal: "I am involved in a most disagreeable scene; a considerable number of the negroes are in the woods in arms. . . . Everything military or civil is in the greatest confusion, and the rainy season has commenced."[36]

It is not surprising therefore that Moore criticized, at least in his journal, the handling of the capitulation, especially as it helped to strengthen the insurgents. He felt that as soon as the French surrendered at Morne Fortuné "large detachments under proper officers ought to have been detached to different parts of the island to encourage and support the proprietors and disarm the blacks." This could have been accomplished in perhaps a week to ten days while the rest of the army dismantled batteries erected for the attack on the French, destroyed roads, and reloaded stores and artillery onto the transports. In this way the British would have done enough to consolidate "a conquest which it took an army of 11,000 men a month to make. As it is," Moore concluded soberly, "the island is left in the most precarious state." Indeed, the French post at Vieux Fort in the south was still not in British hands. Writing home to his father, Moore described affairs in Saint Lucia as "most troublesome & boisterous. I have not had one moment quiet. . . . This would have been in a great measure prevented had the Capitulation . . . not been so hurried. But the sentiments & plan they were to adhere to were dictated to the Negroes before the surrender, and they escaped from the Fort & other Posts with their Arms into the Woods."[37]

Moore's first strategic act as governor was to issue a proclamation to pardon "people of all colours and descriptions who would come in with their arms. I give passes and encourage everybody to return to their habitations," he explained, "and have assured them of indulgence and protection if they remain quiet and attend only to their private affairs." Moore warned returning émigrés, who had fled the island, not to persecute others who had supported the republic, or treat the blacks badly, or they would be punished. He felt it was important for propri- etors to understand that it was in their own best interest "to prevent disturbances," feeling that "however beneficial war might be to me, it was destruction to them." Former royalists and republicans would receive equal treatment. Moore, of course, was not sure about the effects of his initial policy for pacification, but he proceeded on the assumption that if he won over the proprietors "the negroes will soon be brought to submit." This was easier said than done, but the hopeful governor obviously strategized carefully in full recognition of the critical role blacks played in the insurgency, and that peace would be restored first by calming the fears of both blacks and proprietors.[38]

It is clear from Moore's journal that he expected blacks to return to the plantations as slaves and that their masters should treat them humanely. These were the twin foci of his initial approach, but it is hard to see how returning the liberated slaves to even ameliorated slavery could calm the fears of either blacks or proprietors. Moore's views about the proper behavior of masters toward their slaves were quite explicit. When the black insurgents intensified their activities in June 1796, burning plantations and terrorizing British sympathizers in various parts of the island, particularly in the regions of Soufrière and Vieux Fort but also at Micoud on the east coast, Moore was disappointed that the frightened proprietors fled to the coastal towns. He believed that "those in arms in the woods were few, and that the proprietors by remaining upon their estates and treating their negroes kindly would more effectually prevent their joining those in arms, than I should be dispersing the troops through the country." What had Moore to offer the reenslaved blacks other than a promise of good treatment from their masters? Whether they returned to the plantations or remained in the woods, the blacks realized they were taking their chances in a very problematic situation overall. Certainly, proprietors could not be counted on to obey the governor. Indeed, Moore suspected that propri- etors clamored for troops to protect them "in order to tyrannise over the negroes."[39]

During the last part of June 1796, Moore visited "the whole coast and country" from Soufrière to Vieux Fort, including the coastal towns of

Choiseul and Laborie. At public meetings and in private conversations he encouraged proprietors not to abandon their homes and plantations, a course that only strengthened the position of the insurgents; "from policy, if not from humanity," they should "treat their slaves not only with lenity, but even with kindness." How else might reenslavement of the blacks, which was in the interest of proprietors, have a chance to work? Moore reasoned that "men after having been told they were free, and after carrying arms, did not easily return to slavery and labour. It would require management. Kind treatment and good feeling could alone do it. When those in the woods saw the others comfortable and happy, they would naturally join them." The governor was prepared to hunt down insurgents who remained at large, but he insisted on humane treatment for the slaves.[40] He clearly understood the dilemma the insurgents faced. As in 1794–1795 during the governorships of Gordon and Stewart, many blacks chose to fight on, preferring even a contested and precarious freedom to becoming slaves again.

Moore evidently had an overly optimistic or positive view of the nature of slavery and master-slave relations, but he certainly realized that under the circumstances many masters would find it difficult to treat their slaves humanely. After all, these were far from normal times. The normal difficulties of master-slave relations were compounded by the strains and uncertainties of an internal war that was connected with an imperial one between Britain and France. Among proprietors who would continue to treat their slaves harshly were the émigrés. Moore took a special interest in them, and wished "to curb their insolence." He noted that these émigrés "instead of profiting by their misfortunes, seem only to have increased their prejudices, and in their banishment pant for the moment to gratify their revenge and tyrannise over their fellow-creatures. The terms of canaille, coquin, & c., are ever in their mouths, and applied to every person in the lower ranks of life."[41]

Moore's peace plan did not work. He did not, however, abandon it. Instead, he pursued another approach simultaneously by relentlessly tracking down the rebels and their supporters wherever they might be. June 1796 was a busy month. At Vieux Fort during his visit, Moore arrested Rupez Roche, one of many staunch republican agents who had somehow avoided deportation when the British moved in. He also divided the southern and southwest sections of the island, where the insurgents were most active, into two commands. Major Lindsay took responsibility for the region around Vieux Fort and Laborie, while Major Wilson was assigned Soufrière and Choiseul, with orders to guard the plantations, and also the coast, to prevent the landing of reinforcements from the insurgents' comrades at Saint Vincent. Moore spent about a week directing operations in the south. He sent Lindsay to Praslin on the east coast to deal with some trouble there. On the way back to headquarters at Morne Fortuné, he used roads close to the mountains in order to determine the best locations for posting soldiers "to cover the country." The tour through the island's southern quarter furnished Moore with much useful information about the region and people there.

Soon the insurgents became active in the north and northeast around Gros Islet and Dauphin. Fearing that they might be reinforced from Guadeloupe, Moore, who also realized that "it was necessary to quell this species of insurrection before it gained more head," vigorously took the offensive, and later marched to Dennery on the east coast. From the heights above Dennery district he saw much of the area in flames. Blacks who would not cooperate with the insurgents hid out there in the woods. "Negroes, chiefly women, come in daily," Moore wrote. "They were told we should put them to death. This fear will, I hope gradually wear off, and as they find they are sure of protection they will come in." Moore was disappointed by Lindsay's handling of the situation at Praslin because he bungled an opportunity to cripple the insurgents. Lindsay mistakenly treated "the poor brigands, ill led and unnerved, with as much respect as if they were a regular disciplined body." Moore felt that such behavior could not give proprietors and others not sympathetic to the insurgents the confidence needed to restore peace in the country.[42]

After several weeks of striking at the enemy wherever he could, Moore prepared a report so that Abercromby would know just how matters stood in Saint Lucia. He recorded the following portion of the report in his journal:

> The Negroes in the island are to a man attached to the French cause; neither hanging, threats, or money would obtain for me any intelligence from them. Those upon the estates are in league with and connected with those in the woods. Any disembarkation from Guadeloupe of ever so few men and 800 or 1000 stand of arms, will force me to abandon the country, retire my posts, and concentrate everything in the Morne Fortuné, where the want of cover and convenience of every kind, added to the natural unhealthiness of the spot, will soon so reduce the numbers of the garrison as to make the possibility of our having to surrender a thing to be feared.[43]

Moore also argued that if Saint Lucia was truly a "desirable acquisition an immediate stop must be put to the present troubles by sending a body of 800 or 1000 blacks to scour the woods, whilst the British, who

I find from experience incapable of acting in the interior occupy positions on the coast." The man on the spot, Moore felt there was a real possibility the island would be soon lost. "Against the spirit and enterprise of the Republic we have no chance," he wrote emphatically and critically of the conduct of the war in the West Indies.[44] Thoroughly exasperated by a command he had not wanted, Moore wished to be relieved, or better yet sent home. "I am obliged to go from post to post myself, and have the constant dread of arms being landed from Guadeloupe," he complained. "If we keep Saint Lucia it must be by the greatest accident; my situation is irksome to a degree." Abercromby's response was that Moore should be patient; it was his duty "to struggle with difficulties." Moore was therefore left with no choice but to keep up the exasperating fight against the insurgents of Saint Lucia as best he could.[45]

He disagreed with Abercromby that as long as the troops held Morne Fortuné the island was secure: "Were the troops withdrawn from the country, and the coast left open to succours from Guadeloupe, we should instantly be blockaded on Morne Fortuné." The very same fate had befallen Stewart in 1795. Moore, therefore, pursued a very different strategy and continued to take the fight to the very mobile enemy. The troops were ordered to burn houses of blacks discovered "in the wood and on the heights" and destroy their great number of ground provision gardens which kept them fed. "If this is carried out effectually the brigands cannot remain in the interior," Moore calculated. For several days after his disappointing exchange of correspondence with Abercromby, Moore and his troops crisscrossed the rugged country in pursuit of the insurgents. He developed, as a result, a new appreciation for the difficulties of his command. "I am sure I have undergone more fatigue and hardship these last five weeks than most officers suffer in as many campaigns," he wrote in his journal on August 11, 1796. "I have been marching continually in this hot country, where no European ever was before, sleeping almost constantly in the open air, and without tent or any convenience beyond the common soldier." He felt, however, that his exertions could ultimately prove futile because the officers under him were patently incompetent.[46]

On July 21, while in the field at Vieux Fort, Moore took the time to record his reflections on the insurgents and the "guerre des bois"[47] in his journal.

> Their attachment and fidelity to the cause is great; they go to death with indifference. One man the other day denied, and persevered in doing so, that he had ever been with them or knew anything of them.

The instant before he was shot he called out "Vive la république." The actions they commit are shocking; they murder in the most cruel manner even women and children. This I attribute to the people, black and white, who have hitherto directed them. These have been vagabonds from France, of the Robespierre faction, or blacks and men of colour devoid of principle, but with a little education, and some more cunning than the rest. These people have led them to commit every excess and have succeeded in making them perfectly savage; but the blacks have naturally many good qualities. The cause in which they fight is praiseworthy did they not disgrace it by acts which are a shame to human nature. These acts make us feel less remorse in ordering them to be put to death. I do it, however, with pain, being convinced the poor fellows are misled.[48]

The comments, of course, represent Moore's perception of events; they allow a glimpse of the inner man, but at the same time they help shed light on the insurgents' commitment and their tactics of terror in their struggle against the British and their sympathizers, including island royalists. These included some blacks who had not abandoned their masters. They were "equally attached to their cause, and inveterate against the others and against the republican party." But to judge from Moore's remarks about the insurgents and their allies, including even blacks who had returned to the plantations, royalist blacks were in a minority and did not much hinder the insurgents' prosecution of their cause.[49]

When Moore described the insurgents' cause as "great" and "praiseworthy," he was obviously elaborating on his earlier references to the central role of the French emancipation decree of 1794 and the blacks' attachment to freedom. This, more than the general principles of the French Revolution, was the source that invigorated the insurgents' commitment to the struggle. Theirs was not the classical revolt to escape from slavery or to overthrow it, spawned by slaves' opposition to the system itself or by some particularly motivating grievance. Still, by resisting reenslavement they placed themselves in opposition to slavery. The black insurgency in Saint Lucia, while not a slave revolt in the classical sense, does present revealing dimensions of the dynamics that shaped Caribbean slave society and master-slave relations in the context of imperial struggles during the 1790s. Moore understood what he was up against. The enemy was evidently far from weak. He felt that the emancipation decree had changed the character of warfare in the Caribbean and made success against the Saint Lucia insurgents difficult to achieve. In earlier wars, Moore explained, a colony could be considered "conquered and its quiet possession secured" when its chief military posts were taken, "the white people alone being then considered as inhabitants." The small white population was always prepared to bargain for their security through submission. "The negroes were entirely under their control and as passive as any other part of their property." This hyperbole was Moore's way of saying that the slaves in the colonies were unlikely to give the invading forces much trouble. In other words, no counterattack or sustained local resistance was likely from either the whites or their slaves. Now, however, in 1796, the French abolition of slavery had changed everything, had stirred up the blacks against the British. Conquering the colonies was quite a different proposition largely because of black resistance. Ultimately, Moore came to believe, after his experiences in Saint Lucia, that to deal effectively with such resistance in that island several approaches must be employed simultaneously: all posts must be well guarded; whites must submit to British authority; blacks must remain "in subjection" or in slavery; both whites and blacks must be prevented from contacting the French or receiving aid from them by placing troops at posts along the coast; other troops, preferably the black corps, must actively pursue the insurgents in the woods.[50]

At the end of July 1796, Moore received an additional three hundred black troops which allowed him to harass the insurgents in various parts of the island. As a result, many of them returned to the plantations. Moore felt that the plan to destroy their provision grounds was working. He also noticed, however, that none of the blacks who came out of the woods was armed: "these they leave in the Woods for a future opportunity, and our hopes of tranquility depend, upon our being able to embark the majority of those who have carried arms before that opportunity occurs." During much of August in the rainy season the insurgents were not very active, or to the British they did not appear to be active. Moore thought they were "disheartened" and he forecasted the approaching end of the insurgency. Yet he worried about help reaching the rebels from Guadeloupe and tried to get the navy to maintain patrols of the island's windward or eastern coast. He worried, too, about the decimation of the white troops by disease. "The deaths upon Morne Fortuné alone are from sixty to seventy a week." The climate especially during the rainy season from about June to October was only partly responsible for the death toll among the men from yellow fever and malaria. Moore also blamed the high mortality on "a total want of discipline and interior economy in the regiments." In such circumstances he felt that if the war with the insurgents did not end soon "we shall be beaten by equal numbers of the blacks."[51]

Early in September the governor recorded that he had lately arrested a number of people, whites and free people of color, who were allowed to remain on the island by the terms of the capitulation and his proclamation but who had violated those terms by assisting the insurgents with "provisions, ammunition, and intelligence." He explained that he was also forced to use "other violent measures" against enemy collaborators which he first thought would not be necessary, "but true republicanism seems, at least in this country, to be an excuse for every species of treachery, want of faith, and even common honesty, and I begin to think that harsh measures to which the Republic has accustomed them can alone be efficacious." Moore now changed his mind about the war's end being near. He quite simply was not sure he could restore peace. "It depends so much on accident and the efforts of others."[52]

By mid-November the insurgents were on the move again on the windward coast, having received supplies from Guadeloupe. In the island of Saint Vincent the war with the black insurgents and Caribs was largely over, and Moore decided that the services of their commander, Marin Pèdre, a native of Saint Lucia, might prove useful.[53] Before the war, Marin Pèdre, a free person of color, was "an industrious, honest man" with property living in Saint Lucia. During the political strife of the early period of the French Revolution among royalists and republicans, he was a moderate republican and reputedly saved many persons from the guillotine. He was driven to armed opposition during the governorship of Sir Charles Gordon, who detained 300 people arbitrarily and would not release them until they paid. Along with another Saint Lucian free person of color named Marinier,[54] Marin Pèdre led the first groups of insurgents in the woods during the administrations of Gordon and then Stewart, until the arrival of republican commissioner Goyrand from Guadeloupe in 1794. He served as captain of the grenadiers until Stewart evacuated the island, when Goyrand transferred him with reinforcements to Saint Vincent to help the insurgents there. Marin Pèdre was also promoted to the rank of colonel. Goyrand probably sent him to Saint Vincent because he had too much influence among the blacks of Saint Lucia. If so, here was a man who suited Moore's purpose ideally.

Marin Pèdre agreed to help Moore secure the surrender of the insurgents, but he thought a pardon would facilitate matters. Both men stood to gain much. For Moore, the failure he so dreaded would be averted. Marin Pèdre would have his property restored and could live again in a community where he had many relatives and was generally well known and influential. "He wished of all things to see tranquillity restored to this island, where all his relations were," Moore wrote, describing Marin Pèdre also as "a plain man, with great goodness of heart" who could not read or write but possessed "good sense and shrewdness. All the negroes are perfectly acquainted with him. He assumes no airs, and though dressed in his national uniform with two epaulets, he shakes hands and speaks kindly and familiarly with them all. He shows great attachment to and anxiety for his relations."[55] Though Moore had the best man for the plan he had in mind, Marin Pèdre himself would have realized that it would not be a simple matter to negotiate with the insurgents without appearing to take the side of the British.

Moore decided that the proper time to open negotiations would be after he had first given the insurgents "a drubbing." They, presumably, would be at a distinct disadvantage militarily and psychologically and Moore could deal with them from a position of strength. The governor therefore waited until he had inflicted sufficient punishment on the insurgents during the final weeks of 1796, and had placed black troops at posts along the west coast from Castries to Soufrière to prevent landing of supplies from Guadeloupe, before he authorized Marin Pèdre to start negotiations with the insurgents. Moore at the same time kept detachments of his troops "constantly in the woods." On December 19, Moore received a letter from La Croix, who called himself commandant of "L'Armeé française dans les bois," seeking information about the terms of the proposed surrender.[56]

Moore replied that the armed forces in the woods would be treated as prisoners of war after they surrendered with their arms and ammunition. All the blacks who had left the plantations must return to them as slaves and they would be well treated. La Croix asked for a month's cessation of fighting while he discussed these terms with his people. Moore gave him forty-eight hours. La Croix then asked for eight days to work out and relay a definite response. When Moore did not receive any message, he resolved to reopen the fighting. "I rather think still that La Croix and the principal chiefs were sincere in their wish to surrender," he wrote eight days after the truce ended, "but they have since been frightened and persuaded by disaffected people not to come in." These people were collaborators, many of them whites, who were motivated by fear of exposure and punishment should the insurgents surrender. Moore described these whites as "enemies of good order . . . who hope to benefit by the confusion" of war.[57]

By mid-January 1797, Moore had black troops scouring the countryside with renewed intensity. The insurgents, too, were back on the offensive. When they surprised and took the British-held post of Praslin, Moore began to suspect that Marin Pèdre must have had a hand in it because the well-planned operation was "a bolder measure than the brigands had ever attempted." Moore also now thought that Marin Pèdre was guilty of duplicity because, contrary to his advice, it was clear that all along the insurgents had not intended to surrender. After a few more weeks of operations, Moore wrote dejectedly in his journal: "the trouble I have here is infinite, but it goes for nothing, and will never be heard of." The war against the insurgents was taking its toll on him, and he wished instead he were with the British expedition on its way to attack the island of Trinidad. By early May, Abercromby turned his attention to Puerto Rico, and Moore felt that as soon as Victor Hugues at Guadeloupe knew about this he would send reinforcements to the insurgents of Saint Lucia. "My situation is infinitely unpleasant," Moore wrote. "A small force if landed will force me to withdraw my outposts and expose the inhabitants to be murdered, the country to be plundered and devastated. If the officers commanding detachments are not alert, they will risk being cut off" from Morne Fortuné.[58]

Soon, however, Moore had a bad attack of fever. Abercromby pulled him out of Saint Lucia and placed Colonel James Drummond in command. It is true that Moore was relieved to be rid of the worrisome and draining problems of Saint Lucia, but at the same time he was disappointed that he had not beaten the insurgents into submission.[59]

Drummond followed Moore's basic plan of operations against the insurgents. In October 1797, Stanislaus, their main leader, was shot; resistance reportedly waned after that. Brigadier General George Prevost took over from Drummond in July 1798. He had instructions to execute without trial anyone found dealing with the enemy. By that time several leading inhabitants who had fled the island returned. By February 1799, Prevost reported confidently that the "Native Troops" would soon take care of the few remaining insurgents in the woods. The form of government of the island was still military, however, and Prevost recommended that in the interest of restoring peace some civil government might be introduced "so far as concerned private questions of right."[60] With Prevost's encouragement planters began to give serious attention to reorganizing their plantations.[61] By the end of 1799 there were 41 sugar, 318 cotton, 118 coffee, and 67 cocoa plantations. Their size was not recorded. In 1789 there had been 42 sugar, 180 coffee, and 515 cotton plantations, along with an unspecified number where cocoa was cultivated on 400 carrés of land, or 1,280 acres.[62]

One of the difficulties planters faced at the end of the insurgency was the lack of slave labor. The slave population fell from 18,406 in 1790 to 13,391 in 1799. Many were killed, sent away as prisoners of war, captured as insurgents and deported or executed, or joined up with the insurgents at Saint Vincent. Many more also died as a result of the famine caused by the fighting in 1796–1798, when cultivation of provisions on the plantations was abandoned. The British had also systematically destroyed provision grounds in the countryside to starve out the insurgents. The planters of Saint Lucia also discovered that even if some of their slaves were still alive, it was difficult to recover them: some had been stolen or enticed onto other plantations, and others had simply run away.[63] It would seem possible, therefore, that while the British commanders may have ordered them back to the plantations as slaves, many blacks may have manipulated the confused situation to their advantage, not without risk, seeking out plantations and situations that better suited them. They would have found plantation owners who were willing to cooperate.

Saint Lucia remained in British hands until 1802, when it was returned to France by the Treaty of Amiens, but the two European powers went to war again the following year and the British seized the island again in June 1803. This time the British did not have to deal with an insurgency, and the planters continued rebuilding from the ruins of the 1790s. Recovery was slow. At the end of 1803 Governor Robert Brereton reported that the planters were "endeavouring by uncommon industry to resettle their estates, which must take a considerable time to accomplish from want of Negroes or Capital to purchase them."[64] In 1805 the island's total population stood at about 18,886: 1,533 whites, 4,053 free people of color, and 13,300 slaves. If broken and indebted planters were not yet quite out of the fire, the considerable increase of commerce indicated returning confidence in the island's economic future. Perhaps the most striking indication of new commercial vitality was the growth in the number of "mercantile houses," or firms engaged in trade. Shortly before the British took the island in 1803 there were only eight firms in Castries and six in other areas; nearly two years later there were twenty-six firms in Castries and ten elsewhere, an increase of twenty-two. More trading ships now arrived, and even coastal trade revived.[65] Slaves, whose labor power got the plantations going again, numbered nearly 15,000 in 1810 and about 16,000 in 1816, still not sufficient to meet the demand for labor. The abolition of the British slave trade, which took effect in 1808, of course did not help the planters. After several years of hopeful reconstruction, Saint Lucia remained a British colony at the end of the Napoleonic Wars.[66]

If the difficulties of economic reconstruction reminded planters, merchants, and free property owners of the years of the revolution and black insurgency, the slaves also must have had their own recollections.

Faced with the hardships of slavery under the British in the 1800s, the slaves must have mulled over the memory that they had once been free. Their ideological readjustment to slavery, or adjustment to reenslavement, is difficult to reconstruct from existing records, most of which did not discuss the slaves at all. The lives and hopes and strivings of the slaves were lost in the concern for larger economic, constitutional, and military matters. However, some insight into the consciousness of the slaves regarding the years of upheaval, especially their emancipation and reenslavement, emerges from their responses four decades later to the British plan for emancipation.

The British came up with an unwieldy emancipation plan which frustrated the freed people before it fell apart in 1838. One part of the process that caused the ex-slaves much concern was that while they were all nominally free on August 1, 1834, they were to serve a period of apprenticeship to their old masters lasting four years for field workers (predials) and six years for nonfield workers (nonpredials). Both groups could purchase their unexpired term of apprenticeship.[67] During the early months of 1838 leading up to the proposed full emancipation of predial workers, the other workers began to express dissatisfaction that they would have to wait two more years (till 1840) for their full freedom. That is understandable. What is to be made, however, of the report that nonpredials persisted in purchasing what was left of their apprenticeship only months before they were supposed to be fully free by law? Colonel John Alexander Mein, lieutenant governor of Saint Lucia, was persuaded that "doubts still exist in the minds of these people, even as to their ultimate emancipation, notwithstanding I have given directions to the special magistrates to impress upon them the fallacy of the reports of artful and designing persons, who would wish, by creating these doubts, to induce the apprentices to give a higher price for their freedom than they otherwise would."[68]

Why would these workers doubt the approach of full freedom? What was the context within which these uncertainties took shape? Certainly the conditions of partial freedom under apprenticeship were contributing factors. However, the best historically resonant explanation comes from the colored magistrate James Johnston[69] in reference to both groups of apprentices. Johnston noted that some of the nonpredials "appear even to be doubtful as to their being finally emancipated in 1840, and this feeling has arisen from occurrences during the French revolution, still fresh in the recollection of many of the old apprentices, when the slaves were declared free, and were compelled after a short period again to relapse into a state of slavery." As for the nonpredials who were buying the remaining term of their apprenticeship, Johnston commented that they invariably explained that "they prefer buying their freedom, in consequence of obtaining a paper (meaning the Act of affranchisement), which would make their freedom more secure." This feeling was widespread among the apprentices.[70] In 1839 plantation workers were still responding with great anxiety to rumors of reen-slavement.[71]

The perceptions of freedom of the Saint Lucia apprentices during the later 1830s were shaped by the experiences of slavery, by the conditions of the awkward system of apprenticeship, and notably by the apprentices' historical consciousness of the circumstances surround-ing the first emancipation of 1794. It was the British who reimposed slavery. Over forty years later, could their promise of emancipation be regarded as genuine? The wars of the French Revolution in the Carib-bean and black insurgency plunged Saint Lucia into the heat of a military and political conflict which tore the island apart. When it was all over, blacks were still slaves, but for a few years they were important actors and agents at the conjuncture of war, revolution, and slavery in the Caribbean.

NOTES

I am indebted to David Patrick Geggus and Darlene Clark Hine for com-menting on drafts of this chapter.

1. Michael Duffy, *Soldiers, Sugar, and Seapower: The British Expeditions to the West Indies and the War against Revolutionary France* (Oxford: Clarendon Press, 1987); Anne Pérotin-Dumon, "Guerre et révolution dans les Petites Antilles: Le Prix du sucre ou de la liberté?" *Revue Française d'Histoire d'Outre-Mer* 76 (1989): 293–345; David P. Geggus, *Slavery, War, and Revolution: The British Occupation of Saint Domingue 1793–1798* (Oxford: Clarendon Press, 1981); Geggus, "The Anglo-French Conflict in the Caribbean in the 1790s," in *Britain and Revolution-ary France: Conflict, Subversion, and Propaganda,* ed. Colin Jones (Exeter: Univer-sity of Exeter, 1983), pp. 27–39; Roger N. Buckley, *Slaves in Red Coats: The British West India Regiments, 1795–1815* (New Haven: Yale University Press, 1979); Michael Craton, *Testing the Chains: Resistance to Slavery in the British West Indies* (Ithaca: Cornell University Press, 1982), chaps. 15 and 16; Bryan Edwards, "History of the War in the West Indies, from Its Commencement in February 1793," in *The History Civil and Commercial, of the British Colonies in the West Indies* (Philadelphia, 1805–1806), vol. 4, pp. 279–310; Henry H. Breen, *St. Lucia: Historical, Statistical, and Descriptive* (London, 1844; reprint, Frank Cass, 1970), chap. 3; J. H. Parry and P. M. Sherlock, *A Short History of the West Indies* (London: Macmillan, 1965), chap. 11; Robin Blackburn, *The Overthrow of Colonial Slavery 1776–1848* (London: Verso, 1988), chaps. 5 and 6; H. de Poyen, *Les Guerres des Antilles de 1793 à 1815* (Paris, 1896).

2. Memorial of Planters, Proprietors, and Merchants in Britain Trading to Saint Lucia, London, May 6, 1823, *Colonial Office* (hereafter *CO*) 253/17, Public Record Office, Kew, Surrey, England; Brigadier General Robert Brereton to Secretary of State Lord Hobart, November 14, 1803 (private); Saint Lucia Privy

Council Report, February 21, 1824, enclosed in Major James Culley to Secretary of State Earl Bathurst, February 23, 1824, no. 4, *CO 253/18.* The five devastated parishes were Anse la Raye in the west-central quarter and Micoud, Praslin, Dennery, and Dauphin, all on the east or windward coast.

3. Saint Lucia Privy Council Report, February 21, 1824; Breen, *St. Lucia,* chap. 3; Duffy, *Soldiers, Sugar, and Seapower,* pp. 136–156, 221–240; J. W. Fortescue, *A History of the British Army* (London: Macmillan, 1899–1930), vol. 4, pp. 425–430. Similar upheavals occurred simultaneously in Saint Vincent and Grenada to the south of Saint Lucia, though these also possessed striking particular characteristics. At the start of the war with revolutionary France in 1793 these two colonies were in British possession. See n. 19.

4. At the end of the War of American Independence (1783) the British restored Saint Lucia to the French. It remained French until 1794. See J. W. Fortescue, *The British Army 1783–1802* (London: Macmillan, 1905), p. 133. On the economic prospects of Saint Lucia during this period, see Gabriel Debien, "Les Cultures á Sainte-Lucie á la fin du XVIIIe siècle," *Notes D'Histoire Coloniale,* no. 103, extract from *Les Annales des Antilles,* no. 13 (1966), pp. 57–84.

5. Lucien Abenon, Jacques Cauna, and Liliane Chauleau, *Antilles 1789: La Révolution aux Caraïbes* (Editions Nathan, 1989), pp. 171–172; "Extrait d'une lettre de la Souffrière, du 6 Janvier," *Gazette de Sainte Lucie, Nationale et Politique,* January 11, 1791, *CO 71/20.*

6. Breen, *St. Lucia,* pp. 76–79; Sir John Orde to War Secretary Henry Dundas, October 2, 1791, no. 60, October 27, 1791, no. 63, *CO 71/21;* Liliane Chauleau, *Histoire antillaise: La Martinique et la Guadeloupe du XVIIe à la fin du XIXe siècle* (Paris, 1973), pp. 194–195; Abenon, Cauna, and Chauleau, *La Révolution aux Caraïbes,* p. 172. There was reportedly a slave rebellion in the island in 1793. See ibid., p. 174.

7. Breen, *St. Lucia,* pp. 79–81; Duffy, *Soldiers, Sugar, and Seapower,* pp. 59–91, 111; Grey to Dundas, April 4, 1794, *CO 318/13;* April 12, 1794, no. 16, *CO 318/14;* de Bexon to Portland, June 16, 1795, enclosed in Grey to Portland, August 29, 1795, *CO 318/16;* Cooper Willyams, *An Account of the Campaign in the West Indies, in the Year 1794* (London, 1796), pp. 77–84; Edwards, "History of the War in the West Indies"; Fortescue, *History of the British Army,* vol. 4, pp. 362–363; David Buisseret, "The Elusive Deodand: A Study of the Fortified Refuges of the Lesser Antilles," *Journal of Caribbean History* 6 (May 1973): 63–66; de Poyen, *Les Guerres des Antilles,* pp. 58–63.

8. De Bexon to Portland, June 16, 1795, enclosed in Grey to Portland, August 29, 1795, *CO 318/16;* Memorial of Basil Freeland and Thomas Rigsby, May 20, 1797, enclosed in Major General Ralph Abercromby to Dundas, June 3, 1797, no. 18, *War Office* (hereafter *WO*) *1/86,* Public Record Office, Kew, Surrey, England.

9. Breen, *St. Lucia,* p. 81; Duffy, *Soldiers, Sugar, and Seapower,* p. 114; Memorial of John Marie Aquart to Bathurst, August 13, 1816, *CO 253/10.*

10. Grey to Dundas, April 29, 1794, no. 21 ("secret"); July 28, 1794, no. 35; September 9, 1794, no. 38, *CO 318/13;* Dundas to Grey, June 9, 1794, *CO 318/13;* Memorial of J. M. Aquart to Bathurst, August 13, 1816, *CO 253/10.* See also W. Adolphe Roberts, *The French in the West Indies* (Indianapolis: Bobbs-Merrill, 1942), pp. 223–232.

11. Duffy, *Soldiers, Sugar, and Seapower,* pp. 115–156, 136, 217–240; Jacques Adélaïde-Merlande, "Expansion et subversion révolutionnaires dans les isles auvent 1794–1799," paper presented at the twentieth annual meeting of the Association of Caribbean Historians, Basse-Terre, 1989, p. 1. By the end of 1794 the French had recovered all of Guadeloupe.

12. Grey to Dundas, July 17, 1794, no. 33 ("secret"); September 9, 1794, nos. 37 and 38; September 10, 1794, *CO 318/13*.

13. Grey to Dundas, September 9, nos. 37 and 38. In Saint Domingue Commissaire Léger Félicité Sonthonax freed the slaves by decree on August 29, 1793, and so hastened the decree of the National Convention of February 1794, which reached the Antilles much later in the year. See Robert Stein, "The Revolution of 1789 and the Abolition of Slavery," *Canadian Journal of History* 17 (December 1982): 447–467; Stein, "The Abolition of Slavery in the North, West, and South of Saint Domingue," *The Americas* 41 (January 1985): 47–55; Stein, *Léger Félicité Sonthonax: The Lost Sentinel of the Republic* (Rutherford: Fairleigh Dickinson University Press, 1985), chaps. 5–7; David P. Geggus, "From His Most Catholic Majesty to the Godless République: The 'Volte-Face' of Toussaint Louverture and the Ending of Slavery in Saint Domingue," *Revue Française d'Histoire d'Outre-Mer* 65 (1978): 481–499; Geggus, "The French and Haitian Revolutions, and Resistance to Slavery in the Americas: An Overview," ibid., 76 (1989): 107–124; Geggus, "Racial Equality, Slavery, and Colonial Secession during the Constituent Assembly," *American Historical Review* 94 (December 1989): 1290–1308; Jean Tarrade, "Les Colonies et les principes de 1789: Les Assemblées révolutionnaire face au problème de l'esclavage," *Revue Française d'Histoire d'Outre-Mer* 76 (1989): 9–34; Carolyn E. Fick, *The Making of Haiti: The Saint Domingue Revolution from Below* (Knoxville: University of Tennessee Press, 1990), chap. 7; Fick, "Black Peasants and Soldiers in the Saint-Domingue Revolution: Initial Reactions to Freedom in the South Province (1793–1794)," in *History from Below*, ed. Frederick Krantz (New York: Blackwell, 1988), pp. 247–270; Adélaïde-Merlande, "Expansion et subversion."

14. George Rudé, "Ideology and Popular Protest," *Historical Reflections* 3 (Winter 1976): 69–77; E. J. Hobsbawm, "History from Below—Some Reflections," in *History from Below*, pp. 13–27; Buckley, *Slaves in Red Coats*, p. 9; M. A. Lacour, *Histoire de la Guadeloupe* (1855; reprint, Guadeloupe, 1960), vol. 2, p. 402.

15. Major General P. Irving to Dundas, August 1795, no. 10, *WO 1/84*. On the prize-money system implemented by Jervis and Grey, see Duffy, *Soldiers, Sugar, and Seapower*, pp. 106–114. See also Tony Gutridge, "Aspects of Naval Prize Agency 1793–1815," *Mariner's Mirror* 80 (February 1994): 45–53. On the engagement at Dauphin, see Baillie to Grey, August 29, 1794, encl., *CO 318/13*.

16. Duffy, *Soldiers, Sugar, and Seapower*, p. 134; Fortescue, *History of the British Army*, vol. 4, p. 425; Vaughan to Dundas, January 30, 1795, no. 10, *WO 1/83*.

17. Vaughan to Dundas, January 31, 1795, no. 11; February 25, 1795, no. 13 ("secret"), *WO 1/83*. On the Black Carolina Corps, see Joseph W. Barnwell, "The Evacuation of Charleston by the British in 1782," *South Carolina Historical and Genealogical Magazine* 11 (January 1910): 1–26; Buckley, *Slaves in Red Coats*, p. 4; George F. Tyson, Jr., "The Carolina Black Corps: Legacy of Revolution (1782–1798)," *Revista/Review Interamericana* 5 (Winter 1975–1976): 648–664.

18. Vaughan to Dundas, February 25, 1795, no. 13 ("secret"), *WO 1/83*.

19. Vaughan to Dundas, January 30, 1795, no. 10; Fortescue, *History of the British Army*, vol. 4, pp. 426–427. On the troubles in Grenada and Saint Vincent, see, for example, R. P. Devas, *The Island of Grenada (1650–1950)* (Grenada, 1964), pp. 103–200; Craton, *Testing the Chains*, chaps. 15 and 16; Edward L. Cox, "Fedon's Rebellion 1795–1796: Causes and Consequences," *Journal of Negro History* 67 (Spring 1982): 7–19; Cox, *Free Coloreds in the Slave Societies of St. Kitts and Grenada, 1763–1833* (Knoxville: University of Tennessee Press, 1984), chap. 5; Timothy Ashby, "Fedon's Rebellion," *Journal of the Society for Army Historical*

Research (JSAHR) 62 (Autumn 1984): 154–168, and 63 (Winter 1984): 227–235; Duffy, *Soldiers, Sugar, and Seapower,* pp. 136–156, 236–240. See also Bernard Marshall, "Slave Resistance and White Reaction in the British Windward Islands 1763–1833," *Caribbean Quarterly* 28 (September 1982): 33–46.

20. Vaughan to Dundas, March 15, 1795, no. 16 ("secret"); April 16, 1795, no. 22 ("secret"); April 16, 1795, no. 23, *WO 1/83;* Breen, *St. Lucia,* pp. 82–83; Lacour, *Histoire de la Guadeloupe,* pp. 402–403; Adélaïde-Merlande, "Expansion et subversion."

21. Vaughan explained that "instead of making the Sovereignty of the Island their only object," the French and insurgents "endeavour by every means to harass and weaken our regular force, hoping thereby, and by the myriads of negroes they have at their Command ultimately to wrest from us these valuable colonies." Vaughan to Dundas, April 18, 1795 ("most private"), *WO 1/83.* See also, concerning "war of posts" and "general action," Thomas Fleming, "George Washington, General," in *Experience of War,* ed. Robert Cowley (New York: Dell, 1992), pp. 140–143.

22. Vaughan to Dundas, April 19, 1795, with enclosures; April 25, 1795, with enclosures; May 1795, no. 25, encl.; May 11, 1795, no. 26, *WO 1/83.*

23. Vaughan to Dundas, June 16, 1795, *WO 1/83.*

24. Vaughan to Dundas, June 22, 1795, with enclosures, *WO 1/83;* Vaughan to Portland, June 22, 1795, *WO 1/32;* Breen, *St. Lucia,* pp. 84–87; Irving to Dundas, July 8, July 23, 1795, encl., August 1795, no. 10, *WO 1/84;* Adélaïde-Merlande, "Expansion et subversion," p. 2. See also Lacour, *Histoire de la Guadeloupe,* pp. 402–403; de Bexon to Portland, June 16, 1795, encl. in Grey to Portland, August 29, 1795, *CO 318/16.*

25. Langford Lovell to Christopher Bethell, July 11, 1795, Codrington Papers, Nettie Lee Benson Latin American Collection, University of Texas at Austin, microfilm, reel 3.

26. Irving to Dundas, July 8, July 23, 1795, encl., August 1795, no. 10, *WO 1/84.* On Hugues at Guadeloupe, see Chauleau, *Histoire antillaise,* pp. 207–210.

27. De Bexon to Portland, June 16, 1795, encl. in Grey to Portland, August 29, 1795, *CO 318/16.*

28. Duffy, *Soldiers, Sugar, and Seapower,* p. 240.

29. Duffy, *Soldiers, Sugar, and Seapower,* pp. 159–236; Breen, *St. Lucia,* pp. 87–108; "Sir Ralph Abercromby's Original Instructions, 9 October 1795," in *The Haitian Journal of Lieutenant Howard, York Hussars, 1796–1798,* ed. Roger Norman Buckley (Knoxville: University of Tennessee Press, 1985), pp. 139–146.

30. For accounts of the capture of Saint Lucia, see, for example, Abercromby to Dundas, May 4, 1796, no. 13, May 22, 1796, no. 14, May 30, 1796, private, May 31, 1796, private, May 31, 1796, no. 16, Articles of Capitulation encl., *WO 1/85;* Add. MS. 37876, report of May 27, 1796, Windham Papers, British Library (BL), London; Fortescue, *History of the British Army,* vol. 4, pp. 486–492; "Memoirs of Townsend Monckton Hall," in Townsend Monckton Hall Papers, William B. Hamilton Collection; Diary and Commonplace Book of Stephen Prendergast, Perkins Library, Duke University, Durham, North Carolina; *Aventures de guerre aux Antilles (Sainte Lucie, la Martinique, Trinidad) 1796–1805,* ed. G. Debien, in *Notes d'Histoire Coloniale,* no. 200 (1980): 12–27. I am indebted to David Patrick Geggus for bringing this latter source to my attention, and to Marie-Jeanne Rossignol for locating it. See also the informative account from French sources in de Poyen, *Les Guerres des Antilles,* pp. 128–146, which includes Goyrand's journal of events. The journal and correspondence of Brigadier General John Moore, who remained as governor of Saint Lucia, provides a wealth of informa-

tion. For a copy of Moore's journal regarding Saint Lucia, see Add. MS. 57326, 57327, Sir John Moore Papers, vols. 7 and 8 (February 21, 1796–October 24, 1797), British Library, London. The journal is also published as *The Diary of Sir John Moore*, ed. Sir. J. F. Maurice (London: Edward Arnold, 1904), vol. 1, pp. 189–254. In this study I have used this printed copy of the journal, hereafter referred to as "Moore-Journal." For Moore's other correspondence, see Add. MS. 57320, 57321, Sir John Moore Papers, vols. 1 and 2, BL. Portions of the journal and correspondence can also be found in James Carrick Moore, *The Life of Lt. Gen. Sir John Moore*, 2 vols. (London: John Murray, 1834); Beatrice Brownrigg, *The Life and Letters of Sir John Moore* (New York: D. Appleton, 1923), pp. 54–73.

31. J. Perryn to General Lake, May 4, 1796, Add. MS. 37876, Windham Papers, BL.

32. Letter in *The Saint George's Chronicle* and *Grenada Gazette*, July 30, 1796, copy in *CO 101/34*; Abercromby to Dundas, May 31, 1796 (private) *WO 1/85*. See also Debien, *Aventures de guerre aux Antilles*, pp. 24, 26.

33. Fortescue, *History of the British Army*, vol. 4, p. 492; Abercromby to Dundas, May 22, 1796, no. 14, *WO 1/85*; Debien, *Aventures de guerre aux Antilles*, pp. 16–17, 24–25; Moore to his father, August 20, October 11, 1796, Add. MS. 57320, Moore Papers, BL.

34. On disease as a factor in eighteenth-century Caribbean warfare, see, for example, Roger N. Buckley, "The Destruction of the British Army in the West Indies 1793–1815: A Medical History," *JSAHR* 56 (Summer 1978): 79–92; comments on Buckley's article by David Geggus in *JSAHR* 56 (Winter 1978): 238–240 and by R. E. Scouller in *JSAHR* 57 (Spring 1979): 58–59; David Geggus, "Yellow Fever in the 1790s: The British Army in Occupied St. Domingue," *Medical History* 23 (January 1979): 38–58; Duffy, "The British Army and the Caribbean Expeditions of the War against Revolutionary France 1793–1801," *JSAHR* 62 (Summer 1984): 65–73.

35. Perryn to Lake, May 4, 1796, Add. MS. 37876, Windham Papers, BL.

36. Abercromby to Dundas, May 30, 1796, private, *WO 1/85*; Moore-Journal, pp. 219–220; Moore to his father, May 28, 1796, Add. MS. 57320, Moore Papers, BL.

37. Moore-Journal, pp. 221–222; Debien, *Aventures de guerre aux Antilles*, p. 26; Moore to his father, October 11, 1796, Add. MS. 57320, Moore Papers, BL.

38. Moore-Journal, p. 222.

39. Moore-Journal, p. 223; Moore to his father, October 11, 1796, Add. MS. 57320, Moore Papers, BL.

40. Moore-Journal, p. 224.

41. Moore-Journal, pp. 224–225.

42. Moore-Journal, pp. 225–231.

43. Moore-Journal, p. 231.

44. Moore-Journal, pp. 231–232.

45. Moore-Journal, pp. 232–233.

46. Moore-Journal, pp. 233–236; Moore to his father, August 20, 1796, Add. MS. 57320, Moore Papers, BL.

47. Lacour, *Histoire de la Guadeloupe*, vol. 2, p. 402.

48. Moore-Journal, pp. 234–235.

49. Moore-Journal, p. 235.

50. Moore-Journal, pp. 259–260; Moore to Sir Robert Brownrigg, September 4, 1796, Add. MS. 57321, Moore Papers, BL.

51. Moore-Journal, pp. 235–237; Moore to Major General Graham, August 11, 19, 1796, *WO 1/85*. Graham became commander in chief when Abercromby returned to England in August 1796 because of sickness. Fortescue, *History of the Army*, vol. 4, p. 495.

52. Moore-Journal, pp. 237–240.

53. Moore-Journal, pp. 240–241; Graham to Dundas, October 16, 1796, no. 5, *WO 1/86*.

54. On Gordon's handling of affairs in the captured colony, see Kieran Russell Kleczewski, "Martinique and the British Occupation, 1794–1802," Ph.D. diss., Georgetown University, 1988, pp. 204–207. Major General Graham said Marinier was Marin Pèdre's brother. Marinier was also a leader of the insurgents in Saint Vincent. Graham to Dundas, October 16, 1796, no. 5, *WO 1/86*.

55. Moore-Journal, pp. 241–242.

56. Moore-Journal, pp. 242–243.

57. Moore-Journal, pp. 243–244; Moore to his father, August 20, 1796, Add. MS. 57320, Moore Papers, BL.

58. Moore-Journal, pp. 244–250; Moore to his father, February 2, April 1, 1797; Moore to his mother, February 18, 1797, Add. MS. 57320, Moore Papers, BL.

59. Moore-Journal, pp. 250–254; Moore to his father, May 16, 1797, Add. MS. 57320, Moore Papers, BL; Diary and Commonplace Book of Stephen Prendergast.

60. Moore-Journal, pp. 253–254. According to Breen, Drummond succeeded in reducing the insurgents "to such straits" that they finally surrendered before the end of 1797 "at discretion. The only stipulation they made was that, as they had borne arms for so long a period, and had enjoyed the immunities of freemen, under the sanction of the Republican laws, they should not be again reduced to slavery. The British authorities, glad to get rid of such troublesome 'Citoyens' upon any condition, formed them into a regiment, which was sent to the coast of Africa." Breen, *St. Lucia*, p. 107. See also Major General Cornelius Cuyler to Dundas, October 4, 1797, *WO 1/86*; Duffy, *Soldiers, Sugar, and Seapower*, p. 312. For Prevost's comments on the situation in Saint Lucia, see Prevost to Portland, November 24, 1798, February 2, 1799; Draft of Portland's reply to Prevost, April 1, 1799, *CO 253/2*; also Prevost to Portland, March 11, 1801, *CO 253/2*. On the government of the conquered islands, see D. J. Murray, *The West Indies and the Development of Colonial Government 1801–1834* (Oxford: Clarendon Press, 1965), pp. 47–66; Helen Taft Manning, *British Colonial Government after the American Revolution 1782–1820* (New Haven: Yale University Press, 1933; reprint, Hamden: Archon, 1966), pp. 339–392.

61. Prevost to Portland, March 6 1799; Portland to Prevost, May 1, 1799 (draft reply); Prevost to Portland, June 1, 19, 1799; Portland to Prevost, August 26, 1799 (draft reply); Prevost to Portland, November 12, 1799, no. 11, *CO 253/2*.

62. Prevost to Portland, November 12, 1799, nos. 11 and 12, *CO 253/2*; Debien, "Les Cultures à Sainte-Lucie"; M. Lefort de Latour, *Description générale et particulière de l'Ile de Sainte Lucie, 1787*, consulted at Lands and Survey Department, Saint Lucia, West Indies; Brereton to Earl Camden, July 24, 1805, *CO 253/3*. A carré of land is estimated at 3.2 acres.

63. Prevost to Portland, June 19, 1799; Portland to Prevost, July 6, 1799 (draft); Prevost to Portland, September 4, 1799, no. 4; November 12, 1799, nos. 11 and 12; Portland to Prevost, April 18, 1800 (draft), *CO 253/2*; Charles Gachet, *A History of the Roman Catholic Church in St. Lucia* (Port of Spain, Trinidad: Key Caribbean Publications, 1975), p. 24.

64. Charles Jesse, "Sainte Lucie, fille de la Martinique," *Annales des Antilles*, no. 13 (1966): 17; Brereton to Hobart, July 10, November 14, 1803 ("private"), *CO 253/3*.

65. Brereton to Camden, July 24, 1805, *CO 253/3*.

66. Governor Alexander Wood to Earl of Liverpool, January 10, 1812,

enclosure B, *CO 253/7;* Governor Robert Douglass to Bathurst, October 16, 1816, no. 5, *CO 253/10;* M. DeBarbier, "Reflexions sur quelques parties de l'administration de Ste. Lucie" (1815), *CO 253/9.*

67. See, for example, Parry and Sherlock, *Short History of the West Indies,* pp. 175–204; W. L. Burn, *Emancipation and Apprenticeship in the British West Indies* (London: Jonathan Cape, 1937; reprint, New York: Johnson, 1970); William A. Green, *British Slave Emancipation: The Sugar Colonies and the Great Experiment 1830–1865* (Oxford: Clarendon Press, 1991); W. K. Marshall, "The Termination of the Apprenticeship in Barbados and the Windward Islands: An Essay in Colonial Administration and Politics," *Journal of Caribbean History* 2 (May 1971): 1–45.

68. Mein to Lord Glenelg, April 22, 1838, *British Parliamentary Paper (BPP)* (London 1839), vol. 36, p. 267.

69. David Barry Gaspar, "'The Best Years of My Life': James Johnston of St. Lucia and Antigua 1819–1832," paper presented at the fifteenth Conference of Caribbean Historians, Mona, Jamaica, 1983. In spite of his racial origins and color, Johnston achieved the distinction of becoming a stipendiary magistrate in 1838. See Johnston's memorial to Governor Francis Hinks (Barbados), August 22, 1861, *CO 253/129.*

70. Report of J. Johnston, April 8, 1838, enclosure 2 in Mein to Glenelg, April 22, 1838, *BPP,* vol. 36, p. 268; Maurice Halbwachs, *The Collective Memory,* trans. Francis J. Ditter, Jr., and Vida Yazdi Ditter (New York: Harper and Row, 1980); Paul Connerton, *How Societies Remember* (Cambridge: Cambridge University Press, 1989); Richard Price, *First Time: The Historical Vision of an Afro-American People* (Baltimore: Johns Hopkins University Press, 1983), pp. 1–26.

71. *Palladium* (newspaper), May 11, 18, 25, June 1, 1839, *CO 258/1.*

5

Slave Resistance in the Spanish Caribbean in the Mid-1790s

DAVID PATRICK GEGGUS

The few historians who have sought to find patterns in the history of slave resistance in the Americas have produced two main models. One (associated with Michael Craton) stresses internal change within slaveholding societies, particularly the transition from an African- to a creole-dominated slave population.[1] The other (associated with Eugene Genovese) accords overriding significance to the French and Haitian revolutions, whose influence, he believes, gave rise to a new, truly revolutionary type of slave uprising.[2]

In Craton's view, African-led revolts were violent and aimed either at escape from colonial society or its total destruction. The emergence in the early nineteenth century, however, of a creole, that is, locally born, majority among the slaves brought with it new nonviolent tactics and a new willingness to come to terms with the plantation regime. Genovese, on the other hand, sees not increasing moderation but increasing radicalism. Early insurrections were traditionalist and escapist, and they countenanced the enslavement of opponents. Only in the era of the French Revolution, he argues, did slave rebels begin to demand the eradication of slavery as an institution and seek to form "bourgeois-democratic" polities. I have offered critiques of both approaches and suggested that insofar as a new type of uprising did emerge during the age of revolution, it was one in which insurgents claimed to have been already freed by a metropolitan decree that the planter class was refusing to recognize. This feature, I believe, derived as much from the European antislavery movement and late Ancien Régime reformism as from the French Revolution.[3]

This variety of revolt, appealing to a secret emancipation decree, as well as the African/creole and rebellion-to-revolution paradigms, all focus attention on the turn of the nineteenth century. The mid-1790s witnessed one of the most remarkable upsurges of slave resistance in the history of the Americas, affecting English-, French-, Spanish-, Dutch-, and Portuguese-speaking territories from the River Plate to the Mississippi.[4] In a recent study Michel Martin and Alain Yacou write that "it was to the new cries of liberty and equality that there broke out in the same year, 1795, the slave revolts in Puerto Príncipe, Coro, Boca Nigua, Porto Rico, and Grenada. . . ."[5] This chapter examines two of the least known of these rebellions which occurred near Puerto Príncipe in central Cuba and Boca Nigua in Santo Domingo, together with a number of other acts of resistance in the two colonies during the middle and late 1790s. These case studies will be used to explore the forces at work in the generation of slave insurrections and, insofar as the material allows, to cast light on the general themes just outlined.

Both rebellions were short-lived, small-scale affairs, of lesser magnitude than some historians have suggested. They are interesting, however, because they took place in the shadow of the great Haitian Revolution, which destroyed the wealthiest of all Caribbean colonies, French Saint Domingue. Of the tens of thousands of slaves who revolted there in 1791, many claimed to have been freed by the king and adopted a counterrevolutionary discourse. However, after the French Republic abolished slavery in 1794, most eventually allied themselves with the forces of the French Revolution. The two colonies closest to Saint Domingue were Cuba and Santo Domingo (the modern Dominican Republic). Their fortunes were to be profoundly affected by the Haitian Revolution, though in completely divergent ways.

In the early 1790s Cuba was in the throes of rapid change. For over thirty years it had experienced brisk economic expansion through sugar cultivation. The pace of change increased markedly after the slave trade was opened to foreigners in 1789 and after world sugar prices shot up as a result of the slave revolt in Saint Domingue. Cuba's relatively balanced social structure made it less vulnerable to revolt than the typical sugar colony where slaves predominated overwhelmingly. However, the import of enslaved Africans increased at an unprecedented rate after 1789. In 1791–1795 annual slave imports were more than three times their level in the 1780s, and whites ceased to form a majority of the population.[6] If Cuban slavery had had some claim to be considered mild by Caribbean standards, the planters' vehement rejection of the Código Negro Español, the protective slave code drawn up in May 1789, showed that institutional restraints on the master class were no greater there than elsewhere. Moreover, the Cuban tendency to import a high proportion of male slaves was a peculiarly oppressive feature of its slave regime.[7]

Until the 1790s slave revolts had been apparently very uncommon in Cuba. It is noteworthy, however, that the autonomous Cobreros community of blacks, located near Santiago, who had once been slaves of the crown but whose status had become unclear, had been vociferously claiming since 1788 to have been freed by the king.[8] The arrival from Spain and suppression by the administration of the Código Negro also had occasioned much unrest among Cuban slaves, including a brief rebellion on one of the largest sugar estates around the beginning of 1790.[9]

Cuba possessed far and away the strongest military garrison in the Caribbean, but following the outbreak of war with France in 1793 it was substantially reduced over the next two years by troop transfers to Santo Domingo, Florida, and, in May 1795, Louisiana.[10] The fiercely conservative administration, worried as much by white liberals as by nonwhite dissidents, attempted to keep news of the French and Haitian revolutions out of the colony. Despite various restrictions, however, refugees began arriving from strife-torn Saint Domingue bringing their slaves with them.[11] Other blacks were deported from Saint Domingue and sold in Cuba.[12] By late 1794 rumors were running rife of insurrections, by either slaves, white colonists, or French prisoners of war, though all proved groundless.[13]

The tense peace in Cuba was broken early in July 1795 by a small though significant outbreak on a hacienda in the island's central region, about forty miles from the town of Puerto Príncipe (modern Camaguey).[14] Príncipe was among the provinces where the slave population had grown most substantially in the previous twenty years as its ranchers diversified into sugar. But slaves still numbered only about 35 percent of its population, and whites were more prominent there than in the colony in general.[15] The hacienda called Cuatro Compañeros where the outbreak took place belonged to Don Serapio Recio y Miranda, son of the local alguacil mayor (police chief). It was a very small property and had only seven slaves, apparently all men.

Two of the slaves figured most prominently in the rebellion. Romualdo, aged twenty-five and described as "a native of Cobre," seems to have been a former member of the fractious Cobreros community then asserting its rights to freedom. He was certainly Cuban-born. Joseph el Francés ("the Frenchman") was about two years older and probably had come from Saint Domingue. He may have been brought to

Cuba after 1791, either by a refugee colonist or as an illicitly sold pris-
oner of war. However, as no particular significance was attached to his
origins in the investigation of the rebellion, it is quite possible that he
and Juan el Francés, also implicated, had been sold through the interisland slave trade prior to the revolution.[16] Their designation as
"French" identifies them, if not definitely as creoles, then at least as
creolized.

On July 6, 1795, Recio returned to his estate, where he noticed that
the slaves talked in his presence in an uncustomarily noisy manner. On
complaining about it, he was confronted by Romualdo, whom he then
threatened to have whipped. Romualdo thereupon drew his machete
and told Recio, it was later reported, that "if he wanted to mistreat him,
he was mistaken, for all men were equal, and that the whites would
soon see how blacks should be treated."[17] Recio rushed into his house
to get his weapons but found they had been removed by Joseph el
Francés, who cried, "No one has a master now; we are all free." At this
point, Romualdo told Joseph to burn the house, but they found the
palm thatch would not ignite. They shut Recio inside the house, where
Romualdo hit him with a chair. The bewildered proprietor then
adopted a more conciliatory tone, and the slaves thereafter left him
alone.[18]

That night the seven rebels left to gather recruits on neighboring
estates, as Recio was informed by a teenaged mulatto slave. The insurgents talked of the liberty and equality they were to enjoy, and apparently they also used threats. By midmorning another eight or nine
slaves from three other properties had joined them. They had few
weapons. Joseph carried a machete. (What he had done with Recio's
pistols is not explained.) Romualdo had a gun that had been seized
from the manager of a neighboring estate, but he had to cut lead weights
from a fish net for ammunition. Their plan was to obtain more arms by
attacking the military post about fifteen miles away at Santa Cruz. From
there they would march on the town of Puerto Príncipe.

However, by midday the revolt was over. Left unguarded, Recio fled
to his brother's property nearby, and together with three slaves and
another white neighbor they set off to raise the alarm.[19] About five miles
from Cuatro Compañeros they ran into the rebels on the highway. Two
of the insurgents then suddenly turned on their companions. Although
they put up a fierce struggle, the two ringleaders were overpowered
and the rest surrendered, except two who were captured later that day.[20]
The slaves who changed sides were not from Cuatro Compañeros. Both
claimed they had been forced to join the rebels, one after being cut
several times with a machete. The other was a mulatto.

The regional governor in Puerto Príncipe immediately alerted the commandant in Santa Cruz and issued a decree forbidding non-whites to carry any sort of arms. A week later, he reported on the events to Governor Las Casas in Havana. The local whites, he wrote, were filled with fear at the thought that they were facing a repetition of the revolution of Saint Domingue. The extermination of the whites, he claimed, was the rebels' confessed aim. Furthermore, the revolt was unlike the usual type of slave rebellion; it was "something new and directly against the state." He doubtless was referring to the talk of liberty and equality, which at first sight seems clear testimony to the influence of the French Revolution.

The scale of the revolt was much smaller than Alain Yacou implies in recent studies. While making no mention of the numbers involved, he asserts that the rebels won over "a large number" of slaves on surrounding plantations and that the revolt, besides "ravaging" the Recio estate, "enflamed a good part of the Puerto Príncipe region."[21] Yacou also states that the rebels intended to burn the plantations and were inspired by the French emancipation decree, although there is no clear evidence of this, particularly in the single source cited.[22]

There is indeed much uncertainty about the aims of the insurgents. A somewhat different picture from that presented in the local governor's account emerged when a judge was sent from Havana to investigate. In his report, drawn up on August 14, the revolt seems less radical and less destructive in intent. There was no mention of the word "equality." It was said that a rumor had circulated of the arrival in Puerto Príncipe of a royal proclamation emancipating the slaves. The source of the rumor is unclear. Romualdo blamed Emigdio, a local creole slave, well regarded by the Spanish, but this appears to have been a fabrication. Although seven of those interrogated said the plan was to attack Puerto Príncipe, Cuba's second largest city, they all claimed (as did five others) they had been forced by threats to join the uprising. The other four, including the two leaders, claimed their intention was to march on the town and then demand from the governor the freedom he was withholding from them.

All in all the story does not carry much conviction, though the strange fact that no whites were killed and no property seems to have been destroyed does lend credence to it. The governor of Havana in any event decided to reject calls for summary justice and to transfer the case to the Audiencia, the regional appeal court located in Santo Domingo. Only ten men were considered guilty enough to be prosecuted. Three years later the case had yet to be brought to trial, and the ten rebels remained in Puerto Príncipe jail.

What gives this minor event significance is that it forms part of a series of more than twenty American slave conspiracies and uprisings, usually associated with creole slaves, that made use of a rumored emancipation decree and spanned the age of revolution (1776–1848).[23] In some which took on the character of strikes or demonstrations, there seems to have been a genuine belief in the existence of such a decree. In others that were more violently oriented, these rumors appear to have been a smokescreen, a peculiarly bold extension of the slave's proclivity for confronting whites with tall tales told with a straight face. Romualdo may have used the emancipation decree story merely to justify his actions to his interrogators. Conceivably, the story may have circulated among Caribbean blacks as just that, a story of which rebel leaders had made creative, even amusing, use. Yet in view of the way the contemporary press sometimes turned mere rumor into news, it is quite possible that Romualdo, or at least his followers, were genuinely incensed by what they suspected was the suppression of an authentic emancipation decree.

It is not evident that the French emancipation decree of early 1794 was specifically implicated in the Puerto Príncipe revolt. Another possible source of such rumors within the Spanish empire was the suppression of the Código Negro at the end of 1794—a decree regarded as favorable to slaves that had been the subject of a genuine coverup in the colonies. An additional source of confusion in Cuba was the law of February 1795 granting civil rights to certain free coloreds. Acting together they may have aroused the same hopes as the May 15, 1791, decree (regarding free coloreds) had apparently done among Saint Domingue slaves. This would help explain why, more than a year after the emancipation decree of 16 pluviôse and nearly two years after slavery was abolished in Saint Domingue, slaves in Cuba, Spanish Louisiana, Puerto Rico, La Plata, and Venezuela all suddenly started agitating at roughly the same time in spring/early summer 1795, and why most of these plots featured rumors of a suppressed emancipation decree.[24]

It may additionally have been significant that the Puerto Príncipe revolt's leader was a Cobrero. Barely two months after the Cuatro Compañeros affair, the governor of eastern Cuba was complaining of a wave of emancipation rumors and marronage disturbing his district, which he blamed on the Cobrero community near Santiago and the correspondence they were receiving from their representative in Spain, who was seeking to have their free status officially recognized.[25] At the very least, then, one needs to be sensitive to other possible influences operating at this time besides those emanating from Saint Domingue and revolutionary France.

Nevertheless, rumors relating to France soon were circulating in

Cuba. Word went round that Spain intended to sell the island to the French Republic.[26] This rumor was probably inspired by Spain's transfer of Santo Domingo to France, which became known in the Caribbean in September 1795. Then early in 1796 a deportation proclamation aimed at French slaves led some to announce that "as a result of the proclamation all slaves from the French colonies were free." Whether this was a misunderstanding or not, the governor of Puerto Príncipe was not sure, but he suspected the "French" slaves of deliberate "malice." One who had confronted his owner with such claims was brought before the governor to explain himself. In the governor's words, the slave declared "haughtily, with various expressions typical of an ignorant person puffed up with very foolish though seditious principles and ideas, that the blacks of the colony of Cap Français all were free, because they had gained [*adquirido*] their liberty."[27] The next day all the "French" slaves in the town were assembled on the main square to see the man receive one hundred lashes. Around his neck was placed a sign bearing these words: "This is the fruit of the imaginary liberty of the French slaves: in virtue is found true freedom." The slaves remained impassive, the governor noted, but a few weeks later a plot was denounced involving five originally from French colonies.[28]

Two years later the Puerto Príncipe region experienced a much more serious outbreak. About twenty-five slaves launched a violent rebellion on a number of sugar estates several miles from the town.[29] The reported details are somewhat sparse, but it seems the insurgents gathered on one plantation the night of June 11, 1798, and had time to attack three or four other properties before they were driven into the hills by a troop of soldiers and colonists the next morning. One ranch was burned; three overseers were hacked to death and another wounded. One planter, warned by a slave woman, had a narrow escape. It took another day of scouring the hills before the revolt was subdued. Though José Luciano Franco claims the militia made a "frightful carnage" of the rebels, the sources mention only one insurgent killed; another hanged himself. As the average Cuban sugar estate then had about eighty slaves and Puerto Príncipe province then had at least fifty-five estates, it would seem this was not a mass uprising.[30] According to some of the confessions obtained, it would have achieved much greater dimensions had it not broken out two days prematurely.[31] Apparently many urban slaves were implicated, and they included the revolt's leaders. There was said to be an arms cache in town. The rebels reportedly intended to kill all white males and keep the women for themselves. In the end, however, charges were brought against only twenty-three slaves who had participated in the uprising.

Fifteen of these slaves came from two estates; the others each had a different owner. Of the twenty slaves who were punished,[32] the three originators of the plot were hanged and four were sentenced to 200 lashes with ten years' hard labor. Eight men who abandoned the others after the first killings received eight years' hard labor, though those responsible for the killings were not identified in the trial record. The others received lesser punishments, chiefly exile. The origins of sixteen slaves were given. All were Africans except one who was from Azua on the Santo Domingo frontier. He, like three of the Africans, was described as "known as French." They were not the ringleaders, who were all "Carabalí," but played intermediate roles.[33] It was they who received 200 lashes.

The following month a plot was discovered to take over the town of Trinidad, some 150 miles from Puerto Príncipe, and kill the local whites.[34] The conspirators lived in the surrounding countryside. By October five had been prosecuted, of whom two were hanged, though investigations continued thereafter. At least three were Africans; one was from Curaçao and one from Jamaica. Whether they or the "French" slaves in the previous revolt inspired their companions with news of changes in the wider Caribbean is not evident from the documentary record. Soon after the plot was discovered the captain-general observed that the slaves of the province were excited by news of the black victory in Saint Domingue (where British invaders had been forced to evacuate their main positions in May).[35] But in his later accounts of these two affairs, after they had been investigated, he made no reference to the French colony.

Alain Yacou's account of these events, like the pioneering work of Franco, tends to exaggerate both their extent and their links with Saint Domingue. In the course of 1796, he argues, the secret agitation of the *negros franceses* "reached the whole central region," which in 1798 became "a remarkable center of insurrection," indeed of "Haitian messianism."[36] This is a large claim to make on the strength of two small revolts, one belligerent slave whipped for rumor-mongering, and two conspiracies leading to ten arrests.[37] One might imagine that more was involved, but the captain-general's comments on the 1798 affairs make clear this was the sum total for the region over the previous three years—a record he found alarming enough.[38] The Havana region produced only one minor rebellion and two plantation strikes, each confined to one estate and without apparent links to the wider world.[39] Furthermore, Yacou's argument rests on several statements the evidence will not support—that "almost all" the sugar estate work forces of Puerto Príncipe revolted in 1798 and that French slaves were "the true organizers" of that revolt and were also behind the Trinidad conspiracy, which in his recent work Yacou presents as a revolt that ravaged the surrounding region.[40] Marking the beginning of a long cycle of slave resistance in Cuba, these events of the mid-1790s do merit attention, but their true dimensions should not be obscured by romanticizing rhetoric.

Similarly, slaves from Saint Domingue may well have been "messengers of liberty" in Cuba, but that could mean expounding egalitarian doctrine, retailing stories of insurrection, or spreading rumors of imaginary decrees. Here the documentary record is not very helpful. The events of 1795–1796 offer some evidence, albeit equivocal, of the impact of French revolutionary ideology, but also of apparent confusion regarding government decrees combined with more traditionalist thinking. The events of 1798 show merely slaves' hatred for slaveowners— "All whites are bad," said the Puerto Príncipe leader Manuel Carabalí.[41] The potency of the "rumor syndrome," on the other hand, is apparent if one looks forward to the Aponte conspiracy of 1811–1812. Once again, slaves living around Puerto Príncipe planned to march on the town, having heard that "the king had granted freedom, but that the local gentlemen did not want it."[42]

Unlike burgeoning Cuba, Santo Domingo remained one of the most neglected parts of Spain's empire, despite experiencing considerable population growth during the eighteenth century. Its poverty and conservatism contrasted markedly with the worldly dynamism of French Saint Domingue, with which it shared a common frontier. Removal of restrictions on the colony's slave trade led to expansion in sugar cultivation during the late 1780s, but most of the colony's inhabitants were still rural free coloreds and poor whites who engaged in ranching, tobacco farming, and subsistence agriculture.[43]

Though little is known of popular attitudes in Santo Domingo, the Saint Domingue Revolution deepened the mistrust felt at least by the colony's intensely conservative elite for its profane and successful French neighbors. In response to the revolutionary crisis, the governor formed a defensive military cordon along the frontier but maintained a neutral stance toward the contending parties. Spanish colonists and soldiers traded informally with the rebel slaves, who claimed to be fighting for church and king as well as their own freedom, and some of the clergy regarded them as instruments of divine vengeance. When France and Spain went to war in 1793, the administration, on orders from Madrid, recruited thousands of rebel slaves as "auxiliary troops" in the hope of cheaply reconquering the colony lost to France one hundred years before. After early successes, the plan backfired. The black mercenaries under their leaders Jean-François and Biassou proved maddeningly independent, and they made little headway against the republicans once slavery was abolished.[44]

Along with defeat in Europe, this forced Spain to surrender Santo Domingo to France in July 1795.[45] There followed a long and curious twilight period, in which the colony was legally French but the Spanish administration remained in place. The war and revolution in Saint Domingue continued to absorb the republic's attention, and the Spanish wished for an orderly evacuation; hence neither side hurried to implement the treaty. When republican officials briefly visited Santo Domingo in October 1795, they distributed copies of the French emancipation decree, already widely discussed in Santo Domingo,[46] and they declared that slavery was abolished. The Spanish administration denied this, however, and Spanish law remained in force.[47] By the summer of 1796 several thousand colonists and troops had departed, including nearly 800 of the black auxiliaries.[48] Meanwhile the black revolution continued to make strides in the neighboring French colony.

To this point, the Saint Domingue Revolution seems to have evoked little visible response among Santo Domingo's small and scattered slave population. The chief exception was a plot discovered in March 1793 in the border town of Hinche. It was said that all the creole slaves of several frontier towns were involved, but in all only nineteen slaves from ranches and plantations surrounding Hinche were arrested.[49] At least three of them had French names, but as in the Puerto Príncipe affair, this was not singled out for comment in contemporary documents. One of their leaders was Thomas, who said the slaves in the Spanish colony were *pendejos* (penises) for doing nothing while those in Saint Domingue were killing whites. His plan was to seize Hinche during the Holy Week festivities, kill all the whites, and capture the local armory. He claimed that the black general Jean-François (not yet recruited by the Spanish) had given a captain's commission to an urban free black named Andrés Dimini, and that once the general was finished with the French whites, he would make war in Santo Domingo.

As in the Puerto Príncipe case, the accused free black was subsequently found innocent. The promise of outside help was a ploy used in many slave conspiracies to rally support, not least in the 1791 uprising in Saint Domingue by Jean-François and his colleagues, when French royalists were adduced as allies. Dimini, the free black, denied the story about the commission, pointing out that Jean-François enjoyed good relations with the Spanish and supplied them with slaves.[50] Jean-François's conception of slave emancipation indeed was largely limited to that of his own soldiers and their families, and from May 1793 he fought in Spanish pay as at least a nominal defender of slavery against the republicans.[51] Nevertheless, he became a symbol of black pride in the Spanish Caribbean. On learning he had left Santo Domingo for Cuba in late 1795, blacks in Havana organized to celebrate his arrival.[52]

The Hinche plot of 1793 shows clearly the impact of events in Saint Domingue on Spanish slaves in the neighboring colony. Unlike the conspirators in the Puerto Príncipe rebellion, the Hinche conspirators do not seem to have spoken of liberty as an ideal, though it was evidently their goal. This was doubtless because the conspiracy took place before the Saint Domingue slave revolt became allied with the forces of French republicanism and before the slave leaders generally adopted the French Revolution's libertarian rhetoric.[53] This may help explain why the Spanish administration did not pursue the affair vigorously and why none of the accused was executed.[54] Three years later, however, things had changed.

In October 1796 an uprising took place on the Boca Nigua sugar estate that was situated on the coast some fifteen miles west of Santo Domingo City. The plantation had about 200 slaves, of whom 110 to 120 were adult or adolescent males. By the standards of Jamaica or Saint Domingue,[55] the plantation was of only average size, but it was considered the largest and best run in Santo Domingo. Its buildings were new, and it had probably been built up since the opening of the slave trade in 1786.[56] Most of the adult slaves were no doubt Africans. Several of them had French names and may have been fugitives from Saint Domingue or, more likely, had been purchased there.[57] French records show that the plantation manager did business in Cap Français.[58]

Though the plantation belonged to the absentee Marqués de Yranda, it was managed by his nephew, Juan Bautista Oyarzábal, who acted as if it were his own. The work force was said to be well treated, "not like black slaves,"[59] and some of them supposedly acknowledged this fact. Because of the estate's exposed situation, the manager had provided it since the war's outbreak with an armory and two small cannon. As on isolated plantations on Saint Domingue's south coast,[60] the slaves, it seems, were expected to defend the estate against foreign attacks. The artilleryman was Estevan, the slave blacksmith.

There exist four main sources regarding this revolt. Most detailed and important is the report of Manuel Bravo, the investigating judge, who led the expedition sent against the rebels and interrogated all the prisoners. Brief accounts were also written by the colonial governor Joaquín Garcia y Moreno, by the archbishop of Santo Domingo Fernando Portillo y Torres, and by the judges of the Audiencia (appeal court).[61]

The accounts concur in that the plot began as an act of personal revenge by Francisco Sopó, the slave driver. Two or three months before the uprising, an African slave named Benito had committed suicide after being whipped, either for stealing rum or not performing a task. He hoped in death to return to his native land, "as not a few of those wretches believe," commented the investigating judge. Another slave died shortly afterward in the plantation hospital; the slaves blamed the estate doctor for his death. Both men were godsons of Francisco Sopó. According to the judge, Francisco was deeply fond of them. To the archbishop, Francisco was "overwhelmingly besotted and in love with" Benito. Whether it was ritual kinship or homosexual desire that stirred his passions, Francisco determined to take revenge on the white distiller who had punished Benito. He discussed his plan with Antonio the carter, who shared the same hut, and the plot began to snowball. As well as drowning the distiller in a barrel of rum, they decided to kill the white refiner (so they might be put in charge of the refinery, the judge speculated). Their ambitions aroused, they eventually planned to kill all the estate's white staff, including Oyarzábal, and to fortify the plantation, while raising the slaves of the surrounding area.

To learn how the slaves had rebelled in Saint Domingue, Francisco and Antonio contacted three former soldiers of Jean-François's black auxiliaries who were working on the nearby San Juan plantation. All five were Africans of the same ethnic group and regarded one another as "kin" (*parientes*). To gain the confidence of the three ex-soldiers, Francisco and Antonio paid them frequent visits at night, secretly using the plantation's horses, or during the day under the cover of selling pigs. They took them presents of rum and cane syrup. Nevertheless, the ex-soldiers refused to get involved in the plot, telling the slaves that they were well treated. They also refused to take them to Saint Domingue, saying it was too dangerous there.[62]

Over several weeks the two conspirators recruited slaves on the Boca Nigua plantation, initially those of their own ethnic group, it was said, and then others. Tomás Congo Aguirre, a slave "of extremely bad habits" from the neighboring Buenavista estate, seems to have been the only outsider to have joined the plot. This perhaps suggests that the two leaders were "Congo" slaves as well. Bakongo from the Zaire River basin were the most numerous victims of the Atlantic slave trade in the late eighteenth century, and in Saint Domingue they formed by far the largest group of young African males.[63] Other slaves at Boca Nigua who soon became involved in the plot were the elderly Papa Pier, Piti Juan, Christóval Cesar, and Antonio's wife, Ana Maria.

Ana Maria was a domestic slave who worked in the plantation house. Like Francisco, she was said to have been favored by Oyarzábal, though according to the governor she was willing to murder him herself. The ambiguous position of these "elite" slaves is dramatically underscored by their actions during the week before the rebellion. Apparently having second thoughts, Ana Maria approached Francisco about informing the manager of the conspiracy.[64] He dissuaded her, promising he would do so himself at an opportune moment. When on Friday, October 28, the conspirators set the date of the uprising for the following Sunday, Francisco revealed the plot that evening to the white distiller—the very person whom he wanted to kill in the first place. The archbishop later commented smugly that this would seem extraordinary to anyone who was not familiar with blacks. It may be that Francisco was seeking to cover himself in the event of failure or that he and Ana Maria had only reluctantly accepted the extension of the original plan for revenge. Or perhaps it was the refusal that day of the three ex-soldiers to join in the rebellion that caused the slave driver's confidence to desert him.

The former soldiers later told their interrogators that once the date was fixed, they went to Santo Domingo to inform the governor but guards prevented them from entering the city. Though they did not participate in the rebellion, this story was probably untrue. Exactly when Oyarzábal learned of the plot is uncertain. According to the archbishop, he remained in the capital through Saturday and most of Sunday, ignoring repeated warnings from Pedro Abadia, the distiller. This seems likely, since the governor and the investigating judge, who clearly were friends of Oyarzábal, discreetly pass over the matter in their reports. In any event, the manager had returned to the plantation by 4:30 P.M. on Sunday, when Francisco repeated his story to him. Oyarzábal's response was to send away the estate's store of cash and await further developments in the plantation house accompanied by several white and free colored neighbors and the estate's white staff.

Like many other slave conspirators in the Americas, those of Boca Nigua doubtless chose a Sunday evening for their rebellion so they would not have to fight after a full day's work in the fields. At sundown they gathered as usual to receive their weekly allotment of plantains, then suddenly attacked the plantation house armed with an assortment of weapons. These included not only lances, knives, machetes, and sticks fitted with nails, but also hunting rifles, blunderbusses, and pistols, which appear to have been their own.[65] A volley from the house broke the slaves' charge, and they split up into small groups surrounding the building at a distance. Tomás Congo led a second attack but without success. Several slaves were wounded.

Apparently at this point, if not sooner, Francisco joined the whites in the plantation house. During the night he persuaded them to slip out of the house and try to escape through the canefields and winding mountain paths. Though Tomás Congo set fire to a canefield to light up the countryside and, as he truculently said later, to kill any whites hiding in it, all made good their escape. Francisco's behavior perplexed the judges. They were unsure if he had laid a trap for the fleeing whites or had genuinely fallen out with his co-conspirators, perhaps wishing to distinguish between Oyarzábal and his employees.[66]

In the morning the rebels ransacked the plantation house, smashing the furniture and carrying off food and clothing to their huts. Ana Maria helped in the distribution and provided keys to locked doors. Antonio, her husband, was elected "general" in Francisco's absence, while a disappointed Tomás Congo had to accept second in command. The rebels also took muskets and ammunition. Supposedly unfamiliar with the use of screws, they tied together with cord the guns whose locks had not been attached. Artillerymen, guards, and pickets were named, and a cavalry was formed using the plantation animals. The insurgents loaded the estate's two cannon with scrap metal and nails and chose "cannon people" as their watchword, as a reply to "Who goes there?" An expedition led by Papa Pier then went into the nearby hills to recruit slaves on the Nigua estate, which overlooked the plantation. When they arrived, they found its slaves had fled.

The rebels planned to march farther inland the next day to burn the San Christóval plantation and raise its slaves.[67] Thus reinforced they would return and surprise the small fort at Haina on the coast, halfway to Santo Domingo. Some insurgents added they were then to march on the much larger castle of San Gerónimo, which guarded the capital, to seize its weapons. Meanwhile, they decided to hold a feast to celebrate their success, and perhaps to attract more support. Antonio assured his followers he was working for them. He promised freedom to all who would take up arms, but said he would keep as his slaves those who did not.[68] That evening, amid drumming and dancing, the insurgents feasted on the master's meat and wine. Ana Maria presided over the festivities elaborately dressed and "seated beneath an awning where she received the treatment due to a queen, replying with kind words and expressions of generosity." According to the Audiencia's report, Ana Maria and her husband received the titles of queen and king.

The use by slaves of political titles mirroring state authority was common in American societies.[69] Kings and other officials were elected by African slaves involved in conspiracies in Antigua (1736), Louisiana (1791), Trinidad (1805), Jamaica (1816), and Demerara (1823).[70] At the beginning of the Saint Domingue slave revolt, as well, local kings were chosen, and the creole leader Jean François and his wife were supposedly feted as king and queen, though he soon took the title grand admiral.[71] The Boca Nigua insurgents' strange mixture of caution and seeming complacency also might be traced to a ritualized approach to warfare learned in Africa, where dancing was an important part of martial preparation.[72] There was possibly a religious dimension to their actions, too, that escaped the whites' notice. On the other hand, hunger and exhilaration at putting their oppressors to flight might provide a sufficient explanation why they, like slave rebels elsewhere, turned to premature celebration. In addition, one senses a naive confidence stemming from the possession of the two cannon.

During this time, the administration in Santo Domingo had been alerted and preparations were taken to confront the rebels. Two slaves fled the estate during the revolt and early on Monday morning reached the capital, where they informed the plantation steward, Antonio Collar. Some hours later fifty troops of the Cantabrian and Santo Domingo regiments were dispatched together with Manuel Bravo, a judge of the Audiencia who had investigated the colony's two other slave conspiracies of recent years. They had to march about fifteen miles. On the way they learned that Oyarzábal had escaped, helped by the darkness and the local free population. Orders were given to mobilize local residents to cut off access to the region. At nightfall the small expedition reached the still-deserted Nigua plantation on the hill above the insurgents' estate. Down below they could hear the sounds of drumming and celebration, and at 9:00 P.M. the scene was suddenly lit up when a cannon shot set a canefield on fire.

Bravo, the judge, was anxious to kill the "poisonous Hydra" before the revolt spread, but he waited till dawn before crossing the Nigua River. Guided by locals, the soldiers attempted to attack the plantation simultaneously from four directions, but they were brusquely repelled by sustained and heavy fire from muskets and cannon. Falling back to the river with their wounded, they were pursued and a firefight began. After a quarter of an hour, however, the rebels suddenly withdrew and then abandoned the plantation, setting fire to some buildings but failing to burn the green canes. Some surrendered; most fled for the hills. A manhunt then began in the forests between Boca Nigua and Azua, seventy miles away. More troops arrived; but it was the local *monteros*, smallholders armed with lances and machetes, who proved most effective in pursuit. With Oyarzábal offering a reward for recaptured slaves, all but two were retaken within five days. Tomás Congo held out for three weeks. In the attack and following pursuit, six slaves were killed and ten wounded, of whom one later died. The soldiers lost one dead and six wounded.

About one hundred slaves were sent to either hospital or jail in Santo Domingo. The rest were deemed innocent by virtue of their age or sex. Manuel Bravo took ninety-seven depositions, keeping apart those yet to testify from those who had already done so. A white or free colored soldier fluent in "the idiot language that they use" (presumably *bozal* Spanish) was employed as an interpreter. Anxious to make a swift example of the insurgents, the Audiencia passed judgment on November 28, contrasting the "offense" of the Boca Nigua slaves with "the exemplary and praiseworthy conduct of the most loyal Spanish Negroes, by which they have distinguished themselves in the midst of such confusion."[73]

Sentences were carried out during the first days of December. Francisco Sopó, Antonio the carter, Ana Maria, Papa Pier, and Tomás Congo Aguirre were hanged, beheaded, and quartered.[74] Two other leaders were hanged and beheaded. Four slaves were found innocent, but most of the rest received one hundred lashes. Another nineteen, including six women and two girls under age seventeen, were given either fifty or twenty-five lashes each. The three former soldiers of Jean-François were condemned to eight years' hard labor in different Spanish colonies. Most of the slaves who were whipped were additionally sentenced to work for ten years with irons on their legs and neck after their return to the plantation. After the executions, all had to pass under the gallows to witness the dangling corpses of their comrades.

The day of execution was extremely tense, according to Governor Garcia. Afraid that the execution might produce disturbances worthy of the Saint Domingue Revolution, he stationed one hundred soldiers around the gallows, put the rest of the garrison on alert, and closed the city gates. The governor feared both the numerous slaves and free blacks in Santo Domingo and the growing number of French migrants from Saint Domingue, who outnumbered Spaniards on the city streets.[75] Like the *regente* of the Audiencia, Joseph Antonio Urizar, he assumed that the latter included "Philanthropists," partisans of liberty and equality,[76] though Manuel Bravo noted the French were only too pleased by the swift suppression of the uprising. It remains unclear if the population really was "agitated" by the occasion, as one scholar suggests; no source in fact says this.[77]

As to the rebels themselves, contemporaries offered differing assessments. The governor claimed they had planned to capture Santo Domingo City and establish a government like that in Saint Domingue.

The Audiencia asserted their intention was "to take over the plantation, proclaim their general liberty,[78] attract slaves from other plantations, and follow their . . . fatal ideas to the ultimate extreme." These views are echoed in the main published studies of the rebellion, where it is stated that the conspirators' aim was to "proclaim the general liberty of all the colony's slaves."[79] None of this, however, appears in the report of Bravo, the judge who interrogated the prisoners. He wrote nothing of their ultimate intentions and merely opined that if the revolt had spread, it could have had fatal results as in Saint Domingue. The archbishop, who was often critical of the governor, dismissed the rebellion as of little consequence. He saw it as the product of individual resentments and the plantation manager's negligence. It was poorly executed and attracted few slaves from other estates. He denied that the three men from Saint Domingue were behind it. Since Boca Nigua was the sole large plantation in Santo Domingo, he was sure there could be no repetition of the Saint Domingue Revolution in the Spanish colony.[80]

Clearly, the Saint Domingue revolt was influential in the Boca Nigua affair insofar as it provided the rebels with a precedent they wished to learn from; and it may be the French colony was considered as an avenue of escape, especially as some of the slaves may have lived there previously. One would presume that France's defeat of Spain the previous year and the ending of Spanish rule in Santo Domingo were relevant factors as well. Yet remarkably there is no suggestion in the documentary record of the rebels' attempting to speed up the transition to French rule and thus official emancipation. Of course, one can question if such action would have made much sense anyway.[81] Certainly, it is an exaggeration to say, as do Martin and Yacou, that the rebellion was characterized by "the new cries of liberty and equality."[82] There is no trace of libertarian discourse in Bravo's report, and the only mention of "general liberty," the contemporary French term denoting freedom for all, appears somewhat ambiguously in the Audiencia's account.[83] Most important, it seems inconsistent with the leader Antonio's threats, reported by Bravo and Garcia, to enslave those who would not follow him.

The Boca Nigua revolt seems on balance to belong to an older type of slave rebellion, localized in causation, where African ethnic identity and ritual played a central role. Rather than asserting individual liberty as an absolute value, such revolts sometimes included among their aims the enslavement of opponents, as in Tacky's rebellion in Jamaica (1760) and Cuffee's in Berbice (1763). Even while resisting their own enslavement, Africans from societies where slavery was an accepted institution were perhaps less ready than creoles to identify the system as something to eradicate. It was also easier for creoles sharing a common culture to think in terms of the slave population as a whole than it was for Africans conscious of separate identities. Nevertheless, the Boca Nigua revolt was not a narrowly "ethnic rebellion," like some earlier ones in the Caribbean,[84] since it involved Africans from different cultures, although the original conspirators did share a common ethnic background.

I would not claim that these two main case studies—the Puerto Príncipe and Boca Nigua revolts of 1795 and 1796—are clear examples of any particular type of slave insurrection. They illustrate above all the difficulty of reconstructing with limited colonialist sources the nature, and especially the aims, of slave resistance. They illustrate also how published studies in this area sometimes have stretched the evidence further than is warranted.

Yet I think there is evidence here to support the two main paradigms of slave revolt outlined earlier. The Puerto Príncipe 1795 insurrection offers some albeit equivocal testimony to the adoption of the libertarian rhetoric of the French Revolution, even if the French emancipation decree itself was not certainly implicated. In this sense, it would constitute an addition to the short list compiled by Eugene Genovese of the new type of bourgeois-democratic slave revolt. On the other hand, if the rebels were really responding to a rumored royal decree of emancipation, it is most unlikely they were seeking to overthrow the state. Though calling for freedom, the rebels sought legitimacy in the king's name. In terms of European ideologies, the revolt was traditionalist rather than modern, as Jorge Dominguez observed of an earlier example of the phenomenon.[85]

Despite much uncertainty regarding the rebels' origins and ultimate intentions, Craton's African/creole model probably finds most support in these examples each corresponding fairly closely to his archetypes. Though contemporaries and historians have tended to read the meaning of these revolts by the apocalyptic light coming from Saint Domingue, the African insurgents at Boca Nigua and at Puerto Príncipe appear to have acted in largely traditional ways (in both Craton's terms and Genovese's). In contrast, the creole-led insurgents on the hacienda Cuatro Compañeros pursued a somewhat less violent strategy, and their motives seem more connected to external influences. On balance, the exclusively creole conspirators at Hinche in 1793 were those most impressed with events in Saint Domingue, although their apparently destructive plan does not accord with Craton's model.

Even in the shadow of the Haitian Revolution, slave resistance continued to express a diversity that seems closely linked to ethnic origins. The impact of the French and Haitian revolutions is thus not a good principle for typologizing slave revolts. The Africans' familiarity with slavery outside the context of European domination and the creoles' greater access to news and exposure to European culture provide a rationale for why African and creole slaves might have responded differently to the message of the French Revolution. Moreover, when slave insurgents did speak the language of general emancipation it was usually embedded in a traditionalist not a bourgeois-democratic discourse.

NOTES

1. Michael Craton, *Testing the Chains: Resistance to Slavery in the British West Indies* (Ithaca: Cornell University Press, 1982); "The Passion to Exist: Slave Rebellions in the British West Indies, 1629–1832," *Journal of Caribbean History* 13 (1980): 1–20; "Proto-Peasant Revolts? The Late Slave Rebellions in the British West Indies, 1816–1832," *Past & Present* 85 (November 1979): 99–125.

2. Eugene Genovese, *From Rebellion to Revolution: Afro-American Slave Revolts in the Making of the Modern World* (Baton Rouge: Louisiana State University Press, 1979). Michael Mullin, *Africa in America: Slave Acculturation and Resistance in the American South and the British Caribbean, 1736–1831* (Urbana: University of Illinois Press, 1992), offers a model that blends both approaches.

3. David Geggus, *Slave Resistance Studies and the Saint Domingue Slave Revolt* (Miami: Florida International University, 1983); "The Enigma of Jamaica in the 1790s: New Light on the Causation of Slave Rebellions," *William & Mary Quarterly* 44 (April 1987): 274–299; "The Causation of Slave Rebellions: An Overview," *Indian Historical Review* 15 (1987–1988): 116–129; "The French and Haitian Revolutions and Resistance to Slavery in the Americas: An Overview," *Revue Française d'Histoire d'Outre-Mer* 76 (1989): 107–124; chap. 1 in this volume.

4. Geggus, "French and Haitian Revolutions"; chap. 1, table.

5. *De la Révolution française aux révolutions créoles et nègres,* ed. Michel Martin and Alain Yacou (Paris: Editions Caraibéennes, 1989), p. 10 (my translation). Cf. Alain Yacou, "Esclaves et libres français à Cuba au lendemain de la Révolution française," *Jahrbuch für Geschichte von Staat, Wirtschaft und Gesellschaft Lateinamerikas* 28 (1991): 167; Alain Yacou, "Le projet des révoltes serviles de l'Ile de Cuba dans la première moitié du XIXe siècle," *Revue du CERC* (Guadeloupe) 1 (1984): 51. The Boca Nigua revolt in fact took place in 1796. On the revolt at Aguadilla, Puerto Rico, see n. 24.

6. David Eltis, *Economic Growth and the Ending of the Transatlantic Slave Trade* (New York: Oxford University Press, 1987), p. 245; Kenneth Kiple, *Blacks in Colonial Cuba, 1774–1899* (Gainesville: University of Florida Press, 1976), appendix.

7. This high sex ratio of Cuban slave imports probably had material and cultural causes—the bringing of new land into cultivation and Spanish ideas about gender roles. The 1789 slave code, for example, forbade women slaves doing "men's work" and decreed that slave men and women should live and work separately.

8. José Luciano Franco, *Las Minas de Santiago del Prado y la rebelión de los Cobreros, 1530–1800* (Havana: Editorial de Ciencias Sociales, 1975), pp. 58–63;

José Luciano Franco, *Los Palenques de los negros Cimarrones* (Havana: Colección Historia, 1973), pp. 57–87.

9. Julius Scott, "The Common Wind: Currents of Afro-American Communication in the Era of the Haitian Revolution," Ph.D. diss., Duke University, 1986, pp. 151.

10. Geggus, "Enigma of Jamaica," 295–296.

11. Alain Yacou, "Esclaves et libres," and "La présence française dans la partie occidentale de l'Ile de Cuba au lendemain de la Révolution de Saint-Domingue," *Revue Française d'Histoire d'Outre-Mer* 84 (1987): 149–188.

12. Overbrook Seminary, Philadelphia, Rodrigue Papers, box 1, 2/17, Lalanne to D'Orlic, 2 June 1794; Angel Sanz Tapia, *Los Militares emigrados y los prisonieros franceses en Venezuela durante la guerra contra la revolución francesa* (Caracas: Instituto Panamericano de Geografía e Historia, 1977), p. 147.

13. Archivo General de Indias, Sevilla [hereafter, AGI], Estado 14/98, letter by Governor Las Casas, 12 November 1794.

14. Two accounts of the event, written a month apart, survive in Spanish archives: AGI, Ultramar 312, governor of Puerto Príncipe [Afonso de Viana] to Luis de Las Casas, 14 July 1795; AGI, Estado 5/15, Las Casas to Eugenio Llaguno, 18 August 1795, enclosing a report of 14 August by Antonio Marejón y Gato. Various details suggest the latter was the more accurate of the two. The distance from town to plantation was sixteen leagues. The "quatre lieues" in Yacou, "Révolution française," p. 35, is a mistake, as is the date (7 April 1795) there given, so too the implied date (1796) given in Yacou, "Esclaves et libres," p. 167, and "La présence française à Puerto Príncipe de Cuba (Camaguey): Flux et reflux 1791–1809," *Revue du CERC* 4 (1987): 106.

15. Censuses of 1774 and 1792, in Kiple, *Blacks in Colonial Cuba,* appendix.

16. French emigration to the region during the 1790s seems to have been almost nonexistent, though some French had settled there before the Revolution; see Yacou, "Présence française à Puerto Príncipe," pp. 105–106.

17. This appears in the first source, the local governor's summary account, but not the second (see n. 14), which contains no mention of equality.

18. The governor's version has Recio being knocked down prior to the attempt to burn the house, the implications being more damaging for the slaves and more exculpatory for Recio. It conflicts, however, with Marejón y Gato's more detailed report.

19. The first source (see n. 14) mentions "all the slave-drivers and whites of the district," but the second is more specific.

20. The statement in José Luciano Franco, *Ensayos históricos* (Havana: Editorial de Ciencias Sociales, 1974), p. 133, that Serapio left none alive seems without foundation.

21. Yacou, "Révolution française," p. 35, renders the Spanish "para ir sublevar los negros de las haciendas vecinas atraéndoles con la libertad e igualdad que habían de gozar en lo succesivo" as "avec le dessein d'aller soulever les ateliers des propriétés voisines. Ils parviennent assez vite à leurs fins: Les mots de liberté et égalité ont dans leur bouche assez d'attrait pour séduire un grand nombre de leurs congénères."

22. Yacou, "Projet des révoltes," pp. 51–52.

23. See chap. 1.

24. See chap. 1. Guillermo Baralt, *Esclavos rebeldes: Conspiraciones y sublevaciones de esclavos en Puerto Rico* (Rio Piedras: Ed. Huracán, 1981), pp. 16–19, dates the Aguadilla rebellion in Puerto Rico to October 1795, but it clearly took place earlier in the year, almost certainly before August 6. Beyond this,

however, almost nothing is known about it, because the administration failed to investigate it. The island governor wrote only of an "insurrección intentada por algunos negros": AGI, Estado 10/1, Ramón de Castro to Príncipe de la Paz, 22 January 1796.

25. Scott, "Common Wind," p. 23. The free status of the Cobreros was eventually recognized in 1800.

26. Franco, *Ensayos históricos*, p. 99.

27. AGI, Ultramar 312, letter of 9 April 1796. Yacou, "Révolution française," p. 37, assumes the slave had been recently sold by a French refugee, and he does not mention the deportation proclamation.

28. See n. 34. No details were given.

29. AGI, Ultramar 312, "Noticias acaecidas en la villa de Puerto del Príncipe el día 12 de junio de 1798." According to the first news to reach the town, it seemed about fifty slaves were in rebellion, but this apparently proved an exaggeration.

30. Franco, *Ensayos históricos*, p. 133. On plantation size, see Alexander von Humboldt, *The Island of Cuba* (New York: Derby and Jackson, 1856), p. 195; on plantation numbers, see Manuel Moreno Fraginals, *The Sugarmill: The Socioeconomic Complex of Sugar in Cuba* (New York, 1976), p. 69.

31. However, the Saint Domingue slave revolt also broke out two days prematurely; David Geggus, "La cérémonie du Bois Caïman," *Chemins Critiques* (Port-au-Prince) 2 (1992): 66–67.

32. Three cases were held over for further investigation, one of the accused being missing. I assumed that Marcial and Manuel Carabalí, listed in different parts of the trial summary, were the same person.

33. Seven were Carabalí (a term applied narrowly to Ijaw and broadly to all peoples from Biafra); two were Mandinga; one Congo; two Mina (Akan?); two Ganga and one Arará (Aja or Ewe).

34. AGI, Ultramar 312, letter of 19 May 1796.

35. Yacou, "Révolution française," p. 38.

36. Yacou, "Projet des révoltes," p. 52; Alain Yacou, "Le péril haïtien à Cuba: De la révolution nègre à la reconnaissance de l'Indépendance (1791–1825)," *Chemins Critiques* 2 (1992): 85; Franco, *Ensayos históricos*, pp. 133–134; and see nn. 20 and 40.

37. See n. 34.

38. See n. 34.

39. Archivo General de Simancas, Guerra Moderna 6855, reports dated 15, 20, 21 April 1799, enclosed in Miguel Soler to Antonio Cornel, 17 March 1800 (copies kindly supplied by Allan J. Kuethe). The revolt on the Calvo estate in Güines in October 1798 lasted less than one day and involved no violence or destruction. Though described by Yacou as a revolt, the temporary flight of thirty-eight men from the Peñalver estate in August 1798 was a ploy to get an abusive manager dismissed, and it succeeded. A similar attempt on the Ponce de León plantation in February 1799 failed. The packaging of these reports together with copies of all the Puerto Príncipe material by the Havana consulado in April 1799 strongly suggests this was the total number of incidents then known to the administration.

40. Yacou, "Révolution française," pp. 37–38; and see n. 36. Franco, *Ensayos históricos*, p. 134, also calls the Trinidad affair a revolt, and places it in December.

41. See n. 34.

42. Franco, *Ensayos históricos*, p. 156.

43. María Rosario Sevilla Soler, *Santo Domingo: Tierra de frontera (1750–1800)*

(Sevilla: EEHA, 1980); Frank Moya Pons, *Historia colonial de Santo Domingo* (Santiago: Universidad Católica de Madre y Maestra, 1977); Rubén Silié, *Economía, esclavitud y población* (Santo Domingo: Universidad Autónoma de Santo Domingo, 1976).

44. This paragraph is based on AGI, Audiencia de Santo Domingo, 954–957, 1089, etc., and Archivo General de Simancas, Valladolid, Guerra Moderna, 7157–7159. The best published account is Antonio del Monte y Tejada, *Historia de Santo Domingo* (Santo Domingo: Amigos del País, 1890), vols. 3 and 4. For brief published accounts, see Sevilla Soler, *Santo Domingo,* chap. 10; Carlos Esteban Deive, *Los guerrilleros negros* (Santo Domingo: Fundación Cultural Dominicana, 1989), pp. 203–213; David Geggus, "The Great Powers and the Haitian Revolution," in *Tordesillas y sus consecuencias,* (Madrid: Iberoamericana, 1995), ed. Berndt Schröter and Karin Schüller, pp. 114–122.

45. This was not purely a product of the revolutionary situation. The Spanish government valued even undeveloped Trinidad, Puerto Rico, and Florida more than Santo Domingo, and in the peace negotiations ending the American War of Independence it had been willing to cede Santo Domingo to either England or France, though neither power displayed interest in the colony. See *Documentos relativos a la independencia de Norteamérica existentes en archivos españoles* (Madrid: Ministerio de Asuntos Exteriores, 1981), vol. 6, pp. 415–418, 438–443, 447; José Luciano Franco, *Revoluciones y conflictos en el Caribe, 1789–1854* (Havana: Academia de Ciencias, 1965), pp. 5–6. In 1795, the French would have preferred Louisiana to Santo Domingo.

46. Although insisting that the local slaves remained unmoved by French attempts to stir them up and that "they detest[ed] their doctrine and fraternity," the regent of the Audiencia had already thought it prudent to propose a gradual emancipation program (freeing slaves after twenty-five years' service) to counteract French influence; Universidad Católica de Madre y Maestra, Santiago (D.R.), Colección Inchaústegui (typescripts), Urizar to Alcudia, 25 June 1795.

47. Carlos Esteban Deive, *Las Emigraciones dominicanas a Cuba (1795–1808)* (Santo Domingo: Fundación Cultural Dominicana, 1989), pp. 16–17.

48. Deive, *Emigraciones,* pp. 36–44, 132, appears to underestimate the volume of emigration. Cf. AGI, Estado 5a/28 and 61, Estado 13/19. Estimates of the total population in 1795 vary between 70,000 and 180,000: Sevilla Soler, *Santo Domingo,* p. 36; Deive, *Emigraciones,* pp. 19, 131; José Antonio Saco, *Historia de la esclavitud,* (Havana, 1938), vol. 3, p. 32. Deive's "90,000" seems a reasonable guess, but see also Moya Pons, *Historia colonial.*

49. The only African mentioned in these proceedings, José Nago, refused to join the conspiracy; Archivo General de la Nación, Santo Domingo, Fotocopías de Documentos en el Archivo Nacional de Cuba, vol. 4, doc. 43. The main published account is Carlos Esteban Deive, *La Esclavitud en Santo Domingo* (Santo Domingo: Museo del Hombre Dominicano, 1980), vol. 2, pp. 469–471. Nowadays part of Haiti, Hinche and the central savanna then belonged to Santo Domingo.

50. Among the booty taken from Saint Domingue plantations, Jean-François and Biassou sold slaves, chiefly women and children, in their trading with the Spanish; Thomas Madiou, *Histoire d'Haïti* (1847; Port-au-Prince: Fardin, 1989), vol. 1, p. 182.

51. However, as the republicans did not espouse General Emancipation until August 1793, Jean-François's alliance with Spain was not initially as reactionary as it now seems. Moreover, his massacre of 700 French colonists at Fort Dauphin in July 1794 effectively prevented the restoration of slavery in Spanish-occupied Saint Domingue.

52. Emilio Rodríguez Demorizi, *Cesión de Santo Domingo à Francia* (Ciudad Trujillo: Ed. Montalvo, 1958), p. 75. The governor of Havana therefore prevented his disembarkation, and he proceeded to pensioned retirement in Spain. In 1812, after his death, rumors of his return were utilized in the conspiracy of the free black craftsman José Antonio Aponte; Franco, *Ensayos históricos,* pp. 125–190.

53. Madiou, *Histoire d'Haïti* (Port au Prince: Département de l'Instruction Publique, 1922), vol. 1, p. 490; Geggus, "French and Haitian Revolutions," pp. 116–119; David Geggus, "From His Most Catholic Majesty to the Godless Republic: the 'Volte-Face' of Toussaint Louverture and the Ending of Slavery in Saint Domingue," *Revue Française d'Histoire d'Outre-Mer,* 65 (1978): 481–499.

54. A second conspiracy occurred early in 1795 in Samaná on the north coast of Santo Domingo. It involved three white Frenchmen, seven blacks, and a cache of arms. This time the governor wanted exemplary sentences, but the Audiencia again showed what he considered to be lenience; Deive, *Esclavitud,* vol. 2, p. 471.

55. See Michael Craton, *Sinews of Empire* (New York: Anchor, 1974), p. 343; David Geggus, "Sugar and Coffee Cultivation in Saint Domingue and the Shaping of the Slave Labor Force," in *Cultivation and Culture: Labor and the Shaping of Afro-American Culture,* ed. Ira Berlin and Philip Morgan (Charlottesville: University Press of Virginia, 1993), table 1.

56. It was apparently still a ranch in the early 1780s. See Antonio Sánchez Valverde, *Idea del valor de la isla Española* [1785], ed. Cipriano de Utrera and Emiliano Rodríguez Demorizi (Santo Domingo: Editora Nacional, 1971), pp. 113–114; Médéric-Louis-Elie Moreau de Saint-Méry, *Topographical and Political Description of the Spanish Part of Saint-Domingo* (Philadelphia: The Author, 1796), vol. 1, pp. 108–111. The slave driver was African; and of the adult slaves whose origins can be identified very few were creoles.

57. For example, Piti Juan, Raimundo Diamant, Pedro Viejo alias Papa Pier. Hispanization may have disguised many others. Despite the 1777 extradition treaty and laws offering fugitive foreign slaves freedom, runaways from Saint Domingue were often reenslaved by Spanish colonists; Silié, *Economía,* p. 84. During the revolution many fled to Spanish territory and worked for colonists or lived as maroons. In June 1793 the governor decreed that they be sold to Spanish buyers; Archivo General de la Nación, Santo Domingo, Archivo Real de Higüey, legajo 22/52.

58. Archives Nationales, Section d'Outre-Mer, Aix-en-Provence, Notariat de Saint-Domingue, alphabetical index. As early as 1783, the plantation manager had requested permission to import 400 slaves; Carlos Larrazábal Blanco, *Los Negros y la esclavitud en Santo Domingo* (Santo Domingo: Ed. Postigo, 1967), pp. 56, 60. Jamaica supplied many slaves to Santo Domingo; see Frances Armytage, *The Free Port System in the British West Indies* (London: Longmans, Green, 1953), p. 64, and Herbert Klein, *The Middle Passage: Comparative Studies in the Atlantic Slave Trade* (Princeton: Princeton University Press, 1978), pp. 154–155. However, only one of the Boca Nigua slaves was identified as "Inglés."

59. These were the governor's words; see n. 61.

60. Médéric-Louis-Elie Moreau de Saint-Méry, *Description topographique . . . de l'isle Saint-Domingue* [1797], ed. E. Taillemite and B. Maurel (Paris: Société de l'Histoire des Colonies Françaises, 1958), vol. 3, p. 1355.

61. AGI, Estado 16/12, Bravo to García y Moreno, 21 December 1796; Estado 5/202, García y Moreno to Príncipe de la Paz, 31 December 1796; Estado 11/59, Portillo y Torres to Príncipe de la Paz, 12 January 1797; Estado 13/32, "Testimonio de las sentencias," 3 December 1796.

62. The British occupation of the west and south was then at its height, and the position of the republicans and the remaining black auxiliaries was precarious; David Geggus, *Slavery, War and Revolution: The British Occupation of Saint Domingue, 1793–1798* (Oxford: Clarendon Press, 1982), chap. 8.

63. Geggus, "Sugar and Coffee," table 8. One should note, however, that the intermediary who approached Tomás was not one of the two leaders but Simon, whose ethnic affiliation is unknown.

64. Here I follow Manuel Bravo's account, which is quite explicit. The governor's account refers to two women but is more vague.

65. The plantation armory was broken open only the next day. Hence, when the governor stated the slaves used its weapons in the attack, he may have been covering up for Oyarzábal's allowing the slaves to have guns for hunting.

66. Tomás Congo claimed Francisco had participated in the attack.

67. Owned or managed by Gabriel Collar, a former employee of Oyarzábal, the plantation was presumably on the site of the present town of San Cristóbal, some five miles from the coast.

68. The governor's account says "enslave or kill."

69. Roger Bastide, *African Civilizations in the New World* (New York: Harper & Row, 1971), p. 182; Lucien Peytraud, *L'Esclavage aux Antilles françaises avant 1789* (Paris: Hachette, 1897), p. 182.

70. David Barry Gaspar, *Bondmen and Rebels: A Study of Master-Slave Relations in Antigua* (Baltimore: Johns Hopkins University Press, 1985), chap. 11; Ulysses S. Ricard, Jr., "The Pointe Coupée Slave Conspiracy of 1791," in *Proceedings of the Fifteenth Meeting of the French Colonial Historical Society*, ed. Patricia Galloway and Philip Boucher (Lanham: University Press of America, 1992), p. 119; Lionel Fraser, *History of Trinidad* (Port of Spain, 1891–1896), vol. 1, pp. 269–272; *After Africa*, ed. Roger D. Abrahams and John F. Szwed (New Haven: Yale University Press, 1983), p. 297; Mullin, *Africa in America*, p. 251. A duke and a captain-general headed the 1809 conspiracy in Jamaica; George W. Bridges, *The Annals of Jamaica* (London: Murray, 1828), vol. 2, pp. 292–293.

71. *General Advertiser* (Philadelphia) October 11 and November 10, 1791; David Geggus, *The Saint Domingue Slave Revolt and the Rise of Toussaint Louverture*, forthcoming.

72. John K. Thornton, "African Dimensions of the Stono Rebellion," *American Historical Review* 96 (October 1991): 1112. For an unsympathetic description of warfare among the Kongo, see Louis Degrandpré, *Voyage à la côte occidentale de l'Afrique* (Paris, 1797), vol. 1, pp. 136–141. The latter wrote, "they forget the enemy and think only of dancing to drums, and spend the night in rejoicing till morning, worrying very little what the enemy will do" (my translation).

73. This is another reason to suppose the work force was largely African.

74. Their arms and legs were cut off and nailed up in public places in the city; their heads were sent back to the plantation for display. The body of Estevan the blacksmith, who died in hospital, was treated similarly.

75. AGI, Estado 11/1, Portillo y Torres to Príncipe de La Paz, 15 October 1796.

76. AGI, Estado 13/30, Urizar to Príncipe de La Paz, 1 November 1796.

77. Deive, *Guerrilleros*, p. 223.

78. The phrasing was "su libertad general" not "la libertad general."

79. Juan José Andreu Ocariz, "La Rebelión de los esclavos de Boca Nigua," *Anuario de Estudios Americanos* 27 (1970): 558. Deive, *Esclavitud*, vol. 2, pp. 471–474, relies on this article.

80. However, in 1801 (by when Pedro Abadia, the distiller, was the largest

slaveowner in the capital city) an ex-slave army from Saint Domingue invaded Santo Domingo and, temporarily, brought slavery to an end. Toussaint Louverture negotiated the colonists' final surrender on the Boca Nigua estate itself. Shortly afterward, local slaves killed and disemboweled Gabriel Collar, the plantation steward, hanging his intestines round his neck in grisly parody of the execution of four years before. See Emilio Rodríguez Demorizi, *Las Invasiones haitianas de 1801, 1805 y 1822* (Ciudad Trujillo: Editora del Caribe, 1955), pp. 80, 130, 242.

81. Such a rationale might have been more compelling where a transfer of power had not been made but could be envisaged as possible, as in the contemporary slave plots in the former French colonies of Louisiana (1795) and Tobago (1801); Geggus, "French and Haitian Revolutions," p. 115.

82. See n. 5. Franco, *Palenques,* p. 42, presents a similar view.

83. See n. 78.

84. Monica Schuler, "Ethnic Slave Rebellions in the Caribbean and the Guianas," *Journal of Social History* 3 (1970): 374–385. The 1791 Mina conspiracy in Louisiana is another example; Ricard, "Pointe Coupée," pp. 116–129.

85. Jorge Dominguez, *Insurrection or Loyalty: The Breakdown of the Spanish American Empire* (Cambridge: Harvard University Press, 1980), p. 55. Historians of the great Tupac Amarú rebellion of 1781 confront similar problems; see *Resistance, Rebellion, and Consciousness in the Andean Peasant World,* ed. Steve Stern (Madison: University of Wisconsin Press, 1988), chaps. 2–4.

6

Rebellion and Royalism in Spanish Florida
The French Revolution on Spain's Northern Colonial Frontier

JANE G. LANDERS

The French Revolution and its Haitian counterpart had serious political and economic consequences in Spanish Florida, a colony which was still struggling to stabilize after the turmoil of the American Revolution.[1] Alarmed by republican ideology emanating from France, the governors of Spanish Florida, like their counterparts throughout the greater Caribbean, attempted to quarantine the colony by forbidding the introduction of French ideas, books, and citizens, or of slaves originating from French possessions.[2] Despite these efforts, Florida was unable to avoid the contagion, and in 1795 it experienced a French-inspired invasion which resulted in the destruction of valuable plantations, the dislocation of landholders and slaves, political dissension created by sedition trials, and a weakened frontier which, thereafter, was subject to chronic encroachment.[3]

Florida also felt the impact of the French and Haitian revolutions when it received a band of the Black Auxiliaries of Carlos IV from Santo Domingo. These men were seasoned by war against French planters, French and British troops, and their own countrymen, and well acquainted with "dangerous notions" of liberty, equality, and fraternity.[4] The auxiliaries caused consternation not only among the Spanish governors who reluctantly received them but also among the Anglo planters on Florida's borders, who were already disturbed by Spain's racial policies and its reliance on black militias.[5] At a time when slave conspiracies and rebellions, maroon settlements, and Indian war unsettled the southeastern frontier, this new black presence seemed particularly threatening. Ultimately the Spaniards' dependence upon armed black forces contributed to a series of invasions sponsored by the United States and to U.S. acquisition of Florida.[6]

Florida had long held a strategic importance for Spain which outweighed its rather poor (from a European perspective) material and human resources. Originally colonized to prevent French settlement and to protect the rich mines of New Spain and the route of Spain's laden galleons, Florida later served as a buffer against English and, ultimately, United States expansionism. Florida's peninsular conformation provided Spain with ports on both the Atlantic and the Gulf coasts and proximity to key port cities in Cuba, Hispaniola, and Mexico. Its very geography, however, also made Florida attractive and vulnerable to competing European powers with Caribbean interests. Despite repeated challenges to Florida's sovereignty, Spain managed to maintain its tenuous hold on the province from 1565 to 1763. However, at the end of the Anglo-French Seven Years' War, Spain was forced to ransom Havana with Florida, evacuate its colonists to Cuba and Mexico, and cede the province to Britain.

British occupation greatly altered Florida's economic and social development. The new governor and other wealthy investors developed large plantations and imported indentured labor from the Mediterranean and slave labor from Africa.[7] Florida experienced even more dramatic economic and demographic growth during the American Revolution when loyalist refugees from South Carolina and Georgia immigrated with their slaves.[8] A number of these Anglo planters remained in Florida after the colony was retroceded to Spain in 1784, and others were encouraged to immigrate when Spain adopted a generous land grant policy six years later.[9] Moreover, hundreds of slaves belonging to the departing British took advantage of the chaos of the war for American independence and the colonial transfer to escape and claim the religious sanctuary Spain first established in Florida in the seventeenth century.[10] When Spain regained Florida, the returning Spaniards found themselves in the minority in their own colony. Their aggressive and unhappy northern neighbors bitterly contested Florida's fugitive slave policy and resented its friendship with the Creek nation, whose lands they coveted.[11] Spanish administrators rightly feared the Anglos' land hunger and hoped the Indian nations would serve as a buffer to Florida. Governor Vicente Manuel de Zéspedes understood the colony's vulnerable position and complained incessantly to Spain about crumbling defenses, irregular receipt of the government subsidy, and the poor quality of his troops.[12]

The unstable frontier and heterogeneous population made it almost impossible for Zéspedes's successor, Juan Nepomuceno de Quesada, who took office in 1790, to quarantine the colony from the effects of the French Revolution. Quesada received instructions from Spain to screen carefully materials and persons entering the province and to forbid the importation of slaves from French possessions. Although he did his best to comply, Florida was a difficult area to monitor. Long stretches of coastline lay beyond the control of the government located in Saint Augustine, and even the sparsely populated areas surrounding the capital were laced with waterways which provided easy access into the province. Saint Augustine was North America's largest Atlantic port south of Charleston and its cosmopolitan citizenry had many trade connections with the United States, Great Britain, and the Caribbean. News as dramatic as the French Revolution and the largest slave revolt in the history of the Americas at Saint Domingue could not be contained. David Geggus has shown that less than a month after the slave uprising in Saint Domingue, slaves in nearby Jamaica had created songs about the event.[13] There is little doubt that slaves in other circum-Caribbean locations such as Florida would also have had access to the information. Refugees from the revolt in Saint Domingue who passed through or remained in Spanish Florida also provided firsthand accounts, which would have spread rapidly. In addition, Florida merchants, ship captains, and crews traveled frequently to ports such as Cap Français in Saint Domingue and Charleston, where the latest news was traded along with goods.[14]

Floridians quickly learned of the arrival of Edmond Charles Genet, first minister of the French Republic to the United States, in Charleston in 1793. Before taking up his post in Philadelphia, Genet enlisted the French consul to North Carolina, South Carolina, and Georgia in a grand scheme to liberate French and Spanish American colonies from Canada to Mexico. Part of Genet's plan included financing an army to free Florida from Spain's monarchical rule. Genet left Consul Mangourit in charge of the Florida plot and gave him letters of marque to provide naval support for the venture. "The Revolutionary Legion of the Floridas" was soon a reality.[15]

By the spring of 1793, Spain and France were at war, and despite Spain's protests, French warships repeatedly sailed from American ports to attack Spanish vessels. Such blatant violations of President Washington's neutrality orders alienated the last of Genet's supporters, and, finally, Thomas Jefferson was forced to request his recall. Georgia and South Carolina officials who had once assisted Genet and Mangourit became alarmed at their possible culpability and tried to stop the planned invasion of Florida.[16] South Carolina officials seized documents which required commanders and officers of the Florida invasion force to become French citizens. The proposals for enlistment further stated that

East Florida will be considered as a part of the French Republic during the continuation of the war, and as such remains under its immediate protection. At the conclusion of the war, the said country is to become independent to all intents and purposes, with the proviso of adopting a strictly democratical republican government, and the Rights of Man to form the basis of their constitution.[17]

Mangourit wrote Genet's successor, Jean Fauchet, that "we wait only for the fleet and Florida is ours, and the tree of liberty will grow everywhere." Charleston's *City Gazette and Daily Advertiser* featured a long letter addressed to the "Citizens of America" and signed "Republican" which made references to "just and natural rights" and encouraged enlistment in the Florida invasion. "Spain, that proud, that jealous, that indolent nation, is very sensible that she must soon lose the Floridas," it read, and the author assured the readers that "the service you will render posterity by assisting the French in their struggle for liberty will animate the latter, and the former will erect eternal monuments to your praise."[18] By this time, even French officials had become alarmed at the rashness of the Florida venture and attempted to squash it, but the plot had already acquired a momentum of its own.[19] Spain's consul in Charleston kept Governor Quesada apprised of all the rumors of invasion, and Quesada, in turn, informed Spain's representatives in Philadelphia and his immediate superior, the captain general of Cuba, Luis de Las Casas. Quesada had reason to be alarmed. Florida's garrison was chronically undermanned, and the Cuban Third Battalion which provided detachments for Florida consisted largely of deserters, incorrigibles, and other ne'er-do-wells. Quesada depicted his dilemma graphically when he wrote to Las Casas that "half of the soldiers of the Third Battalion are capable of lending a hand to any misdeed and of uniting to flee the province ... and ... together with the Negro fugitives from the United States, who are very detrimental here, and many discontented slaves, convert the province into a theater of horrors."[20]

The troops were not only less than first rate, they had also gone more than a year without pay, and desertions were common. Las Casas, however, was at first reluctant to assign costly assistance to Florida. Forced to rely on the means at hand, Quesada rushed to strengthen provincial defenses. He called on all male citizens over the age of fourteen to report for military duty. All citizens owning slaves were required to present them for paid labor on the fortifications, and a unit of these slaves was organized and trained to man the cannons and relieve the artillery in case of attack.[21]

Despite the governor's stated horror of "detrimental" fugitive and "discontented" slaves, he needed all hands in this emergency. He ordered free blacks to report for paid militia service or be sentenced to three months of shackled and unpaid labor on public works. One propertied member of the free community of color, the merchant Juan Bautista Collins, failed to report on time and even though he was the first sergeant of the free black militia, he was imprisoned on the governor's orders. His mother appealed to the governor's mercy, claiming her son had been away and did not read the notice to report for duty. Although the imprisoned Collins asked permission to enlist, the governor instead sentenced him to hard (and menial) labor on the fortifications as an example to the "rest of his class."[22]

Most of the blacks who reported for duty were former slaves from British colonies to the north who had been granted freedom in Spanish Florida. This free black militia of about fifty men operated land and river patrols on the northern frontier and proved to be a most effective force for the Spaniards. They had their own sergeants, but ultimate command remained with white officers, who were linked to the African community in a number of ways, including kinship.[23] These community connections and the sanctuary available to fugitive slaves in Florida deprived the invaders of support that French Jacobins successfully employed in other areas of the Caribbean, such as Grenada and Saint Vincent.[24]

Early in 1794 Quesada arrested a group of suspected traitors, several of whom carried French commissions, recruitment guidelines, and other incriminating evidence. They were promptly sent off to prison in Havana's Morro Castle, and Cuban authorities began to take the threat of French invasion seriously. The captain general sent troops from Catalonia, Mexico, and Cuba to reinforce the Florida garrison. Some of these units had been destined for Saint Domingue.[25]

Quesada suspected many more might be involved in the republican plot and began to interrogate members of the community. The Revolutionary Legion of the Floridas finally attacked in the summer of 1795, capturing two outlying batteries north of Saint Augustine. With resources stretched thin, Quesada ordered all citizens to remove south of the Saint Johns River. Then, to their great dismay and anger and against the recommendations of his advisors, the governor resorted to a scorched-earth policy, ordering that all the plantations north of that perimeter be burned. As a result he alienated Florida's most important landowners and ruined the most productive plantations in the colony. The political and economic effects were catastrophic.[26]

In August 1795 some of the free black militiamen and allied Indians helped in a Spanish naval assault which retook the occupied riverine posts. Other black militiamen patrolled the southern frontier near Matanzas, allowing Spanish troops to remain near the city. As Florida's earlier governors had discovered, the freed black allies, who had the most to lose should an invasion of unhappy slaveholders succeed, proved to be among Spain's most effective troops. Quesada later commended all the militias and even noted the contributions of "the excellent company of free Negroes."[27] The governor's conflicting opinions about the free blacks of Florida reflected the dilemma faced by Spaniards throughout the Caribbean. Although they frequently disparaged blacks, Spanish administrators depended upon them to maintain a tenuous sovereignty which was under almost constant attack in the eighteenth century. Faced with a chronic shortage of worthy regular troops and inadequate financial and material resources, governors in Spanish Florida repeatedly relied on their black forces. Spain's necessity created opportunities for blacks, who parlayed initiative and military skills into free status. As Africans did throughout the Caribbean, black Floridians became adept at reading the political tides, and they pursued pragmatically their best options during international conflicts. Royalism suited them when the threat of rebel slaveholders loomed.

The 1795 invasion proved a short-lived fiasco. After a series of trials, some of the leaders were imprisoned in the Castillo de San Marcos at Saint Augustine and others served time in Cuba's Morro Castle. All were ultimately pardoned. Despite its comic-opera overtones, however, this episode left lasting scars on Florida. The community had endured almost two years of tense anticipation. In that highly charged atmosphere, suspicion and distrust flourished. Neighbor turned on neighbor; race relations were poisoned; the government suffered a leadership crisis during the invasion; flourishing plantations were burned; pitiful gangs of slaves belonging to sentenced rebels languished and died in embargo; embittered Anglos departed the province with everything they could take; and misery and hardship were widespread. A series of investigations and sedition trials went on for three more years, during which the government confiscated and sold at public auction ten plantations and much property seized from sentenced rebels. While this enabled some Spanish citizens to acquire holdings they may not otherwise have been able to afford, it also discouraged any further capital investment in the colony, and Florida's recovery from the debacle proved to be painfully slow.[28]

Although the immediate threat had passed, the French Revolution as played out in Saint Domingue continued to affect Florida. Only a year after the failed invasion and to the great consternation of Governor Quesada, one of the main figures in the slave revolt against the French,

General Jorge (i.e. Georges) Biassou, caudillo of the Black Auxiliaries of Carlos IV in Santo Domingo, took up residence in Florida with some twenty-five of his followers.[29] Biassou was born to slave parents at Cap Français in Saint Domingue and became the slave of the Fathers of Charity near Le Cap. He rose from slavery to become the self-titled "viceroy of the conquered territories," outranking the more famous Toussaint Louverture, who was his aide and physician to the army Biassou commanded. Biassou was infamous for his alleged fondness for drink and use of *vodun*, as well as his ferocity in battle, but he was also a skilled commander who maintained strict discipline in his untrained and polyglot army, which at its peak numbered 40,000 men.[30]

Biassou and his comrades had early realized their material limitations and, in what C. L. R. James described as "Judas work," offered peace in exchange for their own freedom and the recognition of political rights promised by the French Assembly. The reactionary planters of Saint Domingue rudely rejected their offer, so the bloody fighting continued. When England and Spain went to war with France, both powers courted the rebels. Biassou, Jean-François, and Toussaint accepted the Spanish offer of alliance. Designated the Black Auxiliaries of Carlos IV, they were decorated with gold medals bearing the likeness of the king and presented with documents expressing the gratitude and confidence of the Spanish government. Newly supplied, armed, and dressed and under a Spanish flag, Biassou's forces fought many bloody battles against the French.[31]

However, when the French Assembly abolished slavery, Toussaint broke with Biassou and the Spaniards to offer his services and loyalty to the French Republic. Biassou remained loyal to Spain, thereby losing his chance at a more significant place in history. Before long, Biassou was losing battles against his former aide.[32] Ironically, the very French planters who had once refused to treat with him now hoped for Biassou's success and praised him as one "whose conduct merited general admiration."[33]

Spanish forces withdrew from the fighting in 1795 when the king of Spain and the Directory of the French Republic concluded a peace treaty. By its terms Spain ceded its eastern portion of Hispaniola to the French; the Black Auxiliaries of Carlos IV were disbanded and evacuated from the island. In a "confidential" report to the captain-general of Cuba, the governor of Bayajá expressed his indignation at having had to obey orders to deal with "perfect equality" with the blacks. Now that the war had ended, he felt that such "shameful and perhaps, dangerous indulgences" should also end. He recommended that the Crown abolish black employment and titles immediately. Bothered by the auxiliaries' "pretensions to superiority," he argued that he had seen evidence of their fury, and "although they paint themselves with other colors, they are the same who murdered their owners, violated their wives, and destroyed all those with property."[34]

This confidential report also gives insight into the politics of the auxiliaries. The governor of Bayajá told the leaders they would have to evacuate because the French Republic did not find their presence "compatible," but he urged the "simple soldiers" to remain, as they had been offered freedom by both the French Republic and Spain. The black armies wanted, instead, to maintain their units, ranks, salaries, and rations and embark together for some designated place where they should be given lands to cultivate and be permitted to form a town. They argued that they would then constitute a ready force, able to fight for the king wherever he should care to send them. There was, in fact, royal precedent for this. In 1763 the free black militia and town of Gracia Real de Santa Teresa de Mose outside Saint Augustine in Florida, also composed of former slaves, was evacuated en masse to Cuba, granted homesteads together, and allowed to retain their militia titles.

Despite the governor's opposition, "a considerable number" of soldiers embarked with their leaders for Havana, where, the governor claimed, they expected "the same distinctions, prerogatives, luxury, and excessive tolerance" they had in Bayajá. He assured the captain general of Cuba that he never promised the "venomous vipers" they would be allowed to remain in Havana.[35]

Other Spaniards echoed his racial sentiments. The governor of Santo Domingo, Joaquín García, had once written glowing reports about the exploits of the "valiant warriors" he decorated in the king's name, but as soon as the fighting ceased, he shipped them to Havana. He knew full well their capabilities. The unfortunate troops were not even given time to dispose of their property or settle family affairs.[36] Before leaving Santo Domingo, however, the embittered Biassou lodged a formal complaint against García and urged his dismissal.[37]

Cuba's captain general, Luis de las Casas, was no more anxious than the governors of Bayajá and Santo Domingo to have a large number of unemployed, armed, and experienced "wolves," as they were now referred to, on his hands. A hastily convoked war council decided to deport the black armies, using as their authority the royal order forbidding the introduction of Negroes from French areas. No matter that these particular people had fought against the Republic; they were well acquainted with its ideology and thus represented a threat. Jean-François and twelve other leaders, along with their extended families, sailed for Cádiz. Other groups were dispersed to Trinidad, Guatemala, and Yucatán. When Biassou's entourage arrived in Havana, they were not even permitted to disembark and Biassou himself was given only a night to make a choice between the Isle of Pines, just south of Cuba, and Saint Augustine, Florida, as a place of exile. He chose Saint Augustine.[38] It is possible that Biassou had heard about Saint Augustine from the Florida merchants and sailors who frequented Cap Français before the revolt and that he hoped to make use of those personal connections.

Biassou and his dependents were transported at government expense to Saint Augustine in January 1796. Biassou's household included his wife, Romana Jacobo, Romana's mother, sisters, and brother, and a slave belonging to Biassou. Also with Biassou were at least twenty-five followers whom he referred to as "family" because they paid him allegiance and because he claimed responsibility for them. However, Biassou was forced to leave behind his own mother, whom he had allegedly rescued from slavery in the early years of the revolt.[39] Several months after arriving in Saint Augustine, Biassou petitioned to be allowed to return to Hispaniola and search for his "beloved mother" and for other members of his "family." Spanish authorities in Hispaniola had promised Biassou that any of his dependents left behind would soon be sent to join him, but when he asked them to honor that pledge, the bureaucrats stalled, noting that Biassou's petition did not specify how many "troops" he sought to recover or exactly where they might be located. They were hardly inclined to reunite a force they had gone to such lengths to disperse.[40]

Biassou had enjoyed a position of command for five years before he settled in Florida, and his haughty demeanor immediately alienated Governor Quesada, who arranged lodging for Biassou and his immediate family and sent two nights' supper to the house when they arrived, only to have Biassou complain that he had not been invited to dine at the governor's home. Quesada reported this in amazement to his Cuban superior, warning, "I very much fear the proud and vain character he displays. . . . it is a great problem to decide how to deal with him."[41]

If Quesada had misgivings about Biassou, the white citizenry apparently displayed a mixture of curiosity and dismay toward the unusual newcomers. According to Quesada, who may have been projecting his own concerns, "The slaveowners have viewed his arrival with great disgust, for they fear he will set a bad example for the rest of his class."[42] The garrison soldiers, attracted by the novelty, took to gathering at Biassou's house to ogle him, and Quesada maintained that they, too, expressed disgust. Biassou must have been equally displeased, because he petitioned that the soldiers be forbidden this pastime.[43] No record exists of the reaction of the large population of slaves and free blacks to the arrival of the decorated black military figure and his retinue, but surely all were aware of Biassou's slave origins and his rise above them.

Quesada soon had more to complain about than Biassou's unsuitable pride. Biassou apparently also became a financial burden. Quesada complained that although Biassou had been paid his salary in advance, he spent large sums of money and always asked for more. When Quesada was not forthcoming, Biassou wrote directly to the governor's superior—the captain general of Cuba. To do so, Biassou, who did not write or speak Spanish, used an interpreter from the Cuban Third Battalion whom Quesada had assigned him. Quesada must have regretted his assistance to Biassou when he read the letter to Las Casas:

> The many and valuable services which I have received from your Excellency oblige me to disturb you although you are so importantly occupied. I render all due thanks, although these are never sufficient; neither I nor my family could ever repay you with more than gratitude, which is constant in us; and as proof of it I happily inform you of my arrival at this [port] where I have been paid respects by the governors, the nobles, and the people. I owe this fine reception to the kindness of your Excellency, whom I beg not to fail to forward your desires and orders, which I eagerly look forward to, in order to have the honor of being your most unworthy servant. . . . Sir, I hope to deserve your kindness and that you will order that I be advanced money to buy a house. If I am to subsist in this province I would not be able to manage the costs of rent.[44]

This flowery letter is a masterpiece of veiled sarcasm. Biassou alluded to the supposed favors he had received from Las Casas, whose hospitality, it will be remembered, had not even allowed Biassou to debark in Havana. Biassou also contrasted the implied inconstancy of the Spaniards with his own unceasing gratitude. When he described the way the governor honored him in Saint Augustine (a reception with which Quesada had already reported Biassou was not satisfied), he reminded Las Casas that he was due homage. In begging to be allowed to discharge the captain general's orders, he made an effort to shame Las Casas into some reciprocal feelings of obligation, and perhaps circumvent the local authority of the governor. The effort was in vain. Nor was Biassou advanced money to buy a house, a request which was not illogical because he and the others had abandoned property in Saint Domingue, and the Crown customarily provided for evacuated citizens.[45]

Undaunted, Biassou peppered Governor Quesada and his successor, Enrique White, with complaints.[46] Biassou and his officers were promised that their salaries would continue and that they would be provided with rations and an annual clothing allowance in Florida. However, the Crown made no provision to augment Saint Augustine's subsidy to cover these costs, and the governors' appeals to the viceroy of New Spain for extra funds were denied. After the disasters of the 1795 invasion, the Florida treasury could barely support its regular troops, so the additional burden of supporting Biassou and his band was most unwelcome. Biassou's annual salary (based on that paid in Hispaniola) was 3,840 pesos—not an inconsiderable sum and only 120 pesos less than the annual salary of Florida's governor.

After much wrangling, the treasury officials of Saint Augustine finally agreed to pay Biassou an annual salary of 3,000 pesos, but Quesada warily noted, "since the certificate that he has presented verified the Negro's claims (to the higher salary of 3,000 pesos), he is very dissatisfied, and this added to his high temper and taste for drink, although it has not caused any harm to date, I feel will present a problem."[47]

Indeed, Biassou and the other Black Auxiliaries were quick to protest any grievances, which usually involved their reduced incomes and status in Saint Augustine. In their first year in the colony, both Biassou and one of his followers, Pedro Miguel, complained directly to the captain general of Cuba, who returned the appeals to Florida's new governor, Enrique White. The embarrassed White stiffly admonished all involved that future correspondence be directed through proper channels, meaning himself. Another who identified himself as the sergeant and adjutant to the auxiliary troops of the Spanish island of Santo Domingo, petitioned to receive the salary he had customarily received in Hispaniola, because the single ration he was allowed was insufficient to support his large family. He recalled his service to the king in the war against France, naming five battles in which he took part, but there is no record of the captain general's response.[48]

Despite his reduced circumstances, Biassou attempted to maintain the lifestyle expected of a *caudillo* in Saint Augustine. He wore fine clothes trimmed in gold, a silver-trimmed saber, and a fancy ivory and silver dagger. The gold medal of Charles IV must also have impressed the townspeople of Saint Augustine, unaccustomed to seeing such finery on a black man. Biassou was forced to borrow money to pay the "salary" of dependents for whom he was responsible, such as his brother-in-law and military heir, Juan Jorge Jacobo.

He also borrowed to be able to properly observe religious celebrations such as the Day of Kings (January 6). Allegations about Biassou's practice of *vodun* and his baptism on his deathbed suggest that this celebration may have been observed for its African, rather than Catholic, significance. Fernando Ortiz and others have described the lavish observance of the Day of Kings in nearby Havana. There, lavishly costumed crowds of Africans, free and slave, filled the streets, dancing, drumming, and singing to African music. The participants were organized by nations. Ortiz noted the political organization and social cohesion these festivals promoted, eradicating for a day, the legally imposed distinctions among Africans. All honored their chosen king-for-a-day. As John Thornton and others have noted, hosting entertainments and redistributing wealth were a way an aspirant might attain noble status in some African societies. Biassou's patronage of events such as Day of Kings no doubt reinforced his position as the most important figure in the black community. Thornton has also suggested that through election of kings, national groups "adopted the idiom of the state" and thereby raised suspicions among some colonial officials about their purposes. Although it may have existed, there is no evidence of national organization among Biassou's followers. It does seem clear, however, that Biassou worked hard to maintain a military organization of his own—in effect, a state within a state—and that the Spaniards recognized his leadership and did not attempt to challenge it.[49]

Although Biassou struggled to retain the privileges and position he once enjoyed in Hispaniola, his prestige was damaged when he was no longer able to provide well for his troops and they found they could apply to alternative authorities. When Biassou ordered the arrest of Juan Bautista for fighting, the man appealed to the governor. He argued he was now a civilian, not a soldier, and as Biassou had told them to apply to the governor for rations, he considered that he was no longer subject to the general's (Biassou's) orders. Biassou felt compelled to address the governor about this challenge, always referring to Juan Bautista as a soldier under his command. Biassou stated that he had repeatedly admonished Juan Bautista about his drunkenness. He warned Juan Bautista that he would arrest him should he succumb again. When Biassou gave the order for his arrest, Juan Bautista insolently denied Biassou's authority. Biassou reminded the governor that the Catholic monarch gave him "full powers" to punish and reward those in his service, as Juan Bautista knew full well. Biassou added that even though Juan Bautista may have been ignorant of that fact, he would never before have dared argue with Biassou as he had now done twice. Biassou's honor was clearly at stake in this dispute. He told the governor that he had been too ill to handle the insult previously, but as he did not want to give the town more to talk about, he hoped the governor would support his authority. The governor must have avoided this thicket, for there is no evidence of a response.[50]

Biassou's patronage powers and control may have been reduced, but he was still able to exercise other forms of influence as the titular head of an ever-expanding "family." Despite some conflict, marriage and godparental ties soon linked the former Black Auxiliaries with members of the black community in Saint Augustine, many of whom were former fugitives from the United States. Only three months after arriving, Biassou's brother-in-law, Sergeant Juan Jorge Jacobo, married Rafaela Witten. This union, which may have followed a whirlwind courtship, was important politically. The bride was the daughter of Prince Witten, an escaped slave from South Carolina who had lived in the province for a decade. Witten was a skilled carpenter and property owner whose status in the community was marked by the frequency with which he was chosen as godfather or marriage sponsor. Like Biassou and Jorge Jacobo, Witten was a member of the free black militia and had served well against the Genet-inspired invaders of 1795. The marriage of Biassou's heir, Jorge, and Witten's daughter, Rafaela, united the leading families of both groups of blacks who had allied with the cause of the Spanish king against the forces of French republicanism. Subsequent marriages and baptisms added new layers of connection, and the refugees consistently used the structures of the Catholic Church to strengthen their blended community.[51]

The men of these two communities were also blended into a single militia unit under the command of Jorge Biassou, who by virtue of his service in Santo Domingo used the title of general. Until that time, the highest rank ever achieved by a black militiaman in Florida had been sergeant. Biassou's elevated title raised the status of Florida's black militia.[52]

Although there may have been some objections to such social promotion, Biassou's perquisites came from the king and the circumstances of his appointment assured that governors and captains general forwarded his most controversial memorials to the minister of war in Spain. In 1799 Biassou asked to be allowed to go to Spain and fight for the king, but his request was denied. The following year he asked simply for any other destination. When that request was also rejected, Biassou sent his ailing wife and four members of her family to Havana and asked that they receive the daily subsidy other blacks from Santo Domingo were receiving in Cuba. Finally, Biassou asked to be able to reorganize two separate companies of *pardo* (mulatto) and *moreno* (black) militias, to be placed under his command, and to have equal footing with the white militias.[53] Biassou's efforts seem designed to improve both his social and his financial positions. Florida had not yet fully recovered from the destitution following the invasion, and metropolitan support was becoming increasingly irregular as Spain suffered its own misfortunes.

Like the hard-pressed governors before him, Governor White had to depend heavily on his black guerrilla forces. In 1800 the Seminole and Lower Creek nations elected William Augustus Bowles director of their new state of Muskogee and declared war against Spain. For the next three years Bowles's forces wreaked havoc on Florida, raiding plantations, depriving Saint Augustine of badly needed supplies, and abducting and killing settlers and their slaves. Biassou led several expeditions against the enemy before falling ill.[54] In July 1801 he returned to Saint Augustine, where, after receiving a hasty baptism, he died quietly in his home. The parish priest entered Biassou in the death register as "the renowned caudillo of the black royalists of Santo Domingo."[55]

Biassou's remaining family and followers arranged a wake, and the following day he was buried with full honors. His church Mass included songs, tolling bells, candles, and incense. Governor White and other persons of distinction in the community accompanied Biassou's cortege to the graveyard. Drummers and an honor guard of twenty members of the black militia completed the procession, and these troops discharged a volley at the gravesite. The obligations of military corporatism seem to have outweighed any racial distinctions in this ceremony, the public notary attesting that "every effort was made to accord him the decency due an officer Spain had recognized for military heroism."[56]

Such public ceremonies were much appreciated in Saint Augustine. Festivities marked royal weddings and births and the inaugurations of new governors. Plays, military and religious processions, balls, and visits by Indian delegations all were occasions of enthusiastic and general participation. But Biassou's elaborate burial, carefully staged to honor Florida's only black *caudillo*, was new to Saint Augustine. Biassou was an object lesson which many whites opposed, especially Florida's Anglo planters. He was decorated, militant, independent, and propertied. More alarming in their view, Biassou had fought his way out of slavery in the hemisphere's bloodiest revolution. Indeed, Biassou continued to wage war until death overtook him and was, no doubt, capable of some of the violent acts attributed to him in Saint Domingue. Moreover, he was a proud and difficult man who caused Spanish administrators much annoyance. But the very pride which irritated the Spaniards whom he challenged must also have been a source of comfort to those he led, and perhaps to the larger black community, for in demanding respect for himself, he sought it by extension for all.

The presence of Governor White and other notables at Biassou's funeral must have been encouraged also by the continuing war with the state of Muskogee. The Indians had only recently raided an outlying plantation, abducted a woman and her five children, killed the oldest boy, and taken away ten slaves. For whites it was no time to insult the black militia.

It was, however, a propitious moment for Biassou's brother-in-law, Juan Jorge Jacobo, to press his case. On Biassou's death, Jacobo assumed command of the combined militias, but before he led an expedition in search of the Indians, he petitioned for the salary he had previously enjoyed as a sergeant first class in the royal army in Santo Domingo. He reminded the government of his loyal service at the battles of San Rafael, Plaza Chica de San Miguel, and Barica and of all his previous expeditions out of Saint Augustine. Jacobo declared himself "disappointed . . . but nonetheless . . . willing and ready to serve king and country."[57] The government subsidy had not arrived in some time and Florida was in dire straits, so it seems unlikely a raise was forthcoming. The money, however, was not the sole issue, although Jacobo could have used it. Rather, requests such as his reflected a need to be validated in a society preoccupied with questions of honor and status. Despite his disappointment, Jacobo commanded the black militia through the conclusion of the Indian wars and into the next decade against the so-called Patriot invaders who seized Fernandina and Amelia Island in 1812 and declared an independent "Republic of Florida."[58] Once again, Prince Witten of South Carolina and Benjamin Segui of Santo Domingo were his captains. In an oblique reference to their prior experience in Hispaniola, the governor's war orders enjoined the black commanders not to be "excessively sanguinary" or exceed the limits of "civilized" nations.[59] Florida's use of black militias inspired outrage among the invaders and direct allusions to Santo Domingo. Patriot leader John McIntosh warned President Monroe that

> we have an army of Negroes raked up in this country, and brought from Cuba to be contended with. . . . Saint Augustine, the whole province will be the refuge of fugitive slaves; and from thence emissaries . . . will be detached to bring about the revolt of the black population of the United States.[60]

Other pronouncements by the rebels decried the backwardness of the region, which they attributed to the Spanish monarchy's lethargy and neglect and which they contrasted with the prosperity that would surely be achieved in Florida by republican government. It is clear, however, that the horror of Saint Domingue's race war was clearly the more powerful image in promoting this invasion. Disease, the ferocity of the black and Indian militias, and weakening United States enthusiasm for the land grab eventually ruined the Patriots. Florida was saved for a few more years, but the province was a shambles due to constant political turmoil, and Spain, which had suffered invasions and political turmoil of its own, was in no position to assist its needy colony. The Crown expressed both its poverty and its gratitude to the black militias:

> This government is well satisfied with the noble and loyal spirit which animates all the individuals of this company, and although their zeal for service to their country and our august monarch, Señor Don Fernando VII, does not require other stimulus than the glory of doing their duty, they are assured, nonetheless, in the name of His Majesty, that each one's merit will be magnanimously attended to and compensated with all the advantages the state can assign, and the national government can support for their good services to the country.[61]

In its weakened state, Spain ultimately lost Florida to the territorial ambitions of the United States. In 1821 the province's black auxiliaries and their families joined the departing Spaniards in yet another exodus to Cuba.[62] Prince Witten was sixty-two and Benjamin Segui over fifty when they relocated to Cuba after more than twenty years in the Spanish service. Despite broken promises and sometimes shabby treatment from colonial authorities, the black militiamen were steadfastly loyal to Spain. They had risen out of the chaos of the American and French Revolutions, fought their way out of slavery, and proved formidable and loyal allies of the Crown which freed them.[63] Their efforts helped slow, if not forestall, the tide of republicanism in Saint Domingue and in Florida.

NOTES

1. Franklin Knight demonstrated the multiple effects of conflict, ideology, and economic dislocation on the Caribbean in "The American Revolution and the Caribbean," in *Slavery and Freedom in the Age of the American Revolution*, ed. Ira Berlin and Ronald Hoffman (Urbana: University of Illinois Press, 1986), pp. 237–261. On effects in Florida, see J. Leitch Wright, *Florida in the American Revolution* (Gainesville: University Presses of Florida, 1975).

2. C. L. R. James, *The Black Jacobins: Toussaint L'Ouverture and the San Domingo Revolution* (New York: Vintage, 1963); David Geggus, *Slavery, War, and Revolution: The British Occupation of Saint Domingue, 1793–1798* (Oxford: Clarendon Press, 1982); Alfred N. Hunt, *Haiti's Influence on Antebellum America: Slumbering Volcano in the Caribbean* (Baton Rouge: Louisiana State University Press, 1988); Eugene D. Genovese, *From Rebellion to Revolution: Afro-American Slave Revolts in the Making of the Modern World* (Baton Rouge: Louisiana State University Press, 1979); Julius S. Scott, *The Common Wind: Currents of Afro-American Communication in the Era of the Haitian Revolution* (Oxford University Press, forthcoming).

3. Richard K. Murdoch, *The Georgia-Florida Frontier 1793–1796: Spanish*

Reactions to French Intrigue and American Designs (Berkeley: University of California Press, 1951). As its title indicates, this is primarily a diplomatic history of the era.

4. White fears of such men and their "notions" are described in Michel-Rolph Trouillot, "From Planters' Journals to Academia: The Haitian Revolution as Unthinkable History," *Journal of Caribbean History* 25 (1991): 81–99. See also David Geggus, "Racial Equality, Slavery, and Colonial Secession during the Constituent Assembly, " *American Historical Review* 94 (December 1989): 1290–1308; Jane Landers, "Jorge Biassou: Black Chieftain," in *Clash between Cultures: Spanish East Florida 1784–1821,* ed. Jacqueline K. Fretwell and Susan R. Parker (Saint Augustine: Saint Augustine Historical Society, 1988), pp. 87–100.

5. Herbert Klein points out that approximately one-fourth of the reorganized Cuban army of the late eighteenth century was of African descent. Other Spanish posts in the Caribbean were similarly structured. Herbert Klein, "The Colored Militia of Cuba: 1568–1868," *Caribbean Studies* 6 (July 1966): 17–27.

6. Jane Landers, "Black Society in Spanish St. Augustine, 1784–1821," Ph.D. diss., University of Florida, 1988.

7. Daniel L. Schafer, "'Yellow Silk Ferret Tied Round Their Wrists': African Americans in British East Florida, 1763–1784," in *The African American Heritage of Florida,* ed. David R. Colburn and Jane L. Landers (Gainesville: University Press of Florida, 1995); Schafer, "Plantation Development in British East Florida: A Case Study of the Earl of Egmont," *Florida Historical Quarterly* (October 1984): 172–183; Patricia Griffin, *Mullet on the Beach: The Minorcans of Florida, 1768–1788* (Jacksonville: Saint Augustine Historical Society, 1991).

8. Wilbur Henry Siebert, *Loyalists in East Florida 1783–1785: The Most Important Documents Pertaining Thereto, Edited with an Accompanying Narrative,* 2 vols. (Deland: Florida Historical Society, 1929).

9. Susan R. Parker, "Men without God or King: Rural Planters of East Florida, 1784–1790," *Florida Historical Quarterly* 69 (October 1990): 135–155; *Spanish Land Grants in Florida,* 5 vols. (Tallahassee: State Library Board, 1940–1941).

10. Jane Landers, "Spanish Sanctuary: Fugitive Slaves in Florida, 1687–1790," *Florida Historical Quarterly* 62 (January 1984): 296–313; "Gracia Real de Santa Teresa de Mose: A Free Black Town in Spanish Colonial Florida," *American Historical Review* 95 (February 1991): 9–30.

11. Disputes with Georgians about contested slave property involved diplomatic negotiations of the highest order. More than 250 former slaves were freed by the Spanish before pressure from United States Secretary of State Thomas Jefferson forced Spain to abrogate the sanctuary provision in 1790. The freed slaves appear in the Census of 1784, on microfilm reel 76, East Florida Papers (hereafter cited as EFP), at the P. K. Yonge Library of Florida History, University of Florida, Gainesville (hereafter cited as PKY). For further discussion see Landers, "Spanish Sanctuary."

12. Letters of Vicente Manuel de Zéspedes, included in Miró to Caballo, May 12, 1790, and cited in Derek Noel Kerr, "Petty Felony, Slave Defiance, and Frontier Villainy: Crime and Criminal Justice in Spanish Louisiana, 1770–1803," Ph.D. diss., Tulane University, 1983, p. 194.

13. David Geggus, "The Enigma of Jamaica in the 1790s: New Light on the Causes of Slave Rebellions," *William & Mary Quarterly* 44 (April 1987): 274–299.

14. Among those conducting business in Guarico, as the Spanish called Cap Français, were Miguel Ysnardy, Santos Rodriguez, Joseph Guillén, Pedro Cosifacio, Lorenzo Coll, Isaac Wickes and Francis Fatio. Memorials, EFP, on

microfilm reels 76–78, PKY. In 1792, Don Juan Fatton petitioned the governor of Florida to be allowed to return to Guarico, where he owned a commercial house, to attempt to retrieve 2400 pesos deposited with Porkins Bourlen and Company. Petition of Juan Fatton, May 4, 1792, Memorials 1784–1821, EFP, on microfilm reel 78, PKY. Other trading ventures with Guarico, such as those of José Saby and Sebastián Ortegas, appear in import lists in the EFP.

15. Georgian interests in supplanting Spanish rule related primarily to a desire to break the Indian trade monopoly Spain granted the Panton Leslie Company, a need to stanch the flow of slave runaways, and hopes for evicting the Creek nation from contested settlement areas. One of the Georgia plotters, Samuel Hammond, had commercial interests in the Indian trade and also commanded a militia unit in the Creek War of 1793. Murdoch, *Georgia-Florida Frontier*, pp. 9–15. Also see William S. Coker and Thomas B. Watson, *Indian Traders of the Southeastern Spanish Borderlands: Panton, Leslie & Company and John Forbes & Company, 1783–1847* (Pensacola: University Presses of Florida, 1986), chap. 9.

16. Report of Sebastián Kindelan to Captain General Las Casas, October 15, 1795, enclosing Letter and Proclamation of Governor George Mathews to Governor Bartolomé Morales, Cuba 1439, Archivo General de Indias, Seville, Spain (hereafter cited as AGI).

17. "Proposals for Enlistment in the French Service (1793)," cited in Murdoch, *The Georgia-Florida Frontier*, p. 19. When Britain controlled the territory, it was divided into East and West Florida. East Florida comprised the peninsular area south of the Saint Marys River and west to the Apalachicola River. The Spanish retained that division after 1784.

18. *City Gazette and Daily Advertiser*, Charleston, vol. 12, no. 2445, March 25, 1795. This paper had been sent to Spain by officials in Cuba.

19. President Washington had already warned Georgia that federal troops would intervene in the Creek War, in which Samuel Hammond also participated. Murdoch, *Georgia-Florida Frontier*, pp. 12–25.

20. Juan Nepomuceno de Quesada to Luis de Las Casas, December 10, 1792, Cuba 1439, AGI. Gwendolyn Midlo Hall has described the caliber of the French troops in Louisiana in almost identical terms; *Africans in Colonial Louisiana: The Development of Afro-Creole Culture in the Eighteenth Century* (Baton Rouge: Louisiana State University Press, 1992). Kerr has done the same for the Spanish troops in Louisiana; "Petty Felony." This distrust led Governor Quesada repeatedly to deny land grants to black applicants; he even failed to honor the grants made by his predecessor. Memorials of Villy Villen, October 5, 1790, and Prince Witten, July 14, 1791, EFP, on microfilm reel 77, PKY.

21. Juan Nepomuceno de Quesada to Luis de Las Casas, April 12, 1794, Cuba 1439, AGI.

22. Collins was the son of a white planter from Louisiana, which may have also made him suspect. He became a merchant and beef contractor in Saint Augustine and traveled to Havana, Pensacola, Charleston, and the Indian nations on business. On one such occasion, Quesada approved his license for travel to Havana when Collins presented a letter from his creditors attesting to his "well-known good character." Memorial of J. B. Collins, October 24, 1792, EFP, on microfilm reel 78, PKY.

23. John Leslie, one of the commanders of the free black militia, was a partner in the important southeastern trading company of Panton and Leslie. Like many other important members of the Spanish community, he had mulatto children, whom he recognized and provided for. J. Leitch Wright, "Blacks

in St. Augustine, 1763–1845," typescript, Historic Saint Augustine Preservation Board, n.d. For further examples of interracial unions in Spanish Florida, see Landers, "Black Society." Also see Jane Landers, "Acquisition and Loss on a Spanish Frontier: The Free Black Homesteaders of Florida, 1784–1821," and Daniel L. Schafer, "Shades of Freedom: Anna Kingsley in Senegal, Florida and Haiti," in *Against the Odds: Free Blacks in the Slave Societies of the Americas,* ed. Jane G. Landers (London: Frank Cass, forthcoming).

24. Geggus, "Enigma of Jamaica," p. 279.

25. Among those arrested were Abner Hammond of the Hammond and Fowler Trading Company and wealthy Florida planters, such as John McIntosh, who betrayed the generosity of the Spanish government that granted them their homesteads. Murdoch, *Georgia-Florida Frontier,* p. 42. Inspections of the Commissary of the Army, 1789–1821, EFP, on microfilm reel 31, PKY.

26. Shortly after this episode, Colonel Bartolomé Morales assumed interim command of the plaza. Governor Quesada, who suffered from chronic unidentified fevers and an excitable nature, was said to be "ill." Letters to and from the Spanish Ministers and Consuls in the United States, 1785–1821, June 1795, EFP, on microfilm reels 39–41, PKY.

27. Juan Nepomuceno de Quesada to Luis de Las Casas, October 26, 1795, EFP, on microfilm reel 10, PKY.

28. Records of Criminal Proceedings: Rebellion of 1795, EFP, reels 128–9, PKY.

29. Accounts of the Royal Treasury, 1796–1814, Account of 1796, Santo Domingo (hereafter cited as SD) 2636, AGI.

30. James, *Black Jacobins,* p. 106. James describes Biassou as "a fire-eater, always drunk, always ready for the fiercest and most dangerous exploits" (pp. 93–94). Robert Debs Heinl, Jr., and Nancy Gordon Heinl, *Written in Blood—The Story of the Haitian People 1492–1971* (Boston: Houghton Mifflin, 1978), p. 45, repeat Thomas Madiou's description of Biassou's war tent "filled with kittens of all shades, with snakes, with dead men's bones and other African fetishes. At night huge campfires were lit with naked women dancing horrible dances around them, chanting words understood only on the coast of Africa. When the excitement reached its climax, Biassou would appear with his *bocors* to proclaim in the name of God that every slave killed in battle would re-awaken in his homeland of Africa." Carolyn E. Fick agrees with these characterizations and goes so far as to assert that "among the prominent leaders, it was now Biassou, the fiery and impassioned voodoo adept who, in his more impulsive moments, best incarnated the aspirations and mentality of the insurgent slaves"; see Fick, *The Making of Haiti: The Saint Domingue Revolution from Below* (Knoxville: University of Tennessee Press, 1990), p. 115. To say that Biassou might "incarnate" the "mentality" of the slaves would be a leap in any case, but certainly not because of his impulsive and fiery nature. One might equally argue that Biassou's actions exhibit pragmatic and assiduous pursuit of self-interest.

31. Captain General Joaquín García to the Duque de la Alcudia, February 18 1794, Estado (hereafter cited as ES) 14, document 86, AGI; James, *Black Jacobins,* p. 124. Toussaint's followers in Dondon warned prophetically, "You have received commissions and you have guarantees. Guard your liveries and your parchments. One day they will serve you as the fastidious titles of our former aristocrats served them." Cited in ibid., p. 155.

32. James, *Black Jacobins,* pp. 123–143. Thomas O. Ott, *The Haitian Revolution, 1789–1804* (Knoxville: University of Tennessee Press, 1973), pp. 83–84, asserts that Toussaint's defection from the Spaniards was in part motivated by his own

ambition and that he felt his advancement within the Spanish camp blocked by Biassou and Jean-François. He describes Toussaint's "power struggle" with Biassou and Toussaint's military victories over his former superior. Carolyn Fick agrees; see Fick, *Making of Haiti*, p. 184. Biassou's forces were with the Spaniards at Saint-Raphael when Toussaint surprised and defeated them on May 6, 1794.

33. James, *Black Jacobins*, pp. 131–132.

34. The Marquis of Casa Calvo to Captain General Luis de Las Casas, December 31, 1795, ES 5-A, document 23, AGI. Bayajá was the site of an infamous massacre on July 7, 1794, in which Spanish troops and those of Jean-François killed approximately 1,000 French men, women, and children who had accepted Spanish offers of protection to return from the United States; see James, *Black Jacobins*, p. 151. Although Spaniards were also involved, in the cited document Casa Calvo refers to the incident as a "cruel crime" which "inspired in the sanguinary hearts and entrails [of the blacks] the reckless belief that they had reconquered the town and saved the Spanish garrison from a plot against them by the French emigres."

35. Marquis de Casa Calvo to Captain General Luis de Las Casas, December 31, 1795, ES 5-A, document 23, AGI. Landers, "Gracia Real de Santa Teresa de Mose," pp. 32–33.

36. Petition of Romana Jacobo, October 12, 1801, SD 1268, AGI. The governor of Bayajá wrote disparagingly that some of the black auxiliaries thought the abandonment of their property would excuse their crimes and be proof of fidelity but that their sacrifices were only "illusions" and were made in their own self-interest. Marquis de Casa Calvo to Captain General Luis de Las Casas, December 31, 1795, ES 5-A, AGI.

37. Petition of Jorge Biassou, May 31, 1794, ES 13, document 11, AGI.

38. Captain General Las Casas to the Duque de Alcudia, January 18, 1796, ES 5-A, document 24, AGI.

39. Members of Biassou's immediate family included Romana, her mother, Ana Gran Pres, her sisters, Barbara and Cecilia Gran Pres, and her brother, Juan Jorge Jacobo, Biassou's military successor. All were free blacks from Guarico. In the "extended" family were Juan Luis Menar, a free mulatto from Guarico, who married Barbara Gran Pres; Placido Asil, a free black from San Miguel on the coast of Guinea, who married Biassou's slave Isabel, a black from Villa de Granada; Jorge Brus, a free mulatto from Marmelade, and his wife, María Carlota, a free black from Guarico; Pedro Miguel, a free black; Benjamin Segui, a free mulatto; Peter Yon Frances, ethnicity not given; Leon Duvigneau, a free mulatto, and his black slave wife, Simonett. This group was identified by searching the black baptisms, marriages, and burials for the post-1796 period: Cathedral Parish Records, Diocese of Saint Augustine Catholic Center, Jacksonville (hereafter cited as CPR), on microfilm reels 284 J, K, and L, PKY. This represents only a partial accounting of the refugees, since many may not have been recorded in these registers. In one version of the story of his mother's rescue from the Hospital of the Holy Fathers in le Cap, Biassou murdered all the patients in their beds; see Heinl and Heinl, *Written in Blood*, p. 54.

40. Governor Enrique White to Captain General Las Casas, October 1, 1796, Cuba 1439, AGI.

41. Governor Quesada to Captain General Las Casas, January 25, 1796, Cuba 1439, AGI.

42. Governor Quesada to Captain General Las Casas, March 5, 1796, Cuba 1439, AGI.

43. Ibid.

44. Jorge Biassou to Captain General Las Casas, January 31, 1796, Cuba 1439, AGI. Because Biassou could not write, he customarily marked his correspondence with a specially made black stamp.

45. Biassou was assigned an interpreter from the Cuban Third Battalion who translated Biassou's French dictation into Spanish, and a Spanish amanuensis wrote for Biassou.

46. Quesada to Las Casas, March 5, 1796, Cuba 1439, AGI; Enrique White to Las Casas, July 15, 1796, ibid.

47. Biassou had proof of having received 320 pesos monthly through February 1796, but other documents indicated he had once been paid 250 pesos monthly. Treasury officials seized this excuse to pay the lower rate. Royal Treasury Accounts, 1784–1795, SD 2635, and 1796–1819, SD 2636, AGI.

48. Quesada to Las Casas, March 5, 1796, Cuba 1439, AGI; Enrique White to Las Casas, July 15, 1796, ibid. Petition of Jorge, November 20, 1798, EFP, Letters to the Captain General, on microfilm reel 10, PKY. Jorge recounted his service at battles at the towns of Prus, Plegarias, San Rafael, Plaza Chica de San Miguel, and Barica.

49. Testamentary Proceedings of Jorge Biassou, EFP, on microfilm reel 138, PKY. Fernando Ortiz, "La Fiesta Afro-Cubana del 'Dia de Reyes,'" *Revista Bimestre Cubana* 15 (January–June 1920): 5–17. John Thornton, "African Nations in the New World Experience," paper presented at Vanderbilt University, October 10, 1992.

50. Memorial of Juan Bautista, June 25, 1798, EFP, on microfilm reel 79, PKY. Juan Bautista alleged that English-speaking black militiamen always wanted to fight with him because they knew him to be valiant. Those men replied that Bautista was the instigator of the fights. These charges seem to indicate some division among Saint Augustine's black community along language lines; Memorial of Jorge Biassou, June 26, 1798, ibid. It is interesting to note that Biassou accused Juan Bautista of chronic drunkenness, a charge Spanish officials leveled against Biassou. Perhaps the charge against Juan Bautista was true, but Biassou may also have been using a standard European slur to discredit the soldier.

51. Black Marriages, entry no. 25, April 1796, CPR, on microfilm reel 284L, PKY. Witnesses at the marriage of Jorge Jacobo and Rafaela Witten included the groom's sister and Biassou's wife, Romana, and Rafaela's brother, Francisco. Members of the family later served as the godparents for the children of this union. Black Baptisms, CPR, on microfilm reel 284K, PKY.

52. In one example, correspondence to General Biassou was addressed with the honorific "Don." An unknown hand scratched out "Don" and wrote instead "Señor." Orders to General Biassou, 1801, EFP, on microfilm reel 55, PKY.

53. Memorials of Jorge Biassou, November 2, 1799, December 6, 1799, EFP, on microfilm reel 2, PKY; Captain General Someruelos to Governor White, March 15, 1800, and May 28, 1801, ibid. The request to divide the unit somatically may seem incongruous since Biassou was black, but disciplined units throughout the Spanish Caribbean were similarly divided.

54. Council of War, June 30, 1800, EFP. Orders of General Jorge Biassou, 1801, EFP, on microfilm reel 55, PKY.

55. Black Deaths, entry no. 121, July 14, 1801, on microfilm reel 284L, CPR, PKY.

56. Testamentary Proceedings of Jorge Biassou, EFP, on microfilm reel 138, PKY. Biassou's widow, Romana, remained in Havana. Ill and destitute after Biassou's death, she requested a widow's pension, or half of his monthly salary

of 250 pesos. She received considerably less—a pension equal to that of a captain's widow. Petition of Romana Jacobo, October 12, 1801, SD 1268, AGI.

57. Petition of Jorge Jacobo, February 9, 1802, Cuba 357, AGI.

58. Reviews of the Free Black Militias, October 4, 1802, June 1802, October 12, 1812, Cuba 357, AGI. Review of Garrison, 1807 and 1809, EFP, on microfilm reel 68, PKY. The standard work on the Patriot invasion is Rembert W. Patrick, *Florida Fiasco: Rampant Rebels on the Georgia-Florida Frontier* (Athens: University of Georgia Press, 1950).

59. Orders to Jorge Jacobo, Príncipe Witten, and Benjamin Segui, July 19, 1812, EFP, on microfilm reel 68, PKY. These orders also specify the disposition of seized property. The black militia men could keep horses, cattle, equipment, supplies, clothing, and household goods. Artillery, arms, munitions, and slaves belonged to the king. Nominations for promotions, September 30, 1812, Cuba 357, AGI.

60. Kenneth Wiggins Porter, *The Negro on the American Frontier* (New York: Arno, 1971), pp. 186–194.

61. Royal proclamation, 1812, EFP, on microfilm reel 68, PKY.

62. Relation of the Florida Exiles, August 22, 1821, Cuba 357, AGI. The exiles were granted lands and minimal pensions in Cuba.

63. David Geggus describes the conservative approach of the slave rebels of Saint Domingue and their use of "church-and-king" rhetoric; "Racial Equality," p. 1307. Almost all other scholars agree on the use of the rhetoric, if not on its sincerity.

7

Conflicting Loyalties

The French Revolution and Free People of Color in Spanish
New Orleans

KIMBERLY S. HANGER

During the French Revolution and its diffusion to the Caribbean, the ideas and events associated with French radicalism presented grave problems to the Spanish administrators of Louisiana, as well as to officials in other New World slave societies. Louisiana represented a special case, however: although its population comprised largely slaves of African descent and settlers of French origin, it was ruled by Spain. France established the first settlement at Biloxi in 1699 and founded New Orleans in 1718. After ruling—or actually neglecting—Louisiana for almost seven decades, France ceded its territory west of the Mississippi River, plus the Isle of New Orleans, to Spain following the Seven Years War.[1] Although Spain, like France, considered Louisiana an economic burden, the Crown hoped to utilize it as a protective barrier between mineral-rich New Spain and the increasingly aggressive North American colonies. Preoccupied with restoring order in its war-torn empire, Spain did not officially establish its laws and military power in Louisiana until 1769. Prior to that date, the Crown in 1765 assigned the renowned scientist Antonio de Ulloa, first Spanish governor of Louisiana, the task of preparing the colony for a transfer of power. In November 1768, however, distraught French planters, merchants, and officials banished Ulloa from Louisiana. When Spain sent General Alejandro O'Reilly and 2,100 troops a few months later to restore order, punish the rebellious ringleaders, secure loyalty oaths from the population, and implement the laws and institutions of Castille and the Indies, it sent a definitive message that Louisiana now belonged to His Most Catholic Majesty.[2] Nevertheless, more than one observer of the colony's affairs noted a "distinct aversion of the French for anything Spanish."[3] Local officials precariously balanced social, national, and economic groups in order to avoid potentially explosive situations and to encourage commercial and agricultural prosperity, an especially difficult task in the 1790s.

Threatened repercussions from the French Revolution, already evident in Saint Domingue, included internal subversion and external invasion. With war raging throughout the Spanish empire at this time, the Crown had few troops to send to Louisiana. The prospect of defending the colony with local forces was disheartening. One Spanish official remarked that lower Louisiana, where attacks and uprisings were expected,

> is inhabited by people of French extraction. Although many of them are pacifically inclined, the majority are fond of novelty, have communicated with France and with their possessions in America, and hear with the greatest pleasure of the revolution in that kingdom. Especially do the inhabitants of New Orleans and its vicinity conceal but little their mode of thinking. I fear that if war were declared on France, we would find but few inhabitants of Lower Louisiana who would sincerely defend the country from any undertaking of that nation.[4]

Nevertheless, by fortifying defenses, increasing patrols, improving slave treatment, and suppressing seditious thoughts, words, and actions, officials in Spanish Louisiana endeavored to preserve the colony from French loyalist uprisings, slave rebellions, naval attacks from the Gulf of Mexico, and land attacks from the east. Don Francisco Luis Hector, Barón de Carondelet, governor of the colony from 1791 to 1797 and successor to Governor Esteban Miró, even used propaganda—in the form of correspondence, public announcements, and newspaper reports—to portray the French Revolution at its worst.[5]

Persons of French descent in Louisiana were torn between desires for a reunion with the mother country and apprehensions concerning ideals espoused by the French revolutionaries. Their political views fell along class and economic interest lines. The leading planters and merchants rejected notions of equality and decried efforts by republican France to end slavery in the metropolis and its colonies. In order to halt the flow of "infected" slaves entering Louisiana from the French West Indies, local officials, many of them planters, urged the Spanish governor and Crown to ban such importations, initially from the Caribbean, but later from Africa also. They endeavored not only to check knowledge of and experience with rebellion, but also to decrease the slave to master ratio, and they expected that a strong, centralized Spanish government would provide stability and protect their interests. While influential merchants, of course, resented any infringement on their livelihood and even engaged in contraband trade, most of them also agreed that for the moment a ban on the slave trade was prudent.[6]

On the other hand, several persons of French descent in Louisiana voiced private and public support for fraternity, liberty, and equality and called for the reinstatement of French rule in the colony. Some of them even went so far as to conspire with United States invasionary forces and rebel slaves in order to achieve their goals. Contemporaries commonly blamed the Pointe Coupée slave conspiracy of 1795 on "the influence of St. Domingue on Louisiana's black population."[7] Contemporaries also noted that political disputes had "poisoned the populace, who, through imitation, became in general either partisans of an obnoxious tyranny, or zealous adherents of Robespierre and the disrupting monsters who shared his crimes."[8] Louisiana's white population, however, overcame its internal divisions in order to conceal its frailties from the slave and free black populations. Whites, especially those with property, adamantly wanted to avert a repeat of the upheavals occurring on the French islands at this time. During periods of crisis, such as the 1795 slave conspiracy, government officials and the French populace regularly cooperated to restore order, punish offenders, and prevent future occurrences.[9]

The free population of color in New Orleans also reflected the conflicting loyalties that prevailed in Louisiana. As loyal Spanish subjects and members of the free *pardo* and *moreno* militias, most of the adult males defended the colony against a likely French invasion coming from the gulf and against internal disturbances fomented by pro-French agitators and discontented African and creole slaves. Throughout Spanish America, administrators relied on free people of color to contribute to their colonies' defensive and labor needs, and in Louisiana organized groups of free blacks worked on fortifications, kept guard at strategic points, pursued runaway slaves, and uncovered seditious Jacobin activities.[10] Some free people of color, however, participated in these acts of sedition. They advocated the overthrow of a discriminatory Spanish government and the enactment of liberal French laws that guaranteed free blacks equal rights as citizens and that abolished slavery in France and its colonies.

To avert such disorder the Spanish imperial government enforced its system of checks and balances more rigorously among various corporate groups in society, especially in the unstable Caribbean during the years of the French and Haitian revolutions (1789–1804). Corporate entities comprised part of "a hierarchical order, to be manipulated and counterbalanced against one another." In Louisiana whites, slaves, and free persons of color made up the basic corporate groups, but there were further divisions based on economic and functional standing. Like most Caribbean plantation societies, Louisiana had a three-tiered racial structure, with free persons of color accorded a special legal, economic, military, and social status.[11] Normally fluid, this system allowed free blacks to associate with slaves or to "pass" as whites, and thus relieved racial tension. Some free persons of color, however, overtly rejected their lower status and agitated for rights as citizens equal to white persons; they contributed to legislative petitions and finally open rebellion in Saint Domingue, and conspiracies in Louisiana.[12]

The absence of overt rebellion and the failure of insurrectionary plots in late eighteenth-century Louisiana indicated in part that Spanish officials triumphed in manipulating the various interest groups. French and Spanish wariness of collusion between free people of color and slaves predated the Saint Domingue rebellion, and Louisiana governments had enacted mechanisms for control and separation of these two groups from the colony's beginning. Throughout the Americas white colonials considered free blacks to be a potentially subversive force, liable to combine with slaves to overthrow the "natural" hierarchical order.[13] On the other hand, Spanish authorities in Louisiana were also apprehensive of fraternization between radical whites and free blacks. With insurrection expected from almost every social group, "Spanish prescriptions for safety touched white as well as black behavior," and most Crown officials agreed with Governor Carondelet that "in the course of a war with France, . . . little or nothing could be counted on from most of the inhabitants."[14]

In such a setting, the words and actions of free black persons came under closer scrutiny than usual. Free black immigrants and sailors from Saint Domingue and Cuba brought news of the latest developments and inflammatory notions of liberty and equality, or at least officials and leading *vecinos* (inhabitants) feared they did. During his term Governor Carondelet banished a free black tailor who had recently arrived from Saint Domingue, and his explanation conveyed the anxiety, even paranoia, of the time.

> He is a native of the part of Santo Domingo that belongs to the French and is mixed up in all the intrigues and harassments of the French colony, besides being ungovernable and audacious. Having such a character around under the present circumstances in which I am placed might produce bad results.[15]

Crown representatives associated any pro-French sentiment with the possibility of radicalism and revolt; to them this free person of color "seemed a direct link between the events in St. Domingue and Jacobin attempts to disrupt Spanish rule in Louisiana." When the colony was transferred from Spain to France in 1803, officials continued to express concern about contact between persons of African descent in the Caribbean islands and Louisiana. In August 1803 the French prefect, Pierre Clément de Laussat, asked the Spanish governor, Juan Manuel de Salcedo, to detain five black sailors from Saint Domingue at the mouth of the Mississippi in order to "avoid any communication between these blacks and those of this colony."[16] Colonial officials, however, accused, jailed, and deported many more whites than free blacks for seditious behavior in the 1790s.[17]

This chapter concentrates on the words and activities of the period's foremost free black agitator, Pedro Bailly, a lieutenant in the Compañía de Pardos de la Nueva Orleans. Other free people of color played roles in the 1791 and 1795 Pointe Coupée slave conspiracies and a 1795 conspiracy involving free moreno militiamen and soldiers of the permanent or *fijo* regiment, but Bailly almost singlehandedly tried to incite revolt among free pardos and improve their status.[18] In accordance with a royal decree dated April 27, 1793, Bailly was tried and found guilty in 1794 of "having burst into tirades against the Spanish government and of being a manifest follower of the maxims of the French rebels." In 1791 a tribunal had acquitted Bailly of similar charges.[19] Testimony in these two cases of 1791 and 1794 reveals much of the frustration free pardos experienced in a racially stratified society and their desires to obtain the equality and brotherhood that France appeared to offer. Most free persons of color, however, were reluctant to take up arms against white persons, not only because whites could call on effective, well-trained police forces, but also because, at least on the part of some, they were related by blood.

Military courts under Governors Miró in 1791 and Carondelet in 1794 prosecuted the free pardo militia officer Pedro Bailly for conspiracy, insurrection, and attempted murder. In October 1791 some white persons and free pardos accused Bailly of trying to gather support among the free pardos to instigate a rebellion similar to the revolts that were ravaging Saint Domingue. In particular, Bailly allegedly asked two free pardos if they would consider leading such a movement and be willing to take up arms against the whites if violence were necessary. A month later the free pardo witnesses modified their testimony, and Miró acquitted Bailly. Two and a half years later, when the radical phase of the French Revolution was at its peak, a Carondelet tribunal tried Bailly for espousing notions of equality among whites and free pardos, defaming the Spanish government and its policies, and conspiring to murder the free pardo commander in order to place himself at the head of the company. This testimony was much more convincing and royal anxiety about pro-French subversive activity more exaggerated than in 1791. Consequently, in March 1794 Carondelet found Bailly guilty *por haver profesido especies sugestivas de revolución* (of having professed ideas suggestive of revolution) and sent him to prison in Havana for at least two years.

A perusal of Bailly's personal and military life prior to these cases reveals an aggressive, ambitious man who utilized New Orleans' patrimonial, hierarchical social structure and legal system for his own benefit. He pursued every business opportunity, buying and selling real estate and slaves and borrowing and lending money. In addition, he worked as a carter, blacksmith, wood dealer, and militia officer. Manumitted *graciosamente* (without conditions) by Josef Bailly in 1776 at age twenty-five, Pedro immediately began accumulating property. When he married the recently freed parda Naneta Manuela Carrière, alias Cádiz, in 1778, he possessed 350 pesos (Spanish monetary unit upon which the dollar was based) in silver, wagons and mules used in his trade valued at 120 pesos, and an eighteen-year-old morena slave appraised at 300 pesos. Naneta listed her possessions at that time as 350 pesos in silver and four cows given to her by her mother and valued at forty pesos. Before Naneta died in 1800, she and Bailly had had three children who survived—Pedro, Andrés Pedro, and Naneta Leonard— and two who died—Joseph Pedro and Josef María—at ages nine and three respectively. The godparents for many of Bailly's children were high-ranking Spanish bureaucrats or military personnel and their wives. Bailly purchased his own mother, a morena slave of Don Antonio Mermillion, in 1781 for 250 pesos and freed her two days later. Following the great fire that consumed four-fifths of New Orleans in 1788, Bailly valued his losses at 2,000 pesos in buildings and 675 pesos in personal effects; Naneta signed this statement for him, because like most persons in eighteenth-century New Orleans, Bailly was illiterate.[20]

Bailly's military career appeared as exemplary as his personal and material accomplishments. Between 1779 and 1793 he advanced from corporal second class to first lieutenant in the free pardo militia and served with that unit in the Baton Rouge, Mobile, and Pensacola expeditions against the British during the American Revolution. He and other free pardos also captured runaway slaves, repaired cracks in the levee, and patrolled the streets of New Orleans at night.

However, when the free pardo commander and captain of the first company, Francisco Dorville, and the captain of the second company,

Carlos Simón, brought charges against Bailly in 1794, they cast a much different light on his militia service. According to Dorville and Simón, Bailly consistently feigned illness in order to shirk his responsibilities as a militia officer, responsibilities these two officers took very seriously.[21] They claimed that corporal Bailly reluctantly joined the 1779 Baton Rouge expedition led by Governor Bernardo de Gálvez against the British in the American Revolution, complaining that he was ill and had other more important things to do. Bailly also allegedly often refused to parade through the city with his company on the day of Corpus Christi, and he substituted one of his slaves to work in his place when called to repair cracks in the levee, a tactic usually practiced by wealthy white persons and resented by free blacks. Bailly had lately disobeyed Dorville's orders to assemble the pardo company in order to march to Fort San Felipe de Placaminas (Fort Saint Philip of Plaquemines), where Carondelet detached them to defend the colony from radical French invaders. Fort San Felipe was constructed near the mouth of the Mississippi River in the 1780s to guard against hostile approaches inland from the Gulf of Mexico. Once again Bailly claimed to have better things to do. Dorville and Simón stated that they had questioned royal officials about the promotions in rank that Bailly received despite his disrespectful, insubordinate behavior, but their repeated requests to examine the commission records were turned down.[22]

Indeed, the report Dorville and Simón made contrasted sharply with Bailly's record of rapid promotion in the pardo militia. During the 1791 trial Bailly emphasized his long and loyal service to the Spanish Crown and his excellent reputation as a hard-working inhabitant of New Orleans. Either the pardo officers exaggerated Bailly's insubordination or white officials chose to ignore it. Bailly's white superiors also might have rewarded his material success with promotions; wealth and military titles were often accumulated simultaneously in such strategic areas on the colonial frontier as Louisiana. The pardo officers, however, resented what they considered Bailly's flippant disrespect for an institution they esteemed highly. In addition, long-standing personal conflicts probably tainted Dorville's and Simón's opinion of Bailly. Their 1794 report noted that in the early 1780s and while at Fort San Felipe de Placaminas in November 1793, Bailly had gathered supporters in order to murder Dorville. In the 1790s Dorville experienced several economic failures and owed money to numerous creditors, one of the most persistent being Bailly.[23] Relations between these two men were not harmonious and each sought to discredit the other. Still, one wonders why they waited until 1794 to malign Bailly; perhaps Dorville and Simón, for personal and professional reasons, concocted this entire rationalization ex post facto in order to distance themselves from an individual whom some ruling whites considered dangerous, and they had concrete witnesses to prove it. In the end both triumphed: Dorville rose to command a battalion composed of four companies of free pardos; Bailly spent two years in prison in Havana but returned to New Orleans and resumed his fruitful pursuit of material prosperity.

In the early 1790s Bailly was also involved in monetary disputes with Don Luis Delalande Dapremont, a *negociante* (merchant or dealer) who later accused Bailly of seditious activity. In September 1791 Dapremont sued Bailly to collect a series of debts incurred in the years 1787 and 1788 and totaling 1,270 pesos. The court seized two of Bailly's properties but returned them when he satisfied the debt ten days later. Dapremont concurrently sued Bailly for a debt of 2,346 pesos 4 *reales* (eight reales to the peso), but Bailly argued that he had already paid Dapremont that amount. Dapremont admitted his error and paid all court costs.[24] One month later Bailly prosecuted Dapremont for rental payments. For a period of three years Dapremont had stored some iron at Bailly's warehouse, and now Bailly demanded he pay rent of one peso per month, which Dapremont considered too high. Dapremont called three master blacksmiths to testify that they never charged their customers rent for storage of iron at their warehouses or shops even if they had completed the work long before the iron was removed. Nevertheless, in June 1792 officials ruled in Bailly's favor; Dapremont paid Bailly the thirty-six pesos rent and almost one hundred pesos in court costs.[25]

It was while these cases were before the court that Dapremont presented evidence to Governor Miró accusing Bailly of making criminal statements against the Spanish government. Much of the testimony was hearsay: some free pardos overheard Bailly and recounted the conversation to Claudio Tremé, who told it to Dapremont, who then went to the army surgeon, Don Josef Laby. Dapremont and Laby delivered official letters about the matter to the colonel of the royal armies, Don Francisco Bouligny, and he gave them to Miró.

During this process of transmittal the involved parties altered actual events and words to suit individual purposes. Most of the evidence presented at the trial centered on a conversation between Bailly and the free pardo Esteban Lalande at a dance held at Lalande's house. Dapremont declared that he had heard secondhand that Bailly told Lalande he anxiously awaited letters from the pardos at Cap Français[26] in Saint Domingue *para dar el golpe* (in order to pull off the coup); he wanted to conduct in Louisiana an uprising similar to theirs. Bailly was completely aware that the house was full of whites when he made these remarks. After relaying these observations to Spanish authorities,

Dapremont called on Lalande and two other free pardos who had overheard Bailly—Lalande's cousin Carlos Brulé and Roberto Monplaisir[27]—to substantiate the story. When Lalande, Brulé, and Monplaisir appeared before the tribunal, they elaborated on Bailly's conversation with Lalande but denied that any white person was present on the patio or had overheard their discourse. Monplaisir declared that even he had not seen or participated in the exchange between Bailly and Lalande.[28] In general, Lalande and Brulé stated that before talking with Lalande, Bailly had asked a gentleman who had just arrived from Cap Français if he had any information. The gentleman answered that he had good news about the rebels' success, but did not specify whether he referred to slave attacks on the whites and free blacks or free black confrontations with whites in the city. Bailly then informed Lalande that the morenos and pardos of Cap Français had conducted themselves well against the whites and speculated that in the future a similar movement would take place in New Orleans.[29] The movement only lacked a leader. Lalande replied that he would never lead or even participate in such a rebellion against the better-armed white population, primarily because he refused to sacrifice his life for what he considered a futile effort, and if Bailly insisted on pursuing this topic further, he would ask him to leave.

At that moment Lalande's cousin Carlos Brulé joined Bailly and Lalande, and he too swore to defend the whites. When the court questioned Lalande about communications from Cap Français in Saint Domingue, Lalande stated that Bailly told him that he had not received any letters from the pardos there because they had been prohibited from writing, but he hoped to hear from them soon. Although Lalande noticed that Bailly seemed angry, he did not know whether Bailly was annoyed with him or with the *blancos* (white persons). Considering all the morenos, pardos, and blancos in the house who were not wearing masks, Lalande doubted that Bailly was foolish enough to act overtly hostile toward Lalande's white guests.[30]

Expressing bewilderment over the sudden lack of confidence his creditors had shown him, Bailly asserted his innocence before the tribunal. When he was informed that Dapremont charged him with sedition, Bailly declared that these accusations were malicious and false and had been made only in retaliation to his demands for payment of rent for storing Dapremont's iron in his warehouse. Bailly argued that he had been favored with some fortune, property, and wealth, and that he had established a reputation as a good, loyal servant and had proven his love and zeal for the Crown through participation in numerous military expeditions. He added that in spite of his color, he had merited the esteem of New Orleans' leading citizens, but because of these unfounded charges he was losing this estimation, which would ruin his family.

A month later Bailly again appeared before the tribunal to complain that it had taken no further action to clear his name, and in the meantime he had suffered new setbacks in restoring people's confidence in his conduct and credit. He confessed that he had attended a ball at La-lande's house, but that all they had discussed was the profitability of holding such dances. There had been no talk of Cap Français or insur-rection.

The trial took a strange twist when two of the free pardo witnesses modified their testimony. Lalande now substantiated Bailly's innocence and denounced the accusations as malicious hearsay, only one month after indicating the opposite. He pointed out the unlikelihood that Bailly had provoked a conversation in which he expressed support for revolution like that of the Saint Domingue blacks, considering that Bailly had a family and owned slaves. Besides, the governor and other officials had previously trusted Bailly to command several expeditions to apprehend runaway slaves and other wrongdoers, and he continued to merit their trust. Brulé also altered, or rather clarified, his testimony of a month earlier, stating that he had not explained the situation very well. He emphasized that he had not actually heard the conversation between Bailly and Lalande because he was too far away from them.

Brulé's new testimony also shed light on Dapremont's real motives for bringing conspiracy charges against Bailly. Brulé revealed that when the case went to trial, one of the white deponents had approached him with the news that Bailly had taken wrongful action against Dapremont, demanding rent money for a small quantity of iron stored at his house. This action prompted Dapremont to spread rumors about Bailly. Of course, Dapremont denied any act of vengeance; he stated that he had no reason for harming Bailly and he had always regarded him as a dependable person.

Governor Miró acquitted Bailly. He declared that the judicial in-quiry had not established Bailly's guilt in expressing ideas opposed to the public tranquillity during the discussion he supposedly had con-cerning rebellion in Saint Domingue. Also in Bailly's favor were his honorable conduct, dependability, and good reputation. Furthermore, Miró faulted Lalande with instigating and promoting the content of his conversation with Bailly and with presuming its criminal intent.[31]

Newly accused of maligning the Spanish government and advocat-ing radical French maxims, Bailly stood trial once again in February and March 1794. As decreed by the royal ordinance of May 14, 1793, anyone who espoused ideas that disturbed public order and tranquillity was to be charged with treason and punished accordingly. Late in 1793 Bailly allegedly denounced Spain's social hierarchy and discrimination based on color and praised the equality he perceived in the new French constitution. He did not, however, advocate freedom for bondpersons, despite the fact that in August 1793 Commissioner Léger Félicité Sonthonax had abolished slavery in Saint Domingue.[32] In Governor Carondelet's opinion, officials should restrain Bailly in order to prevent the spread of such pernicious ideas among the discontented. Unfortunately for Bailly, Carondelet expressed these views even before beginning an investigation.

The setting for Bailly's renewed struggle against inequality was Fort San Felipe de Placaminas. As mentioned previously, in November 1793 Carondelet dispatched members of the resident garrison, the white militia, and the free pardo and moreno militias to reinforce that fort and protect the colony against an anticipated French invasion from the Gulf of Mexico. Several of these white and free pardo officers and enlisted men testified about what transpired. After arriving at Placaminas, officers divided the free pardo company between guard duty and manual work on the fortifications. The troops supposedly volunteered for manual labor, but often they were coerced, and they resented it, especially Bailly. He counseled them to present themselves en masse to the commanding officer, Colonel Don Gilberto Antonio de San Maxant (Gilbert Antoine de Saint Maxent), and claim they were too ill to work on the fort. Bailly naturally set an example, disdaining work and remaining in his tent under the pretext of poor health. Indeed, some pardos refused to work together as an organized body or contribute to their assigned tasks. The white officers attributed this to Bailly's influence.

Bailly encouraged insubordination in other ways as well. He preached to whoever would listen that the Spanish government valued the pardos at the time only because they were needed to defend the colony. Officials usually doubted their capabilities and suspected their loyalty to an order dominated by whites. He even went so far as to explain to one white officer that Colonel Maxent referred to individual pardos as *mon fils* (my son, an expression of endearment) and other similar terms during this time of crisis, but afterward he would treat them as if they were dogs. If they were among the French, however, Bailly believed that the pardos would be treated as equals of the whites, as they should be. Maxent's reluctance to drink coffee at the free pardo officers' table and his preference for dining with white officers especially irritated Bailly. Although Maxent gave the pardos all the coffee, salt, butter, sugar, and medicinal wine they requested, Bailly thought that a simple sign of respect, expressed by giving the pardo officers a cup of coffee at his table, would mean more than all these other presents.

Bailly also publicly criticized the actions and demeanor of Dorville, the free pardo commander. Simón testified that Bailly so widely disseminated seditious and insubordinate ideas among the pardo company that he put it in a state of complete disorder. Dorville was forced to leave his sickbed in order to reassert control of his men and remind them of their duty. He also humiliated some of the soldiers and forced them to work on the fortifications. As a result, Bailly's dislike of Dorville intensified, and he poisoned the others against their commander, even encouraging them to murder him. One pardo corporal heard Bailly criticize Dorville several times and refer to him as an idiot, using the French expression *sot*. Bailly intimated that if he headed the company, everyone would benefit because he knew many things about which the others were ignorant. With the inept Dorville gone and Bailly in charge, the corps would win respect. Bailly hinted that he and others could easily arrange Dorville's demise; on one occasion he remarked that if rope were needed to hang Dorville, he would gladly supply it, and at another time he offered to fire the first shot into Dorville's head.

Dorville himself testified that persons had informed him of Bailly's designs on his life, and he complained about Bailly's public attempts to humiliate him, without any respect for his age or rank or for the royal medal he had earned. As for proof of Bailly's insubordinate manner of thinking, one had only to remember that Bailly had been prosecuted previously for having talked with, as well as approached, others in order to persuade them to follow the example of free pardos of Cap Français, who had adopted "maxims of the new French constitution," presumably meaning civil equality with whites. Although the court acquitted Bailly in 1791, Dorville believed that someone had hidden the truth out of compassion for Bailly. He wanted justice to prevail this time.

Testimony given by Don Luis Declouet, second lieutenant of the Louisiana regiment and "Ayudante de las Milicias de Pardos, y Morenos," provided the clearest insights into Bailly's thoughts, words, and actions.[33] While at Placaminas, Bailly approached Declouet and asked for his opinion concerning information about the French enemy. Certain that the French rebels would attack the colony, Declouet responded that Louisiana troops had to prepare to meet and defeat the French, not only because they were enemies of the state and religion, but also because they constituted a foe to all humanity. An aroused Bailly replied: "Humanity! Humanity! I am going to speak frankly to you, sure that you are a man of honor. Sir, I do not see that any acts of inhumanity have been committed. It is true that they have done wrong by murdering their king, but sir, the French are just; they have conceded men their rights."

When Declouet asked to what rights he referred, Bailly answered: "A universal equality among men, us, people of color. We have on the Island of Saint Domingue and other French islands the title *ciudadano activo* (active or participatory citizen); we can speak openly, like any white person and hold the same rank as they. Under our [Louisiana] rule do we have this? No, sir, and it is unjust. All of us being men [rather than slaves], there should be no difference. Only their method of thinking—not color—should differentiate men. Under these circumstances of war the governor treats us with certain semblances, but we are not deceived. Señor Maxent politely received us here at Fort Placaminas, telling us that on this occasion there would be no difference between us and the whites, implying that at other times there are distinctions. Every day Señor Maxent invites officials of the white militia to eat at his table. And why are we not paid this same attention? Are we not officers just as they are?" Declouet tried to calm Bailly and dismiss what he considered ridiculous pretensions by noting that among whites themselves distinctions had existed since the beginning of time and that such differentiation constituted one of the most indispensable and sacred characteristics of human society.

In response Bailly maintained that "whites derive excess benefits from their rights." To demonstrate his point he referred to the inferior status and unjust treatment he experienced as a person of African descent. One day, for example, a Mr. Bernoudy approached him on the levee and said, "my mulatto, you are a good man, do me a favor." This expression upset Bailly, and he responded: *"Mi mulato! Mi mulato!* When was I ever *your* mulatto?" Bailly resented Bernoudy treating him this "foolish way," in other words, as a slave. On another day Bailly was at the notary's office when a Mr. Macarty had the audacity to remark that the free pardos were ruined by their associations with slaves and that if pardos wished to be regarded more highly, they ought to discontinue any fraternization with the tainted slaves. He referred to free pardos as "riffraff, thieves whom the governor should expel from the colony." These remarks angered Bailly, who told Mr. Macarty that if there were among the free people of color such criminals, he should name them and not insult everyone. To which Macarty replied that Bailly was the principal thief and threatened him with his walking stick. Further injustice followed. Although he brought charges against Macarty, officials merely imposed a fine, not for insulting free pardos as a group and Bailly in particular, but rather for showing disrespect for the government by criticizing the governor's policies. Bailly then asked Declouet the rhetorical question of what the government would have done to him if he had talked to a white person the way Macarty had spoken to him. "And you call this justice? No sir, and I am as much an officer as you are."[34] The commanding officers, both white and pardo, considered Bailly's ideas, expressions, and example a dangerous threat to their control over the troops and to an effective defense of Fort San Felipe. Dorville and Simón repeatedly informed their white superiors about Bailly's insubordination, arrogance, and disrespect, especially toward Dorville. Commanding officer Maxent only awaited some pretext to rid the encampment of Bailly, and this opportunity arose when Bailly complained of another illness. Maxent issued Bailly a passport, and he immediately returned to New Orleans. After Bailly's departure Maxent noted more tranquillity and subordination among the pardo militia than before. He reasonably assumed, therefore, that the previous tension stemmed from Bailly's influence. Both Maxent and the pardo captain Simón refused to lead any other expeditions if Bailly joined them; Simón even threatened to resign if Bailly was not discharged from the pardo militia.

On March 26, 1794, Governor Carondelet rendered his judgment. He found Bailly guilty of having followed and adopted the new "constitution" of the French rebels, especially ideas of equality, with such determination that he had not hesitated to make known his sentiments even to the white officers. Moreover, Bailly freely shared his beliefs with individuals of his own color, persuading them to act upon his pernicious notions. They consequently resisted voluntary service and weakened the colony's ability to defend itself from external and internal foes. Bailly also displayed insubordination and lack of respect for his immediate superiors, thereby setting a bad example for others in his company.

Carondelet promptly remitted Bailly to prison in Cuba's Morro Castle, where he remained until 1796.[35] When Bailly returned from Cuba, he resumed his business transactions with whites and free people of color and evidently restored his former honorable reputation as a diligent, trustworthy worker. Although Bailly never served in the militia again, he continued to value his prior rank. Before a notary in 1798 he registered his record of promotion to second lieutenant on September 18, 1792; it stated that he was an industrious and worthy person. Bailly obviously wanted others to appreciate that estimation publicly and formally. A 1798 census of the Faubourg Sainte Marie, the first suburb developed outside of New Orleans' walls, reported that Bailly headed a household of thirteen persons and worked as a wood vendor. Both

Bailly and his son Pedro, a soldier in the free pardo militia, signed an "Address from the Free People of Color" to Governor William C. C. Claiborne on January 17, 1804. In this petition several members of the free pardo and moreno militias clearly outlined their expectations of the new United States government: they emphasized their personal and political freedom as full-fledged citizens and vowed to provide loyal military service, as they had under the previous regime.[36] Thus, even into the American period, Bailly continued his untiring, undaunted struggle to achieve just treatment within a society stratified by race and color, though following his imprisonment he did so through legitimate legal channels.

There were many parallels between Bailly's aims and the goals of the *gens de couleur libres* of Saint Domingue. Like Saint Domingue, Louisiana had a three-tiered social system that accorded free people of color a distinct status inferior to that of whites but more privileged than that of slaves.[37] During the eighteenth century, however, whites in Saint Domingue enacted restrictive legislation that degraded free blacks. The French Revolution gave Saint Domingue free persons of color "a public forum unavailable in the colonies" in which to plead their cause of equality with whites. In France and its colonies free people of color "applied constant pressure against white discrimination based on color rather than on legal and economic status." Their persistence helped persuade French legislators and Louis XVI to grant full racial equality to free nonwhites in April 1792.[38] Bailly did not have such a public forum as the French Assembly, but he tried to convince whoever would listen that one should judge men on their merit, not according to their color.

Bailly also urged his free pardo comrades to join the struggle for equality even if violence were necessary, as it had been in Saint Domingue, but he never advocated a massive slave rebellion. In fact, he never mentioned slaves, only free pardos, when discussing the rights of men. He also appeared unaware that Commissioner Sonthonax had abolished slavery in Saint Domingue in August 1793, and did not anticipate France's emancipation decree of February 4, 1794, which liberated bondpersons in all its colonies.[39] Like many free pardos in Louisiana and Saint Domingue, Bailly owned slaves, supported a plantation slave society, and was not ready to countenance slave revolt. His aim, similar to that of most free blacks in Saint Domingue, was to raise free people of color to the privileged level of whites, not lower them back into slavery. Indeed, during the years of Bailly's "revolutionary" activity, free nonwhites at Cap Français in most instances allied themselves with whites to combat a mutual enemy—the slaves—in anticipation of winning civil equality. Although free persons of color fought whites and slaves in the bloody civil wars that erupted in the West and South provinces of Saint Domingue, they sporadically signed concordats with white residents to ally against slave rebels. In both Louisiana and Saint Domingue many free people of color, particularly property holders, "regarded themselves as superior to and distinct from the black slaves."[40]

In neither Louisiana nor Saint Domingue, however, did free non-whites constitute a monolithic group, and the numerous charges of sedition in late eighteenth-century New Orleans illuminate this diversity. The two Bailly trials and other cases show that free pardos and free morenos often did not exclusively or even frequently conspire together. Evidence from New Orleans supports David Geggus's contention that "during the revolutionary era in the Caribbean, free blacks often aligned themselves either with whites or slaves rather than other free coloreds."[41] Even though morenos made up 31.1 percent of the free non-white population in 1791,[42] Bailly specifically denounced white discrimination directed toward pardos and advocated equality between whites and free pardos. At the Lalande dance (1791) and the Placaminas encampment (1793) Bailly tried to recruit revolutionaries only from among the free pardos, even though free morenos also attended the ball and defended the fort.[43] In Louisiana and other circum-Caribbean areas, "phenotypical distinctions were extremely important . . . they formed the basis of a racial hierarchy and tended in addition to coincide with differences in wealth, literacy, and genealogical distance from slavery."[44]

Testimony and events surrounding the Bailly cases of 1791 and 1794 demonstrated the loyalty most free persons of color sustained for their white kin and the Spanish government. Dorville and Simón contrasted their zealous service to the Crown with Bailly's insubordination and disrespect for military duty. Lalande's words at the dance expressed what most free persons of color recognized: the pardos had received favorable treatment from whites during French rule of the colony and liberty under the Spanish regime.[45] Emphatically stating that they were the sons of whites and had their blood, Lalande, Brulé, and Simón were among several free pardos who testified that they were incapable of murdering their white relatives and benefactors. They opted for peaceful paternalism rather than revolutionary equality.

In addition, the Bailly cases and other conspiracy plots, such as those uncovered at Pointe Coupée in 1791 and 1795, disclosed communication networks operating within Louisiana and between that colony and regions of the circum-Caribbean. Testimony also indicates that much of the information relayed through this system was incorrect, outdated, biased, misunderstood, or manipulated, problems only slightly remedied by today's technology. The radical French ideals of liberty, equality, and fraternity spread quickly to and through Louisiana by means of books, newspapers, correspondence, and such persons as sailors, merchants, and refugees. Free persons of color met with whites and slaves in taverns, billiard rooms, dance halls, shops, and private homes to discuss the latest developments in the ongoing war.[46] Barely two months after the August 1791 outbreak of war in Saint Domingue, Bailly allegedly announced that he awaited letters from the free pardos of that island that would relay their successes, and he expressed support for a similar uprising in Louisiana. At that same party at Lalande's house he asked several whites and free pardos for any information they might have on happenings in Saint Domingue. One gentleman recently arrived from there assured him that the rebels were conducting themselves well against the whites, even though he did not mention specific battles or participants.

The ideals of radical revolutionaries in France and the example set by rebellious free blacks in Saint Domingue and other French islands, coupled with his own personal experiences of racial discrimination, motivated Bailly to speak out against local injustice, perhaps even advocating violent revolution if necessary. Bailly's determined effort to secure equal rights for free pardos did not succeed: he landed in jail, Louisiana never experienced a revolution like the one in Saint Domingue during its early phase, and free black rights and privileges deteriorated even further under United States rule after 1803. Without the protection of a paternalistic Spanish government, free people of color in New Orleans encountered continuing attacks on their status as a distinct group; local whites endeavored to treat all persons of African descent like slaves.[47] Despite his failed attempts, Bailly voiced many of the frustrations free people of color experienced as they contested individually and jointly the anomalous, often tenuous, status they held in three-tiered societies of the circum-Caribbean, and demanded rights equal to those of whites.

NOTES

The inclusive somatic terms *free black* and *free person of color* used in this chapter encompass anyone of African descent. The exclusive terms *moreno* (dark skin-coloring) and *pardo* (light skin-coloring)—preferred by contemporary free blacks over *negro* and *mulato*—are utilized to distinguish elements within the nonwhite population.

Research for this study was supported by generous grants from the Program for Cultural Cooperation between Spain's Ministry of Culture and United States Universities, the Spain-Florida Alliance, the University of Florida Department of History, and the American Historical Association (through an

Albert J. Beveridge Grant for Research in the History of the Western Hemisphere). The author would like to thank Murdo J. MacLeod, Thomas D. Watson, Jane Landers, and the editors for their helpful suggestions and insights. An earlier version of this chapter has been published. See Kimberly Hanger, "Conflicting Loyalties: The French Revolution and Free People of Color in Spanish New Orleans," *Louisiana History* 34 (Winter 1993): 5–33.

1. Mathé Allain, *"Not Worth a Straw": French Colonial Policy and the Early Years of Louisiana* (Lafayette: Center for Louisiana Studies, University of Southwestern Louisiana, 1988); Joseph G. Dawson III, *The Louisiana Governors: From Iberville to Edwards* (Baton Rouge: Louisiana State University Press, 1990), pp. 1–44; *Louisiana: A History*, Bennett H. Wall, ed., 2d ed. (Arlington Heights: Forum Press, 1990), pp. 3–51.

2. Julio Albi, *La Defensa de las Indias (1764–1799)* (Madrid: Instituto de Cooperación Iberoamericana, 1987); Dawson, *Louisiana Governors*, pp. 45–79.

3. Thomas T. McAvoy, *Guide to the Microfilm Edition of the Records of the Diocese of Louisiana and the Floridas, 1576–1803* (Notre Dame: University of Notre Dame Archives, 1967), p. 11.

4. Manuel Gayoso de Lemos, "Political Condition of the Province of Louisiana," Archivo General de Indias, Papeles Procendentes de Cuba (hereafter AGI PPC) 313, July 5, 1792, translated in *Louisiana under the Rule of Spain, France, and the United States, 1785–1807: Social, Economic, and Political Conditions of the Territory Represented in the Louisiana Purchase*, ed. James Alexander Robertson (Cleveland: Arthur H. Clark, 1911), vol. 1, p. 283.

5. For a discussion of Spain's defensive efforts in Louisiana in the 1790s, see Paul F. Lachance, "The Politics of Fear: French Louisianians and the Slave Trade, 1786–1809," *Plantation Slavery in the Americas* 1 (June 1979): 172; Ernest R. Liljegren, "Jacobinism in Spanish Louisiana, 1792–1797," *Louisiana Historical Quarterly* 22 (January 1939): 57–61; Roland C. McConnell, *Negro Troops of Antebellum Louisiana: A History of the Battalion of Free Men of Color* (Baton Rouge: Louisiana State University Press, 1968), pp. 24–27.

6. In the 1790s one of the principal dividing issues was the slave trade; officials debated whether to continue or ban importations from the West Indies and Africa. In "Politics of Fear" Lachance argues that the primary division was between the governors, who generally wanted to keep the trade open, and the cabildo (comprising mainly planters and merchants), which wanted to close it. By middecade the two sides had united to ban the trade entirely in the interest of safety. Liljegren also notes that Spanish officials and local leaders cooperated to protect themselves. Carondelet, even though still suspicious of pro-French sentiment among the planters, turned to them to restore order following the 1795 slave conspiracy. He had them select syndics from among themselves to enforce regulations, keep up patrols, police the areas, and make reports; Liljegren, "Jacobinism in Spanish Louisiana," p. 64. See also Alfred N. Hunt, *Haiti's Influence on Antebellum America: Slumbering Volcano in the Caribbean* (Baton Rouge: Louisiana State University Press, 1988), pp. 25, 27–28.

7. The 1795 slave conspiracy is discussed in Jack D. L. Holmes, "The Abortive Slave Revolt at Pointe Coupée, Louisiana, 1795," *Louisiana History* 11 (Fall 1970): 341–362. More recently, Ulysses S. Ricard, Jr., has examined new documents dealing with the 1791 conspiracy, as has Gwendolyn Midlo Hall for the 1791 and 1795 conspiracies. See Hall's *Africans in Colonial Louisiana: The Development of Afro-Creole Culture in the Eighteenth Century* (Baton Rouge: Louisiana State University Press, 1992), pp. 316–374. On the subject of communication networks, Liljegren asserts that New Orleans served as an entrepôt for

revolutionary propaganda routed into Mexico; Liljegren, "Jacobinism in Spanish Louisiana," p. 60.

8. James Pitot, *Observations on the Colony of Louisiana from 1796 to 1802,* trans. Henry C. Pitot (Baton Rouge: Louisiana State University Press, 1979), p. 3. Pitot apparently advocated moderation.

9. For reaction to the conspiracies, see Hall, *Africans in Colonial Louisiana,* and Holmes, "Abortive Slave Revolt."

10. An informative overview of free blacks in the Caribbean is given by David W. Cohen and Jack P. Greene, Introduction, in *Neither Slave nor Free: The Freedmen of African Descent in the Slave Societies of the New World,* ed. Cohen and Greene (Baltimore: Johns Hopkins University Press, 1972), pp. 1–18. Free black military service in Louisiana is discussed by Kimberly S. Hanger, "A Privilege and Honor to Serve: The Free Black Militia of Spanish New Orleans," *Military History of the Southwest* 21 (Spring 1991): 59–86; Jack D. L. Holmes, *Honor and Fidelity: The Louisiana Infantry Regiment and the Louisiana Militia Companies, 1766–1821* (Birmingham: The Author, 1965); McConnell, *Negro Troops.*

11. Cohen and Greene, in *Neither Slave nor Free;* Laura Foner, "The Free People of Color in Louisiana and St. Domingue: A Comparative Portrait of Two Three-Caste Societies," *Journal of Social History* 3 (Summer 1970): 406–430; Paul F. Lachance, "The 1809 Immigration of Saint Domingue Refugees to New Orleans: Reception, Integration, and Impact," *Louisiana History* 29 (Spring 1988): 109–141; Lachance, "Politics of Fear"; Jane Landers, "Gracia Real de Santa Teresa de Mose: A Free Black Town in Spanish Colonial Florida," *American Historical Review* 95 (February 1990): 9–30; Loren Schweninger, "Prosperous Blacks in the South, 1790–1880," *American Historical Review* 95 (February 1990): 31–56. These all examine the phenomenon of three-caste societies and the anomalous position of free people of color in Louisiana and the Americas.

12. David Geggus, "Racial Equality, Slavery, and Colonial Secession during the Constituent Assembly," *American Historical Review* 94 (December 1989): 1290–1308; Gwendolyn Midlo Hall, "Saint Domingue," in *Neither Slave nor Free,* pp. 172–192.

13. As in other American colonies, government officials in Spanish Louisiana diligently tried to separate and distinguish racial and legal groups. On various occasions the cabildo forbade free blacks and slaves to wear masks or imitate whites during the carnival season, to don fancy headdresses, plumes, or gold jewelry, or to drink together at taverns or dance together at parties. Sacramental records were kept in separate books, one for whites and one for pardos and morenos. Records and Deliberations of the Cabildo [hereafter RDC, housed at the New Orleans Public Library, Louisiana Division], vol. 2, January 19, 1781; Governor Miró's *Bando de buen gobierno,* article 6, RDC, vol. 3, no. 1, June 2, 1786; RDC, vol. 3, no. 2, May 27, 1791; and RDC, vol. 4, no. 3, 7 and February 13, 1800. For information on the incidence of collusion between free blacks and slaves throughout the Americas, see Cohen and Greene, in *Neither Slave nor Free.*

14. Lachance, "Politics of Fear," pp. 173–174; Liljegren, "Jacobinism in Spanish Louisiana," pp. 47–97.

15. Quoted in Hunt, *Haiti's Influence,* pp. 26–27.

16. Quoted in Lachance, "Politics of Fear," p. 177; Hunt, *Haiti's Influence,* p. 26.

17. For example, in July 1793 Carondelet deported sixty-eight suspects. Of special concern was Jean Pierre Pisgignoux and the French agent Auguste de la Chaise. See Hunt, *Haiti's Influence,* p. 25, and Liljegren, "Jacobinism in Spanish Louisiana," pp. 51–58.

18. This discussion of the Pointe Coupée conspiracies is based on notes taken by this author on two papers presented at the Louisiana Historical Association meeting, March 16, 1990: "The 1791 Slave Conspiracy in Pointe Coupée" by Ricard and "The 1795 Slave Conspiracy in Pointe Coupée: The Impact of the French Revolution" by Hall. See also Hall, *Africans in Colonial Louisiana*, pp. 316–374; Holmes, "Abortive Slave Revolt." McConnell, *Negro Troops*, pp. 27–28, provides additional details concerning the conspiracy between white soldiers and free moreno militiamen in 1795.

Slaves of the Mina tribe, discontented with working and living conditions, plotted to attack a settlement store in Pointe Coupée in June 1791. One slave warned the authorities, who captured seventeen slaves and sent them to New Orleans for trial. Under the probable coaching of their interpreters, one of whom was a free Mina, the accused slaves claimed that they were unaware of any conspiracy. A tribunal presided over by Governor Miró acquitted them, and Governor Carondelet later enacted stricter protective measures to regulate slave treatment and thereby prevent additional uprisings.

These measures proved inadequate. Mistreatment, food shortages, harsh work regimes, rumors of impending freedom, organizing activities of Jacobin agents, and the example of Saint Domingue brought together African and creole slaves, free whites, white indentured servants, and free people of color to undertake the overthrow of Louisiana plantation society and its inequalities. Hall's research indicates that intricate communication networks apprised the conspirators of struggles for racial equality and freedom throughout the Caribbean. Informed individuals also knew of the radical French government's attempts to end slavery in its own colonies and to encourage abolition within other nationals' colonies either through legislation or, if necessary, armed conflict. The Spanish government responded to the 1795 Pointe Coupée conspiracy by hanging twenty slaves, sentencing twenty-two blacks and two whites to hard labor, and banishing one white, one slave, and two free blacks from the colony.

Another conspiracy involving members of the Louisiana permanent (fijo) regiment and the free moreno militia was also detected in 1795. In order to protect the colony from an anticipated French invasion launched from the gulf and up the Mississippi River, Carondelet in the fall of 1793 dispatched regular troops and militia members, black as well as white, to Fort San Felipe de Placaminas, located below New Orleans near the river's mouth. During two to three months spent at Placaminas, some of the black and white soldiers stationed there met in makeshift cabins to drink, to amuse themselves, and to discuss the war between France and Spain, the possibility of a French victory in Louisiana, and the policies of the new French leaders, among other things. Back in New Orleans after the threat of invasion had passed, some of these soldiers continued their friendships and attempted to turn talk into action. One white soldier of the permanent garrison named Roland met his acquaintance from Placaminas, the free moreno militiaman Carlos Josef Lange, at a tavern, where Roland reiterated to Lange the French promise of brotherhood and equality. Plotting to destroy the tyrannical Spaniards, Roland promised to secure sixty soldiers, and he urged Lange to gather recruits. Other free moreno militia members instead convinced Lange to turn Roland over to the Spanish authorities and offer his testimony in the case. A military tribunal transferred Roland to Pensacola for punishment.

The free moreno militia members involved in the Roland case were Lange's father-in-law, Francisco Delande, a soldier, and Rafael Bernabé, a corporal first class. Bernabé was a joiner by trade. The philanthropist builder Don Andrés Almonester y Roxas contracted with Bernabé to fashion all the stairways, arches, and other works of wood in the cabildo building that stands in Jackson Square today. By 1801 Bernabé had been promoted to sergeant first class of the first pardo militia company. He was forty-four years old and stood five feet four inches tall (French measure). AGI PPC, 159-B, November 6, 1793; Notarial Acts of Francisco Broutin, Orleans Parish Notarial Archives, no. 46, f. 125, June 19, 1797 (hereafter cited by name of notary, volume number, folio, and date); AGI PPC 160-A, May 1, 1801.

19. The two Bailly trials are: Criminales seguidos de oficio contra el Pardo Libre Pedro Bahy, Louisiana State Museum Historical Center, Spanish Judicial Records (hereafter SJR), October 7, 1791; and Testimonio de la Sumaria contra el Mulato libre Pedro Bailly, Theniente de las Milicias de Pardos de esta Ciudad, por haver prorrumpido especies contra el Govierno Español, y haverse manifestado adicto a las máximas de los Franceses rebeldes, AGI Estado 14, no. 60, February 11, 1794.

20. Bailly appeared in numerous notarial records that registered real estate and slave transactions, receipts for loans and obligations, slave manumissions, guarantees of other persons' loans, and bonds put up for jailed persons. For example, one year after being manumitted, Bailly purchased a twenty-year-old morena slave for 220 pesos and sold her two years later for 400 pesos (Acts of Andrés Almonester y Roxas, f. 297, May 13, 1777 and f. 665, December 14, 1779). The June 1778 census noted that Bailly was a carter living on the left side of Saint Peter Street with his wife, a morena slave, and three other free pardos. Twenty years later he resided in the Faubourg Sainte Marie and worked as a wood dealer.

His household was comprised of thirteen individuals: four free pardos, one free morena, and eight moreno slaves (Recensement du Fauxbourg Ste. Marie, 1798, AGI PC 215-A). Josef Bailly freed his pardo slave Pedro March 28, 1776 (Acts of Andrés Almonester y Roxas, f. 191); Pedro and Naneta recorded their marriage contract before the notary Almonester y Roxas on April 25, 1778, f. 25. For Naneta's will, see Acts of Narciso Broutin, no. 2, f. 13, January 29, 1800, and for records dealing with Bailly's mother, see Acts of Andrés Almonester y Roxas, v. 1, f. 211, June 2, 1781, and f. 214, June 4, 1781. The baptisms and burials of Bailly's children and wife are registered in *Sacramental Records of the Roman Catholic Church of the Archdiocese of New Orleans*, ed. Msgr. Earl C. Woods and Charles E. Nolan (New Orleans: Archdiocese of New Orleans, 1987–1992), vols. 3–5, 7. Examples of influential Spaniards whom Bailly chose to stand for his children include Don Josef de la Peña, captain of the Louisiana permanent regiment and godfather of Joseph Pedro Bailly, and Don Andrés Armesto, secretary of the colonial government and godfather of Andrés Pedro Bailly. Somewhat ironically, the leaders of rebellion historically have had close ties to, and thus a better understanding of, the societies they have sought to change or overthrow. The losses Bailly claimed in the 1788 fire are in Archivo General de Indias, Audiencia de Santo Domingo (hereafter AGI SD) 2576, f. 535, September 30, 1788, and AGI PC 201, f. 44, March 31, 1788. At the time one peso was equivalent to about one U.S. dollar and was the monetary unit upon which the dollar was based.

21. Dorville included his militia rank in every document to which he was a party. In census records he defined his occupation as captain of the pardo militia, even though he was a vendor primarily. He was obviously very proud to be a militia officer.

22. Account of Bailly's Life and Career by Dorville and Simón, AGI Estado 14, no. 60, f. 40–52, February 12, 1794. No other documents have been located to support Dorville's and Simón's claims. Bailly appears as present on all extant militia rosters. As noted in the following text, it is possible that Dorville and Simón made up the whole story. After all, Bailly, like the Pointe Coupée slaves, had been acquitted in 1791 under Governor Miró's jurisdiction; more intense fear of slave revolt and free black/slave collusion most likely would affect Carondelet's decision. Perhaps astute free blacks like Dorville and Simón, who had several personal and material reasons for attacking Bailly, perceived that the paranoid Carondelet would convict Bailly this time around. In the 1794 case, unlike that of 1791, there were several white as well as free black witnesses to Bailly's actions.

23. Refer to Christon I. Archer, *The Army of Bourbon Mexico, 1760–1810* (Albuquerque: University of New Mexico Press, 1977); Leon Campbell, "The Changing Racial and Administrative Structure of the Peruvian Military under the Late Bourbons" *Americas* 32 (July 1975): 117–133; Hanger, "A Privilege and Honor to Serve"; Holmes, *Honor and Fidelity*; Herbert S. Klein, "The Colored Milita of Cuba: 1568–1868," *Caribbean Studies* 6 (July 1966): 17–27; Allan J. Kuethe, *Military Reform and Society in New Granada, 1773–1808* (Gainesville: University Presses of Florida, 1978); Landers, "Gracia Real de Santa Teresa de Mose"; Lyle N. McAlister, *The "Fuero Militar" in New Spain, 1764–1800* (Gainesville: University Presses of Florida, 1957); Joseph P. Sánchez, *Spanish Bluecoats: The Catalonian Volunteers in Northwestern New Spain, 1767–1810* (Albuquerque: University of New Mexico Press, 1990), for further analysis of the prestige a military title conferred upon individuals in the colonies and Spain. Several court proceedings demonstrate the extent of Dorville's economic woes. See Court Proceedings of Francisco Broutin, no. 5, June–August 1791; no. 11, March–April 1792; no. 12, April–June 1792; no. 16, January–March 1793.

24. Court Proceedings of Francisco Broutin, no. 8, f. 75–92, 93–100, September 12, 1791.

25. Pedro Bailly solicitando que Don Luis Lalande Dapremont satisfago el Almazenage de una partida de hierro que atenido es su Almazén de la pertenenda de dicho Dapremont, SJR, October 13, 1791.

26. Cap Français is the modern Cap Haitien, then known to the Spanish as el Guarico.

27. All four free pardos in this case were militia members; Bailly (43 years) and Brulé (50 years) were officers and Lalande (40 years) and Monplaisir (37 years) were soldiers. Interestingly, the soldiers could sign their names, but the officers could not. Lalande was a carpenter and married to the parda libre María Gentilly, the natural daughter of Don Luis Dreux Gentilly. They lived on Bourbon Street. In 1793 a moreno slave sued Lalande for collection of a debt, but Lalande did not have the resources to repay it. He was imprisoned and died a few months later (Court Proceedings of Francisco Broutin, no. 21, f. 1–99, January 31, 1793; Census of New Orleans, November 6, 1791, NOPL). Lalande's cousin Carlos Brulé was also a carpenter. He married María Constancia, daughter of the free pardo silversmith Raymundo Gaillard, in 1777. The pardo officer Francisco Dorville witnessed the marriage. In 1791 Brulé lived on Saint Philip Street with his wife, five children, and four slaves. Between 1791 and 1793 Brulé was promoted from sergeant second class to sergeant first class; Bailly concurrently rose from sergeant second class to lieutenant. By 1801 he was fifty-eight years old and served as captain of the free pardo grenadiers (Woods and Nolan, *Sacramental Records*, vol. 2, p. 38; Census of New Orleans, November 6, 1791,

NOPL; AGI PPC 204, f. 790–791, July 3, 1791; AGI PPC 191, f. 48–49, November 6, 1793; AGI PPC 160-A, f. 354–365, May 1, 1801).

28. Monplaisir declared to the court that although he descended from Dapremont's family and was his kin, he could not tell less than the truth. He said that Dapremont had falsely testified that he (Monplaisir) saw and participated in the exchange between Bailly and Lalande. Rather, Monplaisir was consorting with some women who had gathered on the patio, and he only heard Lalande tell Bailly that he descended from a white person, to which Bailly replied that he did, too. Barely acquainted with Bailly, Monplaisir had never heard him speak about revolution or events in Saint Domingue.

29. Bailly's statements seem confused, most likely attributed to muddled information coming into Louisiana from Saint Domingue. In the early stages of the Haitian Revolution (1791–1792), free people of color at Cap Français in general allied with whites to combat slaves of the Plaine du Nord. Thomas O. Ott states that "many *gens de couleur* [a term, along with *mulattoes*, he uses to encompass free nonwhites of any phenotype] of Le Cap François unexpectedly came to the aid of the whites, took firearms from the king's store, and killed many Insurgents. After all, equality with whites might be their reward," a reward Bailly ultimately sought. It seems that Bailly would have preferred to achieve equality between free people of color and whites peacefully, but he was willing to fight for it, as the free blacks were doing in the West and South provinces of Saint Domingue. The civil war pitting whites, free people of color, and slaves against each other was especially violent in Port-au-Prince. Ott, *The Haitian Revolution, 1789–1804* (Knoxville: University of Tennessee Press, 1973), pp. 47–75. See also Carolyn E. Fick, *The Making of Haiti: The Saint Domingue Revolution from Below* (Knoxville: University of Tennessee Press, 1990).

30. Prior to United States acquisition of Louisiana, free blacks and whites often cavorted together at dances held in private homes. There were also public or subscription balls where entrance fees were charged. The hosts of these private and public dances sometimes requested that guests not wear masks, and at other times specified masked balls, especially during the carnival season. Masking promoted a sense of mystery, secrecy, and adventure, an atmosphere some colonial authorities and inhabitants disapproved. See the author's chapter "Leisure, Family and Social Interaction" in *"Personas de varias clases y colores:* Free People of Color in Spanish New Orleans, 1769–1803," Ph.D diss., University of Florida, 1991.

31. Testimony from Bailly's second trial in 1794, however, reveals that he most likely did await communication from Saint Domingue and advocated racial warfare. Some persons who offered testimony in the 1791 case and others who claimed to have observed Bailly and Lalande conversing but did not come forward at that time served as character witnesses in the later trial. In general repeating the statements he made in 1791, Brulé testified that he had conversed with Monplaisir and Lalande's wife on the patio (evidently Lalande and Bailly were *not* alone) at a carefully placed distance so that he would not have to listen to or join in Lalande's and Bailly's discussion. He could not hear anything. Now a widow due to the death of Lalande in 1792, María Gentilly contradicted Brulé and claimed that Bailly conducted his query in the presence of herself, Lalande, Brulé, and Monplaisir. Although Lalande had not received any information about the French, Bailly stated that he had received letters and that their content was very interesting. Bailly remarked that the pardos of Louisiana subjected themselves to too much scorn and that if they wanted to, they could obtain the same advantages that

the pardos enjoyed at Cap Français, meaning a civil status equal to that of white citizens. Lalande replied that death did not constitute an advantage. Observing Lalande's rising temper, Brulé told Bailly to keep silent and end the conversation because it could be heard by the white guests. The free pardo Carlos Simón also testified that Lalande attempted to involve him in the exchange, asking him if it was possible for a man to fight his father and brothers, but he did not pay any attention to the question.

32. In March 1792 the National Assembly decreed full civil rights as Frenchmen for all free persons of color in the colonies, and in August 1793 a new constitution was approved but never promulgated. In Saint Domingue on June 21, 1793, Sonthonax had granted freedom to all slaves in the North province who fought for the French Republic; he ordered the general abolition of slavery two months later, but like Toussaint, he intended to keep the plantation structure intact. France's National Assembly sanctioned Sonthonax's abolition law and extended freedom to slaves in all the colonies with the Emancipation Decree of February 1794. Geggus, "Racial Equality"; Ott, *Haitian Revolution,* pp. 47–83.

33. Declouet was the son of Don Alexandro Declouet (colonel of the Fixed Infantry Regiment of Louisiana and a native of France) and Doña Luisa Favrot (native of Louisiana). He was a native of Louisiana and a tobacco merchant. In 1791 Declouet was twenty-five years old and lived on Saint Peter Street. He had a natural daughter named Luisa (a mestisa libre, born December 1794) by the parda libre Clara López de Peña. Clara claimed to be of Indian descent and successfully sued to have her daughter's baptismal record transferred from *El Libro de los Negros y Mulatos* to *El Libro de los Blancos* (Census of New Orleans, November 6, 1791, NOPL; Proceedings by Clara López de Peña, Records of the Diocese of Louisiana and the Floridas, Microfilm Roll 8, September 14, 1799).

34. At Fort San Felipe Bailly also discussed the topic of racial equality, or lack of it, with another white officer, Don Manuel García. Following the usual complaint about Maxent's unwillingness to share his table with pardo officers, Bailly proceeded to state that one's skin color was an accident or chance occurrence. Pigmentation should not constitute a reason to differentiate between pardos (with free status implied) and whites. Bailly then praised the French for their correct ideas: they rewarded or punished subjects only on their merit and conduct.

35. As of May 1796 Bailly was still imprisoned in Havana. Unlike four other white prisoners from New Orleans, he was not released in December 1795. He does not appear in the 1795 census of New Orleans or in the notarial records until 1796. Don Luis de las Casas to Señor Príncipe de la Paz, Havana, AGI Estado 5, no. 107, May 8, 1796; El Señor Príncipe de la Paz to el Señor Governador del Consejo, Aranjuez, AGI Estado 5, no. 107, May 15, 1796; el Ph.e Obpo de Salamanca to el Señor Príncipe de la Paz, Madrid, AGI Estado 5, no. 107, May 21, 1796; Recensement du 1er, 2me, et 3m Quartiers, July 1795, AGI PPC 211; Acts of Francisco Broutin, no. 40, f. 328, December 21, 1796.

36. The notarial records indicate that Bailly continued buying and selling slaves with persons of all colors. He frequently borrowed and loaned large sums of money. For example, Don Antonio Cavelier repaid him 2,230 pesos in 1801, and he gave power of attorney to another white person to collect a debt of 3,214 pesos (Acts of Narciso Broutin, no. 3, f. 94, March 23, 1801, and no. 4, f. 56, February 5, 1802). For the registration of Bailly's promotion, see Acts of Francisco Broutin, no. 47, f. 31, March 12, 1798. Also see Recensement du Fauxbourg Ste. Marie, 1798, AGI PPC 215-A; "Address from the Free People of Color,"

January 17, 1804, in *The Territorial Papers of the United States*, ed. Clarence Edwin Carter (Washington, D.C.: United States Government Printing Office, 1940), vol. 9, pp. 174–175. Bailly was involved in the Batture Case of 1807. McConnell notes that rosters of several companies making up the battalion of Chosen Free Men of Color taken in 1814 (just prior to the Battle of New Orleans) included Pierre Bailly, father and son, both of whom were privates. McConnell, *Negro Troops*, pp. 28–29, 68.

37. For evidence of a three-caste (I prefer "three-tiered") system in Louisiana and comparisons with Saint Domingue, see Foner, "Free People of Color in Louisiana and St. Domingue." Hunt identifies "a rigid caste system exist[ing] in eighteenth-century St. Domingue that divided society into four well-defined groups, the *grands blancs* and their rivals, the *petits blancs*, the *gens de couleur* (*affranchis*), and the slaves." Hunt, *Haiti's Influence*, p. 11. The threat of black dominance united whites of all classes in Louisiana, but this threat could not repair the schism dividing Saint Domingue whites. Also see Gwendolyn Midlo Hall, *Social Control in Slave Plantation Societies: A Comparison of St. Domingue and Cuba* (Baltimore: Johns Hopkins University Press, 1971).

38. Geggus, "Racial Equality," pp. 1307, 1308; Hunt, *Haiti's Influence*, p. 13; Ott, *Haitian Revolution*, p. 65.

39. Geggus, "Racial Equality," pp. 1291, 1300; Ott, *Haitian Revolution*, pp. 47–75.

40. Hunt, *Haiti's Influence*, pp. 14, 18.

41. Geggus, "Racial Equality," p. 1297, n. 47.

42. This proportion approached that of Saint Domingue's, where blacks or morenos made up one-third of the free nonwhite population. Census of New Orleans, November 6, 1791, NOPL; Geggus, "Racial Equality," p. 1301, n. 62. Sample data from New Orleans notarial records for the Spanish period show that 56 percent of slaves manumitted were dark-skinned. Hanger, "*Personas de varias clases y colores*," pp. 52–54.

43. Bailly, however, frequently associated with free morenos on both business and personal levels. The godfather of Bailly's son Pedro was Francisco Brantant, a free moreno; Woods and Nolan, *Sacramental Records*, vol. 2, p. 12. Leduf testified that Bailly frequently ate with the officers of the moreno company. This statement also indicated that the free pardo and free moreno officers usually supped separately. For further discussion of social and business relations between free morenos and pardos in Spanish New Orleans, see "Free Blacks at Work" and "Leisure, Family, and Social Interaction," chapters 3 and 6 of Hanger, "*Personas de varias clases y colores*."

44. Geggus, "Racial Equality," p. 1297.

45. The French Code Noir permitted masters over the age of twenty-five to manumit their slaves. Under Spanish law, however, a slave did not have to depend upon the generosity of the master to attain freedom; rather, the slave relied on his or her own efforts and the aid of a favorable legal system. Hans W. Baade, "The Law of Slavery in Spanish Louisiana, 1769–1803," in *Louisiana's Legal Heritage*, ed. Edward F. Haas and Robert R. Macdonald (Pensacola: Perdido Bay Press for the Louisiana State Museum, 1983), pp. 43–86, further compares French and Spanish manumission policies in Louisiana, as does Hanger, "*Personas de varias clases y colores*," pp. 37–109.

46. In "Jacobinism in Spanish Louisiana" Liljegren examines the dissemination of notions considered dangerous by Spanish officials. See n. 13 for sources on the social activities of whites, slaves, and free people of color despite government attempts to prevent interracial gatherings. Authorities especially

tried to prevent slaves from gambling, drinking, dancing, and trading with free blacks and whites.

47. Baade, "Law of Slavery in Spanish Louisiana"; Ira Berlin, *Slaves without Masters: The Free Negro in the Antebellum South* (New York: Pantheon, 1974); John W. Blassingame, *Black New Orleans, 1860–1880* (Chicago: University of Chicago Press, 1973); McConnell, *Negro Troops;* and Judith K. Schafer, "'Open and Notorious Concubinage': The Emancipation of Slave Mistresses by Will and the Supreme Court in Antebellum Louisiana," *Louisiana History* 28, no. 2 (Spring 1987): 165–182, and Shafer, *Slavery, the Civil Law, and the Supreme Court of Louisiana* (Baton Rouge: Louisiana State University Press, 1994), examine the declining status of free people of color in antebellum New Orleans and Louisiana.

8

Revolutionary Saint Domingue in the Making of Territorial Louisiana

ROBERT L. PAQUETTE

The French Revolution stands as the pivotal episode in—arguably—the pivotal period in the making of the modern world. From about the last quarter of the eighteenth century to the middle of the nineteenth, Europe and the Americas experienced unprecedented political upheaval and social transformation. Countries increasingly interlocked within a dynamic, capitalist-driven world market produced disaffected social groups that coalesced into mass insurgencies. These related if discrete insurgencies constituted a vital force in what has been called the age of revolution or age of democratic revolution.[1]

The French Revolution in breaching the old order had expanded the realm of the possible, for reformers as well as for revolutionaries on both sides of the Atlantic. Betrayed promises and bloody excesses notwithstanding, it projected outward one or another vision of human progress, personal freedom, and earthly happiness. It enshrined a revolutionary language that consisted not only of new words but also of old words infused with new meanings. Its champions, proclaiming citizenship, civil liberty, natural rights, and equality, would capture the moral high ground in remarkable quickstep from the defenders of servitude, arbitrary power, privilege, and hierarchy.

Progressive forces in Europe converged during the French Revolution with emancipationist struggles in the Americas, most notably in France's Caribbean colony of Saint Domingue. In 1791 its slaves rose in revolution. They defeated a succession of European armies and, in 1804, created Haiti, the second independent nation in the Americas. The triumph of the slaves and their creation of a black nation in what had been the world's most valuable slave colony raised a standard by which subsequent collective slave resistance, wherever it occurred in the Americas, would be reckoned. Existence proves possibility. Slaves everywhere now had evidence that they could win a confrontation with their supposedly invulnerable masters; masters everywhere now had evidence that collective slave resistance, no matter how small in its beginnings, could turn their world upside down. Much particularist resistance to enslavement mobilized Saint Domingue's oppressed masses, but the revolutionary process also manifested an ecumenical crusade against the system of slavery itself and bore witness to the revolutionary politics and ideology of the wider world. Certainly Saint Domingue's rebel leaders asserted the rights of their people by looking well beyond the referent of their own insular community. As Robin Blackburn, building on the work of C. L. R. James and Eugene Genovese, has argued, "Part of the grandeur of the great French Revolution is that it came to sponsor slave emancipation in the Americas; and part of the grandeur of the great Revolution in St. Domingue/Haiti is that it successfully defended the gains of the French Revolution against France itself."[2]

Defense of those gains shaped the history of the greater Caribbean in ways that scholars have only begun to detail. A full accounting would require volumes. Here one country, territorial Louisiana, will be explored at two levels of analysis—international and local—to suggest the broad and deep influence of revolutionary Saint Domingue.

The story of how Napoleon in the spring of 1803 abandoned his plan to recreate a French empire in the Americas by selling the vast Louisiana territory to the United States has been told many times. But questions persist as to how much credit, if any, Saint Domingue's black Jacobins should receive for Napoleon's decision. Many writers have downplayed the influence of the slave revolution by focusing on Europe and the breakdown of the Peace of Amiens. Simply put, their argument is that Napoleon sold Louisiana because he needed money to prepare for renewed war with Britain. His interest in the east continued to flame, and to reconquer Egypt he had to concentrate on ousting the British from the strategic island of Malta. Selling Louisiana also had the added advantage of improving French relations with the United States and strengthening the most likely candidate to rival Britain for maritime supremacy in the Americas.[3]

Nationalist historians from the United States have gone further. Napoleon, they maintain, offered to sell Louisiana only when he came to understand the depth of United States hostility to France's control of the Mississippi Valley. Whether from Thomas Jefferson and his administration, Congress, or popular protests, clear and abundant signals had reached Napoleon by the first months of 1803 to convince him of United States willingness to go to war over Louisiana and of his consequent vulnerability there and in the Caribbean as well.[4] With war imminent in Europe, Napoleon turned Louisiana to his advantage by selling it to the emerging American power from whom he had little hope of securing it.

Many writers, in apparent harmony with these views, have denied that at the time of Louisiana's sale Napoleon had surrendered his ambitions in Saint Domingue. Thus, Thomas Ott, a historian of the Saint Domingue revolution, contends that even though the great force under General Leclerc sent by Napoleon in 1801 to subdue Saint Domingue suffered terrible losses, among them Leclerc himself, "there is . . . no evidence to prove that Bonaparte considered his Saint Domingue expedition a failure; on the contrary, the First Consul was giving it unprecedented support at the very time he decided to sell Louisiana."[5] Saint Domingue, by extension, gets, at best, a minor, contributing role in Louisiana's sale, and the slave rebels share with epidemic disease the explanation for decimating Napoleon's troops. With reason then did David Geggus recently ask in 1988 for a reconsideration of the issues.[6]

Ott and others seem to equate "failure" with nothing less than capitulation, as if "unprecedented support" entails attainment of an end or even the likely prospect of attaining it. Failure means to fall short of success; success for Napoleon meant far more than a commitment to Saint Domingue but rather the fulfillment of his grander western design, which, in turn, hinged on the firm reestablishment of French authority in Saint Domingue. By the end of March 1803, when Napoleon finally decided to sell Louisiana, he had fallen short of this clearly stated goal, and the costs in Saint Domingue were mounting.

Napoleon derived his western design from ideas and information that had been considered within governmental circles since before the beginning of the French Revolution. In 1789 France's minister to the United States had written a lengthy report on his country's need to recover Louisiana from Spain. If accomplished, "Louisiana could become a center for the northern fur trade, a customer of the mother country, a depot of supplies for the Antilles, and the theatre of a vast trade with the United States."[7] Napoleon resurrected this vision in slightly altered form after he seized the mantle of First Consul. Saint Domingue had accounted for about 40 percent of France's external trade before the French Revolution. Napoleon saw the plantation system once restored to its prerevolutionary order as a mighty commercial engine that would drive France's other American possessions and probably France itself into an interdependent and, above all, self-contained prosperity. French shipping, crippled by years of war with Britain, would regenerate, and France's Caribbean possessions would no longer have to depend on the United States for timber, cattle, and foodstuffs. Indeed, in Louisiana protected French merchants would be poised to carry out an extensive smuggling trade with Mexico and other Spanish possessions.[8]

Leading statesmen in the United States feared the creation of a military colony in Louisiana, which was also considered a convenient outlet for the revolutionary energies of Napoleon's officers and soldiers.[9] Granted land, they could in the process of settling Louisiana readily garrison it for wider conflicts to come. Secret instructions in 1802 tell of "the intention of the First Consul . . . to give Louisiana a degree of strength which will permit him to abandon it without fear in time of war, so that its enemies may be forced to the greatest sacrifice in attempting to attack on it."[10]

Napoleon required respite from war with Britain to implement his western design. He could neither restore order in Saint Domingue nor begin to develop Louisiana so long as a belligerent British navy dominated the sea lanes. The Peace of Amiens (March 27, 1802) provided him with a strategic pause in the world struggle. Refusing to wait on the official signing of the peace, he moved months before, in October 1801, soon after conclusion of its preliminary articles, to prepare an expedition which, in the words of one anxious British official, "surpasses any heretofore seen in the American Archipelago."[11]

Although Napoleon anticipated protests from Britain and the United States over the existence of his great expedition, he gambled that their common fears of a spreading contagion in the greater Caribbean from the black republic in Saint Domingue would allow him to proceed. He thereby veiled his related work in Louisiana. If he could quickly and quietly gain a foothold in Louisiana and gather support from its French-speaking majority, he might not be dislodged without negotiating advantages in other contested regions. François Barbé-Marbois, France's minister of the treasury and Napoleon's close advisor, remembered that Napoleon's plan "consisted in first subjecting the revolted colony, by sending there such considerable forces that he might be justified in regarding success as infallible. After the reduction of the rebels, a part of the army was to be conveyed to Louisiana."[12] Subjected Saint Domingue would thereafter serve as a nearby base for operations in Louisiana.

Only with the enlightenment of hindsight could Napoleon be damned for taking this first step without sufficient forces. His people had amassed most of the available shipping to transport nearly 20,000 men—laureled officers and largely veteran troops at that, fresh from glory on the Continent. Napoleon had thought to send a smaller, separate expedition from Holland at about the same time to occupy Louisiana, but organization lagged, and because of Leclerc's expedition, sufficient transports could not be had.

Concentration on Saint Domingue also seemed logical because by the end of 1801 Spanish officials still had not handed over the documents necessary for the formal transfer of Louisiana, which had been negotiated provisionally more than a year before in the secret treaty of San Ildefonso (October 1, 1800). Had General Leclerc succeeded quickly in Saint Domingue or had sufficient resources been available in Europe, Napoleon might well have ignored formalities. But that would have endangered the truce with Britain and engendered even more than the anticipated protests from both Britain and the United States against the legal retrocession of Louisiana to France.

Napoleon's great expedition, under the command of his brother-in-law, General Leclerc, landed in Saint Domingue in January 1802. Crushing setbacks made quick redeployment of troops in Louisiana foolhardy. In the memorable words of Barbé-Marbois, "There was no longer any question of rebellion. The hostilities had assumed the character of a war between two independent nations."[13]

By the summer of 1802, Napoleon was growing impatient with Spain and with the attendant delays to Louisiana's occupation. In June he informed Denis Decrès, France's minister of navy and colonies, "My intention is that we take possession of Louisiana with the shortest possible delay, that this expedition be organized in the greatest secrecy, and that it have the appearance of being directed toward Saint-Domingue. The troops that I intend for it being on the [river] Scheldt, I should like them to depart from Antwerp or Flushing."[14]

Preparations intensified after Spain finally handed over the royal order of transfer in October 1802. Napoleon and his advisors looked forward to the orderly departure before the end of the year. Secret instructions went out to General Claude P. Victor, chosen by Napoleon to be captain-general of Louisiana, one month later. But rounding up enough ships and ship's stores and finding the money to pay for them plagued Minister Decrès. Lord Whitworth, Britain's minister to France, repeatedly told his superiors near the end of 1802 that Saint Domingue was preoccupying Napoleon's attention. News of ravaged French forces and rebel successes were also circulating widely. "I will content myself with observing," Whitworth wrote in early December, "that such is at this moment the penury of the Government, that it does not possess the means of sending out even the necessary reinforcements for St.

Domingo, and it has only been within these very few days that those means have been very scantily supplied by extorting different sums from the bankers of Paris."[15]

Again, Saint Domingue had intruded. The strain of providing for Leclerc's expedition and the subsequent drain of resources to Saint Domingue disrupted operations in Louisiana that crucially depended on money, coordination, and timing. Napoleon had promised to remove his troops from Holland in September 1802. About three thousand of them remained there well after that date because they were destined for Louisiana. Thousands more had to stay because, as Harold Deutsch has pointed out, "The First Consul was forced by financial embarrassment to maintain a large part of the Republic's forces beyond her borders. His Dutch policy in particular was motivated to a larger extent by this consideration than by any deliberate expansionist program."[16] Britain, however, had made Napoleon's evacuation of Holland a condition of its own evacuation of Malta. Neither happened, and the tenuous Peace of Amiens weakened further.

Months behind schedule, the Louisiana expedition was ready to sail from the Dutch port of Helvoet-Sluys by the start of the new year. By then, however, the weather refused to cooperate, for a cold snap had icebound the ships. Meanwhile Napoleon learned of the death of Leclerc and on January 11, 1803, was reported to have raged, "Damn sugar, damn coffee, damn colonies."[17] To be sure, Napoleon sent thousands of reinforcements to Saint Domingue, but his western design was unraveling. According to Barbé-Marbois, Napoleon, "persisting notwithstanding that event [the death of Leclerc] in his first views, had with reluctance abated his exertions for the speedy departure of the new forces which he purposed sending to America."[18]

In February, as ice still trapped the ships at Helvoet-Sluys and loud opposition from Jefferson and the United States was making an impression, an anxious Napoleon, seeing opportunity slipping away, ordered the Louisiana expedition to sail directly to Louisiana at the first possible moment without stopping at Saint Domingue. Britain watched the massing of forces in Holland and France suspiciously. Napoleon condemned Britain for not living up to the Peace of Amiens. King George III spoke in Parliament of the threat of war. British warships attended the March warming in Holland by positioning themselves outside of Helvoet-Sluys. Once again, the Louisiana expedition sat in port.[19]

Napoleon disliked indecision in his lieutenants and loathed it in himself. In March, he had no doubt that war with Britain was impending. He would still try to salvage what he could in Saint Domingue. If he could not have Louisiana, neither would the British. So, with a seismic shift in strategy, Napoleon opened negotiations with the United States for Louisiana's sale.

The idea that Louisiana's fate was determined solely because of European considerations comes from a rather parochial or tendentious reading of nineteenth-century balance-of-power politics. By this time European conflict had become global conflict. Empire building in the Americas consisted of adding new land and resources to obtain advantage within a circle that, however much it centered in Europe, had nonetheless been widening dramatically overseas, especially in the eighteenth and nineteenth centuries because of the continuing struggle between imperial Britain and imperial France. Not only was revolutionary process in Saint Domingue conspicuously shaped by European balance-of-power politics; it shaped them as well, in some cases decisively. The interconnectedness of Louisiana and Saint Domingue existed not just in Napoleon's mind. By heroically defending the gains of the French Revolution, the rebels of Saint Domingue had drastically limited Napoleon's capacity to fulfill his western design and to project power in the Americas. The precise timing of the collapse of the Peace of Amiens in 1803 and the resumption of war in Europe had much to do with the deployment of French forces in Holland and elsewhere. But certainly that deployment cannot be disassociated from France's preparations for Louisiana and from its general financial woes, aggravated repeatedly by the shocks from Saint Domingue.

Those who connect the sale of Louisiana to Saint Domingue can acknowledge a contribution yet avoid the harder question: Did continued rebellion in Saint Domingue cause Napoleon to sell Louisiana? Put another way, was it a factor whose absence would have obviated the sale?

No sharp line separates causes from counterfactuals. Identifying necessary conditions for historical events invariably leads to the acceptability, given what is known, of certain alternative possible worlds in which, for example, Leclerc's immediate smashing of resistance or a negotiated French protectorate in Saint Domingue freed up sufficient capacity—shipping, soldiers, money, administrative energy—so that Napoleon could have effectively occupied Louisiana. Napoleon surely understood that once in Louisiana he would face foreign opposition; he wanted to be entrenched there before it reached critical mass.

Contrary to standard fare in the United States about the Louisiana purchase as a triumph of Jefferson diplomacy, Robert Tucker and David Hendrickson have cogently argued that by the summer of 1801 Jefferson had no clear understanding of Napoleon's western design. Instead of using Saint Domingue to thwart Napoleon and advance United States interests in the Mississippi Valley, Jefferson actually encouraged Napoleon to secure Saint Domingue from the black rebels, who, in his estimation, posed the greater threat, that of spreading a horrible race war to the southern states.[20] At the very least, bargaining that might have resulted many months or several years later with Napoleon developing Louisiana from an entrenched position would have looked quite different from that which resulted in the sale of all of Louisiana.

Alexander Hamilton, no mean student of national interest and the international balance of power during the age of revolution, welcomed what he saw as the fortuitous conjunction of events that handed Jefferson's administration the opportunity to purchase Louisiana. With due regard to Federalist partisanship, his assessment of Saint Domingue's influence demands respect:

> On the part of France the short interval of peace had been wasted in repeated and fruitless efforts to subjugate St. Domingo; and those means which were originally destined to the colonization of Louisiana, had been gradually exhausted by the unexpected difficulties of this ill-starred enterprize.
>
> To the deadly climate of St. Domingo, and to the courage and obstinate resistance made by its black inhabitants are we indebted for the obstacles which delayed the colonization of Louisiana, till the auspicious moment, when a rupture between England and France gave a new turn to the projects of the latter, and destroyed at once all her schemes as to this favourite object of her ambition.[21]

Possession of Louisiana brought the United States more than 800,000 square miles of ill-defined land populated by foreigners of unknown numbers, concentrated in and above New Orleans. Many of Hamilton's fellow Federalists repudiated this "howling wilderness" and its inhabitants, so lacking in republican virtue and unfit for self-government, or so it was claimed. Heated national debates quickly emerged over the constitutionality of the purchase and Louisiana's proposed status within a democratic republic.[22]

By the beginning of the territorial period, however, lower Louisiana was entering an agricultural and commercial boom. Its economy, like that of western Cuba and other regional enclaves in the greater Caribbean, was benefiting from the demise of war-torn Saint Domingue as the world's leading producer of sugar. Jean-Etienne de Boré's celebrated experiments with sugar culture near New Orleans in 1794–1795 took place with the help of Saint Domingue émigrés and higher sugar prices.[23] By 1804 the rich Mississippi bottomland above and below New Orleans boasted nearly eighty sugar plantations, which may have produced more than five million pounds of sugar.[24] Cotton plantations were also spreading out, above Baton Rouge and northwest along the Red River. Demand for slave labor increased accordingly and outpaced supply. Indeed, the available census data disclose that the Louisiana territory actually had several thousand fewer slaves in 1803 than it did in 1785, when they numbered more than 16,000.[25]

Answering the labor question directly confronted both local and national apprehensions about a replication of the Saint Domingue revolution. In an 1804 bill for Louisiana's territorial government, Congress wrangled over the provision on slave importation. Given the paucity of proslavery commentary from the end of the American Revolution to the War of 1812, these debates offer a significant glimpse into evolving patterns of sectional thought on slavery as well as the slave trade. Three senators from slaveholding states—John Breckinridge of Kentucky, Samuel White of Delaware, and Jesse Franklin of North Carolina—called slavery an evil and conjured up the scarlet image of revolutionary Saint Domingue in seeking to restrict slave importations to Louisiana. "Tis our duty," Senator White declared, "to prevent, as far as possible, the horrid evil of slavery—and thereby avoid the fate of St. Domingo. Nothing but the interposition of Heaven, an unusual thunderstorm, prevented the slaves, only two years since, from destroying Richmond in Virginia."[26] He was referring to Gabriel's conspiracy of 1800, which did, in fact, involve at least one white Frenchmen and seems to have been encouraged by the example of Saint Domingue.[27]

Congress eventually passed a bill that divided the Louisiana territory at the thirty-third parallel into the Orleans territory (essentially what became the state of Louisiana) south of the line and the much larger district of Louisiana north of the line. Section ten forbade, for both territories, "any person or persons to import or bring [slaves] into the said territory, from any port or place without the limits of United States."[28] From within the United States, only those slaves imported before May 1798 and brought into Louisiana by United States citizens intent on settling there could remain.

In particular the *ancienne population*, those French-speaking whites born in Louisiana before its sale to the United States, could not easily understand why rights granted to citizens of the states were denied to them. Properly concerned about social order, they could live with a ban on slave imports from the restive Caribbean as they had after 1800 under Spanish rule. But they wanted access to African sources, whether directly or indirectly through South Carolina, the one state that had reopened the African slave trade before the constitutionally permitted closing in 1808.[29]

Additional congressional legislation passed in March 1805, for Orleans territory only, in effect granted government officials a reprieve from planter discord over the slave trade restrictions. Because this law placed the territorial government of Orleans on exactly the same footing as the territorial government of Mississippi and because its residents possessed the right to import slaves from any state in the United States, residents of Orleans territory ipso facto assumed the same right. John Breckinridge, who in 1804, as senator, had spoken out against the foreign slave trade to the Louisiana territory, in 1805, as United States attorney general, upheld this favorable interpretation by the planting interest. Hence, before 1808, African slaves were able to enter New Orleans by first touching at South Carolina.[30]

William C. C. Claiborne, Thomas Jefferson's handpicked choice as provisional governor of the Louisiana territory and the first and only governor of Orleans territory, had quietly approved the stricter prohibitions of 1804 with his superiors. His prejudices, like those of his president, disposed him more toward free white labor than black slaves. Anglo-American settlers, he also maintained, would come far better prepared to establish the blessings of republican liberty in Louisiana. With slaves and free people of color already comprising more than 40 percent of the total population, he wanted to prevent that "unfortunate race" from overrunning the place. Besides, he wrote, the native whites, debilitated by years of arbitrary rule, had not learned well enough the lessons of Saint Domingue.

> African Negroes are thought here not to be dangerous; but it ought to be recollected that those of St. Domingo were originally from Africa and that slavery Where ever it exists is a galling yoke. I find however that an almost universal sentiment exists in Louisiana in favour of the African traffic.[31]

Like Spanish governors before him, Claiborne had to contend with smugglers who were bringing in slaves from Saint Domingue and other areas of the Caribbean. The French prefect Pierre Clément de Laussat, whom Napoleon had sent ahead of the expedition that never came and from whom Claiborne officially received the transfer of French authority, complained in March 1803 of "criminally greedy traders [who] were bringing in Negroes from Saint Domingue. With each day the evil worsened."[32] Because of his fear of moral contagion from revolutionary Saint Domingue, Claiborne early in 1804 ordered all boats that carried persons of color stopped for inspection at the downriver outpost of

Plaquemines; the boats could not proceed until Claiborne was satisfied that they carried no disruptive elements. Despite this precaution, he conceded, "brigands from St. Domingo" were still slipping in through inhospitable backwaters or concealed in the holds of ships. "I am particularly desirous to exclude those slaves who (from late habits) are accustomed to blood and devastations, and whose Counsel and communication with our present black population may be pregnant with future mischief."[33]

By 1806 slaves and free people of color made up a clear majority of the soaring territorial population. The first official United States census of the territory in 1810 counted 34,311 whites, 34,660 slaves, and 7,585 free persons of color. These figures represented increases from 1803 of 115, 189, and 384 percent, respectively.[34] The relatively equal proportions of whites and slaves and the size of the free colored class, which by 1810 amounted to almost 10 percent of the total population, distinguished lower Louisiana from every state in the union. It bore a far greater resemblance in demography and economy at the same historical moment to the sugar plantation zone around the rising western Cuban port of Matanzas.

To Claiborne's chagrin, a substantial portion of the rapid population growth in Orleans territory derived from legal and illegal immigration from Saint Domingue. Probably more than 15,000 Saint Dominguais resettled in greater New Orleans from the start of the slave revolution to the end of the territorial period in 1812.[35] No immigration stream probably had a more pronounced impact on territorial life. Whites filled roles as legislators, jurists, artists, educators, physicians, and journalists as well as planters, and in the process reinforced besieged French culture; free people of color occupied a wide range of arts and skilled trades, from cabinetry to fencing instruction; slaves provided muscle, skills, and knowledge that contributed to the success of Louisiana's nascent sugar industry.[36]

The number of Saint Domingue immigrants was small in the beginning, probably no more than several hundred by the turn of the century. Some came directly to New Orleans; others gradually moved there after first entering Atlantic ports in the United States. Thousands, including contraband slaves, arrived from 1802 to 1804 with the destruction of Leclerc's forces and his successor's eventual surrender.[37] By far the largest wave of migration crested in 1809. Official and popular hostility to Napoleon's invasion of Spain led to the uprooting of resettled Saint Dominguais in Cuba. More than 9,000 sought refuge in New Orleans within less than a year, according to government records. About 70 percent of them were women and children; about the same proportion were persons of color, almost equally divided between slaves and free coloreds.[38]

Demographic change that increased the proportion of slaves and free persons of color relative to whites and was conspicuously fed by migration from revolutionary Saint Domingue heightened anxieties about governance and social control. Saint Dominguais of all colors spread out from New Orleans to inhabit the prospering river parishes. Territorial officials and planters repeatedly confronted real and imagined rumblings from below, influenced to greater or lesser degrees by Saint Domingue/Haiti.

The influence of Saint Domingue on social order, however, cut in different directions. The vast attention that generations of students have given to the clash of French and Anglo-American cultures in territorial Louisiana has obscured crucial cooperation among whites, regardless of ethnicity, and especially within the planter class. Claiborne's famous *Letter Books* reads almost like a chronicle of his insecurities about the various social groups under his rule. He was naturally suspicious of the white French-speaking inhabitants but, more often than not, registered surprise at their loyalty, or, perhaps better said, restraint. Given the proximity of the French-speaking whites to events in Saint Domingue and their economic stake in a prospering slave system, their preference to avoid collective violence surprised Claiborne too much.

Life was loose and fluid in and around New Orleans. Slaves often lived away from their masters and hired themselves out up and down the Mississippi River. Soldiers of fortune and political firebrands of various ranks and colors struck deals in the grog shops and gaming rooms. Rogues and desperadoes rubbed shoulders with upstart merchants and planters and in many cases were indistinguishable from them. Claiborne repeatedly warned his superiors of the bands of "young adventurers" in New Orleans from France and the French West Indies who are "troublesome for this society," "desperate," and possessed of "revolutionary dispositions."[39]

During the first year of his provisional government, Claiborne had to send troops and arms upriver at the request of more than one hundred French- and English-speaking landholders of Pointe Coupée unnerved by the prospect of slave revolt. This booming cotton plantation district north of Baton Rouge had the largest proportion of slaves to total population (about 70 percent) of any parish in Orleans territory. It also had a history of slave resistance connected to the great revolutions in France and Saint Domingue, dating back to 1795, when it formed the center of a major slave conspiracy that included whites and several free people of color.[40] Claiborne's frightened petitioners claimed,

The news of the revolution of St. Domingo and other places has become common amongst our Blacks—and some here who relate the tragical history of the Revolution of that Island with the General Disposition of the most of our slaves has become very serious—a spirit of revolt and mutyny has crept in amongst them. A few days since we happyly discovered a plan for our distruction.[41]

To borrow Julius Scott's felicitous metaphor, a "common wind" of political ideas was stirring people of all colors and statuses in the greater Caribbean.[42]

Less than a year later, authorities in New Orleans discovered a sophisticated plot to raise slaves and free people of color in revolt throughout the Mississippi Valley. It was formulated by a white Frenchman named Grand Jean who had been a soldier in the French army and had resided for several years in Saint Domingue. In New Orleans he worked as a common laborer in the Faubourg Sainte Marie, a predominantly colored suburb notorious for its lower-class troublemakers. A mulatto slave betrayed the plot, and several free people of color helped to gather evidence against Grand Jean. After his arrest, a search of his trunk revealed a sample of the proclamation he intended to post around as an instrument of recruitment. It was entitled "Le Jugement de la raison humaine."[43]

Existence of a large free-colored class composed of numerous property holders and skilled laborers who had enjoyed certain advantages under Spanish rule presented Claiborne's administration with hard choices. Without question, the promise of republican liberty, better treatment, and more rights under United States rule had wide appeal within the free-colored community. The delivery, however, proved far less generous than the promise. Some free people of color organized to claim their rights; others, looking backward, secretly promoted Spanish interests in the territory. No consistent response emerged, as the Grand Jean conspiracy attests. Like other free-colored classes in the greater Caribbean, that in lower Louisiana behaved according to the ambivalence and vulnerability of its position.

With the maturation of slave society in Orleans territory, free people of color faced growing suspicion and discrimination, and not merely from the Anglo-American elements. The *ancienne population* had long felt, with reason, that the Spanish government used the free people of color against them in order to divide and rule. It was Claiborne a few months before the Grand Jean conspiracy who went against the wishes of New Orleans municipal leaders when he chose not to punish a free mulatto for organizing other free people of color to petition Congress on the question of their rights as citizens. He acted moderately, as he explained to Secretary of State James Madison, because

> I remembered that the events which have Spread blood and desolation in St. Domingo, originated in a dispute between the white and Mulatto inhabitants, and that the too rigid treatment of the former, induced the Latter to seek the support & assistance of the Negroes.[44]

Similar considerations prompted Claiborne to continue long-standing Spanish practice by recommissioning two companies of free-colored militiamen not only against the biases that he carried with him from the southern states but also over the opposition of French-speaking white inhabitants. Jefferson's administration supported Claiborne but urged him to diminish the size of the free-colored militia whenever possible.[45]

In the aftermath of the Grand Jean conspiracy the first Louisiana legislature passed in 1806 a law "to prevent the introduction of Free People of Color from Hispaniola, and other French Islands of America into the Territory of Orleans."[46] It prohibited all free-colored adult males from entering the territory. Those ordered to depart who did not "shall be considered suspicious, and treated as such" until the means were found for their removal. The law explicitly exempted free women of color and free-colored children under the age of fifteen. All free people of color who had removed to the territory from Hispaniola were now required to show proof of their freedom before city or parish officials.

The Saint Domingue émigré group from Cuba in 1809, including more than 6,000 slaves and free persons of color, thus violated federal law in the first case and territorial law in the second case. Initially, Claiborne refused to allow the slaves to land; on reflection, he relented. He had genuine sympathy for the white refugees and worried that strict enforcement of the federal law against their slave attendants would outrage the *ancienne population*. Moreover, the size of the migration was straining community resources. Better that slaves provide for their desperate masters rather than the United States government. The 1808 federal law that prohibited the external slave trade proved vague on how to dispose of seized contraband slaves anyway, so Claiborne allowed refugee masters to take possession of their slaves on posting surety.[47]

Adult males, although probably fewer than 15 percent of the total of more than 3,000 free-colored refugees, received little hospitality from French- or English-speaking whites. Following territorial law, Claiborne ordered all free-colored males above the age of fifteen to leave, and they were instructed to post bond to ensure compliance. "Motives of human-ity induced us to receive the [free-colored] women and children," admitted Claiborne, but "we have at this time a much greater propor-tion of that kind of population than comports with our interests."[48]

James Mather, mayor of New Orleans in 1809, assessed the character of the refugee groups for Claiborne. He conceded that a few malcon-tents were visible among the free people of color, but many of the adult males "possess property, and have useful trades to live upon."[49] When the time came for all free-colored adult males to post bond, many did not comply. Some who did forfeited bond. The authorities had difficulty identifying and rounding up any of them.

In 1804 Claiborne had informed his superiors that at present neither the black nor the mulatto population threatened the public tranquillity. But he warned that "at some future period, this quarter of the Union must (I fear) experience in some degree, the misfortunes of St. Domingo."[50]

His fears and those of the planter class seemed close to realization near the end of the territorial period when in January 1811, lower Louisiana experienced what turned out to be the largest slave revolt in United States history. Judge François-Xavier Martin, an eyewitness to the commotion caused by the revolt in New Orleans and close to the trials of some of the rebels that followed, represented what happened as "a miniature representation of the horrors of St. Domingo."[51]

Hundreds of slaves—perhaps as many as five hundred—revolted in the river parishes of Saint Charles and Saint John the Baptist, the so-called German Coast. They rose on the sugar plantation of Manuel Andry in Saint John the Baptist Parish, less than forty miles northwest of New Orleans. They wounded Andry and killed his second son, then moved south into Saint Charles Parish along the east bank of the river, advancing "rapidly" toward New Orleans. Along the way they burned plantations and destroyed other property and gathered into their ranks slaves from neighboring plantations. White families, some of them warned by loyal slaves, fled before the rebels to New Orleans in panic. White residents there feared communication between persons of color in the city and the German coast slaves. For protection government officials resorted to the truly desperate measure of arming visiting sailors with guns and swords.[52]

Wade Hampton of South Carolina, who had arrived in New Orleans on January 6 as commander in chief of the United States on the Southern Division, moved north to meet the threat with militia and regular troops. Major Homer Virgil Milton, with troops from Baton Rouge, descended the river. Before they united, about a hundred well-armed militiamen from the German Coast under the command of the wounded Andry crossed from the west bank and surprised the rebels on the sugar plantation of Bernard Bernoudi. About seventy slaves, called "banditti" or "brigands" in the official accounts, were killed in battle or summarily executed immediately thereafter. Survivors fled to swamps in the area and were hunted down. Some of those captured stood trial; at least twenty-one were found guilty and put to death. Only two or three whites appear to have been killed.

Authorities ordered executed rebels decapitated, and their heads were stuck on poles for display from Andry's plantation downriver along the east bank to New Orleans. Alcée Fortier, a patrician historian of Louisiana who was attuned to the oral tradition of the revolt and was a descendant of one of the white planting families involved, explained: "The people of the Territory wished, by this terrible warning, to protect themselves against the repetition of the horrors of the revolt in Santo Domingo."[53]

Many questions about the revolt remain to be answered. One of its leaders was Charles Deslondes, allegedly a mulatto slave from Saint Domingue. Was the Louisiana revolt influenced by the Saint Domingue revolution? Do the actions and language of the rebels, at least of the leadership, suggest integration into the age of democratic revolution? Or were the specific causes merely local?

Sugar culture had certainly intensified the work regimen in the lower Mississippi Valley. The German Coast at this time, particularly the east bank, embraced the largest and most productive sugar plantations in Orleans territory. The east bank also contained many of the largest slaveholdings arrayed in an almost unbroken village of estates. On the east bank of Saint Charles Parish, for example, where the revolt was concentrated, they averaged about forty slaves per household.[54]

Slaves of the German Coast seem to have had a tradition of resistance to enslavement. Unrest occurred there in 1795 linked to the Pointe Coupeé conspiracy. And early the next year, disturbances on the estate of the widow Thomassin, Manuel Andry's mother-in-law, led to the discovery of a plot to overthrow the whites.[55] One student of the 1811 revolt has written that the rebels included "men who had participated in the uprising in Hayti, and these took command of the movement. Companies were organized with elected officers to lead them."[56] No source for this assertion, however, was cited. General Hampton charged Spanish agents with inciting the slaves to revolt.[57] No supporting evidence for that charge has surfaced either. Free people of color, who, as a class, were often accused of representing the Spanish interest in the Orleans territory, actually joined with whites in suppressing the revolt and even drew praise for their performance.[58]

Clearly the revolt had an organization and discipline that belies loose talk of contemporaries about drunken and confused banditti. General Hampton first made contact with the rebels in the early morning of January 10 on the Fortier plantation. He found them solidly positioned "within a strong picket fence" and the brick sugar works. He formed his lines to attack, but to his surprise he discovered that the alerted rebels had retreated away "in great silence."[59] The Spanish consul in New Orleans, in passing intelligence about the revolt to his superiors, noted,

> The blacks were not frightened off by the sight of this army [the German Coast militiamen]. They formed themselves in a line, content to fire while they had ammunition. Fifteen or twenty were killed; fifty were taken prisoners, among them three of the chiefs with uniforms and epaulets.[60]

As the territorial period ended, the United States verged on another war with Britain. No less a southern thinker than John Randolph of Roanoke warned Congress that war could bring widespread slave insurrection. John Calhoun, a nationalist war hawk then, tried to counter such worries. The American Revolution, he declared, had not produced any serious cases of slave revolt. And "however the gentleman may frighten himself with the disorganizing effects of French principles, I cannot think our ignorant blacks have felt much of their baneful influence. I dare say no more than one-half of them ever heard of the French Revolution."[61] But as Elizabeth Fox-Genovese and Eugene D. Genovese have noticed, "If half had not, then half already had."[62] And by then, if, as is probable, Calhoun was right, the whites of Louisiana could address a related problem: more than half of their slaves had heard of the Saint Domingue Revolution.

NOTES

1. R. R. Palmer, *The Age of the Democratic Revolution: A Political History of Europe and America, 1760–1800*, 2 vols. (Princeton: Princeton University Press, 1959), and E. J. Hobsbawm, *The Age of Revolution: Europe 1789–1848* (New York: New American Library, 1962), have become the classic introductions to this theme.

2. Robin Blackburn, *The Overthrow of Colonial Slavery, 1776–1848* (London: Verso, 1988), p. 259. See also C. L. R. James, *The Black Jacobins: Toussaint Louverture and the San Domingo Revolution* (New York: Dial Press, 1938); Eugene D. Genovese, *From Rebellion to Revolution: Afro-American Slave Revolts in the*

Making of the Modern World (Baton Rouge: Louisiana State University Press, 1979).

3. Alexander DeConde, *This Affair of Louisiana* (Baton Rouge: Louisiana State University Press, 1978), is the best overall study of the Louisiana purchase. E. Wilson Lyon, *Louisiana in French Diplomacy, 1759–1804* (Norman: University of Oklahoma Press, 1934), and Arthur Preston Whitaker, *The Mississippi Question, 1795–1803: A Study in Trade, Politics, and Diplomacy* (New York: Appleton-Century, 1934), must still be consulted for their insight into the French and Spanish perspective, respectively. I have also benefited from Ronald D. Smith, "Napoleon and Louisiana: Failure of the Proposed Expedition to Occupy and Defend Louisiana, 1801–1803," *Louisiana History* 12 (1971): 21–40. For a recent example of what might be called the Eurocentric interpretation of the Louisiana purchase, see J. Leitch Wright, *Britain and the American Frontier, 1783–1815* (Athens: University of Georgia Press, 1975), p. 135.

4. David A. Carson, "The Role of Congress in the Acquisition of the Louisiana Territory," *Louisiana History* 26 (Fall 1985): 369–383, emphasizes the impact of the hostile Ross resolutions on Napoleon's decision to sell, but disregards Albert H. Bowman, "Pichon, the United States, and Louisiana," *Diplomatic History* 1 (Summer 1977): 257–270, who points out (p. 267) that word of the Ross resolutions reached Napoleon after he had decided to sell. So too did other intelligence, deemed crucially persuasive by some students of the purchase, from France's chargé d'affaires in the United States.

5. Thomas O. Ott, *The Haitian Revolution, 1789–1804* (Knoxville: University of Tennessee Press, 1973), p. 186. See also Carl Ludwig Lokke, *France and the Colonial Question: A Study of Contemporary French Opinion, 1763–1801* (New York: Columbia University Press, 1932), p. 234; Lokke "Leclerc Instructions," *Journal of Negro History* 10 (January 1925): 87–88.

6. David Geggus, review of Alfred N. Hunt, *Haiti's Influence on Antebellum America: Slumbering Volcano in the Caribbean, Louisiana History* 29 (Fall 1988): 389.

7. "Moustier's Memoir on Louisiana," ed. E. Wilson Lyon, *Mississippi Valley Historical Review* 22 (September 1935): 252.

8. DeConde, *Affair of Louisiana*, pp. 91–98; Smith, "Napoleon and Louisiana," pp. 23–24; Lyon, *Louisiana*, pp. 101–109; "Secret Instructions for the Captain-General of Louisiana," in *Louisiana under the Rule of Spain, France, and the United States, 1785–1807*, ed. James Alexander Robertson (Cleveland: A. H. Clark, 1911), vol. 1, pp. 364–374. See David Geggus, *Slavery, War, and Revolution: The British Occupation of Saint Domingue, 1793–1798* (Oxford: Clarendon Press, 1982), p. 6, for Saint Domingue's contribution to France's foreign trade.

9. "Secret Instructions," p. 372; Mildred Fletcher Stahl, "Louisiana As a Factor in French Diplomacy from 1763 to 1800," *Mississippi Valley Historical Review* 17 (December 1930): 374; François Barbé-Marbois, *The History of Louisiana . . .* (Philadelphia: Carey & Lea, 1830), pp. 177, 184, 192, 200–201. See [St. George Tucker], *Reflections on the Cession of Louisiana to the United States* (Washington, D.C.: Samuel Harrison Smith, 1803), p. 4, for an example of United States concern about Louisiana becoming a French military colony.

10. "Secret Instructions," p. 371.

11. Quoted in Barbé-Marbois, *History*, p. 180.

12. Ibid., p. 184.

13. Ibid., p. 190.

14. Quoted in Pierre-Clément de Laussat, *Memoirs of My Life to My Son during the Years 1803 and After . . .*, trans. Agnes-Josephine Pastwa (Baton Rouge: Louisiana State University Press, 1978), p. 114.

15. Letter, Lord Whitworth to Lord Hawkesbury, December 20, 1802, in

England and Napoleon in 1803; Being the Despatches of Lord Whitworth and Others, ed. Oscar Browning (London: Longmans, Green, 1887), p. 29. See also letter, Whitworth to Hawkesbury, November 20, 1802, in ibid., p. 13.

16. Harold C. Deutsch, *The Genesis of Napoleonic Imperialism* (Cambridge: Harvard University Press, 1938), pp. 87–88.

17. Quoted in DeConde, *Affair of Louisiana,* p. 151.

18. Barbé-Marbois, *History,* p. 249.

19. DeConde, *Affair of Louisiana,* pp. 151–154; Smith, "Napoleon and Louisiana," pp. 31–33; Lyon, *Louisiana,* pp. 130–141; Barbé-Marbois, *History,* 250–253.

20. Robert W. Tucker and David C. Hendrickson, *Empire of Liberty: The Statecraft of Thomas Jefferson* (New York: Oxford University Press, 1990), pp. 299–301. In his instructions to Leclerc, Napoleon observed, "The Spanish, the English, and the Americans view with equal anxiety the black republic. . . . Jefferson promised that from the moment that the French army arrives, every measure shall be taken to starve Toussaint and to aid the army." See Lokke, "Leclerc Instructions," p. 93. See also the conclusion reached by Clifford L. Egan in *Neither Peace nor War: Franco-American Relations, 1803–1812* (Baton Rouge: Louisiana State University Press, 1983), p. 24.

21. "Hamilton on the Louisiana Purchase: A Newly Identified Editorial from the *New-York Evening Post," William & Mary Quarterly* 13 (April 1955): 274.

22. Linda K. Kerber, *Federalists in Dissent: Imagery and Ideology in Jeffersonian America* (Ithaca: Cornell University Press, 1970), pp. 41–45, 93, 213; Everett Somerville Brown, *The Constitutional History of the Louisiana Purchase, 1803–1812* (Berkeley: University of California Press, 1920); James E. Scanlon, "A Sudden Conceit: Jefferson and the Louisiana Government Bill of 1804," *Louisiana History* 9 (1968): 139–162.

23. J. Carlyle Sitterson, *Sugar Country: The Cane Sugar Industry in the South, 1753–1950* (Lexington: University of Kentucky Press, 1953), pp. 3–6. For sugar prices, see Noel Deerr, *The History of Sugar* (London: Chapman and Hall, 1949–1950), vol. 2, p. 531.

24. Letter, John Sibley to an unknown correspondent, August 15, 1804, private collection of Mrs. Charles W. Englehard, Far Hills, N.J. Sibley was a physician who settled in Louisiana in 1802 and became a reliable source of information for Governor Claiborne. He carefully counted the sugar plantations on a trip up the Mississippi River. He estimated their sugar production at 75,000 pounds each per annum. See also John G. Clark, *New Orleans, 1718–1812: An Economic History* (Baton Rouge: Louisiana State University Press, 1970), pp. 202–220, esp. p. 219.

25. Census data for 1785 and 1803 are contained in *American State Papers, Class X, Miscellaneous* (Washington: Gales and Seaton, 1834), pp. 381–382. The census of 1803 placed the number of slaves for the entire Louisiana territory and West Florida at only 12,920 but conceded a considerably higher figure because of underestimation and omission. A more accurate census for the Orleans territory in 1806 placed the number of slaves at 22,701 but excluded those of Concordia Parish. Adjusted according to the percentage of slaves in Concordia Parish in 1810, the total for 1806 would rise to 24,880. For the census of 1806, see Territorial Papers of the United States Senate, 1789–1873, Record Group 46, National Archives, Washington, D.C. (microfilm M200, reel 5).

26. *William Plumer's Memorandum of Proceedings in the United States Senate, 1803–1807,* ed. Everett Somerville Brown (New York: Macmillan, 1923), pp. 111–129, esp. pp. 115–116. See also Kerber, *Federalists,* pp. 42–46.

27. Douglas R. Egerton, "Gabriel's Conspiracy and the Election of 1800," *Journal of Southern History* 56 (May 1990): 191–214, esp. 211–213; Genovese, *Rebellion*, p. 95.

28. Francis Newton Thorpe, *The Federal and State Constitutions, Colonial Charters, and Other Organic Laws of the States, Territories, and Colonies . . .* (Washington: Government Printing Office, 1909), vol. 3, p. 1368.

29. Paul F. Lachance, "The Politics of Fear: French Louisianians and the Slave Trade, 1786–1809," *Plantation Society in the Americas* 1 (June 1979): 162–197, is an excellent study; see esp. 176–180. See also letters, Claiborne to Madison, March 10, 1804, in *Official Letter Books of W. C. C. Claiborne, 1801–1816* (Jackson: Mississippi State Department of Archives and History, 1917), vol. 2, pp. 25–26, and Claiborne to Jefferson, April 15, 1804, in *The Territorial Papers of the United States*, ed. Clarence Edwin Carter (Washington: Government Printing Office, 1934–1969), vol. 9, p. 222. French-speaking planters and merchants openly expressed their complaints about the government bill of 1804, including its slave trade provisions, in a memorial to Congress of December 31, 1804, published in *American State Papers, Class X, Miscellaneous*, pp. 396–399.

30. Thorpe, *Federal and State*, vol. 3, p. 1371; Lachance, "Politics of Fear," p. 180. Breckinridge's reasoning on the internal slave trade in 1804 helps to explain his decision in 1805. "I think it good policy to permit slaves to be sent there [Louisiana] from the United States. This will disperse and weaken that race & free the southern states from a part of its black population, and of its danger. If you do not permit slaves from the United States to go there, you will thereby prohibit men of wealth from the southern states going to settle in that country." See *Plumer's Memorandum*, p. 129. For Thomas Jefferson's influence on Breckinridge, see Scanlon, "Sudden Conceit," pp. 152–153.

31. Letter, Claiborne to Madison, July 12, 1804, in *Letter Books*, vol. 2, p. 245. See also Claiborne to Jefferson, April 15, 1804, in *Territorial Papers*, vol. 9, p. 222.

32. Laussat, *Memoirs*, p. 18.

33. Letter, Claiborne to Colonel Freeman, July 17, 1804, in *Letter Books*, vol. 2, pp. 254–255.

34. Third Census of the United States, 1810, Department of Commerce, Record Group 29, National Archives, Washington, D.C. (microfilm, M252 reel 10).

35. René J. Le Gardeur, Jr., "The Refugees from Saint-Domingue," *New Orleans Genesis* 2 (March 1963): 175–176; René R. Nicaud, "The French Colonists from St. Domingue and, in Particular, Louis Moreau Lislet," *Louisiana Bar Journal* 20 (1973): 285–305. My estimate includes imports of contraband slaves from Saint Domingue.

36. Alfred N. Hunt, *Haiti's Influence on Antebellum America: Slumbering Volcano in the Caribbean* (Baton Rouge: Louisiana State University Press, 1988), pp. 45–63; Paul Lachance, "The 1809 Immigration of Saint-Domingue Refugees to New Orleans: Reception, Integration and Impact," *Louisiana History* 29 (Spring 1988): 109–141; Thomas Fiehrer, "Saint-Domingue/Haiti: Louisiana's Caribbean Connection," *Louisiana History* 30 (Fall 1989): 431–433.

37. Gabriel Debien and René Le Gardeur, Jr., "Les Colons de Saint-Domingue réfugiés a la Louisiana," *Revue de Louisiana* 10 (1981): 97–141.

38. Calculated from the table in *Moniteur de la Louisiane* (New Orleans), March 24, 1810.

39. Letters, Claiborne to Madison, January 24, 1804, April 9, 1804, in *Letter Books*, vol. 1, p. 345, and vol. 2, p. 88, respectively.

40. Gwendolyn Midlo Hall, *Africans in Colonial Louisiana: The Development of*

Afro-Creole Culture in the Eighteenth Century (Baton Rouge: Louisiana State University Press, 1992), chap. 11, provides compelling evidence of the engagement of Pointe Coupée's slaves with the revolutionary politics and ideology of the transatlantic world. See also Jack D. L. Holmes, "The Abortive Slave Revolt in Pointe Coupée, Louisiana, 1795," *Louisiana History* 11 (Fall 1979): 341–362; James Thomas McGowan, "Creation of a Slave Society: Louisiana Plantations in the Eighteenth Century" (Ph.D. diss., University of Rochester, 1976), pp. 347–393; Juan José Andreu Ocariz, *Movimientos rebeldes de los esclavos negros durante el dominio español en Luisiana* (Zaragoza: Departamento de Historia Moderna, 1977), pp. 117–177.

41. The petition appears in *Louisiana,* ed. Robertson, vol. 2, pp. 300–301.

42. Julius Sherrard Scott, "The Common Wind: Currents of Afro-American Communication in the Era of the Haitian Revolution," Ph.D. diss., Duke University, 1986.

43. Letter, John Watkins to Secretary Graham, September 6, 1805, in *Territorial Papers,* vol. 9, pp. 500–504. See also Watkins to the City Council, September 28, 1805, Messages of the Mayors, New Orleans Public Library.

44. Letter, Claiborne to Madison, July 12, 1804, in *Letter Books,* vol. 2, p. 245. For a formal response of free-colored leaders to United States rule, see their memorial to Claiborne of January 1804, in *Territorial Papers,* vol. 9, p. 174.

45. Letter, H. Dearborn to Claiborne, February 20, 1804, in *Letter Books,* vol. 2, p. 54. See Roland C. McConnell, *Negro Troops of Antebellum Louisiana: A History of the Battalion of Free Men of Color* (Baton Rouge: Louisiana State University Press, 1968), pp. 33–45, for a detailed discussion of these issues.

46. *Acts Passed at the First Session of the First Legislature of the Territory of Orleans . . .* (New Orleans: Bradford and Anderson, 1807), pp. 126, 128, 130.

47. Letter, Claiborne to Graham, July 19, 1809, in *Letter Books,* vol. 4, pp. 390–391, details his reasoning on the handling of the slaves.

48. Letter, Claiborne to William Savage, November 10, 1809, in *Letter Books,* vol. 5, p. 4. See also Claiborne to Mather, August 9, 1809, in ibid., vol. 4, p. 402.

49. Letter, Mather to Claiborne, July 18, 1809, in *Letter Books,* vol. 4, p. 388.

50. Letter, Claiborne to Madison, July 12, 1804, in *Letter Books,* vol. 2, p. 245.

51. *American and Commercial Daily Advertiser* (Baltimore), February 20, 1811. That Judge Martin authored the letter is clear from a column entitled "Private Correspondence" in the February 26, 1811, issue of the newspaper.

52. James H. Dorman, "The Persistent Specter: Slave Rebellion in Territorial Louisiana," *Louisiana History* 18 (Fall 1977): 389–404, is one of the few scholarly studies of the 1811 revolt. For the response to the revolt in New Orleans and the arming of sailors, see Proceedings of the City Council, Extraordinary session, January 12, 1811, New Orleans Public Library.

53. Alcée Fortier, *A History of Louisiana* (Paris: Goupil, 1904), vol. 3, pp. 78–79.

54. Calculated from data in the census of 1810.

55. Holmes, "Abortive Slave Revolt," p. 358; McGowan, "Creation of a Slave Society," pp. 354, 361–362. On the relationship between Thomassin and Andry, see Glenn R. Conrad, *The German Coast: Abstracts of the Civil Records of St. Charles and St. John the Baptist Parishes, 1804–1812* (Lafayette: Center for Louisiana Studies, 1981), p. 24.

56. John Kendall, "Shadow over the City," *Louisiana Historical Quarterly* 22 (1939): 144.

57. Letter, Hampton to Claiborne, January 12, 1811, in *Territorial Papers,* vol. 9, p. 917.

58. On this point, see the eyewitness account of Charles Perret, a resident of the German Coast and militia leader, published in the *Moniteur de la Louisiane* (New Orleans), January 17, 1811.

59. Letter, Hampton to William Eustis, January 16, 1811, Records of the Office of the Secretary of War, RG 107, National Archives, Washington, D.C.

60. The report of the Spanish consul of January 13, 1811, is excerpted in letter, Eusebio Bardari y Azara to Vicente Folch, February 6, 1811, legajo 221a, Papeles de Cuba, Archivo General de Indias, Seville, Spain (microfilm, Historic New Orleans Collection, New Orleans).

61. Speech, John C. Calhoun, December 12, 1811, in *The Papers of John ∙C. Calhoun*, ed. Clyde N. Wilson (Columbia: University of South Carolina Press, 1959–), vol. 1, p. 81.

62. Elizabeth Fox-Genovese and Eugene D. Genovese, "Political Virtue and the Lessons of the French Revolution: The View from the Slaveholding South," in *Self-Interest: Political Values in the Eighteenth Century*, ed. Richard K. Matthews (Bethlehem, Pennsylvania: Lehigh University Press, 1994).

9

The Admission of Slave Testimony at British Military Courts in the West Indies, 1800–1809

ROGER N. BUCKLEY

African manpower, chiefly slaves, both males and females, played a decisive military role in the development of the British West Indies. Several conditions led to the British army's dependence on slave men and women. These included the absence of conscription, which severely limited the size of the regular army; global wars, which increased the demand for more and more regulars; deadly tropical diseases, particularly among nonimmune Europeans; and, of course, the availability of a large and captive slave population. Africanization, or the critical and widespread exploitation of blacks in virtually all branches of the British military in the West Indies, was recognized during the Seven Years War and the American Revolution.[1]

Like no conflict before, the wars of the French Revolution and Napoleon entailed the unprecedented reliance on African manpower. Several thousand slave laborers, officially designated the "King's Negroes" or "Fort Negroes," were attached to most military installations in the region. They were the property of the British government. Several thousand more were privately owned slaves who were routinely hired out to the army's quartermaster, ordnance, hospital, barracks, and engineering departments.[2] A number of slave jobbers were also rented out as servants to British army officers. The most dramatic and substantive use of black manpower, however, was the large-scale enlistment of African slaves into the British army as regular soldiers soon after the start of the 1792–1815 war. Beginning in 1795, these troops were embodied in special corps which were raised for service in the region and thus were appropriately designated the "West India Regiments." Eight in number, they constituted a new, standing elite force and comprised approximately a third of the total British garrison in the West Indies for much of the long war.[3]

The scale of this unparalleled absorption of slaves as regular soldiers and service troops of all kinds into British army camps had far-reaching consequences. In the delicate area of race relations, the constant sight of black troops expertly executing their duties as British regulars, including the not infrequent example of black noncommissioned officers in command of white troops, must have taken some toll of the then-current belief that Africans were cowardly, lazy, and inferior to whites. The army's resolute use of slave manpower had its most tangible effect on the conduct of court-martial proceedings. Omnipresent by virtue of their large numbers and diverse functions, slaves became critical components of the social organization of British army camp life, with the result that they were drawn increasingly into legal disputes as potential material witnesses in cases involving, for example, white members of the military community. In conformity to colonial custom, however, slaves were prevented from giving testimony at courts-martial. Under the law of evidence with regard to slaves, the testimony of blacks was not admitted for or against free persons. Indeed, special forms of trial which were set aside for slaves, in addition to the limited validity of their evidence, marked slaves off from the rest of the West Indian body politic.[4] Nonetheless, there was mounting need among some elements of the officer corps to admit slave testimony at military tribunals in order to maintain military law and discipline.

The conflict which thus arose was centered to a large extent within the officer corps. Creolized officers, who supported the colonial law of evidence as it pertained to slaves, were pitted against other officers who managed to avoid falling into the trap of colonial conventions and who sought to guard the interests and prerogatives of the imperial army against local interference.

The issue regarding the admissibility of slave testimony at military courts was joined at an unlikely place. In the steamy Dutch colony of Surinam on August 25, 1800, almost exactly one year after its capture by British forces, a British general court-martial found Louis de Weise guilty of the deliberate murder of J. C. Bachoffener and sentenced him to death by hanging.[5] Both de Weise, a captain in the Fifth Battalion, Sixtieth Royal Regiment of Foot, and Bachoffener, an ensign in the White Chasseurs, a Dutch colonial crops, were white.

In accordance with the administration of British military law, the senior officer in the Windward and Leeward Islands Command, whose district included Surinam,[6] forwarded the proceedings of the court-martial to London to the judge advocate general. As the supreme officer responsible for the conduct of prosecutions throughout the army, the judge advocate general also advised the Crown on the confirmation of the findings and sentences of court-martial proceedings referred to him.[7] Lieutenant General Sir Thomas Trigge, a newcomer to the West Indies, also used the opportunity which this communication offered to seek the opinion of the British army's chief legal advisor regarding the lawfulness of the ruling of the presiding deputy judge advocate who conducted the prosecution at the Surinam court-martial. The ruling of August 25, 1800, returned a murder conviction based on presumptive evidence only.[8] Furthermore, the conviction resulted from the refusal of the tribunal to introduce the positive evidence of two material witnesses, both of whom were slaves.[9] The decision to reject their testimony as inadmissible was in strict keeping with West Indian legal practice, which prohibited the use of direct slave evidence against Europeans.

Sir Charles Morgan, judge advocate general at the time, recognized the critical issue raised in Trigge's query: was the imperial army subject to the disciplinary control of authorities constituted under local legislation? On this important question, Morgan admitted that he had not yet made up his mind. Nor had other eminent legal experts, he confessed. Morgan was also uncomfortable with the tribunal's decision to convict on presumptive evidence alone. Such a conviction, he warned, was "of a very nice and delicate nature." In addition to finding the slave witnesses "incontrovertibly capable of stating the real fact, whatever it may have been, from their own knowledge," an opinion that contradicted the British West Indian legal view of the slave as essentially a nonperson, Morgan was also critical of the entire body of colonial slave law, which he considered to be established not upon "natural justice" but upon prudential considerations only. Nevertheless, by upholding the Surinam ruling[10] Morgan recognized the governance of imperial troops by colonial laws. Over the next several years other judge advocates "adopted" the view that because the regular army was subject to the disciplinary control of the colonial assemblies, slave testimony or "black evidence" was prohibited at courts-martial.[11]

Curiously, no mention was made at the time of a set of official imperial instructions prepared in 1764 which gave officers commanding troops in any colony control over regimental interior economy and discipline and put each officer under the immediate command of the senior officer in the district.[12]

By 1809 imperial policies affecting the interests of the West Indies had markedly changed. The decline of the economic wealth of white West Indians in England, the so-called West India bloc, was matched by their decline as a political pressure group.[13] This became evident in that year when the question of the admissibility of slave testimony at military courts was put once again to the judge advocate general for his consideration, this time by the commander in chief at Jamaica, Major General Hugh Carmichael, an embattled regular army officer who opposed the subjection of imperial troops to local institutions and conventions. Withholding his own opinion because of doubts regarding the question, Richard Ryder, judge advocate general of the British army beginning in 1807, forwarded the query to the law officers of the Crown.[14] There being in England no single legal officer corresponding to the minister of justice in other countries, his duties were thus performed by several principal officers, among them the attorney general and the solicitor general. These officers served as legal advisors and representatives of the Crown, but they were also at the service of the state. Moreover, since they were entitled to sit in the House of Commons, where they defended the legality of government actions, their opinions had the weight of government as well as law. The law officers, as well as their assistant, the king's advocate, ruled unanimously that the state of slavery did not incapacitate a slave from being a witness in a court proceeding; the evidence of a slave, therefore, was strictly admissible in military courts.[15] In agreeing with the decisions of his colleagues, the king's advocate opined further that the view which held the testimony of a slave to be inadmissible at a court-martial was "a Rule of Local Policy altogether."[16] This political-legal volte-face meant, in effect, that slaves could now testify against whites in the military at courts-martial in all litigations, ranging from petty theft and disorderly conduct to willful murder and desertion. Slaves could also—in theory, at least—give testimony against white civilians who were litigants in actions brought by military personnel. This was possible since civil offenses, such as treason, murder, and rape, came under the jurisdiction of military courts if they were committed by soldiers on active service.[17]

The British government's landmark decision of 1809 to admit the testimony of slaves at its military courts before the abolition of slavery in 1834 reflected Parliament's growing interference in the affairs of its colonies during the Napoleonic era. Here, that decision will be explored within the context of British West Indian conventions which prohibited slave testimony against whites, the adaptation of the regular army to social and service conditions in the colonies and their consequences; and changing imperial policies regarding the initiative in colonial government.

During the eighteenth century, white creoles in the British West Indies, regardless of their station in society, were united in holding up

their superiority to all other racial groups. This was commonly interpreted as a superiority of race. Some whites believed that blacks,
whether free or slave, were at least culturally backward in comparison
with Europeans.[18] The general and overwhelming presumption, however, among West Indian whites was that slaves, if indeed they were
human, were members of a different and manifestly inferior genus; and
that, as an inevitable consequence of their racial difference, slaves were
dishonest, slothful, dissolute, savage, debased, indiscriminate in their
sexual relations, cowardly, ugly, despotic to their own kin, supersti-
tious, simple, and, of course, demonstrably inferior to Europeans.[19]
John Augustus Waller, a Royal Navy surgeon who resided in the West
Indies between 1807 and 1810, spoke for many of his countrymen when
he unabashedly opined that the English, more than any other European
nation, were inclined to regard their slaves as "an inferior order of
beings." He was also certain that "half the hardships these people
endure, may be traced to that source alone."[20]

One of the best-known attacks on the capacity of blacks was made
by Edward Long, a virulently antiblack planter-historian, in his three-
volume *History of Jamaica,* published in 1774. Long, who resided in
Jamaica from 1757 to 1769, and who inherited large slaveholding properties, utilized the idea of the Great Chain of Being in an attempt to
lower the status of blacks. The Great Chain of Being, as conceived in the
eighteenth century, began with inanimate objects, ranged upward
through the most simple forms of life, through the more intelligent
animals, including man, and continued further upward through the
myriad ranks of celestial creatures until, finally, it reached its summit in
God. No one at the time thought of the Great Chain as originating in
disparities in power and social status between human groups. Forged
by God, the chain was without gaps. Moreover, the progression between the ranks on the scale was nothing more than abstruse modifications which permitted the assembled hierarchy to remain a constant
harmonious whole. Within this hierarchy man was carefully placed in
the middle between the brute and heavenly creation. None of this
prevented Long from applying the rhetoric of the Chain of Being in
commenting on what he held to be appropriate social distinctions in
Jamaica. From this foundation Long made a number of assertions, some
of which were that blacks were a "distinct species" of human; that the
"Negroe race" consisted of "varieties"; that blacks were most analogous
to monkeys and related genera, with whom "some races of black men"
are intimate; and that blacks were cannibals. The conclusion to which
these and other arguments were pointing was that the institution of
African slavery was patterned upon what Winthrop Jordan termed the
"unalterable structure of divinely-ordained Nature."[21]

This assault on the humanity of Africans also found expression in the basic conception of English slave law, which held that slaves were a special kind of property: property in people. Consequently, when purchased and sold in the course of the slave trade, the slave was a commodity of trade. Once purchased, the slave immediately became his or her owner's private property, which was deemed in part real property and in part chattel. As chattel, a slave could be sold for debt. In other cases a slave could be disposed of in accordance with those laws which regulated the inheritance of real estate. Slaves were subject to the widow's right of dower. They could also be entailed, and they could be mortgaged like any other lifeless piece of landed property.

Elsa Goveia has shown that the slave was not completely regarded as mere property, as English slave law tried to suppose in some instances. The slave was a human being, possessing a power of choosing. The slave also demonstrated a particular capacity for violent resistance to slavery, a resistance which must be crushed if white supremacy was to survive. Thus the slave was unwittingly permitted a modicum of *persona* for the exclusive purpose of dealing with her or him under this aspect of the slave's activity as a distinct kind of property. However, insofar as the slave was permitted personality before the law, he or she was regarded almost entirely as a potential criminal. This is at once evident in the police regulations governing virtually all aspects of slave activity.[22]

British West Indian apartheid was the result of the protection and special advantages commonly enjoyed by white creoles and white newcomers to the colonies, and the enforced subordination routinely suffered by blacks. Nowhere was the subordination of blacks to whites more in evidence, and so jealously protected by whites, than in the administration of British West Indian justice. Put baldly, no slave could testify against a white person in any court, regardless of the station of the European in society. (Even in slave courts the testimony of slaves was admissible only against other slaves.) It was unthinkable, given the racist, exploitative, and rigidly subordinated nature of British West Indian society, that a common and thoroughly traduced slave be permitted the solemn opportunity to publicly challenge the integrity of white persons by bringing evidence against them in an institution dominated by, and for, whites only. To do so, it was widely believed, would weaken the very foundation of colonial society. Contemporary drawings of white creoles emphatically portray individuals accustomed to great and unchallengeable personal authority. This was particularly evident when whites were juxtaposed with tyrannized slaves.[23]

Even William Wilberforce, the famous abolitionist, publicly supported the convention that prevented slaves from testifying against whites in West Indian courts. During the course of a debate on his motion for the abolition of the slave trade in April 1792, he admitted that he feared giving slaves the right to offer evidence against whites before their moral condition had improved. (The well-known laxity in morals among white creole males[24] did not, however, undermine their legal rights.) Wilberforce hinted ominously that if this right were granted to blacks, it would likely raise certain political expectations that might well prove incompatible with their status as slaves.[25] The bloody revolution then taking place in the French West Indian colony of Saint Domingue, as Haiti was then called, encouraged Wilberforce to speak against this form of amelioration of the condition of the slaves. Beginning in August 1791, the slaves of the Plain du Nord rose against their white masters, followed quickly by the free mulattoes of the West Province. The killing, racial vengeance, and burning of large areas of the once-prosperous colony presented a new argument against abolition and any other tamperings with the slave system to people in England, who were already badly frightened by the revolution then taking place in France. It is, therefore, not difficult to understand Wilberforce's mood when news of the calamity of the Saint Domingue or Haitian Revolution reached England. Nonetheless, Wilberforce's rationale for opposing the admission of slave evidence against whites revealed not only a flawed logic in his argument but also a disturbing ignorance of the harsh realities of West Indian chattel slavery, for how was the moral condition of the slaves to be improved while they were denied their freedom and their essential humanity and while injustice and exploitation remained the necessary bulwarks of slavery?[26]

The object of the convention that made it illegal for a slave to testify against a white in any court was to ensure the permanence of British West Indian society as envisaged by white creoles. The ruling class, legislating in its own self-interest, was confronted, however, with a serious sociolegal dilemma: the legal subordination of slaves, as established in colonial law, actually facilitated the obstruction of justice for whites. The convention seriously limited the efficacy of certain laws, thereby making it extraordinarily difficult and often impossible to demonstrate that the law had in fact been broken. Drewry Ottley, chief magistrate of Saint Vincent, summed up the situation when, toward the end of the eighteenth century, he wrote: "As the evidence of Slaves is never admitted against White men, the difficulty of legally establishing facts is so great that White men are in a manner put beyond the reach of the law."[27] Throughout the Leewards and undoubtedly in the rest of the British West Indies, it was difficult to convict whites of ill-treating the slaves of others. It also became necessary to provide for the summary examination of those whites suspected of harboring slaves or involved in illicit trade with them. In 1810, the governor of the Leeward Islands, Hugh Elliot, so doubted the efficiency of existing political institutions in the region—particularly where they were invoked against powerful white individuals like Arthur Hodge, a leading inhabitant of Tortola and member of the Council of the Virgin Islands, who took lurid pleasure in torturing several of his slaves to death—that he advised the imperial cabinet to consider the drastic amendment of all colonial institutions. Hodge was subsequently condemned to death for his heinous crimes. The sentence, however, had to be carried out under martial law with a contingent of armed Royal Navy marines and sailors at the ready. Elliot found it necessary to resort to this extraordinary measure only after the jury, which found Hodge guilty of the charge of murdering one of his slaves under circumstances of extreme brutality, nevertheless recommended him to the mercy of the court. In a dispatch to the secretary for war and colonies in London, Elliot disclosed that Hodge's "enormities" would not have come to public attention had Hodge not been exposed by former cronies with whom he had recently quarreled. In 1816 Sir James Leith, Elliot's successor, complained bitterly that he was unable to obtain information with regard to litigations involving slaves because the court records were faulty and those who assisted him in getting evidence jeopardized their position in the community.[28]

The legal subordination of slaves—in fact, blacks in general—similarly obstructed legal actions involving slaves and free people of color. In April 1807 a coroner's inquest at Barbados found Sam Moll, a mulatto, guilty of the deliberate and wanton murder of another slave in Bridgetown. When the coroner issued a writ to apprehend Moll, he avoided arrest by absconding from the island. Subsequently manumitted by his owner, in accordance with the laws of Barbados, Moll inexplicably returned to Barbados, where he promptly surrendered to the authorities and was immediately put on trial at the Court of Sessions. There being no known witnesses at that moment to the murder save several slaves whose positive evidence was inadmissible in ordinary courts which tried felony cases involving free persons (which may explain why Moll returned to Barbados), Moll's acquittal was virtually assured. However, in an eleventh-hour effort by the Barbados attorney general, a "white evidence" was dramatically produced who could corroborate the charge of murder against Moll.[29]

At the close of the eighteenth century, the institution of slavery in the British West Indies was firmly entrenched in both law and custom. That system rested upon the concept of property in people, which was accepted in English statute law and, of course, in the colonies. Slave laws regulated the subordination and control of slaves and effectively served to distinguish them from the rest of society. Most important, the basis of these laws was the routine acceptance of enslavement, which was facilitated by the not unsuccessful attempts of certain intellectuals to demonstrate that all blacks, whether slave or free, were not the equal of whites. For whites, slavery was inextricably linked with their concept of property, power, and freedom, and logically they rejected any revolutionary tampering with their cherished prerogatives by or in the name of people so foreign and inferior as their slaves. It is arguable, perhaps, that the convention that excluded slave testimony against all whites from the judicial process was the chief bulwark of white supremacy in the colonies.

The extraordinary character of the admission of slave testimony at military courts in the British West Indies must also be understood within the context of the adaptation of the regular army to social and service conditions in the colonies. Speedy creolization of the army's officer corps acted as the most continuous and effective method of developing and maintaining compatible interests between the military and the colonies. Royal governors, most if not all of whom were senior regular army officers, shared a deep community of outlook with creole whites. They had, in theory and the understanding of the imperial government, wide powers, and they might exercise their influence to improve the operation of local government and even recommend legislative change. This modus operandi aside, governors knew that what was virtually sacrosanct in their respective colonies was the continuation of a limited form of representative government, dominated by and for creole whites and based upon the strict subordination of the slave population. Their commission and instructions may have entrusted them with the direction of local government, but the institutions created to provide for this direction had been shaped by the colonists so that they, the colonists, could largely govern themselves. Needing exceptional popularity to govern their usually impatient subjects effectively, royal governors frequently resembled traditional West Indian grandees in their social habits and politics. They owned slaves and plantations and were dependent, like any other West Indian proprietor, on local merchants.[30]

Other army officers were similarly socialized. Some purchased slaves as personal attendants and even trafficked in slaves.[31] In Barbados and no doubt elsewhere in the British West Indies, Royal Army officers sometimes purchased their slave mistresses from their owners and subsequently manumitted them in accordance with local law.[32] All officers, it appears, from green subalterns to senior field officers, had slave servants, a practice deeply rooted in local custom and decreed by army orders. War Office regulations of October 27, 1794, allowed three slave servants for each field officer, two for a captain, and one for a lowly subaltern. A "just Sum," provided by the Commissary General, enabled officers to rent slave jobbers as servants.[33] Several thousand additional slaves, females as well as males, from common laborers to skilled stonemasons, were employed at military installations throughout the West Indies by the army's many departments. Countless other slaves involved in the local food trade and prostitution were a fixture at military camps.[34] Slaves, consequently, were omnipresent at British army camps. Moreover, the ease with which they came and went in the camp suggests their integral place in the social structure of British army life in the West Indies. Military areas were thus places of permanent interracial concourse. Although junior officers ordinarily found it difficult to live on their army pay, the number of occupants in the lodgings of Captain de Weise in Paramaribo, Surinam's principal city, confirms that he was absolutely determined to live the debauched and extravagant life of a creole grandee. In addition to the customary white military man-servant permitted all British army officers, de Weise's housemates included two rented mulatto house slaves, a boy and a girl, and two live-in mulatto women. The latter were undoubtedly there to perform domestic as well as sexual functions, given the pervasive practice of sexual exploitation of women of African descent by white men in the Caribbean.[35]

There were also, as to be expected, marriages between Royal Army and Navy officers and creole women, unions which undoubtedly socialized the outsider to the complex of customs centering upon white society. The famous Horatio Nelson, British hero of the battle of Trafalgar in 1805, was among those who succumbed to the charms and wealth of a white West Indian woman. The Royal Navy backed West Indian economic interests. The West Indian station was considered the "station for honor," and slave owners routinely feted admirals. Nelson's marriage to a propertied heiress from the tiny island of Nevis played no small part in his undisguised support of the slave system. "I was bred in the good old school, and taught to appreciate the value of our West Indian possessions," he boasted defiantly and unequivocally, "and neither in the field nor Senate shall their just rights be infringed, while I have an arm to fight in their defence, or a tongue to launch my voice against the damnable doctrine of Wilberforce and his hypocritical allies."[36]

Of course, there were those officers who for various reasons ran

afoul of creole society and its tropical truths. Some publicly demonstrated their opposition to the depravity and misery of West Indian
slavery during their service in the region. Angered over the brutal
murder of a female slave in Saint Lucia in 1804, Lieutenant General Sir
William Myers, commander in chief, Windward and Leeward Islands,
issued a tough proclamation which undoubtedly reverberated throughout the Caribbean. Slave owners convicted of mutilation were to be
fined and imprisoned. Those found guilty of murder were to be executed "without benefit of Clergy."[37] Another officer, Lieutenant Leach,
who served at Antigua from 1803 to 1805, regarded slavery as the
epitome of evil. He used extraordinary means to stop a slave driver
from whipping an aged female slave: he shot the driver in the legs with
a fowling piece.[38] Others still, like Major General Hugh Carmichael,
often steadfastly represented imperial interests over local concerns.
Officers who held various outsider attitudes were not, apparently,
typical of the officer corps. Given their dissenting views, they could not
be expected to win friends and influence others within the local society.
Most officers, it seems, either had an overall favorable view of slavery or
were indifferent to its many evils.[39]

The opinions of Lieutenant Thomas Howard regarding slavery
were typical of these officers. Howard, who served in Saint Domingue
and Jamaica from 1796 to 1801 in the York Hussars, initially expressed
compassion for slaves who were victims of cruelty. After spending,
however, more than a year in Saint Domingue, where he was evidently
subjected to what Edward Brathwaite calls "cultural action" or social
processing,[40] Howard admitted in his journal that he now viewed
slavery very differently. In a revealing passage, the young cavalry
officer, now thoroughly creolized, concluded that "when I first came
into this Country, I had the most horrid Idea of the treatment the Slaves
received from their Masters that could possibly be formed; every time I
heard the Lash Sound over the Back of a Negro my very Blood boiled
and I was ready to take away the whip and lash the Master. Since that
time I do not think, nay I am persuaded my Heart is not grown harder
than it was, yet I see the Business in a very different Light." Furthermore, while trivializing certain crushing disabilities slaves were forced
to suffer, Howard employed some of the standard proslavery arguments in his passionate defense of African slavery:

> A Slave is not permitted to strike a white Man under Penalty of losing
> his right Hand; he is not permitted, also, to wear shoes, which depri-
> vation is a Badge of Slavery. His Evidence cannot be taken against a
> White Man, tho' his Deposition may go toward Substantiating facts.
> Except these prohibitions, I do not see why they may not live as

happily as any Class of Men. This I am Assured of: they have less Cares [than English peasants] and, therefore, of course, ought to be Happier. As to the Idea of Slavery embittering their Lives, I deny it, except in some particular Cases; for except their Nobles, Princes and great Men, speaking of their own Country, I believe the Commonality are born Slaves and, therefore, by being Imported into the West Indies, only change Masters; which, was I to judge by the manner they treat their Slaves, for there are many Negroes, [who are] Slaves to Negroes, I should imagine must be infinitely easier than the Servitude they have been brought-up in, and as to the Vicissitudes of Fortune, sometimes experienced perhaps by their Chieftains and great Men, I will ask: is Africk alone the Country wherein that happens? or cannot France within these five Years shew Examples infinitely more numerous and cruel than any the African can complain of? Could not Siberia relate Anecdotes of Princes, Statesmen, Soldiers and every description [of people], who have enjoyed Honor, Wealth, Power and Luxury, pining in a state of Servitude and Banishment, infinitely more Cruel and further from their Native Homes than the African? who cannot feel his situation half so forcibly as another from having been born, bred and brought-up in servitude. That Law and Regulations might be enacted and adopted for the greater Security of the Slaves from personal Injury I do not wish to deny, and make no doubt but ere long that will be the Case, when instead of looking down on their Situations with Pity, I shall, on the contrary, consider them as infinitely better off than any day-labouring Set of Men in Europe: [for they are] less worked, better fed, Clothed, taken Care of and Housed.[41]

Howard and other officers who shared his views assimilated into the dominant group without much apparent difficulty.

Like wax softened by heat, Captain Philpot, the presiding deputy judge advocate at the Surinam tribunal in 1800, and the other fourteen members of the court conformed to the compelling pressure of creole society. The ruling of the court, as well as the management of the prosecution, reflected how far officers would go in sacrificing the critical interests of the imperial army in order to accommodate local needs and sensibilities. The testimony of several witnesses placed the two rented domestic slaves of Captain de Weise squarely at the murder scene. The court also allowed what appeared to be the unscheduled testimony of a prominent Surinam planter, who, as if to remind the army of the convention which prohibited slave testimony against whites, verified the slaves' legal status. Philpot admitted their evidence was "very material" to the prosecution, but he nevertheless ruled that their testimony was inadmissible "according to the Laws of all British Colonies"[42] (Surinam, of course, not being among them).

It is likely that the Surinam decision encouraged other creolized regular army officers to rule similarly. Major General Hugh Carmichael complained angrily in 1809 that several deputy judge advocates in Jamaica had "adopted" the position that local laws regulated courts-martial.[43]

Paradoxically, it was the deputy judge advocate who raised the admissibility issue and not the local proprietor, whose convenient appearance before the court has already been noted. The introduction of this question served the defense only. (In fact, had the slaves been allowed to testify, de Weise would have been convicted on positive evidence and speedily executed, a fate he escaped[44] as a direct consequence of his conviction on inference and probable reasoning.) Moreover, whether it was due to ignorance of military law or to extreme deference to creole institutions and conventions, the court failed to challenge the colonial claim of joint responsibility in the governance of the British army, which was explicit in the ruling of the Surinam tribunal.[45] No mention was made that this interpretation was diametrically opposite to the long-established metropolitan view that the imperial army was governed by its own statutory powers, which it took overseas and which transcended colonial enactments.

If the natural tendency of armies is toward self-government, tolerating no external influences, as Alfred Vagts has argued,[46] this principle met with early failure in the British army. In the early history of the army, troops on active service were harshly governed by the Articles of War issued under the prerogative authority of the Crown. Military law in times of peace was first provided in 1689 by the Mutiny Act, subsequently passed annually by Parliament. Successive amendments to the act throughout the eighteenth century expanded it to a comprehensive statute covering the recruitment, billeting, movement, and discipline of the army. The system of governing British soldiers during wartime by the Articles of War, decreed under the power of the Crown, was superseded by a corresponding statutory power, the Mutiny Act of 1803. Thus, at the beginning of the nineteenth century, the British army, both in peace and war, was governed by the annual Mutiny Act and statutory articles.[47]

Some members of Parliament recognized that Parliament was restricted in the use of its powers in relation to the colonies. To some, as the eighteenth century came to a close, it was a convention of the Constitution, to others a simple matter of political expediency. On the other hand, members of Parliament were also certain of the primacy of the law of Parliament, that is, their abstract right to legislate for the colonies. Moreover, the sovereign power vested in the king and Parliament was assumed in England to extend naturally to the colonies. This view of

Parliament's legislative supremacy was made explicit by the Declaratory Act of 1765, which declared the colonies "subordinate unto, and dependent upon, the Imperial Crown and Parliament of Great Britain." It also asserted, unequivocally, that the king and Parliament had "full Power and Authority to make Laws and Statutes of sufficient force and Validity to bind the Colonies and People of America, Subjects of the Crown of Great Britain, in all Cases whatsoever." Additionally, William Blackstone, the eminent jurist, had claimed that there must exist in every state "a supreme, irresistible, absolute, uncontrolled authority in which the jura summa imperii, or right of sovereignty, reside." Even during the period beginning with the events of the American Revolution, when the practice of noninterference in colonial affairs was in accord with opinion in Parliament, members of Parliament agreed that the imperial assembly, by means of its transcendent powers, could legislate for the colonies in cases of emergency.[48]

In 1767, General Thomas Gage, commander in chief in America, cited these arguments while specifically making the case for the supremacy of military law after being advised that the Bermuda assembly was then considering an act which would regulate courts-martial. Recently embroiled in efforts to amend the Mutiny Act in order to extend it to North America,[49] Gage was unswerving in his fulmination against the pending legislation and the actions of the assembly. Not only was it presumptuous of an "Inferior" legislature to "Interfere" in the laws of Parliament and the governance of the royal troops, but the action represented a "Precedent of the most dangerous Tendency, a high Invasion of the Prerogative of the Crown, and of the Rights of Parliament." Moreover, "it is Illegal, and inconsistent with the British Constitution." Concerned, perhaps, that officers in the Bermuda garrison might not be knowledgeable of their responsibilities while conducting court-martial proceedings, the commanding officer was reminded of the solemn conditions which all members of courts-martial were bound to observe. Gage underscored these: *"Duly to Administer Justice According to the Rules and Articles for the better Government of His Majesty's Forces and according to an Act of Parliament."* Finally, he sternly and explicitly ordered the Bermuda commander

> absolutely to refuse Obedience to this Provincial Law made for the Military Government of His Majesty's Forces under Your Command. That neither you or any Officer or Soldier under Your Command shall Acknowledge or Submit to the Authority of any Miliary Court of Justice that shall be Assembled by Virtue of the Provincial Act in Question. That you do reject their Authority and protest against all their Proceedings. And Lastly, that the Rules and Articles for the better

Government of His Majesty's Forces, the Act of Parliament for the Punishing of Mutiny and Desertion, and the Customs of War, shall be Your Sole Rule and Guidance, and no other, in the Government of the Troops entrusted to Your Care.[50]

In theory, Parliament believed it held an ultimate authority over the West Indian assemblies. In practice, there were vigilant watchdogs of metropolitan interests, like feisty General Gage. Yet London concurred with the Surinam ruling in 1800 and, by so doing, recognized the juridical right of the colonies to co-govern the British army. What forces compelled London to agree to a situation that was inherently detrimental to the governance of the Royal Army in the West Indies?

At the time of the murder, February 8, 1800, Britain was busy consolidating its position in Surinam and wished to avoid conflict with the Dutch, who had surrendered the colony without resistance. Ensign Bachoffener's murder at the hands of a British officer undoubtedly heightened tensions. To have violated a sacrosanct convention by permitting slaves to testify directly against whites might have jeopardized Britain's hold on the conquered colony. To this was added the planters' fear of a slave rebellion like that of Saint Domingue. It was therefore imperative to be on good terms with the Dutch, the majority of whom supported the occupation. In fact, a few days after the capitulation of the colony, on August 31, 1799, the entire Dutch garrison took service in the British army.[51] Lieutenant General Trigge, the conqueror of Surinam, was fully aware of this when he informed London that the Dutch governor had proposed to give the Corps of Black Chasseurs to the British government, provided the unit was taken into the British army as a regular regiment. Trigge was mindful of the need for cordial relations with the local planters when he encouraged London to "accede to the wishes of the Colony."[52]

More important was the late eighteenth-century practice in Parliament of caution and noninterference in colonial matters. The initiative in everything related to the internal affairs of the islands resided with the local assemblies, and in Britain colonial governments were understood to function in this way. To permit slaves to give evidence at courts-martial would be considered a serious breach of this principle, which had become fixed as a result of the shock of the American Revolution. Although there is direct evidence that the Surinam case was brought to the attention of George III,[53] as was the custom, there is no known record which cites the employment of the principle of noninterference of the British government in colonial affairs by the law officers in support of the Surinam decision. Fortunately, however, the same argument was employed by the law officers in a different but related case in 1799, for which documentary evidence is available. This case concerned several thousand slave-soldiers serving as regulars in the British army, and deserves attention as a window into the actions of Parliament in respect to the legislative rights of the colonies.

In 1795 the War Office took an unprecedented step in the war against revolutionary France when it established a permanent army of professional slave-soldiers, the West India Regiments. In 1795 two regiments were raised; by 1798 there were twelve, each with an establishment of 1,000 rank and file. Maintained clandestinely by the odious slave trade, these troops were kept in the legal status of slavery. The measure was exceedingly unpopular in the colonies, and the colonists quickly attempted to destroy the experiment by enforcing statutes which prohibited slaves from carrying weapons. In November 1798 the home secretary, the Duke of Portland, requested the opinion of the law officers on two critical questions: Does military service in the British army relieve blacks serving in the West India Regiments from colonial police regulations? If West India soldiers are subject to colonial slave laws, can they be manumitted by an act of the king or would it be more advisable to do so by an act of Parliament?[54] The law officers decided that being in British military service did not place black soldiers beyond the slave laws, insofar as those laws affected them personally. As to the second question, West India soldiers could evade the jurisdiction of colonial laws only if granted freedom according to the laws of the assemblies. Portland was cautioned, however, that manumission would not release black troops from all disabilities since they would still be subject to restrictive colonial laws that controlled the activities of free blacks. As for Portland's suggestion to manumit West India soldiers by an act of Parliament, the law officers wrote that "we presume your Grace did not mean to require of us an opinion on [a] matter of political expediency, but to require our opinion as to the legal operation of such an act. Upon this subject we beg leave to submit to Your Grace's consideration, whether any Law to be passed by the Parliament here would not be an interference with the internal Legislation of the Colonies, which Parliament has of late not been disposed to exercise."[55]

Twice more, in 1801, almost identical inquiries were put to the law officers. In each the attorney and solicitor generals reminded London that parliamentary enfranchisement of black soldiers would constitute "interference" with the colonial legislatures. It is clear from the tone of these opinions that noninterference of Parliament in the internal operations of the colonies was in the period 1799 to 1801 a set political principle.[56]

In May 1808, two months before Hugh Lyle Carmichel assumed

command of the Jamaica garrison, thirty-three African recruits of his own regiment, the Second West India Regiment, mutinied, killing two of their officers. The remainder of the Second, which at the time had a strength of about one thousand men, quickly suppressed the mutiny, killing nine of the mutineers in the process. In an effort to diminish the possibility of a clash between black West India soldiers and angry whites, three hundred men of the regiment were first interned on board a ship-of-war during the enquiry into the mutiny, then dispatched on an expedition against the French at Santo Domingo. Seeking to use this disturbance to prove the justness of their criticism of black troops, the Jamaica Assembly summoned Carmichael and other officers to appear as witnesses, and also requested copies of the proceedings of the court-martial and court of enquiry. Carmichael refused all requests, and the resulting discord in the Assembly compelled the Duke of Manchester, then governor of the island, to prorogue that body. Both the Crown's attorney general and the secretary of war and colonies considered Carmichael's refusal to comply with the Assembly's request unconstitutional. Carmichael was duly ordered to furnish the Assembly with the documents requested and to testify before the legislature. Having already incurred colonial wrath as a result of the Slave Trade Abolition Act of 1807, which the colonists regarded to be an infringement of both their property rights and their constitutional rights to legislate in internal matters, London ordered that the Second West India Regiment and Carmichael both be removed from Jamaica. The Second left the island toward the end of 1809. Carmichael, who had hoped to be reassigned to either Europe or the East Indies, was given a staff post in the Windward and Leeward Islands Command and departed Jamaica in August of the same year.[57]

Before taking leave of Jamaica, Carmichael, dauntless and determined as ever to protect the interests of the Royal Army from what he judged to be the dangerous consequences of colonial interference, sought the counsel of the judge advocate general concerning the actions of several army officers who had rejected slave testimony at military tribunals on the grounds that such evidence was prohibited by local law. Carmichael was outraged that on three occasions "the most distinct and incontrovertible Evidence" was denied. In one case, justice was defeated, he fumed, when the testimony of an "intelligent and sensible" woman was rejected because she was a slave. These objections, he mused, were not allowed under the Mutiny Act. Implicit in this remark was the basic question: which law, colonial or imperial, governs courts-martial in the West Indies?[58]

Because of personal doubts as well as the importance of the question, Richard Ryder, the judge advocate general at the time, sought the counsel of the law officers.[59] On June 26, 1809, from Lincoln's Inn, they rendered their opinion. "We think," they concluded, that Jamaica colonial law

> does not govern this case, because a Court Martial is not one of the Courts of the Island. The Question therefore is whether generally, the State of Slavery incapacitates those who are subject to it from being Witnesses in a Court of Justice, and we do not conceive that it does. We are not aware of any authority to that effect, and therefore we think that such evidence is strictly admissible.[60]

The king's advocate concurred "entirely" with the opinion, adding, flippantly, that the legal basis for the rejection of slave witnesses at military courts in the West Indies was "a Rule of Local Policy altogether."[61]

The historic decision of 1809 became the standard in subsequent similar cases. In 1811, when the question was brought once more to the attention of the judge advocate general for his consideration, he advised that "with regard to the admissibility of the Evidence of a Slave against a free Person before a Court Martial I will take the opportunity of referring you to a Case Submitted to the King's Advocate and the Attorney and Solicitor General in the Year 1809, who concurred in Opinion, that such Evidence was admissible."[62] It may have also inspired Robert Scott when he wrote in his authoritative *Military Law of England:* "In all cases, where neither the statutory nor common law of the army will suffice, the deficiency must naturally be supplied from the parental source, the common law of England."[63]

In a masterful and enduring study of the development of British colonial government from 1782 to 1820, Helen Manning commented that during this period London treated the colonial legislatures with excessive deference. Imperial ministers may have been mesmerized by colonial representatives, she continues, thus delaying the inevitable tightening control of London over the colonial assemblies until after 1815. Parliament, as a result, guided by the practice of noninterference in the internal affairs of the colonies, avoided passing laws that might offend the susceptibilities of the colonists. As evidence of London's "tenderness" for the sensitivity of the colonists, Manning cites, among other examples, Carmichael's dispute with Jamaica and the resolution of it by the banishment of Carmichael to Demerara (modern-day Guyana) and the redeployment of the Second West India Regiment to the Bahamas.[64] If London did not tamper with the constitutional and legal rights of the colonists, imperial ministers showed little hesitation during the Napoleonic era in assuming a greater direct role in colonial government over the heated objections of the colonists. The law officers' opinion of 1809 can hardly be viewed as a sign of submission to the colonial party. In fact, their ruling was part of the escalation in metropolitan-colonial friction over the administration of the colonies well before 1815.

As the eighteenth century came to an end, the power of the initiative in colonial government was in the process of shifting from the colonial assemblies to Parliament. This reversal, as pointed out by David Murray, was due to the widespread condemnation in Britain of the local assemblies for their unwillingness to remodel their slave codes at the urging of the antislavery movement. As evidence of the initiative in colonial government having passed to Parliament during the Napoleonic Wars, Murray cites the creation of the Colonial Office in 1801; the growth of centralized administration, the forerunner of Crown Colony government, in captured Dutch, French, and Spanish colonies; and the abolition of the slave trade in 1807.[65] Missing from this telling list are several additional imperial initiatives, particularly those which relate to the role of the Royal Army in the defense of the British West Indies during the wars of the French Revolution and Napoleon. When in 1795 London established the West India Regiments, the colonists immediately opposed the measure. In June 1795 the standing committee of the West Indian planters and merchants in London was advised that numerous planters in the Leeward Islands were unalterably opposed to the use of armed and trained slaves on the grounds that the employment of this force "to serve as Military Corps in the British West Indies was a measure of the most dangerous consequences to the Lives and properties of the Inhabitants and Owners of Estates in these Islands." The committee, which held similar views, quickly resolved on making a strong protest to London.[66] In an effort to thwart stubborn and persistent colonial attempts to destroy the West India army, Parliament included a clause in the 1807 Mutiny Act which manumitted all slaves in British military service. As a direct consequence of this enactment, a course of action that had been discouraged by the law officers in 1799 and again in 1801, approximately 10,000 West India soldiers were manumitted in what must certainly have been the largest number of slaves freed by a single act of manumission in preemancipation society in the British West Indies.[67] The manumission of thousands of black troops was part of a new, yet unpopular epoch in interracial relations. Then, faced with the need to resist certain creolizing influences in the officer corps, which hampered the day-to-day government of the Royal Army, the law officers in 1809 reminded colonists and soldiers alike that the imperial army was not regulated by local laws, conventions, or tropical truths; rather, it was self-governing, governed by the statutory articles and the Mutiny Act only.

Beginning with the events of the American Revolution, when the practice of noninterference in colonial affairs was in accord with opinion in Parliament, and continuing into the nineteenth century, members of Parliament agreed that Parliament could take the initiative in regulating matters for the colonies in cases of emergency. In the case of these imperial initiatives, it was assumed that Parliament was exercising its transcendent powers in matters of vital interest to the imperial government.

The law officers' decision of 1809 coincided with Britain's energetic conduct of the war against Napoleon and his allies. For instance, in September 1807 the Danish fleet was seized at Copenhagen. Orders in Council were issued to destroy French foreign trade in November 1807. In July 1808 an expeditionary force landed in Portugal. At sea, the Royal Navy decisively defeated the French in a small but lively action near La Rochelle in the spring of 1809. In August of the same year a large amphibious assault was launched against the French satellite kingdom of Holland.[68] In the West Indies, French resistance was crushed when an expedition captured Guadeloupe in February 1810.

The importance of the law officers' ruling went significantly beyond the struggle between Parliament and the colonies for the initiative in colonial government. It also represented a major assault against certain fundamentals of slavery. The ability of a slave to give direct evidence against a free individual, particularly a white person, gave the slave access to the highest authority. The slave was now a public participant in the solemnity, ritual, and drama of a white man's court. Here was a deep invasion of white privilege. Along with legal redress came a proportionate reduction in the slave's traditional powerlessness in relation to another person[69] and an increase in the slave's self-esteem. Furthermore, not only did the ruling permit a slave access to power; it also challenged the basic concept of disability and eternal loss which was an indispensable component of British West Indian slavery. Because of the inherent restrictive nature of slavery, the status of the slave was characterized by separation, subordination, and the lack of rights. In finding that the condition of slavery did not automatically impair a slave's sense of judgment and ability to think critically, the 1809 ruling in effect exposed the purely bogus, artificial, and arbitrary nature of British slavery. Implied in the ruling was the belief that a slave was also a normal human being, a belief which advocates of slavery such as Long had sought to deny. Carmichael said as much when he described the frustrated slave witness as an "intelligent and sensible" person. It is to Carmichael's lasting credit that despite a long exposure to seductive and perverting creolizing influences, he could recognize the essential humanity of a normal human being when he beheld a slave. To question these concepts, as the law officers did in 1809, was to challenge the basis of social organization in the British West Indies.

The economic structure and legal basis of British West Indian slavery came to an abrupt end in 1834 with Parliament's legislative termination of slavery. The destructive process was well under way before 1834, however. The implacable will of the slave to resist slavery by any act, passive and violent, was joined with elements of what Seymour Drescher calls British "abolitionism."[70]

The former resulted in relentless sabotage and periodic rebellion throughout the period of slavery, making life in the West Indies for whites both costly and dangerous. The latter led to, among other things, the abolition of the slave trade in 1807 by an act of Parliament. Additionally, there were new economic forces and concomitant social and political factors at work toward the end of the eighteenth century in Britain, and these forces would eventually redefine Britain's relationship with her colonies. All this resulted in Parliament's effort to wrest the initiative in colonial government away from the local assemblies. The law officers' ruling of 1809 was an important aspect of mounting and determined imperial interference in colonial affairs during the Napoleonic era. That decision was also a radical response befitting a revolutionary age.

NOTES

The research for this article was financed by an award from the National Endowment for the Humanities, Washington, D.C. The author wishes to thank the following scholars for their helpful comments and criticisms: Riva Berlant-Schiller, Mavis Campbell, Seymour Drescher, Edward Cox, Susan Debevec, Stanley Engerman, David Fieldhouse, and David J. Murray.

1. Egremont to Lyttleton, n.d., January 1762, London, Public Record Office, *Colonial Office Papers* (hereafter *CO*) 137/61; Calder to Jenkinson, October 29, 1779, *War Office Papers* (hereafter *WO*) 1/51; Vaughan to Jenkinson, September 21, 1780, ibid.

2. See Jones to Cuyler, September 20, 1797, *WO* 1/86. See "Preparations Made by the Quarter Master General [Knox] for the Army to Serve under the Orders of His Excellency Sir Ralph Abercromby K.B.," enclosed in Abercromby to Dundas, April 9, 1796, *WO* 1/85.

3. For the history of these regiments during the wars of the French Revolution and Napoleon, see Roger Norman Buckley, *Slaves in Red Coats: The British West India Regiments, 1795–1815* (New Haven: Yale University Press, 1979). In August 1807, the combined effective strength of the West India Regiments was 7,950; see ibid., pp. 130–131.

4. Elsa V. Goveia, "The West Indian Slave Laws of the 18th Century," *Chapters in Caribbean History* (Eagle Hall, Barbados: Caribbean Universities Press, 1970), p. 34.

5. Proceedings of a General Court-Martial of Captain Louis de Weise, 5th Battalion/60th Foot, held at Surinam, August 2–25, 1800, *WO 71/187* (hereafter referred to as the "de Weise Proceedings").

6. During this time, the military administration of the British West Indies comprised two principal sectors, the Windward and Leeward Islands Command and the Jamaica Command. The former included garrisons at Barbados, Saint Vincent, Grenada, Antigua, Saint Kitts, Dominica, Saint Lucia, Tobago, and Trinidad. This command was also responsible for the defense of the conquered colonies of Saint Eustatius, the Saints, Martinique, Demerara, Essequibo, Berbice, Surinam, Saint Martin, Curaçao, Saint Croix, Saint Johns, Saint Thomas, and Saint Bartholomew. The Jamaica Command, which reported separately to London on the state of its garrisons, included posts at Jamaica, Bermuda, the Bahamas, and the Honduras Settlement.

7. Thomas Reide, *A Treatise on the Duty of Infantry Officers, and the Present System of British Military Discipline* (Dublin: P. Byrne, 1797), p. 74; O. Hood Phillips, *Constitutional and Administrative Law* (London: Sweet and Maxwell, 1967), p. 342.

8. Morgan to Trigge, private, February 5, 1801, *WO 81/27*. Trigge arrived in the West Indies in 1799.

9. Ibid. and de Weise Proceedings, *WO 71/187*. There is no known record of a successful earlier attempt on the part of the British army to similarly introduce slave testimony at a court-martial.

10. Morgan to Trigge, private, February 5, 1801, *WO 81/27*.

11. Carmichael to Judge Advocate General, April 30, 1809, *WO 72/30*.

12. Helen T. Manning, *British Colonial Government after the American Revolution, 1782–1820* (New Haven: Yale University Press, 1933; reprint, Hamden: Archon, 1966), p. 123.

13. Elsa V. Goveia, *Slave Society in the British Leeward Islands at the End of the Eighteenth Century* (New Haven: Yale University Press, 1969), p. 100.

14. Ryder to Gordon, June 17, 1809, *WO 81/40*.

15. William R. Anson, *The Law and Custom of the Constitution*, 4th ed. (Oxford: Clarendon Press, 1935), vol. 2 (part 1), pp. 220–222; Phillips, *Constitutional and Administrative Law*, pp. 316–319; A. Lawrence Lowell, *The Government of England* (New York: Macmillan, 1916), vol. 1, pp. 131–134; Theodore F. Plucknett, *A Concise History of the Common Law*, 5th ed. (Boston: Little, Brown, 1956), pp. 228–230; and Opinion of the Attorney and Solicitor Generals, June 26, 1809, and Opinion of the King's Advocate, June 30, 1809, *WO 72/30*.

16. Opinion of the King's Advocate, June 30, 1809, *WO 72/30*.

17. *Manual of Military Law* (British War Office, 1914), pp. 11–14, 85.

18. Goveia, *Slave Society*, p. 213.

19. Edward Brathwaite, *The Development of Creole Society in Jamaica, 1770–1820* (Oxford: Clarendon Press, 1971), p. 181.

20. Quoted in Goveia, *Slave Society*, pp. 213–214.

21. For all this, see Winthrop D. Jordan, *White over Black: American Attitudes toward the Negro, 1550–1812* (Chapel Hill: University of North Carolina Press, 1968), pp. 216–219, 228, 493; and Brathwaite, *Development of Creole Society*, pp. 73, 181–182.

22. Goveia, "West Indian Slave Laws," pp. 21, 25.

23. See "A West India Sportsman," London, 1807. The merciless and extravagant use of slaves to accommodate any and every need and whim of

whites is not an exaggeration. For instance, a crowd of slaves waited on Dr. George Pinckard, a British army regimental surgeon, and his associates during a typical creole outing. "The accommodation of the day's journey," wrote Pinckard, who served in the West Indies at the end of the eighteenth century, "were quite West Indian, each had a slave running at his horse's side, or holding at his tail; and each slave was loaded either with a trunk of clothes upon his head, or a bottle of Madeira wine, of rum, or of water in his hand. . . . The negroes kept pace with us throughout the whole of the journey, and were not only at hand to give us drink on the road, but were likewise in readiness to supply us with dry clothes on our arrival." See George Pinckard, *Notes on the West Indies: Written during the Expedition under the Command of the Late General Sir Ralph Abercromby* (London: Longman, Hurst, Rees and Orme, 1806), vol. 2, pp. 398–399. See also Brathwaite, *Development of Creole Society*, pp. 117–118.

24. Orlando Patterson, *The Sociology of Slavery: An Analysis of the Origins, Development, and Structure of Negro Slave Society in Jamaica* (Rutherford: Fairleigh Dickinson University Press, 1969), pp. 41–42.

25. Goveia, *Slave Society*, p. 190.

26. The author has been unable to determine when or if Wilberforce reversed himself on the admissibility of slave evidence against whites before the abolition of slavery in 1834.

27. Quoted in Goveia, *Slave Society*, p. 189.

28. Goveia, *Slave Society*, pp. 188, 201; Manning, *British Colonial Government*, p. 492.

29. *Barbados Chronicle: or Caribbean Courier*, June 4–11, 15–18, 1808.

30. David J. Murray, *The West Indies and the Development of Colonial Government, 1801–1834* (Oxford: Clarendon Press, 1965), pp. 13–23.

31. For the case of Brigadier General Stehelin's runaway slave and the general's attempt to regain possession of him, see Beckwith to Castlereagh, no. 27, October 31, 1808, enclosures, *CO 318/34*, and Beckwith to Liverpool, no. 135, February 14, 1812, and enclosure, *CO 318/46*.

32. Jerome S. Handler, *The Unappropriated People: Freedmen in the Slave Society of Barbados* (Baltimore: Johns Hopkins University Press, 1974), p. 37.

33. "REGULATIONS for the Use of His Majesty's Troops, Upon their Arrival in the West Indies," in [Henry Dundas], *Facts Relative to the Conduct of the War in the West Indies* (London: J. Owen, 1796), p. 193.

34. The "King's Negroes," for instance, was a corps of slave laborers, units of which were attached to each principal fortification in the British West Indies by the 1770s. These men were quartered in barracks set aside for their specific use. See the location of the "King's Negroes" barracks in Jamaican fortifications in the following manuscripts: New York, Hispanic Society of America, Thomas Craskell, "State of the Forts and Batteries in Jamaica," 1773 (HC 336/2294-Craskell); and Jones and Ratzer, "Plans and Sketches of the Forts and Batteries in Jamaica," 1774 (HC 336/2315-Jones). For slaves involved in the food trade see Goveia, *Slave Society*, pp. 226–227. For military prostitution, see Brathwaite, *Development of Creole Society*, p. 160.

35. See de Weise Proceedings, *WO 71/187*; Goviea, *Slave Society*, pp. 215–217. De Weise's preference for mulatto domestic slaves (i.e., slaves of mixed black and white ancestry) was in keeping with British West Indian practice. See Patterson, *Sociology of Slavery*, p. 59; Lowell Ragatz, *The Fall of the Planter Class in the British Caribbean, 1763–1833* (New York: Appleton-Century-Crofts, 1928; reprint, New York: Octagon, 1971), p. 8.

36. Quoted in Eric Williams, *Capitalism and Slavery* (Chapel Hill: University of North Carolina Press, 1944; reprint, New York: Capricorn, 1966), p. 44.

37. The legality of this proclamation was later questioned by the army's high command in the Windward and Leeward Islands. Beckwith to Castlereagh, no. 28, November 2, 1808, and enclosure, *CO 318/34*.

38. Leach was scarred by his experiences with slavery, however. He later wrote in his autobiography: "I have too often witnessed the application of the lash to old and young, male and female, and have too frequently heard their cries and lamentations, ever to forget it:—nor shall I ever cease to hold in utter destestation and abhorrence this infernal system." J. Leach, *Rough Sketches of the Life of an Older Soldier* (London: Longman, Rees, Orme, Brown, and Green, 1831), p. 21.

39. Although there is a vast manuscript and printed literature, a full study of the British garrison in the West Indies remains to be written. This unfortunate situation necessitates inferring from inconclusive evidence.

40. Brathwaite, *Development of Creole Society*, p. 296.

41. *The Haitian Journal of Lieutenant Howard, York Hussars, 1796–1798*, ed. Roger N. Buckley (Knoxville: University of Tennessee Press, 1985), pp. 108–109.

42. De Weise Proceedings, *WO 71/187*.

43. Carmichael to Judge Advocate General, April 30, 1809, *WO 72/30*.

44. Morgan to Trigge, February 5, 1801, *WO 71/187;* Morgan to Trigge, April 8, 1802; and Morgan to Trigge, private, September 19, 1801, *WO 81/27*.

45. De Weise Proceedings, *WO 71/187*.

46. Alfred Vagts, *A History of Militarism, Civilian and Military*, revised ed. (New York: Free Press, n.d.), p. 296.

47. *Manual of Military Law*, pp. 1–13.

48. Murray, *West Indies*, pp. 1–4.

49. John Shy, *Toward Lexington: The Role of the British Army in the Coming of the American Revolution* (Princeton: Princeton University Press, 1975), pp. 163–181.

50. Gage to Delacherois, October 14, 1767, *CO 37/31*.

51. *WO 1/87*, returns on pp. 469, 473. The French occupation of the Republic of the United Provinces, as the Netherlands was then called, in 1795, did not have the complete support of the Dutch people, particularly the colonial party. The call in Amsterdam in 1796–1797 for the outright emancipation of all Dutch slaves in the empire, as well as the abolition of the slave trade, compelled the Dutch planters in Surinam to deal peacefully with the British, who represented the status quo in the West Indies.

52. Trigge to Dundas, November 17, 1799, *WO 1/87*.

53. Morgan to Trigge, private, February 5, 1801, *WO 81/27*.

54. Portland to Attorney and Solicitor Generals, November 12, 1798, *CO 153/31*.

55. Attorney and Solicitor Generals' Report to Portland, March 11, 1799, enclosed in King to Huskisson, March 11, 1799, *WO 1/88*.

56. For a full discussion of all three opinions, see Roger N. Buckley, "Slave or Freedman: The Question of the Legal Status of the British West India Soldier, 1795–1807," *Caribbean Studies* 17 (October 1977–January 1978): 83–113.

57. At the time of the mutiny, Carmichael had commanded the regiment in the field for eleven years as its lieutenant colonel. Official records dealing with the mutiny are found chiefly in *CO 137/122, 123, 126*.

58. Carmichael to Judge Advocate General (Ryder), April 30, 1809, and enclosure no. 2, *WO 72/30*.

59. Ryder to Gordon, June 17, 1809, *WO 81/40*.

60. Opinion of the Attorney and Solicitor Generals (Gibbs and Plumer), June 26, 1809, *WO 72/30*.

61. Opinion of the King's Advocate, June 30, 1809, *WO 72/30*.

62. Sutton to Beckwith, May 4, 1811, *WO 81/44*. Also see Fergusson to Campbell, July 15, 1834, *WO 81/87*.

63. Robert Scott, *The Military Law of England* (London: T. Goddard, 1810), p. 8.

64. Manning, *British Colonial Government*, pp. 143–149. Also see Carmichael to Castlereagh, May 19, 1809, *CO 137/126*.

65. Murray, *West Indies*, pp. xii–xiv, 1–31.

66. Goveia, *Slave Society*, p. 148.

67. Buckley, *Slaves in Red Coats*, pp. 77–80. This figure is compiled chiefly from the army's periodic return of December 1807, which shows the effective strength of these corps. The total number manumitted would be substantially higher if an indeterminate number of blacks in the Royal Navy and in white regiments were included.

68. During the period of the French Revolution and Napoleon, the Netherlands was successively known as the Republic of the United Provinces (to 1795), the Batavian Republic (1795–1805), the Batavian Commonwealth (1805–1806), the Kingdom of Holland (1806–1810), Departments of the French Empire (1810–1813), and the Kingdom of the United Netherlands (1814–1830). See Simon Schama, *Patriots and Liberators: Revolution in the Netherlands, 1780–1813* (London: Collins, 1977), p. xvii.

69. On the question of power relationships under slavery, see Orlando Patterson, *Slavery and Social Death: A Comparative Study* (Cambridge: Harvard University Press, 1982), pp. 1–6.

70. Seymour Drescher, *Capitalism and Antislavery: British Mobilization in Comparative Perspective* (New York: Oxford, 1987).

CONTRIBUTORS

Roger N. Buckley, Professor of History at the University of Connecticut at Storrs, is the author of *Slaves in Red Coats: The British West India Regiments, 1795–1815* and the editor of *The Haitian Journal of Lieutenant Howard, York Hussars, 1796–1798* and *The Napoleonic War Journal of Captain Thomas Henry Browne, 1807–1816*.

Michael Duffy is Senior Lecturer in History at the University of Exeter. His publications include *The Englishman and the Foreigner* and *Soldiers, Sugar and Seapower: The British Expeditions to the Caribbean and the War against Revolutionary France*.

Carolyn E. Fick, Associate Professor of Caribbean and Latin American History in the Department of History at Concordia University (Montreal), is the author of *The Making of Haiti: The Saint Domingue Revolution from Below*.

David Barry Gaspar, Professor of History at Duke University, is the author of *Bondmen and Rebels*, co-editor of *More Than Chattel*, and author of several articles about dimensions of the African diaspora.

David Patrick Geggus, Professor of History at the University of Florida, is the author of *Slavery, War and Revolution* and of more than sixty scholarly articles concerning slavery and the Caribbean.

Kimberly S. Hanger, Assistant Professor of Latin American History at the University of Tulsa, previously served as historian for the Louisiana State Museum. In addition to articles on race relations in Spanish Louisiana, she is the author of *Bounded Lives, Bounded Places: Free Black Society in Colonial New Orleans, 1769–1803*.

Jane G. Landers is Assistant Professor of History and a member of the Center for Latin American and Iberian Studies at Vanderbilt University. She is the editor of *Against the Odds: Free Blacks in the Slave Societies of the Americas* and co-editor of *African American Heritage of Florida*.

Robert L. Paquette, Publius Virgilius Rogers Professor of American History at Hamilton College, is the author of *Sugar Is Made with Blood*, which was awarded the Elsa Goveia Prize of the Association of Caribbean Historians.

INDEX